Thriving in Mind
The Natural Key to Sustainable Neurofitness

Benziger Breakthrough Core Library

Revised Edition

by Katherine Benziger, Ph.D.

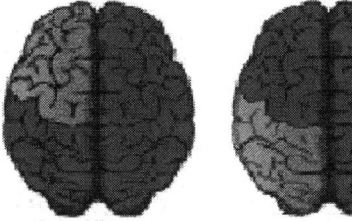 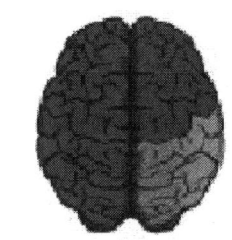 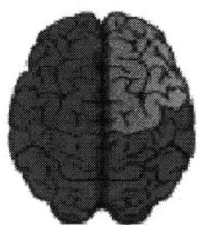

Copyright © 2013 by Katherine Benziger, Ph.D. All rights reserved.
Part of the Benziger Breakthrough Core Library

Printed in the United States of America. No part of this book may be used or reproduced in any manner whatsoever without written permission except in the case of brief quotations embodied in articles and reviews.

Contact info: www.benziger.org, dr.benziger@benziger.org

ISBN #: 978-1492802471

This book is dedicated with gratitude to Isabel Hamilton Rey, my maternal grandmother, who studied with Carl G. Jung in Switzerland in 1932-33, establishing a family commitment to personal growth; and to my mother, Patricia Rey Benziger for reminding me that Jung's work has a healing and empowering value in today's world.

And to:

- Karl Pribram, M.D. Ph.D. for his insights, contributions and ongoing encouragement for almost three decades. Karl's original insights, shared with me almost 30 years ago, were 20-30 years ahead of most neuroscience. His generous sharing of his time and his own expert knowledge allowed me to develop the model that is helping so many people. Karl's instinct and intuition about the location of Jung's functions as well as the reason one of the 3 non-dominant functions was definitely a weakness, as well as the insight that the brain is structured so elegantly that when neurons are functionally-specialized, they will perceive only what they need to perceive to do their specialized job! Thank you, Karl.

- Don Williams for his goodwill, friendship and ongoing support of my efforts to share my discoveries and work. Don has opened doors and opportunities inside the community of Jungian Analysis and elsewhere for more than a decade and a half. His intermittent help with my own website as well as his invitations to teach on his site's interactive, global workshops gave my work exposure and recognition that it could not have gotten elsewhere.

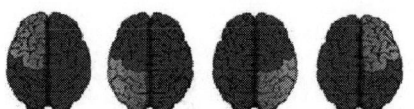

Table of Contents

Introduction to 2012 Edition — 5

Forward 2011 Edition Falsification of Type — 19

Chapter 1: You, Your Brain and Your Dominance — 24
- Four Functionally Specialized Types of Thinking — 24
- The Law of Dominance — 29
- Life's Two Rules of Thumb and Maslow's Hierarchy — 30
- Brain Dominance Self-Assessment Part 1 — 31
- Brain Dominance Self-Assessment Part 2 — 38
- Describing Your Dominance — 40

Chapter 2: Dominance is Natural — 42
- Questions and Answers About Dominance — 45

Chapter 3: Two Hands, Four Brains — 49
- The Left Posterior Convexity Sequential Mode — 49
- The Right Posterior Convexity Feeling / Harmonizing Mode — 55
- The Frontal Right: Internal Image-Generating Mode — 62
- The Frontal Left Analytic Mode — 70
- Four Brains, One System — 76
- Questions and Answers — 80

Chapter 4: The Other Key Piece — 86
- Introversion and Extraversion — 86
- Introversion, Extraversion and the Arousal System — 90

Chapter 5: Working Right, Working Easy — 93
- Career Selection and Success: The Basic Principle — 93
- Brain Dominance and The Business Community — 95
- Brain Dominance and The Helping Professions — 106
- Brain Dominance and The Fine Arts — 116
- Brain Dominance and Leadership — 119

Chapter 6: When Work Doesn't Work — 123
- Career Shifts Driven by Mismatches — 123
- Career Shifts Driven by the Need for Novelty — 126
- Procrastination — 129
- Problems with Time — 134
- Dominance and Decision Making — 136
- Work Rhythms, Hours and Speed — 137
- Questions and Answers about Work — 138

Chapter 7: You've Got to be Kidding — **143**
- Friends and Mirrors — 143
- Marriage — 147
- Family Life With Children — 165
- How to Validate Your Child's Preference — 176
- Kids and School — 178

Chapter 8: Your Whole Brain Over Your Lifetime — **188**
- Being True To Yourself — 188
- Falsifying Type — 189
- Defending the Self — 193
- Bringing It All Together — 193
- Questions and Answers about Falsification of Type — 194

Chapter 9: Developing Competencies — **217**
- Competencies — 217
- 4-Step Plan for Competency Development — 217
- Activities For Developing Competencies — 220
- 7-Step Success Strategy — 223
- Life's Two Rules of Thumb — 230

Chapter 10: Getting Along and Communicating Clearly — **231**
- Communicating — 231
- Communicating With Employees at Work — 231
- Guidelines for Communicating At Home — 246

Chapter 11: Managing Preferences to Maximize Effectiveness — **254**
- Leveraging Your Preference — 254
- Managing Your Weaknesses — 258
- Strategies for Managing Weaknesses — 260

Appendices — **272**
- Appendix A: The Tradition of Thinking About Thinking — 272
- Appendix B: Physiological Bases for the Model — 284
- Appendix C: Limbic & Reptilian Activation Indicators — 294
- Appendix D: A Glossary for the Jargon Lover — 296
- Appendix E: Bibliography — 303

Index — **310**

KBA's Life-Building Tools — **316**

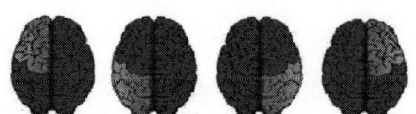

Introduction to 2012 Edition

Today, millions of people around the world, like you, are asking for help to manage the stress, anxiety and depression in their lives and, at the same time, keep their brains fit! These people want to live longer, healthier lives! They want to grow old while retaining their ability to enjoy their family and their ability to think, act and live independently. For all these people three things are important: diet, lifestyle, and leveraging their brain's natural preference's gifts! For all of these people, Thriving in Mind, along with the BTSA Assessment, is a must! Together with Thriving in Mind: The Workbook they make up what Dr. Benziger calls her core tools for empowering individuals around the world.

A complete library of books written by Dr. Benziger are available as part of the Benziger Breakthrough family of products – in Spanish and English – including: Thriving in Mind: The Natural Path for Sustainable Neuro-fitness; Thriving in Mind: The Workbook; Falsification of Type; Overcoming Depression; The Physiological Bases of Jung's Typology Model and The BTSA User Manual.

For professional coaches and trainers in HR, OD or Management Consulting, as well as health care professionals interested in wellness, who want to use Dr. Benziger's tools in their product or service line, a 5-day 40-hour ICF-accredited workshop is available in English and Spanish – the Benziger Breakthrough Licensing Workshop!

Here is the big picture and how it fits together. In the area of stress management, leaders of goodwill around the world, like best selling authors Sir Michael Marmot (The Status Syndrome, 2004), in London, and Professor Robert Sapolsky (Why Zebras Don't Get Ulcers, 1994), in California, are actively seeking to educate people about the findings from Marmot's 40 year long, global study, and their 30 year long collaboration to help people understand and manage stress. These findings are that in the industrialized world, your position in the hierarchy affects how much control you have and, in the end, according to both Marmot and Sapolsky, drives your health (see Stress Portrait of a Killer PBS, DVD, 2008). People at the top of the hierarchy, with the most control, are hardy and healthy. You might say they are chronically well! But those lower down on the hierarchy, in positions with less power and less control over their own lives, are chronically ill. Indeed the lower they are on the hierarchy, the more severe their health problems. And because hierarchies typify the way the world is organized today, in the early 21st century, and most people are not at the top of the hierarchy, this is a very important fact of life for most people – one they need to understand, accept and work with if they want to live a happier, healthier life.

From our point of view, another way of stating Marmot's finding is, your position in the hierarchy means if you are at the top, you will have the freedom and control to use and be rewarded for using your natural gifts. But, if you are not at the top of the hierarchy, you will not have the control you need to structure your own work day so that you are able to use your preference – and find you must falsify type to continue holding your job or get a promotion.

In the area of anxiety and depression, best selling physicians Mark Hyman, M.D. (The UltraMind Solution, 2009), in Boston, and Daniel Amen, M.D. (Change Your Brain, Change Your Life, 1998), in California, both in PBS specials to help people improve the quality of their own lives, are actively seeking to educate people so they understand and manage anxiety and depression – without using drugs, but through life-style changes. Both physicians seek to help people identify and manage sources of anxiety and depression so they can live empowered lives, with sharp minds and healthy bodies. From our point of view, their approaches are wonderful and empowering, and can be most effective if the person using them learns about Falsifying Type, and uses this book, Thriving in Mind, and the BTSA to guide life and career decisions. Significantly, anxiety and depression can both be caused by either Falsifying Type or the invalidation of type – subjects discussed in Chapter 8 of Thriving in Mind.

In the new, emerging and rapidly growing area of wellness known as brain fitness, doctors and researchers, like Dr. Michael Merzenich, appearing in the PBS special and DVD The Brain Fitness Program, 2008, Sharon Begley, author of Train Your Mind Change Your Brain, 2007, and Martin Seligman, author of Authentic Happiness, 2002, are trying to help people understand that happiness is the natural human condition, despite the fact that many people currently feel chronically overwhelmed by the stress in their lives, or chronically depressed. Indeed, several researchers in this area believe people have "a happiness set point" – which may have been dragged down by the chronic stress in their lives, a set point they can regain if they use the brain fitness techniques to release the chronic stress and raise their happiness level by consciously leveraging their brain's natural positive plasticity. Indeed, they encourage everyone to embrace this new knowledge so that everyone can be healthier. Moreover, several including Sharon Begley, who appears in the DVD above with Dr. Merzenich, and who has written and authored Train Your Mind, Change Your Brain in 2007, is advising people who are seeking to apply these brain fitness techniques to their own lives – by selecting and doing more new activities in which they are learning new skills – not simply do something they have heard is good for the brain (i.e. read, join a dance club), but by consciously doing (i.e. selecting and engaging in) new activities they themselves truly enjoy! From our point of view, Begley is correct! Two friends or a couple may both want to learn new skills to keep their brains healthy by triggering positive plasticity – but they may need to do very different new things, because they have different preferences.

If a person's natural gifts don't match the skills they have been using in life, the skills they have been rewarded for and paid well to perform, then, it is very likely that they are suffering from the high levels of chronic stress, anxiety and or depression in their lives caused by their falsifying type.

For the past thirty years it has been difficult for people whose gifts are in the Frontal Right or Right Posterior Convexity (Basal Right) to find opportunities at the top of the hierarchy without falsifying type. But today, with the collapse of some parts of global business culture and the increasing pressure to find new solutions to complex global problems (all things Frontal Rights do brilliantly), and to find new and powerful ways to build trust, good-will and real peace (all things Right Posterior Convexities do brilliantly) there is a global need for the gifts of both the Frontal Right and the Right Posterior Convexity. So, it is possible now to act. Dr. Benziger's books and assessment tools can help you identify and embrace your natural gifts – and then go get a job actually using them!

Much of the important understanding in the difference between what the Left and Right do has been contributed by Paul Ekman, Ph.D., whose research on non-verbal communication and its real power was detailed in his book Emotions Revealed: Recognizing Faces and Feelings to Improve Communication and Emotional Life, 2003. Ekman's findings became common folk wisdom, when they were shared with the world in Malcolm Gladwell's Blink: The Power of Thinking Without Thinking, in 2005. Indeed, some authors, such as Jill Bolte Taylor, Ph.D., in My Stroke of Insight: A Brain Scientist's Personal Journey, 2006, are actively encouraging everyone to use both Right Brain modes more!

In her book, Bolte Taylor, confirms what Dr. Benziger has said, that almost everyone today is using their Left Brains a great deal, even if their preference is not in the Left Brain. Dr. Benziger emphasizes that doing so has tremendous costs, because those who do not have a preference in one of the Brain's two left modes, are Falsifying Type and harming their brains and health.

Bolte Taylor, who is not aware of this falsifying type and its costs, simply says, functionally "left brain dominant" because we are a highly verbal society in which everyone speaks and reads language many hours of the day.

Bolte Taylor explains that a part of the Left Posterior Convexity (Basal Left) of our brain hears words, hears the higher frequencies which are used to speak words. Moreover, she explains, it is a region, which is located in the Left Posterior Convexity, which also sees/reads written words and sees solid rectangular objects because the Left Posterior Convexity sees the shorter wavelengths which allow us to see edges and boundaries which make up solid rectangular objects. More precisely the left sees and focuses on edges and boundaries, including written letters and words which are perceived by the Left Posterior Convexity as small objects. These discoveries ground Dr. Benziger's model as the Left Posterior Convexity is the region she identifies as doing routine procedures with objects. Using words to both identify the objects and the detailed, proceduralized tasks which must be done.

By contrast, Bolte Taylor explains, it is a region, which is located in the Right Posterior Convexity, which understands and hears the person's non-verbals and knows what the person is really feeling, because the Right Posterior Convexity hears the lower frequencies which are used to communicate the tonal non-verbals! Moreover, the Right Posterior Convexity sees the non-verbal communication because it sees the longer wave-lengths which allow the person to see past the edges to see and connect with / relate to their environment and all that is in it – to see what surrounds them and to relate to that whether it is human or non-human. These discoveries ground Dr. Benziger's model as the Basal Region is the region she identifies as doing harmonizing, trust-building relating. Using non-verbals (tonals, body language, facial expressions) to communicate with the purpose of building authentic good will and trust using honest communication supported by congruent non-verbals.

Importantly, for many who have read some of the new best sellers such as Bolte Taylors book, or Daniel J. Levitin's This Is Your Brain on Music, 2008, what Dr. Benziger has written in Thriving in Mind will seem to match so completely what these two best selling authors are saying about brain specialization, that they

may miss the reasons Dr. Benziger's work is so important. The two vital points Dr. Benziger makes, which neither Bolte Taylor nor Levitin mention are the following:

Many people who have mastered tasks are actually falsifying type so that while they are being recognized as experts for having mastered these tasks, in fact, their brain is being damaged by the repeated performance of tasks which are not actually managed by their natural preference, but by a different area in the brain.

Competency and Preference are not the same. Everyone can and generally does develop competencies in every mode. Some of the competencies they develop are very high level, i.e. mastery. It is possible for someone to have this kind of mastery in more than one of these four specialized regions. But each person only has one preference. That is they have one and only one specialized region which has natural efficiency that allows it to use only 1/100th the energy which the person needs to use in his or her other three modes. Competency alone may improve efficiency by 1-2 percent. While, the person's one and only one Preference improves it by 100 percent. In other words, thinking with our preference uses so little energy; we feel it is easy and effortless. This was shown originally more than 10 years ago by Dr. Richard Haier, and was subsequently shown to be true by several other independent researchers, including Dr. Karl Pribram.

It is not so much right and left or the four lobes which many authors refer, including Levitin and Taylor, i.e. Frontal, Parietal, Occipital, Temporal. The four specialized areas which Dr. Benziger has proposed and which function as discreet areas are: The Frontal Right, Frontal Left, Left Posterior Cortical Convexity (includes Left temporal, left occipital, left parietal) and Right Posterior Cortical Convexity (includes Right temporal, right occipital, right parietal).

See the four functionally specialized areas of the human brain.

One has a Frontal Left	Another has a Left Posterior Convexity	Another has a Right Posterior Convexity	Another has a Frontal Right
	Left Posterior Convexity	Right Posterior Convexity	
Preference	Preference	Preference	Preference

Dr. Benziger had the good fortune, at the time she developed her model and for the next twenty years, to be coached personally by Dr. Karl Pribram, who, in 1980, suggested she focus on what he saw as the 4 functionally specialized areas of the human cortex[1]. Pribram added that the huge size of the bridges connecting the right and left cerebral hemispheres was such that all communication between the right and left was relatively easy.

For Pribram, the real problem, which led to real difficulties in communication and collaboration on teams and between couples and in families, was between the posterior cortical convexity and the frontal lobes. Pribram believed based on his expert knowledge and personal experience as a brain researcher, professor, husband and father that the more serious problem was between concrete thinkers and abstract conceptual thinkers. And based on what Dr. Pribram telling Dr. Benziger, concrete thinking is managed in the posterior convexity, while abstract thinking is managed in the frontal lobes. To help those having this kind of communication problem, Dr. Benziger has provided detailed coaching in both chapters 7 and 8 of this book on personal and professional communication.

When she was starting to work with Pribram on her model, Dr. Pribram told her that if what she was observing was true, and people were using these four Types and moving around them in the manner she described, over time, then these four types of thinking were being managed in the human cortex. In a transformative organizing of this information, Dr. Pribram showed Dr. Benziger how Jung's four specialized Types were actually the four functionally specialized types of cortical thinking, alerting her that if each was doing a different job it would then actually be receiving very different input – the input it needed to do the highly specialized job it was doing. He told her this could happen in many ways but that generally each specialized function had physiological screens which allowed it to receive only the data it needed to do its job. Some would be screens that excluded data and others would be screens that included data. Below is a summary presentation of this information which identifies the four functionally specialized areas of the human cortex Dr. Karl Pribram identified for Dr. Benziger; the four functionally specialized types of cortical thinking they each manage followed by a label identifying the corresponding Jungian Type. Following that core of information about how each "functions", Dr. Benziger has added specific words and phrases to help you understand how differently each mode actually thinks:

Analytical Logical Thinking, Jung's Thinking, is in the Left Frontal Lobe. This specialized type of thinking perceives structure and structural weakness. It does the goal-focused planning and the naming of objects and precision analysis of the mathematical information of the physical structures using precision tools and precision measurements.

---

[1] Importantly, Dario Nardi Ph.D., a highly respected, award-winning UCLA professor, in his 2011 book Neuroscience of Personality, confirmed with his own comprehensive EEG research that these 4 area Pribram identified for Dr. Benziger 30 years ago, do indeed perform the tasks and skills which Jung and Jungians called/call the 4 Functions. In other words,, Nardi's studies confirm that Dr. Benziger's work over the past 30 years was focusing on the correct areas of the human cortex, the frontal lobes and the posterior convextiles! Neuroscience of Personality Brain Savvy Insights for All Types of People, Copyright July 2011 Dario Nardi. Published by Radiance House, Los Angeles, USA.

Sequential Routine Thinking, Jung's Sensing, is in the Left Posterior Cortical Convexity. This specialized type of thinking sees and processes the short visual wave lengths which allow it to see the hard edges and boundaries. It touches, holds and moves bounded shapes and people to perform a desired, scheduled procedure. And it hears and processes the high auditory frequencies which are the words and phrases which identify objects and describe these detailed procedures.

Harmonic Relationship-building Thinking, Jung's Feeling, is in the Right Posterior Cortical Convexity. This specialized type of thinking sees and processes the long visual wave lengths which allow it to see past the boundaries to see total close environment so that the person experiences everything as connected. People with a natural preference in this area naturally build bridges. The natural skills and focus allow this area to perform dressing, grooming tasks that connect with and nurture themselves and others. People with this lead touch others on the skin in ways which build connection and trust. They also see the facial expressions, eye contact and non-verbal body language of others which allow them to know and respond to what the other person is really feeling. They also hear and process the low auditory frequencies which allow people with this preference to hear how the person is speaking – their vocals and tonals – which communicate the truth about how the other person is feeling and whether they are telling the truth or are lying. This part is intuitive about people.

Creative Thinking, Jung's Intuition, is in the Right Frontal Lobe. This specialized type of thinking makes the gestures while they talk, gestures which when studied are found to support the words/ideas the person is speaking. This person also sees the abstract patterns in their environment which allow them to do spatial planning and spatial problem solving. They see patterns in the world at large which allow them to identify breakthrough ideas which respond to trends they have seen. They see the trends in the big, dynamic, chaotic picture, the landscape, which allow them to invent and make appropriate changes – often before others have realized it is necessary to make them. They are generally seen as change makers. This part is intuitive about ideas.

Now, look at the four functionally specialized areas of the human brain again. Which one is your Preference? Which one is the one you enjoy the most? Or remember enjoying the most when you were young?

One has a Frontal Left	Another has a Basal Left	Another has a Basal Right	Another has a Frontal Right
	Left Posterior Convexity	Right Posterior Convexity	
Preference	Preference	Preference	Preference

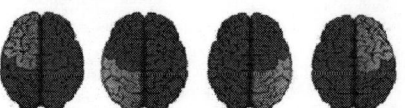

In each case, the person with a specific preference sees and hears easily what their brain needs to see and hear to do the tasks which their preference manages! You can see that a person has only one area which is efficient and three areas which are all highly inefficient. It matters where your natural gifts are! If you are living in a culture which will not reward you unless you develop the left and use it to speak, listen, read and write then you will use the left brain areas and suffer the consequences – unless your preference is in the left brain of course!

Look at how a person with a natural lead in the Frontal Left or Left Posterior Convexity would be able to live – and generally "speaking in many places today" does live enjoying a job which uses and rewards one of these two Left modes. Indeed it is quite clear that while he was still alive Abraham Maslow did think about these problems when he wrote:

"The first and overarching Big Problem is to make The Good Person. We must have better human beings or else it is quite possible that we may all be wiped out, and even if not wiped out, certainly live in tension and anxiety as a species….The equally Big Problem as urgent as the one I have already mentioned is to make the Good Society. There is a kind of a feedback between the Good Society and the Good Person. They need each other…. I wave aside the problem of which comes first. It is quite clear that they develop simultaneously and in tandem. It would in any case be impossible to achieve either one without the other."[2] From Dr. Benziger's work, over thirty years, as well as Carl Jung's and Abraham Maslow's the answers to both of these Big Problems seems clear and self-evident. We create Good People by creating truly healthy, happy people – by providing everyone with work/activities that use their natural lead function in an environment that also uses, honors, rewards their natural level of Extraversion/Introversion!

See Abraham Maslow Hierarchy illustration on the next page.

---

[2] Abraham H. Maslow, The Farther Reaches of Human Nature (Penguin Books in Arkana 1993) pages 18-19.

Living true to Type, keeps your brain operating in cool blue!

Living true to type
Keeps your brain Operating in cool blue.
It is healthy and promotes wellness! It is sustainable!

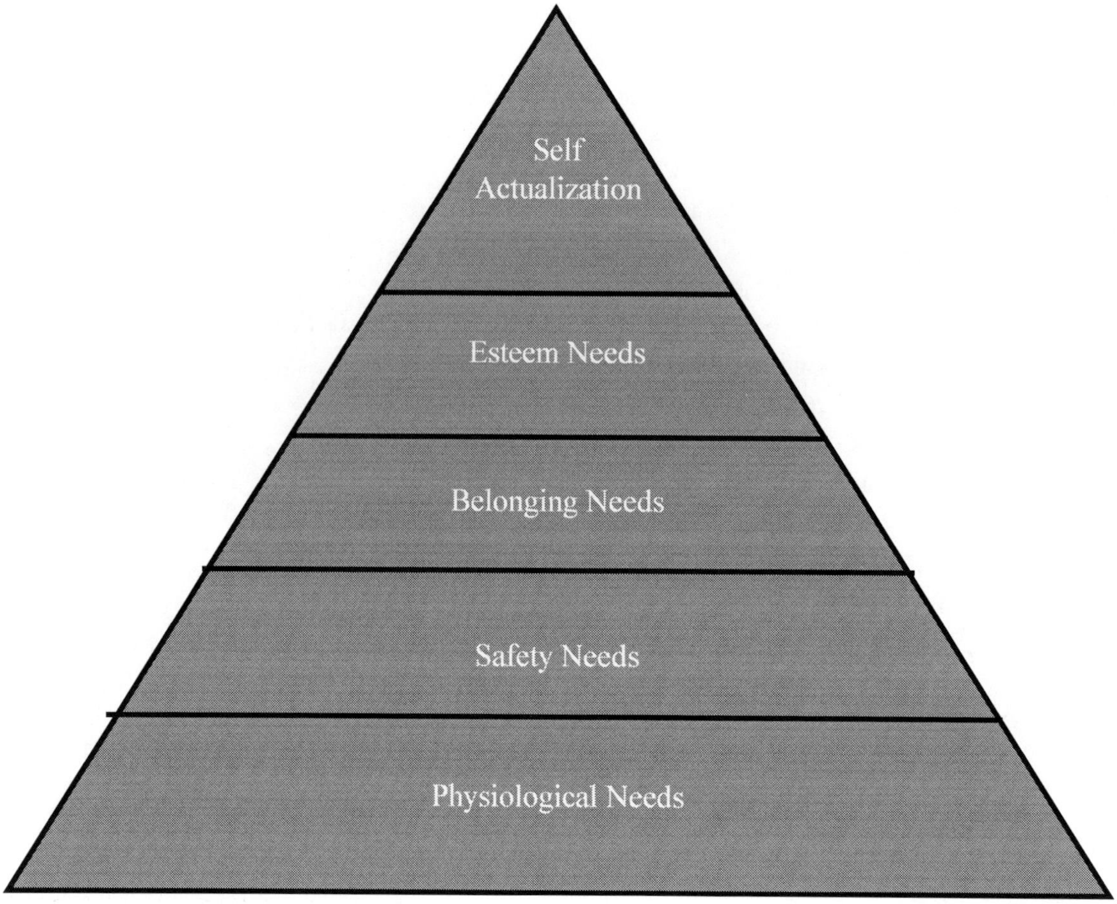

(Pyramid diagram from top to bottom: Self Actualization, Esteem Needs, Belonging Needs, Safety Needs, Physiological Needs)

Now, look at how a person with a natural lead in the Frontal Right or Right Posterior Convexity would be able to live. To hold most jobs today they have to falsify type. That is they are thinking hot, frying their brain. Recent research shows that 80% of the strokes are occurring in the Left Hemisphere because in this highly verbal 21st century world where everyone must read and write and use goals and logical planning, everyone is practically speaking living a life which is left brained according to Jill Bolte Taylor. So, those with gifts in the right are indeed suffering the ultimate costs of falsifying type almost all the time.

See Abraham Maslow Hierarchy illustration on next page.

Falsifying Type, makes your brain red hot – fries your brain!

Falsifying type
Forces Your brain to Overheat & Fries your brain.
It is not healthy! It is not sustainable!

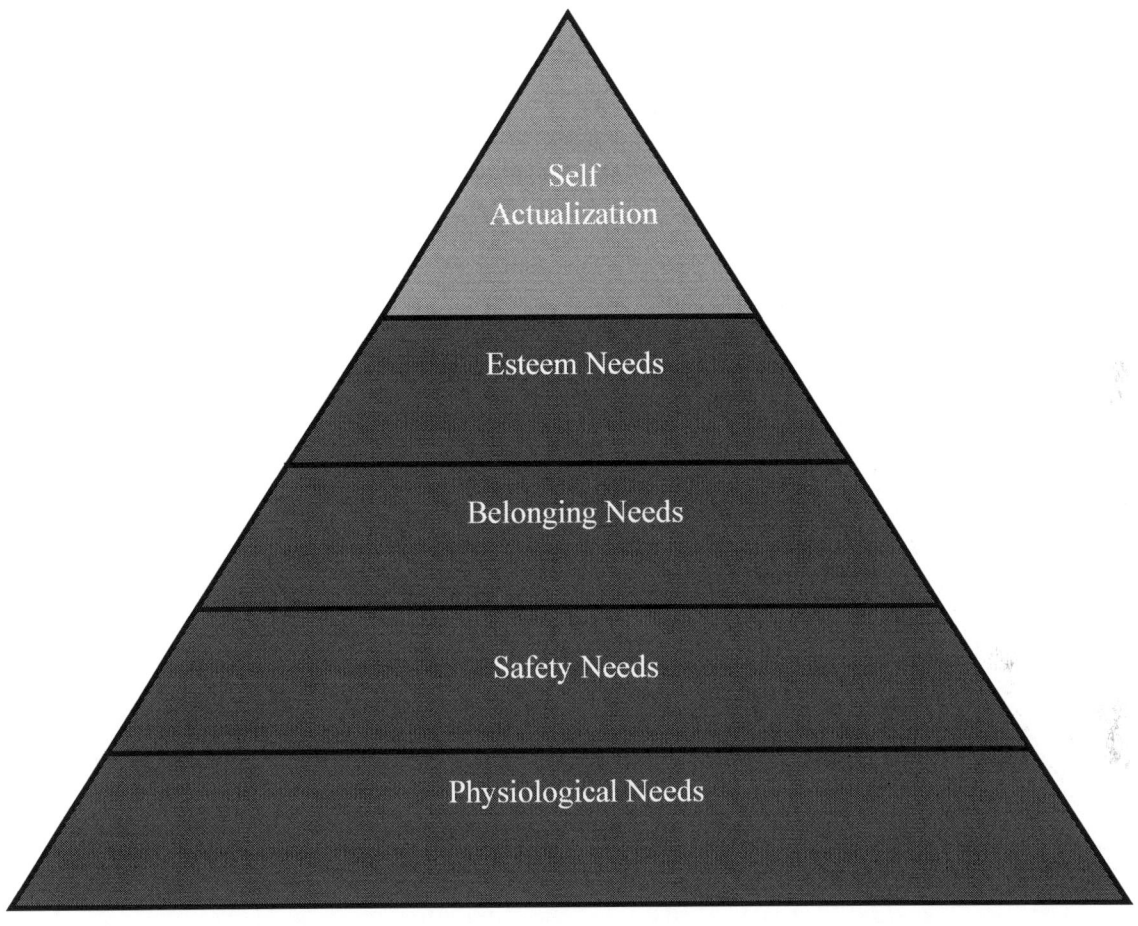

Now, let's look at how each of the four modes actually functions in more detail, so we can begin to ask ourselves which of the four modes is actually my true north or preference, the mode that allows me to act and react naturally, easily effortlessly.

Frontal Left's Life-skill set #1: Structure: lead and develop the business. This person is naturally gifted when these things need to be done and he or she is asked and rewarded for doing them! New research is confirming that this is the part of the cerebral cortex which manages and structures speech, structures music and structures perceptions in general – including the goal setting and logical decisions in our life about what we want to do when we are actively logically evaluating our options and making logical decisions about how best to proceed at any time. And breakthroughs in neuroscience supporting this, have shown that this is the part of the brain that does the naming, the goal-focused, logical problem solving.

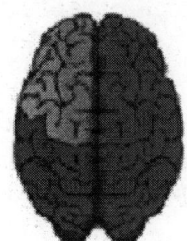

Frontal Left's are powerful analytical thinkers.

Left Posterior Convexity's (Basal Left's) Life-skill set #2: Maintain – build and maintain solid foundations for production. This person is naturally gifted when these things need to be done and he or she is asked and rewarded for doing them! New research is confirming that this is the part of the cerebral cortex that does hear words and manage our vocabulary and our known established routine phrases – and see all the "bounded shapes" in our world because it sees edges – vertical, horizontal edges which create and see boundaries and which sees the boundary of our own body and experiences it as separate from others, and each other person as separate from his or her neighbor or friend or coworker. Breakthroughs in neuroscience supporting this have shown that the areas within the left posterior cortical convexity (left occipital) see the short wave lengths which allow this area to see the edges and boundaries between objects. Particularly, those lines and edges which are straight horizontal, vertical and oblique lines – including very small objects with edge which the brain interprets as written language, i.e. words and phrases. While additional research in neuroscience has shown that others areas within the Left Posterior Cortical Convexity (left temporal lobes) hear high frequencies which the brain recognizes as spoken words.

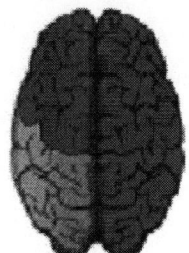

Left Posterior Convexity's are powerful proceduralized production thinkers.

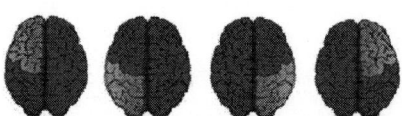

Right Posterior Convexity's (Basal Right's) Life-skill set #3: Communicate Feedback: harmonize the present feedback for change and new growth. This person is naturally gifted when these things need to be done and he or she is asked and rewarded for doing them! New research is confirming that this is the part of the cerebral cortex that does not see edges or boundaries, but sees the connections with others and hears and sees all the non-verbal communication which allows people to easily understand what someone is truly thinking and feeling and build trust and good will with others, as well as performs the many tasks which are considering grooming in baboons, and serves to connect and nurture others. Research in neuroscience supporting this, has shown that the areas within the right posterior cortical convexity (right occipital) see the long wave lengthswhich allow this area to see past the edges and objects to see and connect with the environment. In particular the right occipital sees non-verbal body language including smiles and posture which tell another person the truth about how someone is really feeling and what they are really thinking. While additional research in neuroscience has shown that other areas within the Right Posterior Cortical Convexity (right temporal lobes) hear low frequencies which the brain recognizes the non-verbal elements of speech such as vocal, tonal elements that again, tell the person the truth about what another person is really thinking and feeling. The long wave lengths soften or blur edges and allow you to see more outside your personal space and relate to it, by grooming and dressing yourself and grooming and dressing your family and friends and low auditory frequencies we process as non-verbals – tone, pitch, timbre which helps the Basal Right build and nurture trust and honest relationships.

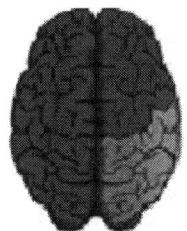

Right Posterior Convexity's are powerful harmonizing thinkers.

Frontal Right's Life-skill set #4: Start: inspire, create the future using vision & innovations. This person is naturally gifted when these things need to be done and he or she is asked and rewarded for doing them! New research is confirming that this is the part of the cerebral cortex which manages gesturing – including the gesturing done by people who are blind and using sign language. And not seeing the edges and boundaries or structure sees past these to the bigger environment to see the patterns and trends which are going on in large, dynamic, chaotic areas of life. Breakthroughs in neuroscience are supporting this. Research has shown that this is the part of the brain that does the spatial planning and problem solving as well as the gesturing.

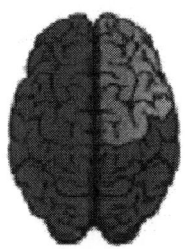

Frontal Right's are powerful creative thinkers.

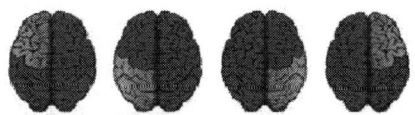

Dr. Benziger sees a future filled with opportunity and hope. When each person is allowed to identify, develop, use and be rewarded for using their brain's natural gifts, then Thriving is possible for all people! This means identifying, building and developing work places which allow Right Posterior Convexities and Frontal Rights to spend the day using and being rewarded for using their natural gifts, not just Frontal Lefts and Left Posterior Convexities. The good news is that in 2009 the world not only needs superior Frontal Left logical problem solvers and superior Left Posterior Convexity production people, it also needs superior Right Posterior Convexity thinkers who can build trust and good will between individuals, communities and nations, and superior Frontal Right thinkers who can and will discover and invent new solutions to the complex dynamic problems (global poverty, global warming, clean affordable water) we are currently facing as a world. So the news is good. This is the time when the world is ready to fully embrace the full spectrum of diversity of human intelligence and to move forward into a time of shared peace and prosperity.

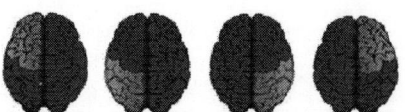

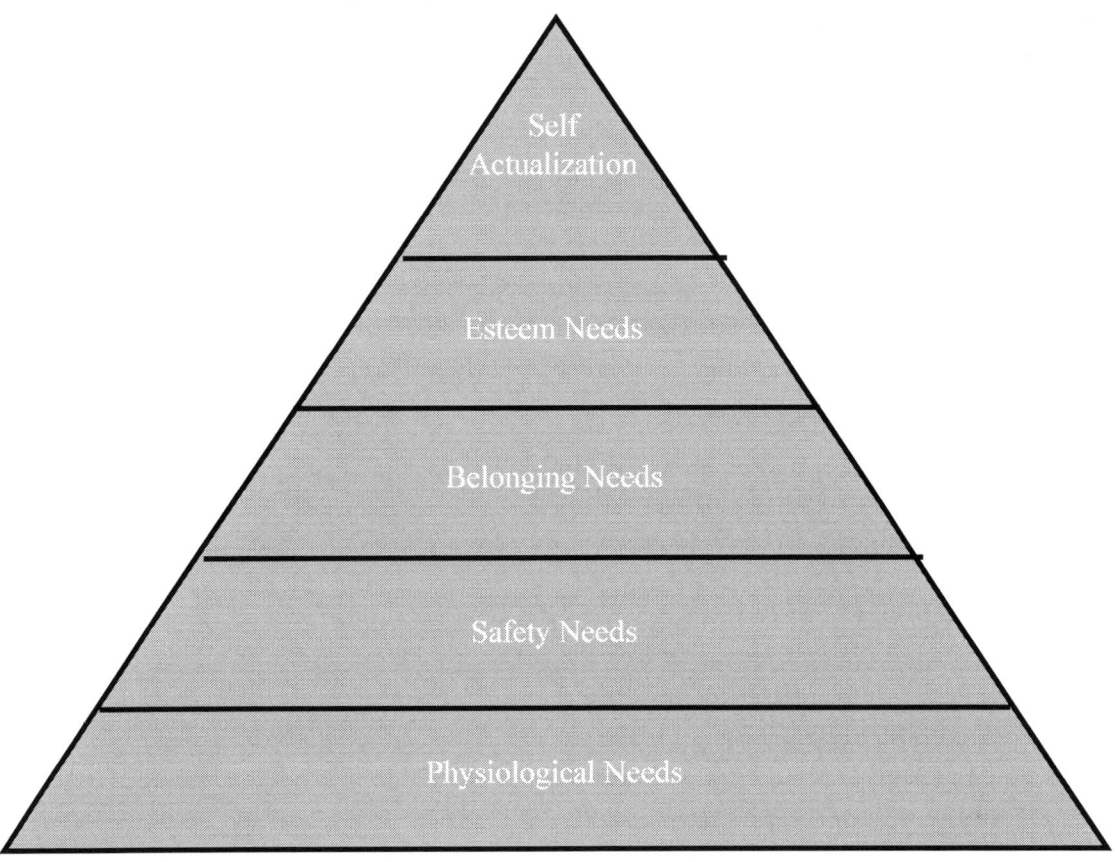

Living true to type
Keeps your brain Operating in cool blue.
It is healthy and promotes wellness! It is sustainable!

- Self Actualization
- Esteem Needs
- Belonging Needs
- Safety Needs
- Physiological Needs

Significantly, Dr. Benziger's books and assessment include not just help understanding if and how you have been falsifying type with respect to your own brain's natural specialized way of thinking, but also in-depth analysis of the person's level of introversion or extraversion over their lifetime. Here her source was the global leader in this area, Hans Eysenck. His breakthrough understanding in the final 10 years of his life was that each person had a stable set point which identified how awake they were when they woke up caused by the level of nor-epinephrine in their brain stem. Indeed Dr. Benziger's work is again unique in helping people understand that while everyone does have a natural set point in this area, as Eysenck found, over time if the person is living under chronic anxiety their effective level of extraversion will decrease. This may stay altered for several months or several years – as long as the chronic anxiety is in their lives. Then, when that chronic anxiety leaves, the person naturally (with no conscious effort) returns to their natural set point.

With a highly developed expertise in all three areas (Jung, Neuroscience and Human Resources Management) Dr. Benziger was able to see and appreciate the implications of Falsifying Type and accumulate more than 10,000 hours in studying the life patterns of people from childhood through adulthood in which Falsifying

Type and its costs were visible to her, by 1986. Since that time her work has been available to help others and those who study and apply it in Africa, Europe and Latin America find the same life patterns of Falsifying Type and its costs.

This book is an eye-opening and empowering book for anyone exploring how to live sustainably. It is a powerful, decision-making guide to help individuals and teams manage job stress and performance. Significantly, when working with teams, Dr. Benziger points out that when people are falsifying type they tend to feel exhausted, angry, anxious and are not easy to get along with. Indeed they are often miserable and make others miserable. So it is when working with teams, accepting that 80% of the people are falsifying type, it is wise to meet and work with every team member to help them identify, embrace and contribute the skills managed by their preference, so they will be easy and fun to work with! Dr. Benziger's observations have also like the global research and work on Stress Management, Depression and Anxiety as well as Fitness, and her findings in this area are Working with You is Killing Me, 2007, by Katherine Crowley and Kathi Elster, 2003 by Roy H. Lubit

And for those working alone, Thriving in Mind can be used to pro-actively design and use an effective self-help program in "Brain Fitness" which will allow them to select new skills and areas to learn which will use their natural preference, so that they can leverage positive neuro-plasticity to enhance their own wellness!

For those leaders who want to learn more about this global problem which Dr. Benziger is the only one working on specifically Falsification to Type, we recommend you read the 2009 Edition of Falsification of Type, the book included in this series which was written for Global leaders after completing Thriving in Mind and taking the eBTSA. Included here, now, to help you understand the book's content and value is the Forward to the 2009 Edition of Falsifying Type.

FORWARD for 2011 EDITION Falsification of Type

Today more than ever before people are voicing their desire to **thrive** - to be healthy, happy and actively engaged in life. People are pressing neuroscientists to discover and structure the human "keys to youth" so they can grow old, **sustaining** their health, vitality and mental acuity. As neuroscientists identify weakened or defective features of our neurological anatomy and develop techniques for healing and re-energizing them, other neuroscientists confirm and extend their understanding that much of what goes wrong in us is due to stress, which they reiterate we, as individuals and a society, must manage better to sustain wellness and to prevent premature aging in otherwise healthy people.

Having studied and worked with Falsification of Type and stress management for more than thirty years, I believe Falsification of Type to be one of the most insidious and least understood causes of stress in the world, one which anyone seeking to thrive must understand and honor as they go about their daily life. This book is for those who want to understand Falsification of Type fully so they can act and help others act to help themselves and the world.

In the thirteen years since this book was originally published in 1995, Arlene Taylor, Ph.D., completed a decade-long study of the human costs of falsifying type and subsequently in November 1999, Arlene Taylor, Ph.D. and I co-authored an article in which we reported the findings of her study, *The Physiological Foundations of Falsification of Type and PASS*. The findings corroborated my own findings and identified PASS, the Prolonged Adaption Stress Syndrome, as a previously unrecognized factor in chronic fatigue and depression. The complete family of symptoms that Taylor's work identified as linked to extended Falsification of Type, was: fatigue, hyper-vigilance, immune system alterations, memory impairment, altered brain chemistry, diminished frontal lobe functions, discouragement and/or depression, and self-esteem problems. An in-depth account of these symptoms is reported in Chapter 8 of <u>Thriving in Mind</u> by Katherine Benziger, Ph.D. To help the reader, a summary of these is included here below:

The Critical Costs of Falsifying Type

1. Fatigue - prolonged Falsification of Type requires the brain to work up to 100 times harder, which quite naturally creates fatigue.

2. Hyper-Vigilance - prolonged Falsification of Type can create a state of hyper-vigilance as the brain goes on protective alertness. This is a safety mechanism that can show up in a variety of different ways.

3. Immune System Alteration - Falsifying Type can be thought of as the individual living a lie at some level. Lying can suppress immune system function (i.e. can temporarily shrink the Thymus gland) that can negatively impact one's health.

4. Memory Impairment - Cortisol, released under stress, can interfere with memory functions.

5. Altered Brain Chemistry - prolonged Falsification of Type can interfere with hypothalamus and pituitary function that, in turn, can interfere with hormonal balance.

6. Diminished Frontal Lobe Functions - prolonged Falsification of Type as a significant stressor can interfere with functions typically associated with the frontal lobes of the cerebrum.

7. Discouragement or Depression - prolonged Falsification of Type can lead to the repeated triggering of the Conserve/ Withdraw reaction to stress. This can be especially true for high introverts, although it can be observed in extraverts who, as years go by, continue to perceive a mismatch between who they are as individuals and societal expectations and/or repeated episodes of failure. This can lead to discouragement, especially as fatigue increases, and can contribute to the development of depression or to the exacerbation of existing depression. Estimates suggest that upwards of 20 million individuals in the USA are depressed, 15 percent of whom are suicidal. Prolonged Falsification of Type would appear to be a key factor in at least some of these cases.

8. Self-Esteem Problems - any or all of the other symptoms can contribute to a perceived diminished overall success in life. In turn, this throws one's self-esteem off balance. Problems in this area can appear as low self-esteem or inflated self-esteem or flip back and forth between them.

Significantly, a recent global study done by David G. Blanchflower and Andrew J. Oswald on well-being reported in Issue 8, April 2008, of the Journal of Social Science found that life satisfaction in the industrial countries dips in middle age when increased depression is being reported. This fact is consistent with my own findings, as reported in this book and especially in Chapter IV Findings and Chapter V Summary, Conclusions and Recommendations. Chart G on the next page (taken from Chapter IV) allows you to truly see and appreciate the critical nature of the problem. Leaders need to reevaluate what they are doing so that all people will have the opportunity to use and be rewarded for using their natural gifts.

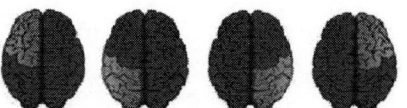

CHART G: SOCIETAL CRITICALITY EVALUATION MATRIX
SERIOUSNESS OF RAMIFICATIONS TO SOCIETY
Updated in 2006
This important information for business and government leaders is shown in detail on page 87 of the 2008 Edition of Falsification of Type

Very Serious Almost always lethal Maximally debilitating Brief duration Highly infectious	4 Ebola Virus Fall out from an atom bomb Failure of an atomic reactor	5 AIDS – country dependent	6 AIDS – country dependent	7	8
Serious Often lethal Heavily debilitating Chronic Rarely infectious	3 Strokes Alzheimer's Heart Disease Cancer	4 AIDS – country dependent	5	6	7
Moderately serious Rarely lethal Moderately debilitating Chronic Rarely infectious	2	3 Depression Anxiety High Blood Pressure	4	5 Falsification of Type and PASS – Prolonged Adaption Stress Syndrome	6
Minimally serious Not lethal Minimally debilitating Brief duration Infectious	1	2	3 Colds Flu Allergies	4	5
Not serious Not lethal Minimally debilitating Brief duration Not infectious	0	1	2	3	4
	0-1% rare or infrequent 5%	6% moderately frequent 30%	31% frequent 69%	70% very frequent 94%	91% Universal Omnipresent 100%

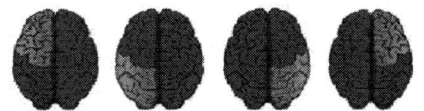

So take a moment to look at Chart G on the previous page. As you do, you will see that Falsifying Type is a very serious a global problem. Allow yourself to see and accept that Falsifying Type is truly an urgent human need which leaders who are embracing the 2nd industrial revolution in the 21st century must resolve by honoring that the world and its people truly need not just Left Posterior Convexity procedural jobs which give production certainty and Frontal Left logical/analytical jobs which provide clarity and alignment with goals and priorities, jobs which dominated the training and education in the 19th and 20th centuries and during 1st industrial revolution. The world and its people also need workers who can contribute Frontal Right creativity and Basal Right empathy, trust and community.

NOTE: A convention in this book is to use Jungian terms. Some terms used by Dr. Benziger such as Left Posterior Convexity, Right Posterior Convexity, Frontal Left or Frontal Right each have equivalent meanings to Jung's Sensing, Feeling, Thinking, Intuition. Also, because she invented the Benziger Breakthrough model at a time when the term Posterior Convexity was not yet being used, Dr. Benziger' early work uses the term Basal. This is a term Dr. Benziger invented so she would not have to use the term Sensory Lobes. Now that others understand that the Sensory Lobes are doing more than sensing, the convention in neuroscience is to use the term Posterior Convexity, to identify this same region of the cortex which in the past had been identified as the Sensory Lobes.[3]

---

3 Again, Dario Nardi Ph.D. in his 2011 book Neuroscience of Personality, confirmed with his own excellent and comprehensive EEG research that these 4 areas Pribram identified for Dr. Benziger 30 years ago do indeed perform the tasks and skills which Jung called the 4 Functions. Moreover with his excellent **EEG** studies Nardi has also identified and detailed the smaller cortical regions which make up each of the 4 larger cortical areas, and details the specific sub-functions each of the smaller regions perform, which together make up on Dr. Benziger's/Pribram's Frontal Left and Frontal Right; as well as identified and detailed the specific sub-functions of each of the smaller regions which together make up on Dr. Benziger's/Pribram's Left Posterior Convexity and Right Posterior Convexity. For these reason's Nardi's work can be understood to work with and support Dr. Benziger's and is helpful to anyone seeking the most up to date information about how Benziger's/Pribram's act out each of Jung's 4 functions.

More specifically, as part of the:
<u>Left Frontal</u>, Nardi is testing/studying the Left Prefrontal fp1, Left Frontal f3 and Left Frontal f7
<u>Right Frontal</u>, Nardi is testing/studying the Right Prefrontal fp2, Right Frontal f4 and Right Frontal f8
<u>Left Posterior Convexity</u> or what has been known as the Left Sensory Lobes, Nardi is testing/studying the Left Temporal T3, Left Temporal T5, Left Parietal C3, Left Parietal P3 and Left Occipital O1
<u>Right Posterior Convexity</u> or what has been known as the Right Sensory Lobes, Nardi is testing/studying the Right Temporal T4, Right Temporal T6, Right Parietal C4, Right Parietal P4 and Right Occipital O2

That said, it is important to say what Nardi did not do.
1. Nardi did not conduct his studies using a PET scan so he was only able to tell us what part of the brain each person was/is using not how much energy their brains are consuming to access these areas. Based on Benziger work it is an excellent guess that two things would be found. First that those who report being energized and uplifted by doing these tasks are actually using 1/100th the energy that other people use accessing the identical regions. Second that some people in the group who excel at these tasks are using 100 times the energy and actually frying their brain, even if they are feeling a joy/satisfaction from satisfying some Maslow Need.
2. Nardi did not conduct his studies overtime or re-assess the same person several months or years later while also identifying a person's emotional tone to also know how the person generally feels about their life at this time. Dr. Benziger's work tracking people's emotional tones over 30 years has shown that people can and do Falsify Type for years without recognizing it because are getting powerful validation for what they are doing and and or no one has told them it is no one has actually told them it is possible to falsify type.

Neuroscience of Personality Brain Savy Insights for All Types of People, Copyright July 2011 Dario Nardi. Published by Radiance House, Los Angeles, USA.

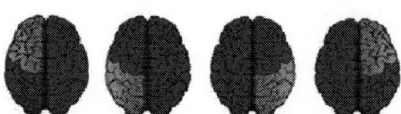

Taken from page 70 of Dario Nardi's 2011 book,
NEUROSCIENCE OF PERSONALITY

Table 4-1: Cognitive Skill-Sets Check List

Region	Region	Skills
Left Prefrontal	Fp1	Chief Judge: Focus on explaining, making decisions, noting errors, and screening out distracting information.
Right Prefrontal	Fp2	Process Manager: Focuss on preoecess, either step-by-step for tasks, or open-ended creative brainstorming, or both.
Left Frontal	F7	Imaginative Mimic: Morror others' behavior, pick up skills by observing others, and make imaginative inferences.
Left Frontal	F3	Deductive Analyst: Follow a chain of logical deductions and backtrack to correct thinking due to reasoning errors.
Right Frontal	F4	Expert Classifier: Accurately place concepts by testing them against many catergories are once to find a best-fit.
Right Frontal	F8	Grounded Believer: Evaluate people and activities in terms of like or dislike, and/or recall details with high accuracy.
Left Temporal	T3	Precise Speaker: Focus on content of the spoken word, attend to proper grammar, usage, enunciation, and diction.
Left Parietal	C3	Factual Storekeeper: Easily memorize and execute steps of movemnet (dance steps, etc.) and/or recall facts.
Right Temporal	T4	Intuitive listener: Focus on voice tone and other affective qualities of sound. Speak in a holistic way to influence.
Right Parietal	C4	Flowing Artist: Draw, paint, dance or otherwise use your body in a flowing, spontaneous, and/or artistic manner.
Left Temporal	T5	Sensitive Mediator: Attend to how others respond to you and alter your behavior to get more desirable results.
Left Parietal	P3	Tactical Navigator: Integrate physical space, motion, and visual clues to move skillfully though the environment.
Right Parietal	P4	Strategic Gamer: Weigh many pros and cons, risks and uncertainties at once in order to finesses complex situations.
Right Temporal	T6	Purposeful Futurist: State what will surely happen in the future, and/or apply a symbolic meaing to a situaion.
Left Occipital	O1	Visual Engineer: Mentally rotate, measure, arrange, assemble and explore objects with a focus on funtionality.
Right Occipital	O2	Abstract Imprssionist: Notice holistic themes, patterns, and raltionships in photos, paintings, and similar images.

Neuroscience of Personality Brain Savvy Insights for All Types of People, Copyright July 2011 Dario Nardi. Published by Radiance House, Los Angeles, USA

Chapter 1: You, Your Brain and Your Dominance

▲ Four Functionally Specialized Types of Thinking

Understanding how your brain works well enough to find and use your inner compass is not hard! Thinking takes place in the part of your brain called the cortex, the part often referred to as your gray matter.

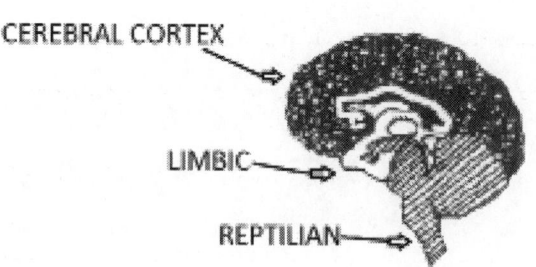

PAUL MacLEAN'S TRIUNE BRAIN

• The reptilian system	Manages our energy level, our wakefulness, sleep cycles, heart rate and breathing
• The limbic system	Manages the storage and retrieval of memories, our blood pressure, body temperature, sex drive and appetite
• The cerebral cortex	Manages our thinking

Your cerebral cortex thinks about the past, present and future utilizing the capabilities of your limbic and reptilian brains to supply it with data and to carry your thinking into action.

Two intersecting fissures, or cuts, the central fissure and the longitudinal fissure, divide the cortex into four essentially equal-sized areas.

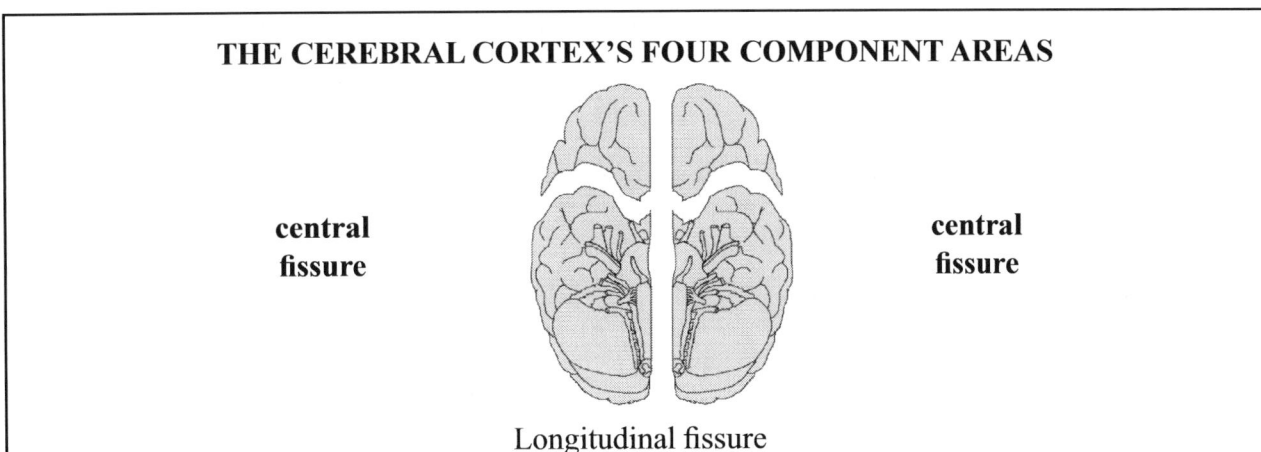

Each area can be seen as having its own job – the way it contributes to your life and to the world. Each is like a specialized machine or specialized software that needs the correct input in order to do its job. The result, not surprisingly is that each has a distinct way in which it gets or accesses information and a distinct way in which it thinks or processes information.

Thinking: The Modes			
Cortical Region	**Benziger**	**Processing**	**Jungian Function**
Left Frontal (Anterior) Lobe	Frontal Left	Analytical	Thinking
Right Frontal (Anterior) Lobe	Frontal Right	Internal Imaging	Intuition
Left Posterior Convexity	Left Posterior Convexity	Sequential	Sensation
Right Posterior Convexity	Right Posterior Convexity	Feeling	Feeling

At this point it is important to insert a note on terminology to explain how and why I chose and use the term *posterior convexity* to identify the posterior areas. Older books in neuroscience identify four lobes or sections within each hemisphere: frontal, temporal, parietal, occipital. In these books, the latter three lobes, the temporal, parietal and occipital, were referred to jointly as the sensory cortex. As neuroscience reinvents itself, terminology changes to reflect new discoveries about how the brain works. Today, the term *sensory cortex* is no longer used and the portion of our cortex behind the central fissure is referred to as the *posterior convexity*. The shift in terminology came about because scientists discovered that sensory data or input goes to all four areas of the cortex, not just to those in the back of the brain and that all four areas actively process the information they receive. That is, all four areas think.

The work I am sharing with you here is consistent with contemporary neuroscience. I created the model 15 years ago guided at the time by breakthrough observations from Dr. Karl Pribram, before most neuroscientists had accepted that the active processing and thinking go on in the posterior convexity.

I had to create a new word for what was then identified as the sensory cortex because to use that term reinforced the common belief that these areas were only for data storage and not capable of active thinking. The term I created 15 years ago was *basal*, a term commonly used to mean under or behind. The posterior convexities are behind and a bit under the frontal lobes.

You may be asking why don't you use Jung's terms *thinking, sensing, feeling, and intuition* to identify the four areas. It's an excellent question. It is true, I believe these four areas are the body's home for Dr. Jung's four functions. So, why not just use his terms.

The problem for me is that our society mistakenly identifies *thinking* as the brighter or superior, as more valuable in life. By creating and working in a more neutral language you and others can learn to value and embrace all four functions as equal. It is actually an interesting point that all four of Jung's functions appear today to be specialized *types of thinking* managed by a functionally specialized region of the human cortex. Again, given how highly our society values thinking, it is helpful to teach everyone that each of Jung's functions is actually a specialized type of thinking.

Having addressed the question of terminology, let's return to look at the human cortex and its functionally specialized regions, each with its own specialized perception and equally specialized type of thinking.

Let's look at the posterior convexities first. Recent breakthroughs in neuroscience confirm that each attends to very different information. The Left Posterior Convexity (Basal Left) takes in information about objects and masses. Two very different examples, both of which are perceived and taken in by the posterior left, are a machine and the letter *e*. Both are perceived as objects. Once the posterior left has taken in information, it uses its unique ability to sequence that information so that the information can be retrieved and used dependably. Its sequential processing is most easily appreciated as the ability to learn and perform an established sequence of movements–a procedure or routine–generally involving objects. Examples, that remind us how powerful and valuable this specialized type of thinking is, include properly assembling a machine, working on an assembly line, focusing on words by writing and reading.

By contrast, the Right Posterior Convexity Posterior (Basal Right) takes in and attends to concrete harmonic information about relationships between different tonal qualities or pitches in someone's voice; different notes on a scale; different rhythms (in music, speech, movement); different colors; different body positions and different facial expressions. Once it has taken in information, the posterior right uses its unique ability to distinguish harmonious relationships from discordant relationships and to act to harmonize whatever material it is working with. Its specialized type of concrete processing is most easily appreciated as the ability to create and sustain harmony by welcoming, connecting with and nurturing other people, children, animals, plants, the world.

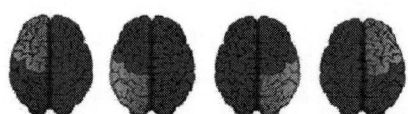

Now let's look at the frontal lobes. Again each lobe has its own specialized screen that determines what it sees and takes in as well as its own specialized type of processing or thinking. First, the Frontal Left notices structure and breaks, weaknesses or malfunctioning in that structure. Its attention is drawn to the break. It asks for and receives additional focusing energy from the deepest parts of the brainstem and subsequently is able to focus with tremendous precision on all the relevant details that might explain why the break happened and how it might be repaired. Once it has taken in information, the Frontal Left Lobe uses its unique ability to logically evaluate and solve problems to determine if the break can be repaired and how to repair it. Its specialized type of processing is most easily appreciated as the ability to diagnose and repair a malfunctioning or broken watch, human body, automobile, machine or company.

The Frontal Right lobe perceives abstract pattern and bleeps of pattern rather than structure **and breaks in structure**. Structure has both "structured" or rigid form and function. It holds something up. Abstract Patterns, like trends in the weather or human behavior, are very different and serve a different purpose.

The Frontal Right lobe perceives abstract patterns, that lead it to see how things may have developed or may be developing, as well as the absence of that pattern, that suggest something important from the whole is missing. Again, once it has taken in information, the Frontal Right lobe uses its unique ability to generate metaphors (e.g. life is a bowl of cherries, a family tree has branches, the child is blossoming) that reflect the essence of something and generate and manipulate internal images of abstract or complex spatial, patterned information to identify trends and developing or evolving needs. Its specialized type of processing is most easily appreciated as the ability to anticipate changes in its environment, invent new solutions and lead people through difficult times with a vision of what is possible.

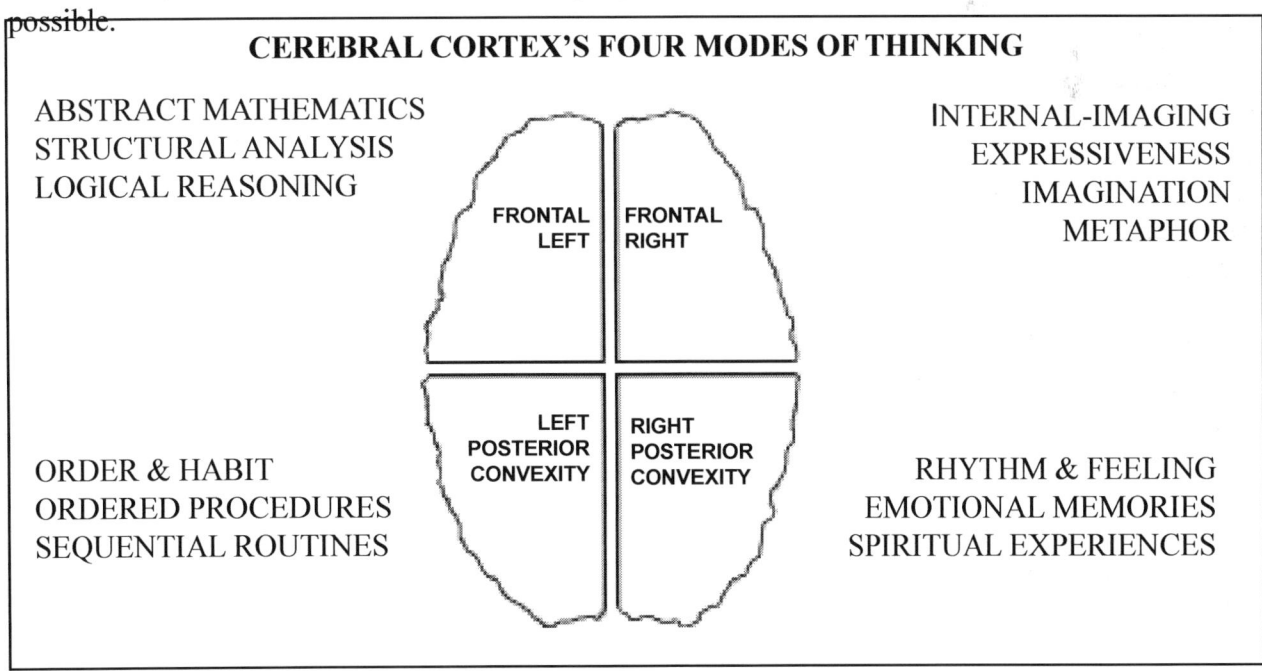

Combining this new image of the cortex with more in-depth information about how each of the four areas thinks, we can create the model of our cerebral brain shown here.

Importantly, although each of the four key areas of our cortex has its own function or specialty, the individual areas were not designed to function alone, but in concert with each other as part of one unified brain system. In fact, only by working together can they accomplish their shared purpose: *to ensure human survival, growth and evolution.* Although each area has a specialized function and each is of equal importance, human life as we know it would not be possible if any one of the four modes were absent. Given this, one might assume that every human being is born with equal access to all four modes. Paradoxically, when we explore the second element of the model, the Law of Dominance, which describes the model's internal dynamics, we find the contrary to be true.

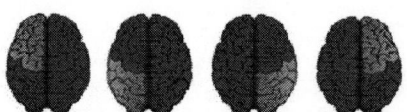

▲ The Law of Dominance

The Law of Dominance, which governs your brain's internal dynamics, tells us that far from being born with four equally available and equally strong thinking modes, each of us is born with:
- one clearly *preferred* mode, in which we have tremendous natural speed and efficiency, and
- three *non-preferred* modes, each of which is more difficult for us to use as they are substantially slower and less efficient.

According to research done by Dr. Richard Haier in at San Diego we "prefer" one mode because our brain is naturally more efficient in that mode. According to Haier, the "electrical" resistance within and between neurons in our area of preference is so much lower that we only use 1/100th the oxygen or energy when we use it to think. In other words, when we use our natural lead, thinking feels easy and effortless. By contrast, when using our other areas, each of which uses 100 times the energy – thinking is literally more difficult and exhausting.

What is important to note is, physiologically, dominance is natural and normal. As a matter of fact, dominance governs much of our physiology. And yet, as natural as dominance is, it is frequently not understood or not accepted as valid and it's implications are often ignored. Moreover, this simple lack of understanding results in many people finding themselves confused, tired or overwhelmed by problems and blocked from the joyous, effective and healthy life they seek.

This universal fact of life – that each person has only one naturally preferred type of thinking – was noted earlier in the 20th century, as many of you know, by the Swiss psychologist Carl Jung and even earlier by the Native American tribes who saw life as a huge medicine wheel with four primary directions. According to their tradition, each of us is born at a specific location on the wheel of life and each carries with us, throughout our life, the perspective – the attitudes and values inherent in that location.[4]

Another law that governs our brain's internal dynamics involves introversion and extraversion. These inner self-descriptors – describing how we see ourselves and relate to our world – identify our normal, inner level of wakefulness – whether we naturally and rapidly wake up wide awake or normally need time and some additional stimulus to wake up and stay awake. Introversion and extraversion are important elements of Jung's model, but were not included in my original research and book as their scientific foundations were not understood 15 years ago. Key discoveries about the scientific foundations for introversion and extraversion made by Dr. Hans Eysenck in the early 1990's allowed me to integrate them into my work. To help you benefit from this new information, this aspect of the model is presented in Chapter 4 - *The Other Key Piece: Introversion and Extraversion*, in the BTSA Personal Feedback Document and in articles on my website www.benziger.org.

---

[4] For additional information about these and other models describing human thinking see Appendix A: *The Tradition of Thinking About Thinking*

▲ Life's Two Rules of Thumb and Maslow's Hierarchy

These two rules of thumb govern your brain's interaction with its environment. I discovered these two rules while working with clients who sought to apply my work to their everyday lives, to empower themselves to be happier, healthier and more effective. They reveal what you need to do to succeed, be effective, happy and healthy.

Life's Two Rules of Thumb

Rule 1: To develop or nurture your self-esteem, as well as ensure your immediate effectiveness and success, select activities and people that match your preference.

Rule 2: To assure your survival, as well as guarantee your long-term effectiveness and success, manage activities and people not matching your preference consciously and carefully and, if possible, enlist assistance from others with complementary brains.

Given what you already understand about dominance and these rules, you might guess that almost everyone uses their natural lead most of the time. If all else were equal, you would be right. The problem is that a wide range of factors – including our society's historic over-valuing of the left cortical modes (Thinking and Sensing) and under-valuing of the right cortical modes (Intuition and Feeling) – mean all else is not equal. Every day, the majority of us face external pressures to survive, belong and fit in or, alternatively, we face our own inner needs to be respected and rewarded. When facing these pressures and needs, so aptly identified by Abraham Maslow, many people choose to Falsify Type. That is, they try to do or be something that runs counter to their preference. To manage their own lives better these people need to learn that Falsifying Type, while satisfying a need identified by Maslow, also causes them to be tired, irritable and anxious.

The rest of the book will help you decide to what extent you may have been Falsifying Type; how Falsifying Type has affected your life; how to identify your natural lead as well as apply the Two Rules of Thumb to your own life. Before exploring any further, you need a picture of your own brain dominance – which modes you've developed through use, which one you prefer, which, if any, you avoid and whether you've Falsified Type. The following self-assessment will help you do this.

▲ Brain Dominance Self-Assessment Part 1[5]

General Directions: Part 1 is in four sections, one for each mode. In each section you will find a descriptive paragraph followed by 15 statements designed to assist you in evaluating your strength in that mode exclusively. As you read, keep in mind two things:

1. Dominance is *normal* and *natural*. Do not expect or try to score high on all four modes. Most people will (and should) have high scores in only one or two areas.

2. There is an important difference between preference and competency. Don't identify what you can do; *identify what you like to do and what you do easily and effortlessly.*

For these reasons, as you read through the assessment, consider how you think and act *at work and at home*. Read slowly, and notice the degree of *real comfort, familiarity and identification you have with the specific words and phrases* used for each particular mode. Be sensitive to the fact that you may have developed many competencies or mental skills in areas which you do not necessarily prefer, just as a child born left-handed may have developed a competency in using his or her right hand. If you do something well, but do not feel comfort, ease, satisfaction, and delight in it as you do it, your ability may not be a preference.

Lastly, **do not paraphrase.** The more comfort you feel applying these *specific words* and *phrases* to yourself, the more likely it is that you have a natural preference for that mode.

---

[5] This self-assessment will assist most of you to identify your strongest and weakest modes. However, due to people's tendency to Falsify Type that is to develop and identify with competencies in a non-preferred mode in order to survive or fit in where their dominance is not accepted or rewarded – the results of this short assessment are not always accurate. For a more complete analysis of your profile, your tendency to Falsify Type, your introversion extraversion needs and emotional tone, arrange to take the Benziger Thinking Styles Assessment (BTSA). For more information about the BTSA see KBA's Life Building Tools in the section at the end of this book or Dr. Benziger's website at *www.benziger.org.*

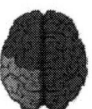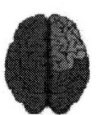

MODE I

Mode I thinking is ordered and procedural, distinguished by the ability to *repeat an action consistently and accurately over time.* True Mode I thinkers derive satisfaction and a sense of accomplishment from following *established routines and procedures*. They are masters at attending to the details. Loyal, dependable and reliable, they may remain with the same company for years where they are valued for the *consistency* of their work and the *thoroughness* with which they complete tasks. Naturally *conservative*, they appreciate *traditional* values and prefer to approach tasks and solve problems in a step-by-step manner.

Now, on a scale of *0* (not at all) to *5* (completely), how comfortable are you with this paragraph as a description of yourself? Write that number here:

Part A: 2

Next, read through the following 15 statements, putting a checkmark next to those that are *very descriptive of you*. Leave blank any that don't apply or are only somewhat descriptive of you.

1. I excel at keeping things organized. ✗
2. I like working with details. ✗
3. I am very productive, reliable and self-disciplined. ✗
4. I enjoy sorting, filing, planning and making labels.
5. I think rules are important and should be followed.
6. I prefer to have specific instructions and procedures to work by. ✗
7. I consider myself to be conservative and traditional.
8. Both at work and home, I like to have specific places for everything. ✗
9. I use a step-by-step method for solving problems and approaching tasks.
10. I actively dislike ambiguity, uncertainty and unpredictability.
11. I complete assignments on time and in an orderly way.
12. I prefer to associate with and most highly approve of people who have their emotions under control and behave appropriately. ✗
13. I always read the directions completely before beginning a project.
14. I enjoy having regular routines and following them. ✗
15. I prefer to schedule both my personal and professional life and am upset when I have to deviate from that schedule.

To calculate your score for Part B, count the number of checkmarks above, and give yourself one (1) point for each. Write your total here:

Part B: 9

Now, add the numbers from Part A and Part B and write the total below:

TOTAL MODE I SCORE: 9

MODE II

Mode II thinking is *spiritual, symbolic and feeling-based*. It *picks up the subtleties* and shifts in others' moods, emotions and *nonverbal signals*. Strong mode II thinkers are often highly expressive, instinctively *reaching out to comfort*, encourage or connect with others through words and gestures. Naturally caring, they believe that *how someone feels* is of utmost importance and they bring this *concern for compassion, relationship and interpersonal harmony* to both their personal and professional lives. Given their ability to relate positively and empathetically, Mode II thinkers also excel at motivating others to join in by sharing their own excitement, enthusiasm and support.

Now, on a scale of *0* (not at all) to *5* (completely), how comfortable are you with this paragraph as a description of yourself? Write that number here:

Part A: 2

Next, read through the following 15 statements, putting a checkmark next to those that are *very descriptive of you*. Leave blank any that don't apply or are only somewhat descriptive of you.

1. I pay particular attention to and am skilled at understanding body language and nonverbal communication.
2. I believe feelings are truer and more important than thoughts. ✗
3. I enjoy verbally "connecting" with others, listening to their problems and sharing feelings.
4. I consider myself a highly spiritual person.
5. I relate to others empathetically and find it easy to feel what they feel. ✗
6. I excel at creating enthusiasm and positively motivating others. ✗
7. I often spontaneously touch others in nurturing and encouraging ways. ✗
8. I automatically watch someone's face when talking with him or her.
9. I love to sing, dance and listen to music. ✗
10. I believe *personal growth* and development are extremely important. ✗
11. I define success by the quality of my experience.
12. I consider my relationships to be the most important part of my life.
13. I feel uneasy in conflict situations. ✗
14. I consider *cooperation* and *harmony* the most important human values.
15. I always want to know how people *feel* and how they are *relating*.

To calculate your score for Part B, count the number of checkmarks above and give yourself one (1) point for each. Write your total here:

Part B: 7

Now, add the numbers from Part A and Part B and write the total below:

TOTAL MODE II SCORE: 9

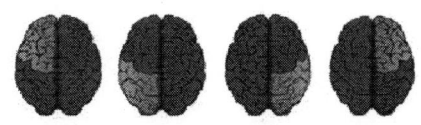

MODE III

Mode III thinking is *visual, spatial and nonverbal.* It is metaphoric and conceptual, expressing itself as *internal pictures or movies,* that the Mode III thinker delights in viewing and which naturally makes them masters of *integration, innovation and imagination.* Easily bored, they constantly *seek the stimulation of new concepts,* new information and new adventures. They are readily identified by their visual filing system that stores material in stacks or piles around their homes and offices; and their quirky, sometimes off the wall sense of humor. As *conceptual humanitarians* they are interested in humanity and its evolution even though they may not be especially adept at relating one on one.

Now, on a scale of *0* (not at all) to *5* (completely), how comfortable are you with this paragraph as a description of yourself? Write that number here:

Part A: 5

Next, read through the following 15 statements, putting a checkmark next to those that are *very descriptive of you.* Leave blank any that don't apply or are only somewhat descriptive of you.

1. I focus more on the "Big Picture" than "tetchy" details, such as spelling or balancing my checkbook. ✗
2. I regularly come up with innovative ideas and creative solutions. ✗
3. I am recognized as a highly energetic and expressive person. ✗
4. I actively dislike and get quickly bored with routine tasks or activities. ✗
5. I excel at synthesizing disparate ideas or items into new "wholes". ✗
6. I prefer to work simultaneously, processing lots of ideas and tasks at the same time. ✗
7. I consider *novelty, originality* and *evolution* the most important values. ✗
8. I find information easily in the stacks I use to organize my personal space at home and at work. ✗
9. I use metaphors and visual analogies to explain my thinking to others. ✗
10. I get excited by others' novel or "off the wall" ideas. ✗
11. I rely on hunches and my intuition when solving problems. ✗
12. I have a sense of humor that's gotten me into trouble for not behaving appropriately.
13. I get some of my best ideas while doing "nothing in particular". ✗
14. I have well developed spatial skills, can easily "see" how to rearrange a room, re-pack a suitcase or car so everything fits in. ✗
15. I have artistic talent. ✗

To calculate your score for Part B, count the number of checkmarks above and give yourself one (1) point for each. Write your total here:

Part B: 20

Now, add the numbers from Part A and Part B and write the total below:

TOTAL MODE III SCORE: _____

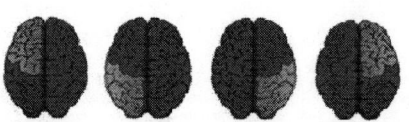

MODE IV

Mode IV thinking is logical and mathematical, excelling at critical analysis, diagnostic problem-solving, and in the use of tools and machines. Mode IV thinkers have well-defined goals and the ability to calculate the most direct, efficient and cost-effective strategies for any situation. This leads them towards positions of leadership in which they can control key decisions and manipulate circumstances into alignment with their desired results. Given their ability to be critical and precise, it is not surprising they prefer technical, mechanical or financial work.

Now, on a scale of 0 (not at all) to 5 (completely), how comfortable are you with this paragraph as a description of yourself? Write that number here:

Part A: 2

Next, read through the following 15 statements, putting a checkmark next to those that are very descriptive of you. Leave blank any that don't apply or are somewhat descriptive of you.

1. I prefer to work with technical or financial matters. ____
2. I like doing critical and analytical thinking. ____
3. I have good diagnostic and technical problem-solving skills. X
4. I excel at studying science, finance, math or logic. ____
5. I find I enjoy and am energized by verbal argumentation or debate. X
6. I excel at understanding machines and enjoy using tools & building or fixing things. ____
7. I prefer to have the final responsibility for making decisions and setting priorities. ____
8. I consider thinking *significantly* more important than feeling. ____
9. I excel at making investments and in managing and leveraging key resources such as time and money. X
10. I consider myself a primarily logical thinker. ____
11. I excel at delegating and giving orders. X
12. I regularly organize material into key points and operational principles. ____
13. I evaluate m success by the actual results I produce and by the bottom line. X
14. I consider myself a powerful, decisive and effective leader. ____
15. I value *effectiveness and rationality* above all else. ____

To calculate your score for Part B, count the number of checkmarks above and give yourself one (1) point for each. Write your total here:

Part B: 7

Now, add all the numbers from Part A and Part B and write the total below:

TOTAL MODE IV SCORE: 7

▲ Interpreting your Scores Part 1

In order to understand your own brain better, transfer your total for each mode to the space below.

MODE I Left Posterior Convexity	**MODE II** Right Posterior Convexity	**MODE III** Frontal Right	**MODE IV** Frontal Left
9	9	20	7

By looking at your scores together, you can begin to see how you yourself are using your brain. You can see immediately whether one or perhaps two of your scores are noticeably higher than the others.

Significantly, we all have *only one natural preference* or lead, which we can use alone or in conjunction with non-preferred competencies in one or more of our three non-preferred modes. If we are living true to our natural preference, using our brain as it was designed to be used, leading with our natural lead; our scores show our natural preference as highest **and our greatest natural weakness - located diagonally across the brain from our natural preference - as lowest. The other two modes, called auxiliaries, may be minimally to strongly developed.** Whatever the case, when you are using your brain effectively, you are using your natural preference significantly more **than either of your auxiliaries.**

If you are currently leading with your natural preference, you are probably generally happy, energized and healthy because you are using your brain in the way it was designed to be used. **If this is true for you, then your modal scores indicate the following.**

20: a very high score indicates a **Commitment** to one's preference. If you scored this high, it means you consciously choose to think in this way, have many competencies you have developed using this mode, believe it is the best way to think and possibly believe that everyone else should think this way.

13 to 19: a high score indicates a **Developed Preference**. Your competencies in this mode are the most dependable part of your bag of tricks and the way you most often want to do things.

6 to 12: a moderate score indicates **Non-Preferred, Developed Competencies** in an auxiliary. You will generally find that you can access and use such a mode *at will* and with the conscious choice to do so, especially when what you want it to do serves a greater purpose, one aligned with your preferred mode. Continued focus in this area, however, over time, will fatigue and drain you.

0 to 5: a low score indicates a lack of preference for and often an actual **Avoidance** in a mode. Situations requiring you to perform in this area may evoke a strong sense of resistance in you, induce you to immediate or motivate you to leave the room, procrastinate, daydream, doodle or make lists of what you really want to do.

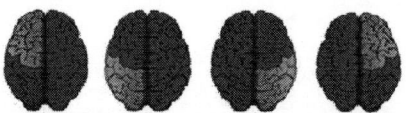

Generally, people who are living true to type, leading with their natural preference have the following natural patterns of relative, developed strength in their brains. Mode I thinkers have 13-20 in Mode I, 6-12 in Mode II, 0-5 in Mode III and 6-12 in Mode IV. Mode II thinkers have 6-12 in Mode I, 13-20 in Mode II, 6-12 in Mode III and 0-5 in Mode IV. Mode III thinkers have 0-5 in Mode I, 6-12 in Mode II, 13-20 in Mode III and 6-12 in Mode IV. Mode IV thinkers have 6-12 in Mode I, 0-5 in Mode II, 6-12 in Mode III and 13-20 in Mode IV. Again, the above meanings apply *only* if you are living over center, leading with your preference (e.g. using your preference first and using your preference more than other modes). Statistically speaking, that will only be about 20 percent of you.

Significantly, according to research done by myself in the 1980's, and duplicated by The Gallup International (reported in *Now, Discover Your Strengths*, by Marcus Buckingham, 2001), 70 to 80 percent of people living in the our modern industrial and post-industrial, global culture are falsifying type (e.g. leading with a mode other than their brain's natural lead), to survive (support themselves or their family), fit in (be accepted, included or loved), belong or be rewarded.

If you are part of the majority, part of the 80 percent who are falsifying type, your data may identify how you are currently using your brain, but not your preference. Your high scores, even if they are 13-20 show **Developed Competencies in Non-Preferred modes.** This means that you can do these things but that the cost to your brain is chronic fatigue, irritability and anxiety. So, if your scores fall into one of the above patterns, but you are chronically fatigued and irritable, or if you have two or more scores that are 13-20, you are probably falsifying type. For this reason, to help you understand what your data really means, take a minute to complete Part 2 of the Self-Assessment.

Brain Dominance Self-Assessment Part 2

Take a minute to read and answer the three sets of questions below.

1. During and following the work day:
   - Do you find your job *boring*?   NO _____   YES _____
   - Do you suffer from chronic *fatigue*?   NO _____   YES ✗
   - Do you suffer from *headaches*?   NO _____   YES ✗
   - Do you suffer from *irritability*?   NO _____   YES ✗
   - Do you experience a *lack of joy*?   NO _____   YES ✗
   - Do you frequently consume *sugar, coffee or caffeine drinks*?   NO _____   YES 4

                                        total **YES**   4

The more *YES* answers you have, the greater the probability you are Falsifying Type.

2. During and following the work day:
   - Does someone often want or need you to do things outside your area of giftedness?   NO _____   YES ✗
   - Does someone often put you down for doing what you enjoy or what comes easily for you?   NO _____   YES ✗
   - Does someone often tell you are wrong, silly or stupid?   NO _____   YES ✗
   - Does someone often dismiss your ideas?   NO _____   YES ✗
   - Does someone often correct things you say or do?   NO _____   YES ✗

                                        total **YES**   5

The more *YES* answers you have, the greater the probability that you are being *invalidated* regularly by one or more persons around you and, as a result, you are Falsifying Type to please others and reduce your emotional pain or discomfort.

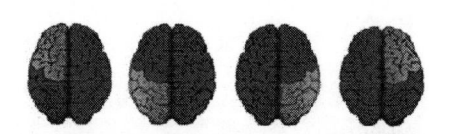

3. During and following the work day: **a**   **b**

- When you walk into your office or home do you find yourself
  a) comfortable, or
  b) uncomfortable?   ___   _X_

- When in your office or home do you find yourself
  a) feeling alive and alert, or
  b) bored and falling asleep?   ___   _X_

- When in your office or home do you find yourself
  a) focused and absorbed in what you are doing, or
  b) unable to focus?   ___   _X_

- When in your office or home do you find you become
  a) lost in what you are doing and lose track of time, or
  b) does time pass slowly?   _X_   ___

- When in your office or home, do you
  a) settle in and want to stay put, or
  b) leave or go out to find some stimulation?   ___   _X_

The more *b* answers you chose, the greater the probability that you are Falsifying Type as a result of living or working in an environment that does not speak to your gifts.

Significantly, persons who are Falsifying Type report experiencing frequent anxiety, exhaustion and/or increasing health problems. If you experience these problems; or if your memory of yourself as a child differs significantly from how you are today; and/or if your answers to Part 2 suggest you may be Falsifying Type, read Chapters 1-5 and 7 of this book and then retake this self-assessment test or arrange to take the BTSA itself to gain a deeper understanding of your natural preference.

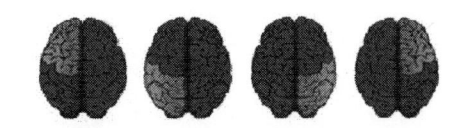

The Benziger Breakthrough

▲ Describing Your Dominance

In describing people's patterns, it can be useful to use phrases that give a dynamic picture of the person's pattern. Importantly, each pattern contributes differently.

Quarter-brainers may be described by affixing the phrase "quarter-brain" to the preferred or most developed mode (i.e. a "quarter-brain Frontal Left" or a "quarter-brain Right Posterior Convexity"). Some see this pattern as too focused or narrow. Yet, quarter-brainers are often seen as loners. If they are more extraverted, they may work in commission sales. Otherwise, as true experts in their field, they contribute superbly as technical advisors and resource persons to individuals or teams.

Half-brainers may be described as being: "double right" (someone with highly developed skills in both right modes), "double frontal" (someone with highly developed skills in both frontal modes), "double left" (someone with highly developed skills in both left modes), "double posterior convexity" (someone with highly developed skills in both posterior convexity modes) and "diagonal" (someone with highly developed skills in the Left Posterior Convexity and Frontal Right, or alternately, in the Frontal Left and Right Posterior Convexity). Doubles tend to function well on teams. They contribute from their preference and use their abilities in their second mode to connect with other team or family members.

Triple-brainers, also called Translators, may be described by indicating their area of weakness: a "triple translator with a weakness in the Left Posterior Convexity" or a "triple translator with a weakness in the Frontal Left". Significantly, people with highly developed skills in three modes – their natural lead and both of their auxiliary modes – tend to do well as supervisors and managers, in positions that use their ability to help people accept, value and understand each other so that they can all work together as a team.

Finally, whole-brain patterns may be referred to as whole-brained. Such a pattern can be powerful particularly if it has been developed slowly over decades. Indeed, for Jung, "integrating one's fourth function" was in some ways one of the goals of life. The difficulty occurs when the pattern is developed prematurely as a result of early Falsification of Type. Here, it reflects an ability and tendency to fit in, or do whatever anyone else wants, rather than an ability to lead. Using the above information, describe your own pattern:

My pattern is that of a _____

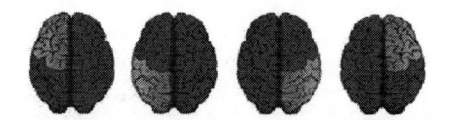

A graph or *kite* can also be made from a person's scores as illustrated below. The scores are graphed on a drawing of the brain like the one depicted earlier in this chapter. The score for each mode is *scaled* (20 = 100) and recorded on a line that runs through the middle of each mode. 100 is placed at the outer edge of the brain. Such graphs often convey more effectively the dynamic energy that accompanies each pattern. They are also linear abstractions, like caricatures and models. As such, they communicate well with the Frontal Right mode that really doesn't understand words and numbers very well.

For now, spend a few moments studying these sample graphs. Do some appear to be more balanced? Some more skewed? Some more uplifted? Some more grounded? Some more focused?

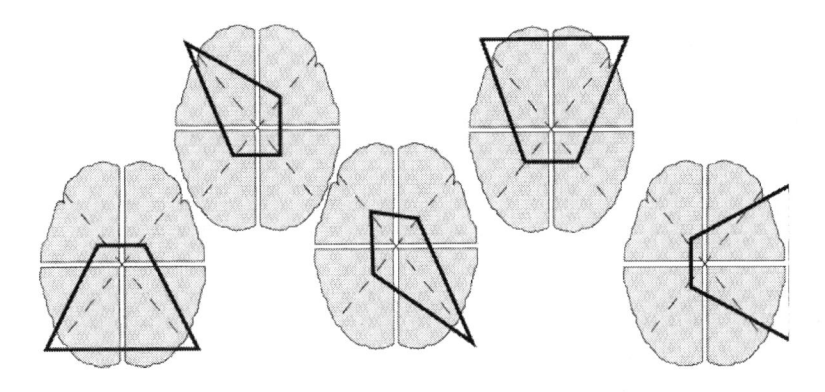

Given what you already know about the four modes, which ones identify people who would be likely to attend to details or deadlines? To how you are feeling and whether or not you are feeling welcome? To trends? To be analyzing the mechanical or technical cause of an accident?

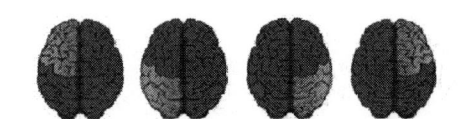

The Benziger Breakthrough

Chapter 2: Dominance is Natural

There is a great deal more I want to share with you about your four types of thinking, but before I do, I want to tell you about *dominance*. Dominance is the natural law governing your brain's internal dynamics. Dominance makes it easier for you to use one mode. And, dominance makes it easier for you to use some modes in combination, such as your Right Posterior Convexity and Left Posterior Convexity, than to use others in combination, such as your Left Posterior Convexity and Frontal Right.

As I explained in Chapter 1, your neurochemistry creates your dominance by setting up one mode in your brain that is easy to use because the electrochemical resistance in that area is very low. Practically speaking you don't have to work hard when you use it. It is your preferred mode or preference. What's more, that same neurochemistry makes it much more difficult for you to use your other three modes. Indeed, these modes, your non-preferred modes, require you to use *one hundred times the energy to think*. Thinking with your preference is easy and fun. Thinking with your non-preferred modes is hard work. The easy feeling you have when using your preference is your body's biofeedback to you. It is your inner compass pointing to the path that will bring you the most joy and satisfaction in life.

Using your brain structure, your dominance also determines which of your non-preferred modes you are most likely to use. Two of your less efficient modes are more available to you because they are located next to your preference and are connected to it by substantial neuronal bridges. Where such bridges exist, communication between modes and consequently iterative thinking is faster and easier. It is these two non-preferred modes, connected to your preference that you can use as auxiliaries.

Mutually Available Modes	Bridges Connecting Them
--Frontal Right	Corpus callosum
Left Posterior Convexity – --Right Posterior Convexity	Corpus callosum
Frontal Left --Left Posterior Convexity	Conduit between Broca's and Wernicke's
Frontal Right – Right Posterior Convexity	Conduit between two unnamed, similarly located areas, in right hemisphere

Your third non-preferred mode, the one that is not next to your preference and is not connected to it by a bridge built of neurons, is your natural weakness. It is as inefficient as your other non-preferred modes and it is located diagonally across the brain from your preference. As no diagonal bridges exist in the brain, getting from your preference to this non-preferred mode is difficult. And, communication between this mode and your preference is significantly more work.

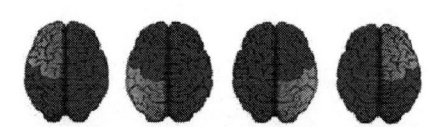

Modes Not Connected
Frontal Left and the Right Posterior Convexity
Frontal Right and the Left Posterior Convexity

It is this third non-preferred mode, the one that is not connected to your preference, that you cannot readily use as an auxiliary and that you must ultimately accept as your weakest mode or inferior function.

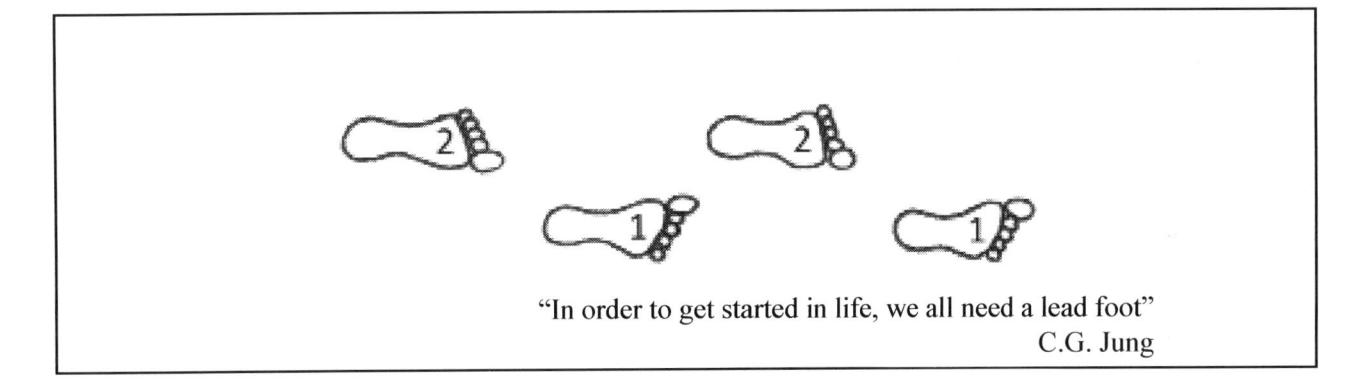

"In order to get started in life, we all need a lead foot"
C.G. Jung

Some people have difficulty with the concept of dominance. These people often associate it with the word *dominating*, an unfortunate association that suggests controlling, limiting and overbearing behavior. Actually, in scientific terms, *dominance* simply means that within a given system, comprised of discrete elements, one part of the system leads while the others follow – an organizing organizing scheme that is found in countless systems, both natural and man-made.

Geese fly south, in formation, following their leader.

SOUTH ⟶

Dominance in nature organizes animals into groups that follow the lead indicated by their leader, the dominant male or female in the group.

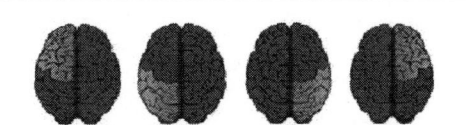

We even use this structure to describe how we, as humans, co-function or collaborate:
- when two people dance together, one usually leads while the other follows,
- when an orchestra performs, its members follow the lead of the conductor,
- when the violin section plays, its members follow the lead of the 1st violinist,
- when a group of boy scouts go on a hike, they follow their pack leader, who sets the direction, and
- when a corporate team brainstorms how to solve a marketing problem, they follow the facilitation of their manager.

What's more, dominance in thinking is just one of the many ways in which dominance governs your body and behavior. You experience dominance within your own body most immediately through your handedness. You are also: armed, footed, legged, eyed and often eared. In other words, one arm is naturally stronger, one foot generally leads, one leg is naturally stronger, one eye does most of our focusing, and one ear most of the hearing so that you generally hold that ear to the phone when talking – whether you realize it or not.

Stopping to think about handedness can give you an appreciation for dominance as well as how dominance affects your life. Handedness is normal. Most people, 95 percent of us, have a clear left or right-handedness. Although this is true, it is important to add that handedness does not limit you to the use of only one hand or minimize the importance of your non-dominant hand. Rather, it defines the role of your non-dominant hand as that of a follower or supporter. You need and depend on your two hands working together, to cooperate when you must do a two-handed job.

Consider what happens when you write a letter. Naturally you do the actual writing with your dominant hand. In order to keep the paper from moving, and perhaps to get the cap off the pen in the first place, you will, however, invariably need and use your non-dominant hand. Your two hands work together, one leading, and one supporting, to successfully complete the task. Similarly with brainedness, having a lead in one mode does not make your other modes unimportant.

Finally, by looking at what you already know about handedness, you can see that when your environment suits your dominance, you are able to perform effortlessly and well, but when your environment does not match your dominance you are uncomfortable and often function poorly. Consider the example of the left-handed person who has only right-handed scissors for cutting or the left-handed person sitting immediately to the right of a right-handed person at the dinner table. When the environment does not suit a particular instance of dominance, the person or group has difficulty.

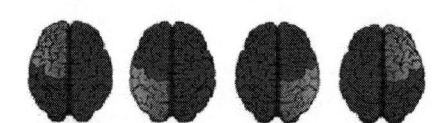

As you consider these other examples of dominance, you can begin to appreciate that what is true for dominance in handedness is true for brainedness. When you are in an environment that matches, feeds and uses your brain's preference, you are mentally alert and on top. But, when you are in an environment that does not allow you to use your brain's preference, you become bored, or tired and have difficulty continuing to pay attention.

Once you understand that brain dominance is as common and natural as handedness, it becomes easy to understand how and why two people with similar backgrounds, even within the same family, can think very differently about the same idea, topic or event. Many interpersonal conflicts and much miscommunication have their roots in people's differing patterns of dominance.

In summary, the Law of Dominance governs your ability to develop and use the four types of thinking as well as your ability to solve a particular problem without help and or get along with others whose help you need and want.

▲ Questions and Answers About Dominance

What is the difference between *preference*, *dominance* and *competency*?

Your preference is your predisposition for one type of thinking based on its superior natural efficiency that makes using it fun and effortless. You are born with this preference. It is a key part of who you are and it never changes. Thus, originally, when people began to look at brain dominance, in the 1970's *dominance* was used to indicate a person's natural *preference*.

Practically speaking, however, because so many assessment instruments measure a person's practical dominance and mistakenly identify it as that person's natural dominance, I prefer to use qualifying adjectives when talking about dominance:
- *Natural dominance*: a person's preference
- *Practical dominance:* a person's developed pattern, which may or may not be natural.

Finally, *competencies* are skills developed by study, practice and repetition. The most important thing to understand is that you can and do develop competencies in your non-preferred modes as well as in your preference. Naturally, the competencies you find most energizing are those you develop in your preference, they are your *preferred competencies*. If we are allowed to do the things that we enjoy that energize us, things that use our *preferred competencies*, we will quite naturally develop more competencies in our preference than in any of our other modes, and enjoy *natural dominance*. Practically speaking, however, life may lead us to develop and use more competencies outside our preference. When this happens, we are Falsifying Type and our effective or practical dominance will reflect this Falsification of Type rather than our true preference or natural dominance.

How many different patterns of mental dominance are there?

There are only four patterns of *natural dominance*. These are the four quarter-brained patterns in which only one mode is highly developed and that mode is also the person's natural preference or lead. By contrast there are fifteen patterns of *practical or effective dominance* that can occur as a result of a person developing and using non-preferred competencies. These are:

- four quarter-brained patterns in which only one mode is highly developed and that mode is *not* the person's natural preference. This pattern involves falsification of type and is not very effective or dependable.
- six half-brained patterns in which two modes are highly developed, one of which may or may not be the person's natural preference. If the highest mode is the person's natural lead then this pattern can be highly effective and dependable in life. If the highest is not the person's natural lead this pattern involves falsifying type and is not very effective or dependable.
- four patterns in which three modes are highly developed, one of which may or may not be the person's natural preference. If the highest is in the middle and is also the person's natural lead then this pattern can be highly effective and dependable in life. If the highest is not the person's natural lead or is not in the middle this pattern involves falsifying type and is not very effective or dependable.
- one pattern in which all four modes are highly developed, although only one is the person's natural preference. When developed early in life this pattern is not dependable. When developed later in life it may be highly dependable and effective if the person is leading with their natural preference.

In general, people are healthiest and most effective when their natural preference is included in their developed dominance pattern and it is also their most developed or strongest mode. Problems are more likely to occur when a person's natural preference is not included in their practical dominance; and/or when their practical dominance scores indicate that their greatest natural weakness (diagonally opposite their natural preference) is being used more than the person's natural preference or auxiliaries.

Which pattern is the most common?

Statistically speaking, the most frequent pattern is the one with two very strong modes, the half-brainers. Approximately 55 percent of the population has two strongly developed modes. What's more, as explained in Chapter 1, half-brainers come in several varieties. They might be double frontal, double posterior convexity, double left, double right, or even a diagonal combination of the Left Posterior Convexity and Frontal Right. This insight with respect to the range and variety of patterns is particularly important and contrary to hypotheses in the 1960's and 1970's that we were all either "left-brained" (i.e. double lefts) or "right-brained" (i.e. double rights).

What is the approximate frequency of the other patterns?

Approximately 25 percent of the population has only one highly developed, dominant mode. When these persons are in a situation that demands the expertise of their lead, they tend to come across as experts. When the context shifts and the necessary skills are outside their single area of strength, however, these same persons may be seen as too narrowly focused or narrow-minded. An example of such context-dependent, negative labeling is the strong Frontal Left thinker, who is respected for his

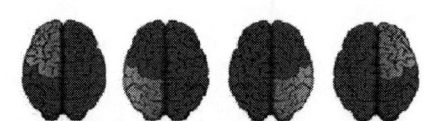

analytic skill in structuring contracts yet is seen as a dud the same evening at a cocktail party.
By contrast the 55 percent of the population with two strongly developed modes is seen as more flexible and broad-minded. Nonetheless, even these persons can be seen, by others, as distinctly skewed. This seems to be most obvious when the person in question is a double left or a double right thinker.

Tri-modal thinkers are far more rare, making up only about 15 percent of the population. These individuals, with their wide-ranging developed competencies, enjoy a flexible strength. They are often recognized as *translators* as they find themselves being asked to assist people with differing and narrower patterns to understand each other. Although many people look at triple translators with a sense of envy or admiration, the pattern is not without its disadvantages, one of which is difficulty in decision-making. With three equally developed modes all vying for control, it is not uncommon for tri-modals to feel confused or terribly at odds with themselves.

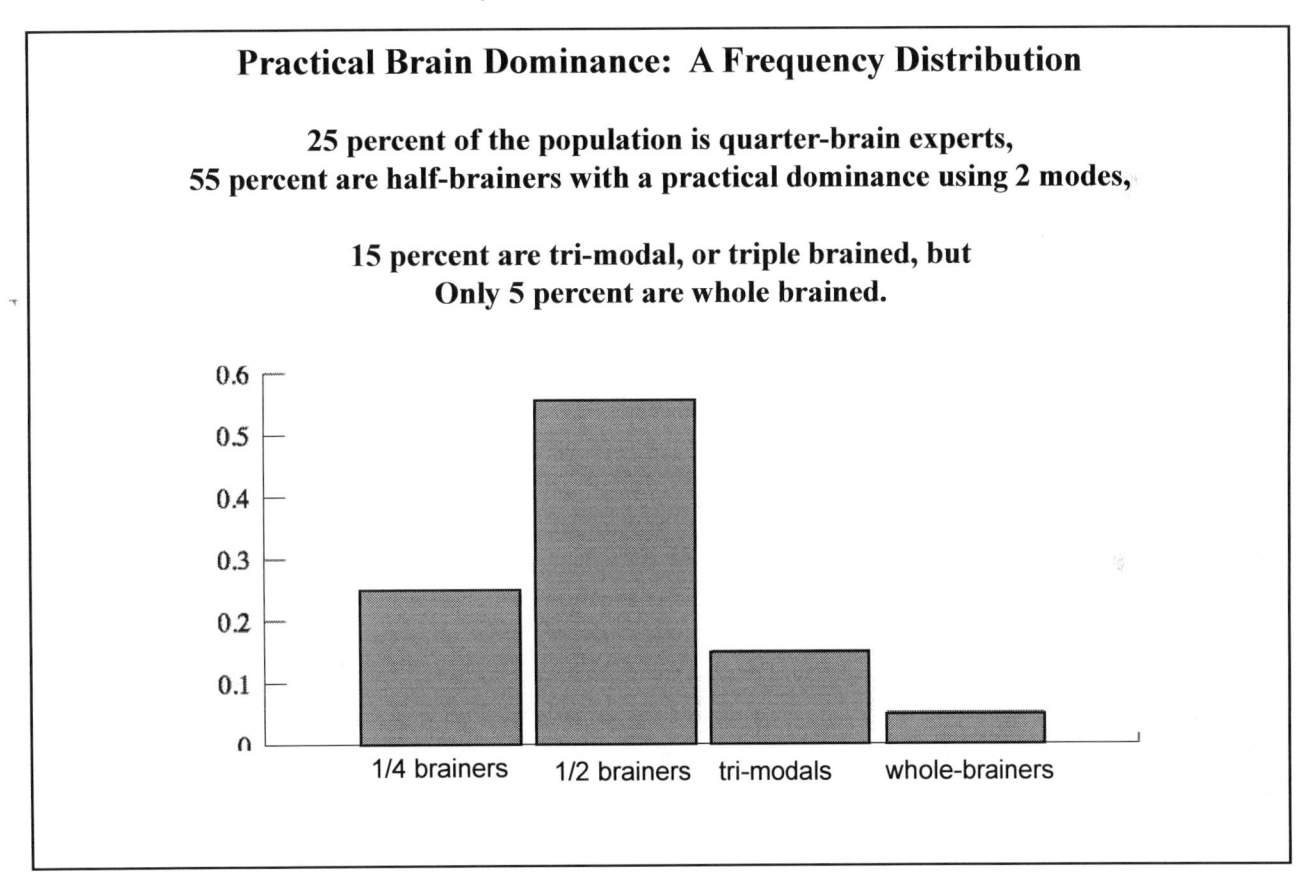

Practical Brain Dominance: A Frequency Distribution

**25 percent of the population is quarter-brain experts,
55 percent are half-brainers with a practical dominance using 2 modes,**

**15 percent are tri-modal, or triple brained, but
Only 5 percent are whole brained.**

	1/4 brainers	1/2 brainers	tri-modals	whole-brainers
	0.25	0.55	0.15	0.05

The last of the general patterns, in which all four of the modes are strongly developed, is referred to as whole-brained. The pattern is found in only a small portion of the population, approximately 5 percent, and is noted for either its high degree of flexibility or its indecisiveness, depending on the context.

What is important to keep in mind, however, is that all patterns can be equally valid and equally useful in life. The energy and drive that the quarter-brain expert focuses in one mode enable him or her to devote countless hours and concentrated effort to accomplishing things for which a more broad-minded person would not sit still. At the same time, the breadth and holistic understanding of the more whole-brained person enable him/her to communicate more readily and effectively with a wide range of persons, a task that would confound and exhaust the narrowly focused brain.

What is the most important point about dominance?

The most important question to ask yourself is whether your present lead is your natural lead and the preference that energizes you by its high degree of natural efficiency. When you have answered that, then you can ask yourself whether the additional modes you are using are your natural auxiliaries.

To honor and work with your natural dominance, you need to value it, use it and leverage it. Over time we are energized and uplifted by leading with our natural preference and by using one or both of our natural auxiliaries to support our preference – by living over center. By contrast, we are made irritable, anxious, exhausted and depressed by: trying to lead with one of our natural auxiliaries or trying to use our natural weakness as our lead or even as a primary auxiliary. That is the rule. That is the way our dominance works.[6]

Your Brain's Auxiliaries and Weakness		
Your Preference is most efficient	Its Natural Auxiliaries are less efficient and easy accessible	Its Natural Weakness is less efficient and not easily accessible
Frontal Left	Frontal Right; + Left Posterior Convexity	Right Posterior Convexity
Frontal Right	Frontal Left; + Right Posterior Convexity	Left Posterior Convexity
Left Posterior Convexity	Right Posterior Convexity; + Frontal Left	Frontal Right
Right Posterior Convexity	Left Posterior Convexity; + Frontal Right	Frontal Left

---

6 See Chapter 11 pages 268-275 for details on using preferences with auxiliaries

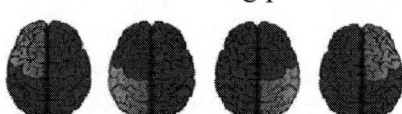

Chapter 3: Two Hands, Four Brains

Now that you understand a bit about dominance, I want to tell you more about your brain's four specialized types of thinking. As you learn about each mode in more depth, you will begin to appreciate how exquisitely designed each is to handle certain kinds of problems. And, as your understanding and appreciation for all four grows, you will see how these four types of thinking, functioning together as a interactive, dynamic set of capabilities (competencies), provide you, and indeed the entire human race with the flexibility and requisite variety to survive and ultimately to thrive.

As you read these in-depth descriptions and characterizations about your brain's four expert systems, ask yourself, have I, because of my strength or weakness in this mode:

- ever been teased or shamed?
- found it easier or more difficult to be accepted?
- found it easier or more difficult to make friends?
- found it easier or more difficult to marry or partner?
- found it easier or more difficult to get through school?
- found it easier or more difficult to hold a job?

Now, let me tell you about your Left Posterior Convexity.

▲ The Left Posterior Convexity: Sequential Mode

This mode has screens that shape its perception of the world so that it sees, hears and tactically perceives the following part of the total picture: rectangular objects with mass, i.e. books, boxes, furniture, cars; small objects with mass, i.e. numbers, numerals, the letters of the alphabet and combinations of letters (words), stamps, coins, keys; spoken and written words, vocabulary; tactile confirmation of a mass obtained through grasping and handling objects.

When and as it perceives any of the above masses, this mode seeks to *sequence* what it has perceived. It *alphabetizes* a set of files. It orders a set of documents *chronologically*. It carries out tasks in a *step-by-step* manner.

We often describe this kind of activity as routine and it is *routine work* or routine thinking that is the province of our left hemisphere's posterior convexity. Its ability to focus on concrete details and to proceduralize enables it to successfully execute routine tasks and groups of routine tasks again and again and again, dependably.

Although some of us use this brain a great deal more than others, everyone has and uses this type of specialized thinking. To appreciate how much you depend on it take a look at your own morning routine. What do you do and have to do every morning? Exercise? Bathe? Dress? Make coffee?

> **SEQUENTIAL ORGANIZING SYSTEMS
> FOR MANAGING DATA, SCHEDULES, PROCEDURES**
>
> A, B, C, D, E, F, G, H, I, J, K, L, M,
> N, O, P, Q, R, S, T, U, V, W, X, Y, Z
> 1, 2, 3, 4, 5, 6, 7, 8, 9, 10
> 1900, 1901, 1902, 1903, 1904, 1905, 1906
> I, II, III, IV, V, VI, VII, VIII, IX, X
> 1:00, 1:15, 1:30, 1:45, 2:00, 2:15, 2:30

Prepare and eat breakfast? Feed the children? The cat? If you work outside the home, do you leave at a particular time? By a particular mode of transportation?

What constitutes a routine is that you do the *same things* every day, in the *same order*, in approximately the *same amount of time*. Some people have only three or four steps in their routine. Others have 15 or 20 steps. For some people one step like bathing can be broken down into an entire sub-routine: start hot water running, make sure soap, shampoo and wash cloth are within reach, adjust water to desired temperature, turn on shower, remove robe, hang it on hook, get in shower, wet hair and wash with shampoo, rinse hair, put conditioner on hair, wash body with soap, rinse off conditioner, turn off shower, reach for towels, put one towel on hair, dry body with second towel, get out of bath tub, hang wet towels over shower rod, etc. In other words, although at first glance a routine might appear to have just a few steps, when examined more closely, this routine may be found to have dozens or even hundreds of discrete, detailed steps arranged in a pre-established sequence.

Recognizing that people who do and enjoy doing lots of routine activities are using this Left Posterior Convexity sequential mode of thinking is an important first step in understanding this specialized type of thinking. Seeing the value of this mode as part of the entire system and appreciating its contribution are necessary next steps.

The first value of routine thinking is that it is *efficient*; it allows you to accomplish a great deal in a short amount of time. Compare the days on which you follow your morning routine (work days) with the days you don't (weekends). Following the routine you are able to get yourself up, dressed, and moving in a short period of time. On weekends, it may take you hours to get through the same steps (if you get through them at all!). Routines help you accomplish tasks and groups of tasks efficiently by locking in a set of decisions or acceptable choices, making it unnecessary to re-decide every day or time what needs to be done. Not having to decide: "Should I exercise or not?" "Should I jog around two blocks or three this morning?" "Should I take a bath or a shower?" "Should I eat cereal or make time to cook pancakes?" keeps you from wasting time prioritizing and deciding.

Another way to view this is that routine enables you to *predict and control* the amount of time it takes to do something. This characteristic of routine thinking is tremendously beneficial in our personal as well as work lives. It allows us to roll over for another five minutes of snooze-time in the morning. It enables parents to know how much time they need to allow to get to work – given they have to dress the kids first. It enables companies to know how many people to hire to accomplish a specific amount of work. As such, it is recognized as important in operational planning.

Another value of routine thinking is that it *frees your mind* to think about other things that may need your attention. Look again at yourself. What goes on as you move through your morning routine? Do you actually, actively think about each of the things you do? If you're like most of us, the answer is "No, of course not". You're functioning on automatic, letting your Left Posterior Convexity mode manage the routine activity while the rest of you thinks about something else, often totally unrelated. This unrelated, second thinking process may be passive or active. You may simply be enjoying memories of a recent pleasurable event, such as a pleasant evening the night before. Or, you may be actively strategizing about the best way to approach the boss to get her support. Either way, routine thinking allows you to have *two thinks for the price of one*. In this way, its efficiency saves you time and energy.

The third value of routine processing is that it is *dependable*, even under stress. Have you ever gotten to work and suddenly wondered: "Did I turn off the iron?" or "Did I remember to lock the house?" You called a neighbor or drove home yourself to check, only to discover that there had been no cause for alarm. Everything was as it should be: the iron was off, the house locked. This type of experience usually happens when we are either heavily preoccupied ourselves or accidentally interrupted during the course of carrying out a routine. At these times, the semi-conscious monitoring, which we characteristically do to ensure that our routine is run completely and correctly, is forgotten. Nonetheless, because our Left Posterior Convexity mode operates as dependably as a computer, programmed to complete any set of routines it begins, we generally find that even when we have been distracted, everything in our routine has been accomplished.

Bringing all these positive traits together, a fitting motto for the Left Posterior Convexity mode might be: "Count on me for double efficiency with dependability".

A point to be made here is that while the Left Posterior Convexity mode functions in an ordered, step-by-step manner, the Left Posterior Convexity thinker is no happier working on a production line than anyone else, doing an isolated task, which in and of itself completes nothing. Indeed, by definition, a procedure moves in a step-by-step way towards a goal.

Of course, there are drawbacks to using the routine mode. For one thing, it does not handle the unpredicted, the unexpected or interruptions well. By its very nature, sequential thinking adheres to a specified format that does not vary or change. Thus, when a change or interruption occurs, it reacts like a computer whose data has been entered incorrectly. It registers confusion. If there are too many interruptions or irregularities in the schedule or environment, a person with a natural lead in this type of thinking may actually crash or shut down while someone with a more active, decision-making mode for a preference comes in to sort out the problem.

LEFT POSTERIOR CONVEXITY FOUNDATION-BUILDING TASKS

A Partial Listing

Buying Groceries	Purchasing Supplies
Keeping Supplies Orderly	Filling Orders
Paying Bills or Taxes	Balancing a Check Book
Invoicing Clients	Writing Pay Checks
Preparing Monthly Statements	Following a Recipe
Washing Clothes or Dishes	Folding Clothes
Routine Cleaning	Preparing Routine Meals
Assembling a toy according to the instructions provided	Assembling a stereo system using the instructions provided

---

Another point is that although our brain's overall thinking system is designed to function on an appropriateness model, passing control to whichever area can best handle the issue or task at hand, in practice, each mode tends to resist giving up control. Hence, the Left Posterior Convexity might respond to an interruption by saying: "We don't need to change the way we do this. It works just fine. It's been working just fine for 40 years."

And yet, despite these drawbacks, the Left Posterior Convexity is a necessary and extremely valuable mode for all of us. Viewed from a systems perspective, this mode performs the meta-function of building and maintaining orderly foundations in our lives. With its attention to detail, dependability and efficiency, it keeps us organized at work and at home. And because it is *on* so much of the time, ensuring a strong foundation, it frees us to learn, explore, enjoy and grow.

Creativity and innovation are wondrous, but constantly having to reinvent the wheel uses up unnecessary time and energy. Procedural, knowledge-based foundations are necessary for individual, family and corporate life: a tree grows only as tall as its roots allow; a building can only climb as high as its foundation can support; and, the best logical argument is no stronger than the data used.

This then is the meta-function of our Left Posterior Convexity Sequential Thinking Mode. As life and human civilization continue to evolve, the strong orderly foundations it provides are what ultimately enable us to live broader and more expansive lives.

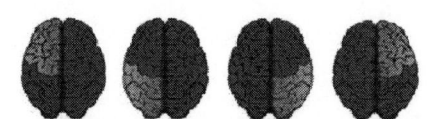

To review what you have read, as well as check to see what you might have missed, look at the above chart. Then, read through the chart below on the Left Posterior Convexity Thinker, asking yourself as you go, "Who do I know that thinks this way? Myself? My mother or father? My child? My friend? My spouse? My brother or sister? My co-worker? My boss?" When someone comes to mind, ask yourself in what way he or she has provided you with foundations.

THE LEFT POSTERIOR CONVEXITY
ITS STRUCTURE, VALUE & META-FUNCTION

THE LEFT POSTERIOR CONVEXITY

STRUCTURE:	SEQUENTIAL
	DETAILED
	PROCEDURAL
VALUE:	DEPENDABILITY
	TIME-SAVING
	LIBERATING
META-FUNCTION:	THE BUILDING AND
	MANTAINIG OF ORDERLY FOUNDATIO[NS]

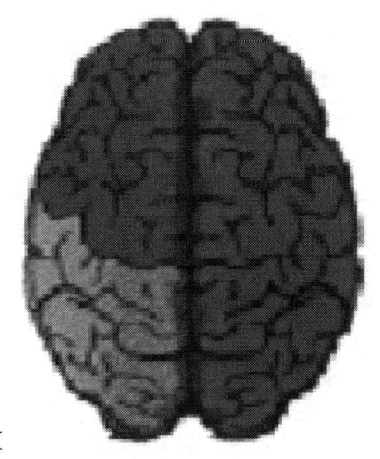

The Benziger Breakthrough

LEFT POSTERIOR CONVEXITY THINKER

ARCHETYPES:
The Adding Machine or Plow Horse

SYMBOL: An Anchor

MOST ATTENTIVE TO: Following the instructions. Matching action to the prescribed routine or procedure. Doing things by the book.

VALUES LEARNING: Procedural applications that have immediate and clear use, and are presented in an organized, pre-digested or step-by-step manner.

INTERNAL LANGUAGE: Data in, data out. The sequential playback of previously experienced or learned events, rules or procedures such as: "Always put the horse before the cart." "Always file your tax return by April 15."

USES LANGUAGE TO: Communicate the prescribed order, or to communicate that something is wrong, that is, something is out of order.

FAVORED MODE OF COMMUNICATION: Written forms that maximize efficiency by requiring or enabling check marks.

PATTERN OR RHYTHM OF SPEECH: Slow and even or steady. Often talking only to verbalize existing expectations, or report what is wrong and the sequence of events leading to the moment in time the problem was discovered.

CHARACTERISTIC THOUGHT PATTERN: Is visceral more than conceptual, preferring to work with things rather than ideas. Also prefers to work with things rather than people.

TYPICAL PHRASES: "Just tell me what to do and I'll do it." "Let's play it safe..." "The law is..." "The rule book says..." "It's important to establish good habits." "Self-discipline is important." "We do it this way here..." "Good fences make good neighbors..."

SELF-PERCEPTION: A highly productive worker.

AS SEEN BY OTHERS: Boring, non-imaginative, a stick in the mud, not an original bone in their body; workhorse who grinds out the task.

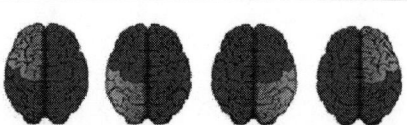

▲The Right Posterior Convexity: Feeling / Harmonizing Mode

This mode has screens that shape its perception of the world so that it sees, hears and tactically perceives the following part of the total picture: information about *things* that relate harmonically not sequentially. For example, musical notes, musical parts, colors, non-verbal body language, facial expressions and voice tone and pitch.

When it perceives any of these, this specialized type of thinking seeks to *harmonize* what it has perceived. Just as the posterior left sequences things to put them in order so they are available to use, the posterior right harmonizes, adjusting the diverse elements until they are in harmony – ready to use. Harmony is not merely nice, it is necessary to continued life. Internal harmony, the kind you feel when you are using your natural preference, makes you feel happy and energized. External harmony, between elements within your environment and between individual members of your family or work team, or between families in your neighborhood or congregation, allows you and those you know to live safer more effective lives, building rather than destroying your community and world. Moreover, internal harmony contributes to external harmony, because when you are happy and energized you find it easier to get along with others, at home and on the job.

Strong Right Posterior Convexities harmonize by singing in harmony, dancing in harmony, dressing in harmony and by matching or mirroring with their own body language the nonverbals they pick up, including easily adopting a dialect or accent from those with whom they are hanging out, or from a region they are visiting, or the pronunciation of foreign languages they encounter when traveling. They become openly enthusiastic when they sense another's excitement and demonstrably sad as they sense another's sadness. Their mood matching response to others is distinctive and impressive. It includes a repertoire of nonverbal gestures – smiles, frowns, pats, hugs, intonation – as well as noises they use like words to *connect* and *communicate*, but which strictly speaking have no literal, left-brained meaning.

Strong Right Posterior Convexities also respond openly to disharmony or *discord*. When someone is upset or uncomfortable, they provide the soft words and caring touch needed to re-establish harmony. They frequently amaze or astound others with:

- their revealing post-meeting or post-party observations about others' emotional states (i.e. "What do you suppose has Mary so upset?", "I wonder what was bothering John. He certainly was preoccupied with something."); as well as with
- their penchant for getting involved in others' lives and showing no hesitation about intervening in what might be considered a person's private life. (i.e. "I think I'll go talk with John. Perhaps I can help." Or, "I think I'll ask Mary if she'd like to have a cup of coffee. I'll bet she needs to talk with someone.").

Although people lacking Right Posterior Convexity access find the ability to read other people's minds and feelings magical, it is only magical because they don't have a Right Posterior Convexity preference. For Right Posterior Convexities, this type of magic is natural.

Scientific research shows this area of the cortex recognizes *faces* and differentiates one person from another more rapidly and efficiently. Some research even suggests that when our brains are damaged in this area, we are unable to distinguish even those we have known well for years. (*The Man Who Mistook His Wife for a Hat* by Oliver Sacks, 1986).

Not surprisingly, Right Posterior Convexities prefer to interact with others often and regularly, preferably face to face.

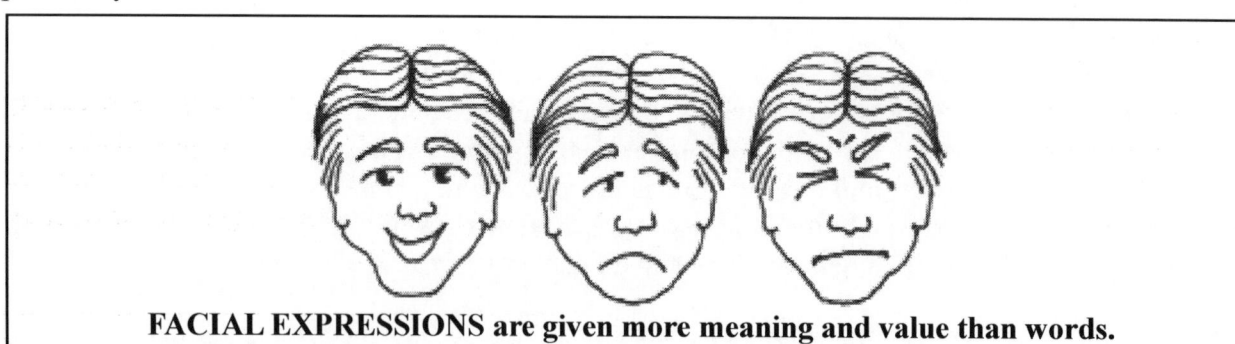

FACIAL EXPRESSIONS are given more meaning and value than words.

At The Mayo Clinic, within the community of operating room physicians and nurses, with whom I worked for many years, the nurses, many of whom are natural Right Posterior Convexities, have relatively little difficulty recognizing a fellow operating room team member once he or she is fully garbed (at which point his/her hair and some of his/her face is no longer visible). By contrast, the surgeons, most of whom have double frontal patterns, with a natural lead in the Frontal Left or Frontal Right and only a minimal access to the Right Posterior Convexity often use the wrong name when addressing one of their team, a mistake that upsets smooth team functioning, but is understandable given what we know about brain dominance. To these physicians, the simple fact that the Right Posterior Convexity team members can recognize others in the OR is remarkable.

Another act of magic is that natural Right Posterior Convexities are able to recognize faces over time – even when a person has aged substantially and others might not recognize them.

Recognizing that people who enjoy activities containing lots of harmonically rich data and easily recognize faces are using the Right Posterior Convexity is an important first step in understanding this specialized type of thinking. Seeing the Right Posterior Convexity's value as part of the entire system and appreciating its contribution are necessary next steps.

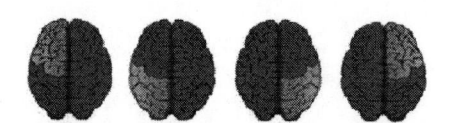

The first value of this type of thinking is that it contributes to human understanding and communication. In his landmark analysis of *human communication*, done in the 1970's at UCLA (University of California at Los Angeles), Dr. Albert Morabian, who has made this area his life's work and is currently head of communication department at UCLA, showed that 55 percent of any message conveyed through speech is contained in the speaker's nonverbal signals and cues (facial expressions and body language),

35 percent in their vocals (voice tone and rhythm) and only 10 percent in the actual words and their meanings. Morabian's findings suggest that more left-brained people often only get 10 percent of what you are saying, but that Right Posterior Convexities, who may not perceive or make sense of specific words, especially those dealing with precision or measurement, can and do understand more of your *total message* than any other single specialized type of thinker

– because they read your face and body in the same way the left brain reads books and listens to the spoken word.

Significantly, when listening to another person Right Posterior Convexities seem to be particularly sensitive to the consistency or inconsistency of the total package of nonverbal signals as well as to the congruency or lack of congruency between their nonverbals and the verbals. This ability to perceive and evaluate the person's communication often allows the Right Posterior Convexity to know whether a person means what they say, will follow through, are lying or telling the truth.

For Right Posterior Convexities
EYE CONTACT is the essence of connecting

If you watch and listen closely to someone with a strong preference for this mode, you'll also notice that they are particularly interested in eyes and tend to watch eyes closely. Some will tell you they can tell what whether a person is lying just by watching their eyes. Others will tell you the eyes are the windows to the soul.

The second value of this type of thinking is that it values and operates to increase connection. This value shows up in the Right Posterior Convexity's use of language. Left-brainers use speech as they use any other tool, to accomplish the tasks for which they are responsible, such as communicating the results of a decision, an expectation, a goal or a set of instructions.

Right Posterior Convexities, on the other hand, talk with others in order to *connect*. Touch frequently

accompanies their verbal expression, to let you know they know you are there, and/or to express their emotional support for you. Unfortunately, *touching to connect* is not fully sanctioned in our culture. It is permitted between lovers, as well as between parents and children, but is discouraged strongly between men and between employees. Where touching is taboo, Right Posterior Convexities use language to touch people. This specialized use of language might even be called *verbal hugs*. Not surprisingly, Right Posterior Convexities need to talk more in an environment where touching is forbidden or taboo.

Right Posterior Convexities regularly reach out and touch someone over the phone or through greeting cards or by sending a special smile or a questioning frown across a crowded room. And, when they do these things, it is to connect or communicate intimacy and acceptance, not to pass along instructions or decisions. The Right Posterior Convexity's use of language is about relating and *relationships*, not information. This aspect of relatedness is key to how the Right Posterior Convexity processes data. A specialized way in which they apply their ability to connect with others is in welcoming and including others. The importance of this is that the more people are connected to each other, the more loyalty and less violence there is among them.

The third value of this type of thinking is that it responds to emotional information and situations with empathy. People and smiles are important to them! After all, the smile, if authentic, is the sign that everything is ok – that everyone is feeling ok. The outward and visible sign of their inner reality is the smiling face they doodle on their notes, buy and stick on a card and use to personalize their e-mails. But when they see someone who is not happy, their discomfort with that directs them to connect – inviting the person to talk about what is bothering them. On a deep level, Right Posterior Convexities know that things go better for everyone when everyone is feeling happy and energized.

This deep level of knowing has been given some scientific foundations and explanation by the research of Candace B. Pert, Ph.D. (*Molecules of Emotion: Why You Feel The Way You Feel*). Significantly Pert's breakthrough work is showing that our emotions – enthusiasm, happiness, anger, fear, sadness, hopelessness – have a physical basis in our bodies – in our brains, along our spines, in our guts. According to Pert, only 2 percent of the self-communication that goes on in our brains is electrical, e.g. moving across neuronal synapses. The rest, 98 percent, is chemical and is mediated by molecules of neuro-peptides on all our cells. So when *we have an emotion*, it is taking place all over our body and not surprisingly Right Posterior Convexities, who are so in touch with and in tune with the human body, are more likely to feel and recognize that emotion than people with other preferences. It is an important and powerful addition to the Right Posterior Convexity's talents. By knowing before others know that they themselves or you are unhappy, they can act to resolve the problem before it results in someone leaving or someone getting hurt.

It is worth repeating that we all have emotions. It is just that Right Posterior Convexities are more aware of what emotions are being felt and who is feeling what as it affects their own internal harmony as well as the interpersonal harmony around them – both of which they want to safeguard.

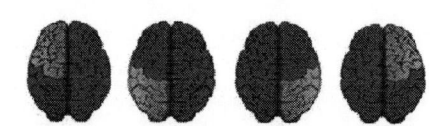

Right Posterior Convexities are particularly sensitive to harmony on all levels. They might notice the visual harmony that exists between certain colors and remark: "That dress looks good on her. It goes well with her coloring." Because the act of dressing is managed in the Right Posterior Convexity, Right Posterior Convexities particularly have outfits that are coordinated and harmonized with multiple colors that look well together. Given the chance, even very young Right Posterior Convexities play dress up or change clothes several times a day. Later, adolescent and adult Right Posterior Convexities spend their leisure time shopping – trying on clothes to see what looks good, feels right or fits the occasion. They might notice the harmony between two scents: "That perfume didn't suit me (with my body's natural odor), but it smells wonderful on you (with your body's natural odor)." And, of course, they notice and appreciate vocal and instrumental harmony. They are helpful in determining which clothing might help someone look and feel better and which food is fresh and safe to consume.

What is the meta-function of this specialized type of thinking? Consider what it is trying to accomplish. By reaching out to connect, it is attempting to bridge the gap that exists between people, to create peace and unity. Its ability to sense clearly what others are feeling and to respond to that awareness with a gesture or word is a powerful tool to experience and affirm our human connectedness.

Significant research in the area of successful, long-term relationships and collaboration by L.K. Steil[7] suggests that the foundation for a *mutual, predictable problem-solving capability* – the ability to work things through without recourse to violence – is the *phatic bond*. This bond is nothing more or less than seeing in another person something of yourself. If Steil is correct, those with the strongest natural ability to see what connects them to others at the deepest level are the natural collaborators and champions of peace.

Life itself is created through the connection of one person to another. The posterior portion of the right cortex is engineered to ensure those connections. It helps us bond and motivates us to nurture each other. It fosters our awareness that we are all one and that to do harm to any of us is to do harm to all. The mega trend High Tech/High Touch, identified by John Naisbitt, in 1982 in Megatrends, suggests that the success and intensity of our technological progress will naturally give birth, in time, to a time when the need for Right Posterior Convexities to contribute to humanity will be recognized and welcomed. Consider the Right Posterior Convexity function as our early warning system – if we utilize it, we can create stronger and more powerful communities – and a strong connected global village. If we do not welcome and use it, we will be forced over and over again to use our own inner resources and those of the world as a whole to repeatedly respond to one crisis after another.

The Right Posterior Convexity's internally pre-structured drive for peace and harmony operates to ensure survival of the species. It excels at sustaining meaningful contact, connections, communications and community. By constantly striving to bridge the gap between itself and others, monitoring hurt

---

[7] LK Steil was a researcher-psychologist hired in the 70's to identify the basis of trust – the type of trust important to team performance – which he defined as the confidence when something happens that might cause someone to distrust another person and react by either distancing or quarreling or blaming, that together you will work through the problem. (Steil did not to my knowledge write books but he did teach workshops throughout the USA for IBM one of which I attended.)

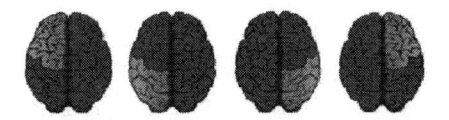

feelings and sadness, and exuding a passion for enthusiasm and connection, it actively works to bring about the peace necessary for our survival. It is the guardian of vitality, peace and harmony, and it becomes clear why its motto must be: "United we stand, divided we fall."

Before reading further, take a moment to review what you have learned about the Right Posterior Convexity's specialized type of thinking. Then, look at the chart on the Right Posterior Convexity Thinker, asking yourself as you read: "Who do I know that thinks this way? Myself? My mother? Father? My child? A Friend? My lover or spouse? My colleague? My boss?" Each time someone occurs to you, ask yourself, "How has this person contributed to the building and or maintaining of life-sustaining, peaceful connections and harmonious foundations in my life?"

THE RIGHT POSTERIOR CONVEXITY
ITS STRUCTURE, VALUE & META-FUNCTION

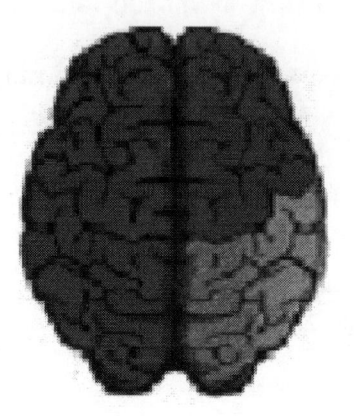

THE RIGHT POSTERIOR CONVEXITY

STRUCTURE:	**RHYTHMICAL**
	NONVERBAL
	FEELING
VALUE:	**INTERPERSONAL**
	SENSITIVE
	NURTURING
META-FUNCTION:	**PEACE & HARMONY**

RIGHT POESTERIOR CONVEXITY THINKER

ARCHETYPES: Reverend Jesse Jackson, Earth Mother, the Shaman, Florence Nightingale, Moth er Theresa, Princess Diana, the Jewish Mother.

SYMBOL: An egg, a smiling face, a bouquet of mixed flowers, a pregnant woman's belly.

MOST ATTENTIVE TO: Relationships and people.

VALUES LEARNING: How to harmonize and identify information that proves the underlying unity or equality of all people/life; or enables them to connect with god and god's creation (i.e. meditation and prayer), and people (i.e. active listening and empathy training).

INTERNAL LANGUAGE: Feelings, felt harmony

USES LANGUAGE TO: Express or share their own feelings, to reach out and touch someone or to harmonize the environment.

FAVORED MODE OF COMMUNICATION: Singing, dancing, speaking with the eyes and touching.

PATTERN OR RHYTHM OF SPEECH: Intonation emphasized. sometimes slow, often flowing or modulated, clearly louder and more pronounced if angry and in sync with whatever they're feeling O.K.

CHARACTERISTIC THOUGHT PATTERN: Visceral more than conceptual, sometimes to the point of being earthy. Jumps quickly to a level of enthusiasm that may seem almost child-like in response to good news (such as the news that someone special is coming to visit).

TYPICAL PHRASES: "I care about you." "I empathize with you." "Tell me what you feel." "Let's do something together." "Oh, it will be fun, we can share." "Teamwork" and "Participation" "When life gives you lemons, make lemonade." "Personal growth"

SELF-PERCEPTION: A caring person.

AS SEEN BY OTHERS: Touchy-feely, a soft touch, a non-stop talker, a chatterbox, fluff, Little Goody Two Shoes.

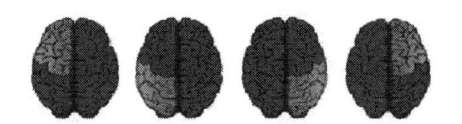

▲ The Frontal Right: Internal Image-Generating Mode

This mode has screens that shape its perception of the world so that it sees and hears the following part of the total picture: abstract, dynamic visual – spatial patterns. For example, patterns revealing trends, natural space, architectural space, caricatures and mime. When it perceives these abstract patterns, this specialized type of thinking seeks to *synthesize* or *interpret* what it has perceived so that what was perceived is useful in predicting changes and in inventing novel solutions to new or unsolved problems. It might synthesize one theory with another as in physics. It might interpret a pattern it perceived through generating a *metaphor* that captures the message. One place to notice this specialized type of thinking is when you are moving furniture. Although many pieces require only brute strength, others require more spatial intelligence. Most of us have been in this situation. We have a large, heavy piece of furniture that we want to move through a doorway. Despite the concerted effort of two or three persons, we are unable to successfully accomplish the task. In fact, after 20 minutes or an hour, all we have managed to do is scratch the table, chip the door jam and exhaust ourselves. We have all agreed that the table simply will not fit through the door and are about to give up when a passerby stops and casually suggests a new angle. Following their suggestion, we discover in a matter of seconds that the table will fit through the door easily!

How did the passerby do it? This kind of spatial problem solving is as magical to those not gifted in the Frontal Right as the Right Posterior Convexity's mind reading is to people not gifted in the Right Posterior Convexity's specialized type of thinking. How does spatial thinking work? Actually it's quite simple for someone with a Frontal Right preference. First, you capture both the image (the table) and the shape (the doorway) on this lobe's internal screen. Then you rotate the two forms until the needed position becomes clear. It is nothing more or less than the ability to *manipulate images spatially* in your imagination. More people do this well than we realize. Some have done it so brilliantly that entire books have been written about how they thought. Find a book or articles about Nikola Tesla, M.C. Escher or Benoit Mandlebrot, the founder of Chaos Theory, or to learn how these Frontal Right skills can be economically profitable – read: *Oil is First Found in the Mind: The Philosophy of Exploration* by Norman H. Foster and published by the American Association of Geologists.

Another characteristic behavior of Frontal Right thinkers connected to their spatial intelligence is *visual filing or stacking*. The system is a simple one. Incoming and working documents are arranged in piles. And, over time, these piles grow into stacks, which cover the desk, the shelves, and the chairs and even, eventually, much of the floor area. Although to a non-stacker such a system appears messy, to the Frontal Right the consistent and stable visual stimulation it provides is essential for success. A more traditional organizing system, using filing cabinets and drawers (Left Posterior Convexity), removes the files and information from the field of vision, and hence make it likely they will be totally forgotten by the spatial thinker. In fact, it occurs to us that the saying "out of sight, out of mind" must have been developed to describe the Frontal Right propensity for losing track of things that have been stored in filing cabinets, even when the files in the cabinet are carefully marked.

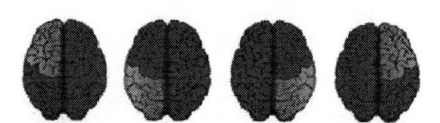

An important advantage of visual filing for Frontal Right thinkers is that it is generally label-free thereby enabling the storage of many bits of information whose precise category or relationship to the problem is as yet unclear. More traditional systems that are grounded in labels would make storing such vague data impossible. When we relate this to the Frontal Right's function to anticipate and facilitate successful change, the value of this flexible storage pattern becomes even clearer. For the data Frontal Rights work with that helps them anticipate change are – for them – like so many pieces of a jigsaw puzzle that cannot be placed as yet because not enough of the picture has been completed. To complete the jigsaw puzzle and to be successful creative thinkers, one must keep those odd-shaped pieces that do not yet go anywhere around and visible.

Another characteristic of visual filing is that the specific spatial location or *context* of each file, relative to their own body, other files or objects is significant in the mind of the Frontal Right thinker. This of course is fine, unless a helpful relative or clerical worker helps by straightening up your office.

Frontal Right prefer to store their information in STACKS

My office, illustrated above, is a typical stacker's office. And, despite nice furniture, my personal office often resembles a paper-recycling plant, especially if I am in the process of creating something new. Many years ago, when I first hired a full-time secretary, problems naturally arose due to my Frontal Right approach to filing. Since the only key to the order in my stacks was inextricably stored in my own spatial brain, it became necessary on occasion for my secretary to phone me long distance when she couldn't find something.

> "Where is the CMC file? Oh, yes, it's there. Go to the desk, stand facing the west window. Put out your left hand. Move three stacks over to the left. Go down about half way. It's under a purple file and has a small piece of torn lime green paper clipped to the front with a phone number."

The Benziger Breakthrough

As you might imagine, this procedure fostered resentment on the part of the secretary whose efficiency and productivity were affected each time she needed a file or document I had been using.

In the end, we resolved the problem by agreeing that my secretary had total control of the files that had to do with program administration and the daily operations of the business. Such a division appears normal and natural, but in the day-to-day running of a business what seems rational is not always what feels right.

Not surprisingly, many research scientists have a Frontal Right preference and need to work out the same sort of boundaries with their technical assistants and co-workers, including their managers. In fact, one of our favorite Frontal Right stories involves Dr. Richard Feynman[8], the Nobel prize-winning physicist, in just such a situation.

During the Second World War, Feynman was asked to join the team of scientists working at Los Alamos. From the moment he set to work, his style of thinking was apparent. As he thought and doodled and listened and doodled, the papers relevant to the project began to a mass. Feynman understood from his own past experience working on difficult problems that his ability to work comfortably and successfully was linked to his notes and papers being left out and undisturbed. Unfortunately, those in charge of project security for the project thought his work was a matter of national security and should be locked up nightly in an office vault. You can imagine, knowing what you now know, the frustration such a requirement would engender in a spatial thinker. As Feynman put it: "You asked me to leave my job and to move three thousand miles to help you because you need my brain, and yet you insist on handicapping it."

This would be a good, illustrative Frontal Right story if it ended here. What makes it an even better one is what Feynman did to deal with the handicap. Over the years, as a hobby, he had learned how to break into safes. This turned out to be just the skill he needed now. At night when his papers were locked safely away, Feynman broke into the compound, eluded both guards and guard dogs, entered the building (picking locks along the way) and finally broke into the safe in which his papers were securely stored to leave a note attached to them which said: "Feynman was here."

As predicted by Feynman, his prank evoked both anger and frustration. And yet, had anyone there understood brain dominance, all of his behavior might have been both anticipated and accepted. As a Frontal Right with a strong preference for change, innovation and mental risk, Feynman had little use for procedural rules or securing things. Additionally, Frontal Rights frequently report getting a kick out of breaking rules simply to see what happens. Although this behavior appears counterproductive to most people, it is only counterproductive when the goal is to keep things as they are. If your goal is to create new solutions or engender change, testing or challenging the boundaries may actually be necessary.

---

8 For those interested in other stories about Feynman, his own autobiography is excellent and enlightening reading: *Surely You're Joking Mr. Feynman, Adventures of a Curious Character*, released in 1985, just a few years prior to his death, by W.W. Norton & Co.

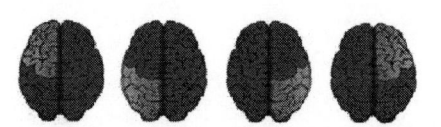

Another element in this tale is Feynman's characteristically *bizarre and quirky sense of humor.* Another person angered by having his hands tied might have behaved more brutally or destructively. Yet, for Feynman, the kick was in demonstrating the other side was not right and leaving a flippant note. With a natural gift for imaging, it was easy for Feynman to picture the project manager opening the safe, as well as the anger, confusion and helplessness the manager would feel as he read Feynman's note and realized Feynman had broken through his trusted security system – again.

Again, the important point is: these skills are critical to the high functioning of Frontal Rights – wherever they are working. Some years ago, a client needed to foster creative thinking in his company. The BTSA confirmed that he had several Frontal Rights working for him, so the suggestion was made that the problem lay in the company's climate. I then related the above Feynman tale to illustrate how legitimate company policies can inadvertently curb creative thinkers. As I recall, the chief executive's face began to break into a smile as I talked, as if a light bulb had gone on inside his head. He had been attached to the military defense industry for some time, and recalled working on a project where all the creative types had had the same spatial stacking habits/needs. Although at the time he thought it was their generally recalcitrant natures, he recalled the project manager had taken the need very seriously. So seriously in fact that he had a safe-room constructed so that when the Frontal Rights arrived in the morning they entered it, worked to their heart's and mind's content all day and left everything out and intact – because the entire room was a locked safe. Bizarre? Only if one doesn't understand the value of undisturbed stacks and papers to those using spatial intelligence to solve problems.

To learn more about this type of thinking look at the books and articles written by Howard Gruber in the 1980's and 1990's. Gruber has made his life's work understanding and describing creative Frontal Right thinkers including: Darwin, Piaget and Einstein.

Yet another odd behavior that characterizes most Frontal Right thinkers is their *tendency to laugh* when no one else is laughing. This behavior, when unexplained, confuses others and raises their suspicions as to the sanity of their Frontal Right colleagues or relatives. In point of fact, the explanation is both simple and rational. As noted, in order to think, the Frontal Right brain must translate everything it sees and experiences into pictures. This translating is most relevant and valuable when the person is attempting to solve a complex problem creatively. It does, however, go on intermittently all the time, which means that while the Frontal Right thinker is listening to or watching anything some of what he is experiencing will automatically be translated into pictorial form so that his preferred mode can process what's happening. These translations are often bizarre and humorous. If the speaker is loud and forceful, the Frontal Right thinker might unthinkingly observe a picture floating across his mind of the speaker transformed into a bull elephant. Or, if the speaker is going over detailed notes, which to the Frontal Right might seem unnecessarily time consuming, the Frontal Right might look at the speaker and see a turtle in a business suit. No wonder they laugh. Wouldn't anyone who saw those pictures?

Thus, many behaviors that characterize Frontal Rights, which may appear quirky to the world, are the necessary and instinctual result of their strong spatial intelligence. But to say or think that spatial thinking is all that this brain does would be a mistake. The Frontal Right lobe is structured to perceive abstract or broad stroke patterns. As such it is the part of our brain that draws and recognizes caricatures as well as models. It does not process all the rhythms and details of a person's face, as does the Right Posterior Convexity. Instead it sees key lines and captures the overall effect. It is interesting to note that if an individual damages his Right Posterior Convexity brain to the extent that he is no longer able to recognize the photograph or face of a friend or loved one; he will still be able to recognize a *caricature* of the person providing his Frontal Right is undamaged. Often, while listening or talking, Frontal Rights capture the force and direction of what is being said in doodles. Although such doodles have not been seen as valuable until fairly recently, we now understand that they are a dynamic map of what the Frontal Right is picturing and when properly decoded, often hold valuable insights about the problem or issue being discussed.

Although this may seem a bit too simplistic, it is an important reminder that as a functionally specialized type of thinking the Frontal Right is totally visual. Technically, you might say it is both dumb and mute for it neither understands nor expresses itself in words or numbers. In order for it to learn or think, everything it sees in the world around it must be translated into internal images. As it takes in more information and translates it into pictures, patterns begin to emerge. The phenomenon is simple. And yet, describing the patterns it perceives can be very difficult. For one thing, the degree of complexity and the multiple relationships conveyed by an image exceed anything that can be captured in simple verbal reporting. Hence the old adage: "a picture is worth a thousand words".

Add to this the fact that the pictures being viewed internally by the Frontal Right thinker are frequently dynamic and moving, rather than still, and you can begin to grasp the magnitude of the problem. Imagine that you are looking at a still image and trying to describe what you see to someone who cannot see the photograph. Then imagine that every 15 seconds the image shifts noticeably. What would happen if you continued to attempt to describe the images aloud? First, your speech might become very rapid as you attempt to describe all of what you see (and how the various parts relate). Then, as the images begin to outpace you, you find yourself dropping an idea mid-sentence in an effort to keep up. You might also give up attempting to capture the shifting details in an effort to fully describe the result. Or, you might lapse into long periods of silence as you get absorbed in watching everything that's happening. All of these – rapid speech, dropped ideas, non-sequential reporting and lapses into silence – are typical speech patterns for strong visual thinkers.

This confused communication pattern is exacerbated when the Frontal Right thinker attempts to solve a problem and talk at the same time. When the mode is actively being used to solve a problem, the speed of the pictures increases. By the time a few words have been spoken, 10 pictures have moved across the Frontal Right thinker's internal screen and, no matter how hard they try, they can't keep up with their pictorial brain. The best they can do is annotating the film inside their head with captions much like those used in silent movies. The only problem is that the listener in this case has only the captions of the film (which is going on inside the speaker's head).

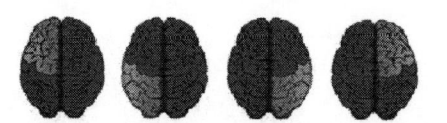

So now we know that there are people who think in internally generated cartoons, caricatures and filmstrips. So what? Why create a discrete specialized type of thinking that works exclusively with silent abstract moving pictures? One clue lies in the role it plays with furniture moving in which this ability was the key to success. Another clue comes to us from the chronicles of Nikola Tesla, an inventor par excellence, who consciously used this ability to design and test new machines in his head. Both examples suggest that the meta-function of this mode is to be the part of our brain that can *envision* a different way of doing things. Thus, just as we have one functionally-specialized type of thinking part of our brain that focuses on keeping things stable and anchored, and a second functionally-specialized type of thinking that focuses on building and sustaining sound human relationships, we also have a third functionally-specialized type of thinking focused on making changes to help us adapt as life and our world changes. For those who trust this specialized type of thinking it is a tremendously efficient, cost effective research and development lab: no salaries, no costly supplies or machines, just the ability to do rapid, low risk experimentation, which can have real world applications.

It is indeed exciting that we are beginning to understand how much humanity owes to this part of our brain. And, yet, we are still beginners at consciously developing and using the Frontal Right's abilities. Some of the ways that are currently being developed include the conscious use of *guided visualization*, a technique based on the Frontal Right's internal image generating skills, to assist in wellness and behavior change. This technique is being used and tested in two very different applications: in health and in improved athletic performance.

In the area of health, The Carl O. Simonton Cancer Treatment Center has demonstrated that when people repeatedly vividly imagine, or visualize, their own white blood cells destroying the cancer cells in their body, they increase the actual rate and strength of this natural disease fighting mechanism, sometimes to the extent of actual recovery. The breakthrough made by the Simontons was the discovery that for those persons for whom visualization was difficult (i.e. they had difficulty in seeing any pictures at all, in creating images which were specific and recognizable, and in manipulating the images so that the dynamic aspect of the white cells destroying the cancerous cells was clear), a film or video showing the desired images and action functioned as an effective training aid, increasing the success of the process.

In the area of improved athletic performance, Sybervision designed a similar approach, under the guidance of Dr. Karl Pribram, who was at the time head of Stanford's Behavioral Research Lab. Here, in a program to improve one's tennis game, videotaped, broad-stroke line drawings of the desired muscle and movement patterns are used to seed the user's imagination.

In both examples, the specific desired future condition is known: in the first, the white cells must attack and destroy the cancer cells and in the second, the muscles must coordinate in a specific known manner. In other words, neither example is seeking to train people to discover or create a new solution. Nonetheless, it is significant that the abilities of the Frontal Right appear to be useful in manifesting, or actualizing, a pre-known vision.

In other companies such as Pillsbury, Apple Computer, Dupont, General Electric, Shell Oil and Proctor & Gamble, people are hiring creativity consultants to go one step further and to consciously develop Frontal Right thinking in order to increase their creative abilities to solve problems by inventing new solutions. It is easy to see how this latter use of our Frontal Right internal image-generating abilities is a more advanced, and perhaps more difficult, application. And yet, both applications have value.

In summary, the Frontal Right is a specialized type of thinking that processes by generating and manipulating internal images. Its meta-function is today more clearly understood and its unique contribution valued. It helps us adapt and make change whether in response to our own internal need to learn and grow (i.e. Abraham Maslow identified the need to actualize at the top of his hierarchy of needs) or in response to the external demands of a changing environment.

Characteristics of this functionally specialized type of thinking are that it needs to work with information spatially and create stacks wherever it goes, that it frequently laughs at the visual representations it creates, that it tends to break rules and procedures as a matter of course. Some of these behaviors alienate others. Nonetheless, because its internal images are transferred into cartoons, jokes or mime (i.e. Robin Williams), the Frontal Right could also be called the Guardian of our Amusement & Humor.

So, take time to review what you have learned about this type of thinking. When you have completed your review, then begin exploring the following chart on The Frontal Right Thinker, asking yourself as you read: "Who you know that thinks this way?" And, as before, when you identify the Frontal Rights in your life, ask yourself: "In what way do these people contribute to life, especially to my ability to adapt and be flexible?"

THE FRONTAL RIGHT
ITS STRUCTURE, VALUE & META-FUNCTION

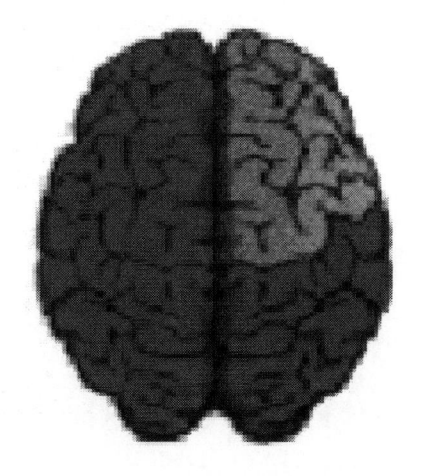

	FRONTAL RIGHT
STRUCTURE:	INTERNAL IMAGES NONVERBAL SPATIAL DYNAMIC
VALUE:	INNOVATIVE AMUSEMENT
META-FUNCTION:	GROWTH & ADAPTATION

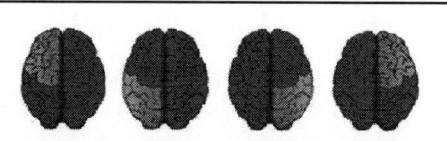

FRONTAL RIGHT THINKER

ARCHETYPES: Mad scientist: Nikola Tesla, Richard Feynman, Benoit Mandlebrot; Dreamer: Martin Luther King "I have a dream" & John F. Kennedy "Ask not what your country can do for you, but what you can do for your country"; Grand architect & Futurists: Patrick Geddes, Buckminster Fuller

SYMBOL: Rainbow, butterfly, eagle wings, sail

MOST ATTENTIVE TO: New ideas, Abstract patterns, Big trends.

VALUES LEARNING: New Concepts, New World Views, New Perspectives

INTERNAL LANGUAGE: Patterns and Images.

USES LANGUAGE TO: Think out loud, to think out a problem or idea they have been looking at inside in symbolic or imaged form.

FAVORED MODE OF COMMUNICATION: Metaphoric or symbolic images or word-pictures such as, "I hit a log jam".

PATTERN OR RHYTHM OF SPEECH: Rapid, trying to capture the picture in words, punctuated at times by silences when they've gone within to look closely at something and they are lost to the world.

CHARACTERISTIC THOUGHT PATTERN: Metaphoric, pictorial. Very conceptual, sometimes to the point of losing touch with reality.

TYPICAL PHRASES: "When all else fails, read the instructions." "Wing it." "Let's play with that idea." "Take an idea and run with it." "It's new." "Being on the cutting edge", "linkages" or "synergistic". "Getting the big picture." "Using a wide angle lens."

SELF-PERCEPTION:
A visionary leader of people, a lighthouse.

AS SEEN BY OTHERS: A space cadet, a dreamer, someone who can't focus, or who has his/her head in the clouds.

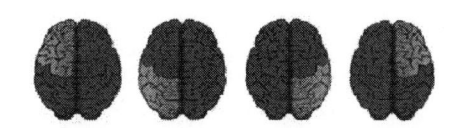

▲ The Frontal Left: Analytic Mode

We now have three of the four functionally-specialized types of thinking in place: one to build strong, stable foundations in our lives, one to ensure that we live in peace and harmony with others, and one to assist us in adapting and making change. All that we lack is the *analytic* ability to monitor our environment and decide which of the modes is best suited to handle the situations in which we find ourselves. Not surprisingly, this is part of the Frontal Left's job description.

This mode has screens that shape its perception of the world so that it sees and hears the following part of the total picture: precise functional structural relationships and the breakdowns in functional structural relationships. For example, how a lever pulley system provides mechanical advantage; how one part of a machine functions and interacts with other parts of that machine to do the specific job it was built to do. When it perceives these functional structural relationships, this specialized type of thinking seeks to *analyze* and *evaluate* what it has perceived, to see if the structure or machine is working correctly and doing the best possible job. When it perceives the function *has broken down*, it analyzes it to repair or fix it so that it is working again.

To say that Frontal Left thinking is analytic is to say, according to Webster, that it is capable of separating a whole into its component parts. A key ability of this mode is critical analysis, the ability to chunk or group items into significant *categories* or *components without the use of pre-established guidelines*. This ability to divide and classify, without pre-existing rules or direction, is an important function of the Frontal Left. Also important is the Frontal Left's ability to create and use signs. Indeed, because of this ability, this chunking may be done symbolically, as is the case with *mathematics*.

A key application of this skill is the act of labeling or naming. The Left Posterior Convexity may store a piece of information from a sensory experience, but unless that experience or key component of it is labeled, it will be difficult to retrieve the memory. Recent research on memory retention suggests that this is precisely the reason many of us have so much difficulty retrieving our early childhood memories; without a well-developed labeling system in place at the time, we did not classify them in ways we can now easily access and recall.

Obviously the ability to name is strongly tied to the ability to develop a growing body of knowledge. A word or concept once named may be stored and retrieved. It may also be explained to or discussed by others. All of us have this ability to name and use labels, but it is the analytic brain that excels in the area of creating new names and classification systems. Thus, it is the Frontal Left that is responsible for the division of experience and information into functional parts with discrete meanings and applications.

Frontal Lefts excel at symbolic logic, but the Frontal Left is not a symbolic brain. This apparent contradiction is explained by the fact that symbolic logic does not actually use symbols. It, in fact, uses signs (which are a specialty of the Frontal Left). A sign is something that has, at any moment in time, one and only one set of meanings. As such, signs are specific and exclusive.

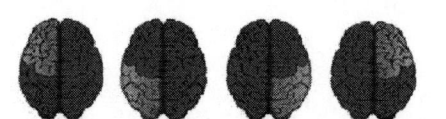

SIGNS AND THEIR MEANINGS		
Chair		Any of a variety of pieces of furniture designed to be sat on
$F(X)=Y$	F	Stands for a specific function
	X	Stands for a specific set of variables
	Y	Stands for the specific set of solutions generated when the specified function is applied to each variable in the referenced set X
$C=\pi r^2$	π	Is a sign for the value 3.14159265
	r	Is a sign for the length of the radius
	c	Is a sign for the circumference of a given circle generated by its radius

By way of contrast, *true symbols*, which are processed by either one or both of the right brain modes, have *layers of meaning* and are more generalized and all inclusive than signs. Consider the symbol for circle. It may describe a closed, unified system like a prayer circle, a healing circle or a sewing *circle*. It can also signify unity or a stable cycle of repetition. Another point about symbols is that they often include an emotional element lacking in signs. The symbol *birth*, for example, which can signify any number of new beginnings, also carries with it a good deal of emotional content like positive and hopeful. Contrast this to the sign for radius (r) that has no emotional over- or under-tones.

This differentiation is important because the Frontal Left has none of the emotion we associate with symbols. Skilled in the use of sign language, it is most adept at cool, logical, non-emotional decision-making. In fact, you might say that part of the value of this mode is that it is non-emotional.

SIGNS DENOTE

SYMBOLS CONNOTE

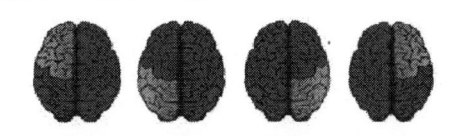

The Benziger Breakthrough

When this cool, analytic mode applies itself to an external, physical reality (such as a machine), its key concern is to identify the object's significant parts and their functional relationships. This type of processing, which focuses on seeing *cause* and *effect* is called *diagnostic thinking*. Frontal Left thinkers excel not only at discovering what is wrong with and repairing broken machines, but also at analyzing and diagnosing the cause of illness in a sick body.

Not surprisingly, when this same Frontal Left analytic approach applies itself to an idea or concept, much the same process takes place. For example, if a strongly Frontal Left manager is given a proposal for a new program, he is likely to see the proposal as a single component in his total operation and to try to understand how it will affect the other components and the structure of the whole system. If, after due analysis, he determines that the overall effectiveness of the operation will be enhanced by the new program, he is likely to approve it. If he doesn't see how it fits in *functionally*, he is likely to turn it down.

Not surprisingly, this mode also excels at comparing differing realities in order to make a recommendation or decision. For example, if you wanted to compare apples, oranges, celery and veal, although you might have a difficult time getting a meaningful answer from the other modes, the analytic brain would have no trouble whatsoever. It would immediately sort out the information and establish that there are many possible answers depending on the intended purpose or use. In other words, it would seek a basis for the comparison. Depending on the basis, the above items might be compared by their cost, weight, protein value, calories, vitamin A content, regional availability or income value to produce. Thus, the analytic thinker begins processing by asking you: "What is the purpose of this comparison and what are you trying to find out?" Once the purpose is known, it identifies appropriate criteria and the desired comparison becomes a matter of mere calculation.

Another frequently used application of this Frontal Left skill is the act of prioritizing. For prioritizing, whether applied to tasks at work or a child's requests for Christmas gifts, involves the comparison of disparate things. Although everyone manages in some way or another to prioritize, many of us feel we muddle through the task. For a strong Frontal Left thinker, however, any and every task that involves the setting of priorities is a welcome opportunity to analyze, categorize, chunk and evaluate.

Another characteristic of analytic thinkers is that they are exceptionally good at staying on track. They are adept at looking at and evaluating various chunks or components with one eye, while simultaneously keeping their other eye on the ultimate purpose of their actions and the direction they want things to go. In other words, they are not only excellent at *goal setting;* they are also equally adept at *goal achievement*. This skill tends to lead them to manipulate the variables in a given situation in order to bring them into alignment with their chosen direction. Perhaps for these reasons, many of us sense capable Frontal Lefts to be very *goal-directed*.

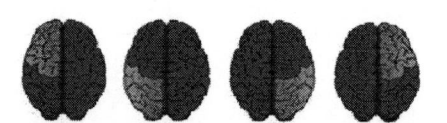

Perhaps because machines tend to embody analytic thinking in its purest form – that is, they have specific, precisely defined components each of which has a contributing function – Frontal Lefts often show a liking for and comfort with machines. Sometimes this liking shows up in an unexpected interest in personally assessing a new office machine or appliance. Often it shows up in their tendency to acquire tools and machines that they assemble into a workshop. Most often, this particular affinity is observable in their characteristic use of *mechanical metaphors* to describe and understand other less mechanical things. An analytic thinker, for example, may talk about *getting a mechanical advantage* in a difficult situation or about managing to get *leverage*. They also "nail things down" and "put the screws" to someone or some organization. And, when referring to a collection of personal skills, they describe them as "my tool kit". This machine talk reflects the way they think about things. They are not usually using it to be poetic or colorful, but simply because it is the most natural way for them to think.

Yet another characteristic behavior of Frontal Left thinkers is verbal fencing. Because critical analysis is their most valued personal tool, and because one's ability to use a tool well is derived from frequent practice, analytic thinkers often play with this skill for the pure pleasure they derive from doing so. Thus, when you observe two lawyers or two physicians in what appears to be a heated argument, you may not be seeing a fight, but rather two adept mental swordsmen practicing the art of mental fencing in order to hone and polish their most valued tool. That they are getting as much fun out of doing so as an NBA player gets shooting a few baskets while crossing a gym floor may be difficult for some of us to understand, but it is, nonetheless, true. Verbal argumentation or debate is actually energizing for Frontal Lefts and they seek out opportunities to engage in it. They simply do not perceive it as fighting, even if others around them do.

In summary, we might say that the Frontal Left, with its ability to compare disparate realities and to analyze complex situations, is the specialized type of thinking that enables us to be *responsive* and *responsible* managers of our own lives and the lives of others. In the final analysis, it is this mode that is intended to direct the operations of the total system, making sure each of the functionally specialized modes contributes in a useful and appropriate way to the success of the whole.

Now, read through the following chart on the Frontal Left Mode. As you read, see if you can explain each word on the chart and give an example of how it typifies this mode.

THE FRONTAL LEFT
ITS STRUCTURE, VALUE & META-FUNCTION

FRONTAL LEFT

STRUCTURE: USES 'SING' LANGUAGE
ANALYTICAL
LOGICAL

VALUE: NONE-EMOTIONAL
NAMING
DECISION-MAKING

META-FUNCTION: MANAGEMENT

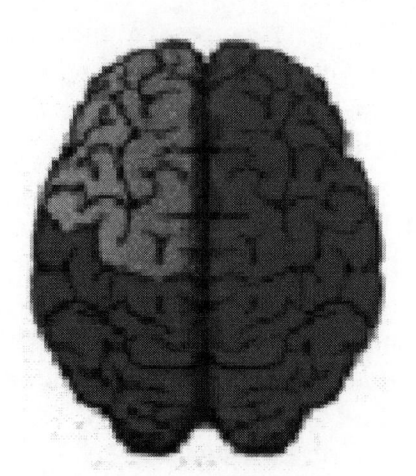

And now, continue to develop your understanding and mastery of the model by reading the chart below on the Frontal Left Thinker. As with the other functionally specialized modes, as you read the chart, ask yourself, "Whom do I know who thinks this way?" When you have identified a couple of people, stop to consider how or in what way these people contribute to your ability to make difficult decisions, to remain goal-directed when it's important. What specifically have they done to assist you?

FRONTAL LEFT THINKER

ARCHETYPES:
The King, King Solomon, The Judge
SYMBOL: A Scepter, Scales, Gavel

MOST ATTENTIVE TO: Operational Principles that enable the efficient use of resources and facilitate technical problem-solving and decision-making.

VALUES LEARNING: General Operational Principles

INTERNAL LANGUAGE: Logic

USES LANGUAGE TO: Communicate the results of their thinking, frequently a decision they have made.

FAVORED MODE OF COMMUNICATION: The half-page summary and verbal debate, verbal fencing.

PATTERN OR RHYTHM OF SPEECH: Short, crisp, chopped, dry.

CHARACTERISTIC THOUGHT PATTERN: More conceptual than visceral, often preferring to weigh the variables, make a decision, and then delegate the doing of the task to another person. Records information by chunks or key concepts, allowing for easier transfer and application of an idea from one area or field of study to another because in each situation the same operating principle is found.

TYPICAL PHRASES: "How do we strengthen our position" "What's it worth to us" "According to my calculations…" "See if you can get some leverage for us" "What's the bottom line" "Weigh all the variables" "Look at the penalty clause" "Do a critical analysis" "Break it down," "Take it apart" "Fundamentally speaking…" "A key point to be reckoned with is…"

SELF-PERCEPTION:
A strong leader, competent decision-maker.

AS SEEN BY OTHERS: Powerful, but often also uncaring, unfeeling, overly critical and calculating in a manipulative manner.

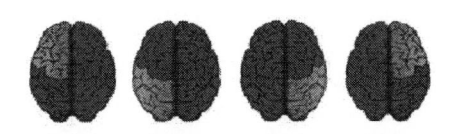

▲ Four Brains, One System

By now you probably have a good feel for each of the brain's four functionally specialized types of thinking. And, you probably realize that they are really separate machines designed to do very different tasks. Now, take a few minutes to scan the following pages. They have been designed with an eye towards whimsy, to assist you in locking in your understanding of how differently these four types of thinking see the world around them. Scanning them will help you to integrate your understanding of the four separate modes into one whole brain model. When you have finished looking at the charts, continue with the question and answer section of this chapter.

Some Other Ways to View Each Mode

How each mode thinks – a symbolic summary

A = A   The Left Posterior Convexity remembers definitions. To it, what IS, is.

         The Right Posterior Convexity picks up the "emotional tone" in the communication or situation. What IS is not as important as how we feel about it.

A = B   The Frontal Right, unable to access and use words directly, generally captures the essence of experiences and data using pictorial, metaphoric analogies. What IS, is seen as something else.

A = A   The Frontal Left, with its focus on using sensed data to made decisions, uses logical functions to convert the raw data into useful data. What IS is analyzed to generate new information.

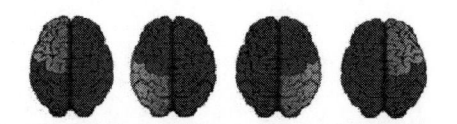

**A Symbolic Graphic Perspective, or
Frontal Right Summary of the Model**

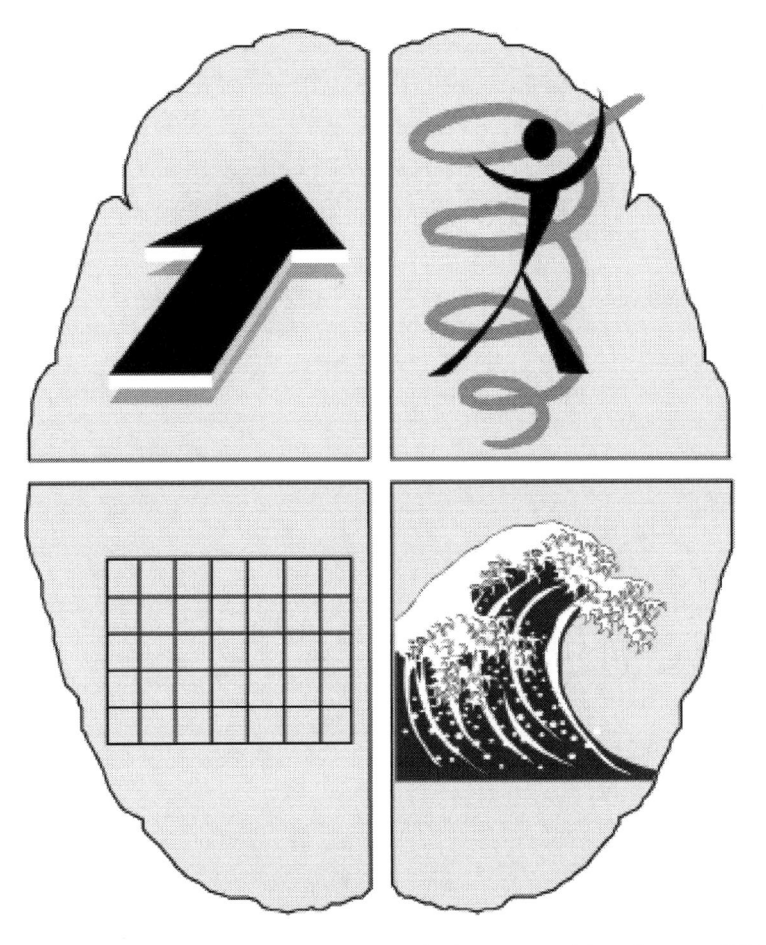

The Left Posterior Convexity pigeonholes everything into a **GRID**.

The Right Posterior Convexity goes with the flow, like a **WAVE**.

The Frontal Right **SPIRALS** high, playing with an idea.

The Frontal Left focuses in on the target, like an **ARROW**.

A Playful Perspective in Pictures
or, yet another right–brained perspective

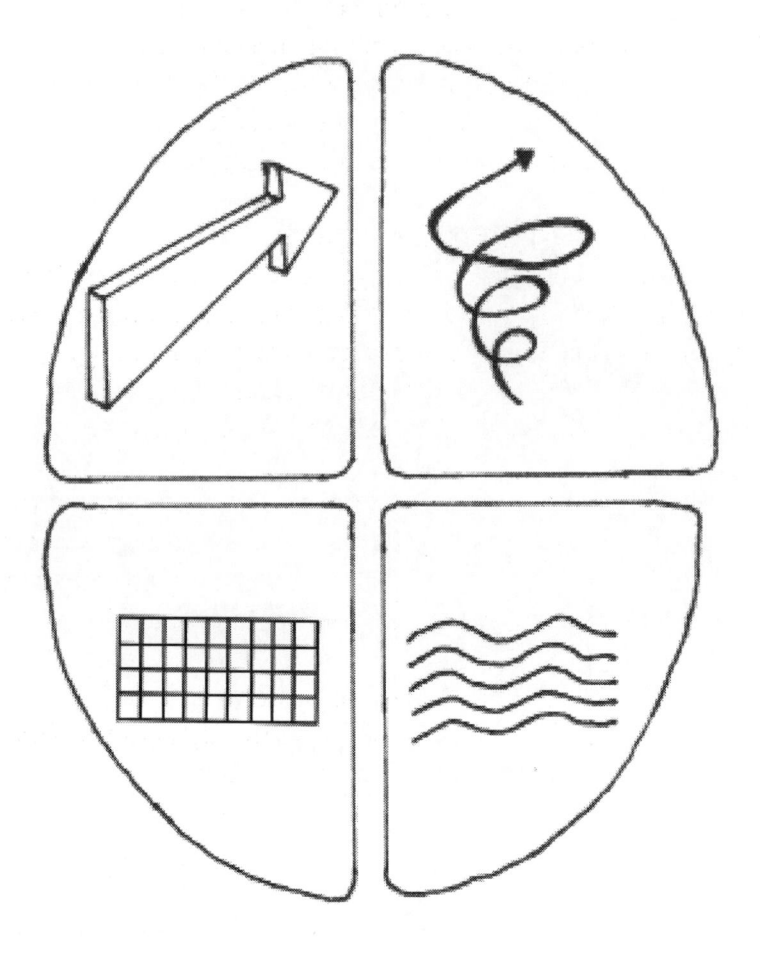

The Left Posterior Convexity **maintains order** by having a place and time for everything and everything in its time and place.

The Right Posterior Convexity **fosters peace and unity** by harmonizing with others.

The Frontal Right **accomplishes the impossible** by using visionary guidance to leap over tall buildings and broad canyons in a single bound.

The Frontal Left **makes difficult decisions** by using logic to compare seemingly dissimilar options.

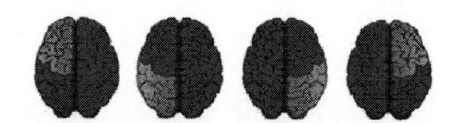

Four Perspectives on Artistic Composition

Given that
The frontal lobes are conceptual and idea-driven;
The (basal) posterior convexities are visceral and sensory;
The left modes are parts-focused;
The right modes experience the gestalt;

It might be said that
The Left Posterior Convexity focuses on sensed pieces or tangible objects
The Right Posterior Convexity focuses on the sensed connection or relationship
The Frontal Right focuses on an abstracted totality,
a unifying symbolic image
The Frontal Left focuses on abstracted pieces or key concepts

Frost's *The Road Not Taken* can be viewed from four perspectives:
The Left Posterior Convexity notices **and** values the words, the written poem.
The Right Posterior Convexity notices **and** values the feelings: discomfort and sadness commonly felt by people who reflect on a lost opportunity.
The Frontal Right notices **and** values the unifying symbolic image – a fork in a road as a time of both opportunity and decision.
The Frontal Left notices **and** values the meter, measure, form
used to structure this great poem.

Beethoven's **Ninth Symphony** might be appreciated
For its diversity of powerful characteristics
The Left Posterior Convexity notices **and** values the notes, the written score and the theme repeated over and over.
The Right Posterior Convexity notices **and** values the feeling of harmony or discord conveyed by the relationship of each note to those around it and
by the tonals - flat or sharp,
loudness, softness, increasing or decreasing pace, silences.
The Frontal Right notices **and** values the unifying symbolic image
of lightning and storm clouds.
The Frontal Left notices **and** values the tools that were used to create the masterpiece, such as meter and percussion instruments.

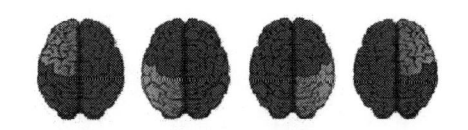

Questions and Answers

You've spent a good deal of time describing and detailing the positive aspects of each functionally specialized type of thinking. What are some of the negative behaviors that we might encounter or experience with each?

The Left Posterior Convexity sequential thinker, while highly productive and necessary can at the same time be a drag in situations when change is needed. Their increased sense of stress at these times can cause them to sabotage others' efforts or to become rigid in their adherence to what is. It is also true that when in conflict with another person, strong Left Posterior Convexities tend to resort to rules and procedures for mediating the conflict rather than trying to process the feelings involved. This approach, particularly if used in family and personal relations, can cause unresolved bad feelings to remain even after the crisis has been solved.

The Right Posterior Convexity feeling-focused thinker, while excellent at nurturing and bridge building, may have difficulty in making and presenting unpopular decisions. Their fear of causing upsets can lead them to avoid the realities of life. As well, if a Right Posterior Convexity decides they do not like you, they may turn on you and use all their intuitive understanding about you to hurt or punish you by making sure you feel cut off and isolated.

The Frontal Right adaptive thinker, while unparalleled in the ability to respond creatively, may nonetheless cause problems for others because he cannot let well enough alone. He will make unnecessary changes simply because adhering to sameness is counter to his internal nature. As well, many Frontal Rights, although committed to a positive and humanitarian vision, may inadvertently walk on people or offend them simply because the Frontal Right pays little attention to their needs, feelings and non-verbal signals.

And finally, the Frontal Left analytic thinker, while perhaps most adept at setting and attaining goals, can become too easily attached to a win-lose scenario in which he intends to win and thus sets others up as losers. In addition, most Frontal Lefts have a weakness in the feeling mode, which means that, like the Frontal Right, they may walk on others and offend them without realizing it and without even sensing or understanding the inherent wrongness in doing such a thing.

The negative behaviors that characterize any given person are a complex matter that arises from the individual's self-esteem and general psychological make up as well as his brain dominance. We can, however, note that, at least in part, our characteristic negative behaviors are determined by how many strengths we have. A half-brainer who has strong developed competencies in both the Left Posterior Convexity and Right Posterior Convexity, with a natural lead in one or the other, will probably not engender as many bad feelings in the process of resolving conflicts as either the quarter-brain Left Posterior Convexity or the half-brainer who is using the Left Posterior Convexity along with the Frontal Left, both of which lack strength in the specialized type of thinking done by the feeling, bonding, peace engendering Right Posterior Convexity mode.

According to your model, the only real logical thinker is the Frontal Left. And yet, many people I know who are clearly not Frontal Lefts consider themselves to be very logical. Can you explain this?

Actually, your experience is not as unusual as you might think. As a society we value logic so much that everyone wanting to fit in seeks to be logical. It is also true, according to our own research that many people simply do not understand what the term *logical* really means.

Indeed, once logic is truly understood, it becomes easy for most people to see whether they are or are not logical. When some difficulty arises it usually comes from one of two sources. The first is the strong Left Posterior Convexity thinker who adheres assiduously to routines and procedures originally established by logical thinking. Such an individual may well confuse his adherence to a logically derived procedure with being logical. The way to assist such a person to realize his confusion is to point out that when a true Frontal Left thinker engages in any procedure, he is likely to stop first to ask: "What, if anything, has changed? What, if anything, is different?" Their purpose in doing this is to determine whether the logical rule applies in the present situation. If he determines everything is the same, he will follow the procedure. If he determines, however, that there is a significant difference in some aspect of the situation, he will first, by logically analyzing what has happened, adjust the procedure so that he has a revised procedure to use. In contrast, the purely Left Posterior Convexity person tends to simply plunge forward into the procedure regardless of the change in circumstances.

The other source of confusion comes from Right Posterior Convexities who see themselves as rational because their behavior and decisions are based on reasons. Our society has lost sight of Jung's understanding that feeling-based decisions are based on reasons and are, as such, rational. Moreover, because we tend to equate *rational* with *logical*, many Right Posterior Convexities confuse these two terms, asserting to themselves and others that they are indeed rational and logical when in point of fact they are rational but not logical. In such cases, a person can be helped to understand their misperception of themselves most easily if they are validated and recognized as rational, and their feeling-based information is recognized, valued and used in problem-solving and decision-making.

I understand the concept that people with differing mental preferences might see the same reality quite differently. Would you give us some examples that illustrate these differences in perspective?

The following seven questions, which cover a wide range of everyday issues and concerns, should help develop your understanding of the *differences in point of view* between the four specialized types of thinking.

Take time to read through these examples slowly. As you do so, consider how you would answer each question. Which answer is most comfortable for you? Which answer is most uncomfortable or unlike you? How do your answers match up with your dominance? Remember, life experience leads us to adopt particular habits of mind that may not actually reflect our natural preference – but rather the preference of one of our parents, teachers or bosses. These are the times and situations when we have been pushed or pulled to abandon our true lead or preference or to Falsify Type.

**How the Brain's Specialized Types of Thinking
See the Same World Differently**

QUESTION #1:	**How do you manage your income?**
LEFT POSTERIOR CONVEXITY:	I budget my income: 20 percent for housing, 30 percent food, 10 percent clothing, 5 percent car payment; 5 percent insurance premiums, 5 percent entertainment and 5 percent towards my annual vacation. The remaining 20 percent goes to the bank into a savings account.
RIGHT POSTERIOR CONVEXITY:	I go easy at the end of the month.
FRONTAL RIGHT:	I don't know. Managing money is a detail in life. I can't seem to focus on it. But I'm lucky and things generally turn out all right.
FRONTAL LEFT:	I get my money to work for me.
QUESTION #2:	**How did you select your last car?**
LEFT POSTERIOR CONVEXITY:	I decided how much I could afford to spend based on my savings and income. And I read *Consumers Guide* to determine which of the bigger, safer cars had the best performance rating.
RIGHT POSTERIOR CONVEXITY:	I talked with several friends and decided to get the kind my best friend has. Oh, except that I wanted a blue car. Hers is red.
FRONTAL RIGHT:	I like cars that are different. Fast. Generally, I buy foreign cars.
FRONTAL LEFT:	The car I own must have a powerful engine and precision handling so that it holds the road.

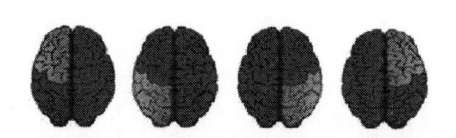

How the Brain's Specialized Types of Thinking See the Same World Differently

QUESTION #3: Are you presently successful?

LEFT POSTERIOR CONVEXITY: Yes, we are successful because we have a daily goal of processing 50 people and today we processed 50 people. Yesterday was not a good day because we only saw 40 people.

RIGHT POSTERIOR CONVEXITY:: Some of the staff are not very happy about what's been happening around here. But I think it's going to change. I noticed the boss had a twinkle in her eye when she came back from the board meeting.

FRONTAL RIGHT: We're really doing well. Batting a hundred. Yesterday didn't look like such a good day at first, but in the last inning, we hit one out of the ballpark.

FRONTAL LEFT: We had a successful day today because we have a goal of processing 50 people a day and today we saw 60. On the other hand, yesterday was also a good day, despite the fact that we only saw 40 people, because one of the people we saw gave us a contract worth eight times one of our normal sales.

QUESTION #4: Why do you do what you're doing in that way?

LEFT POSTERIOR CONVEXITY:: This is how we do it because we have a procedures manual that says to do it this way.

RIGHT POSTERIOR CONVEXITY: I feel comfortable doing it this way.

FRONTAL RIGHT: Our department is a war zone. Most of the time I try to stay in the trenches.

FRONTAL LEFT: This is how we do it because, despite what the manual states, we have found that things work faster and are safer when we do it this way.

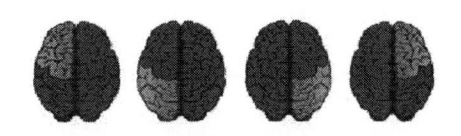

How the Brain's Specialized Types of Thinking See the Same World Differently

QUESTION #5: **If someone came to you with a new way of doing your job, how would you respond?**

LEFT POSTERIOR CONVEXITY: I'd be very cautious. A lot of new ideas are hare-brained. Trying them just wastes time and money.

RIGHT POSTERIOR CONVEXITY: If they seemed to care about me, I'd be appreciative and enthusiastic.

FRONTAL RIGHT: I'd probably listen to what they had to say. New ideas are like a fresh breeze, they stir your imagination. Perhaps later I'd play with the idea to see how it might relate to some of my own ideas.

FRONTAL LEFT: I'd test its feasibility: Can it be done? Can it be done cost effectively? Will it sell?

QUESTION #6: **If you were standing at a <u>crossroads</u> at a place <u>unknown</u> to you, how would you decide which direction to go in?**

LEFT POSTERIOR CONVEXITY: I'd probably go along the most well-worn path.

RIGHT POSTERIOR CONVEXITY: I'd go where there were people and something happening.

FRONTAL RIGHT: Ah yes, "Two roads diverged in a yellow wood…" Well, naturally I'd take the road less traveled, to seek adventure and excitement.

FRONTAL LEFT: I'd go where I could accomplish something, where there was a phone, a bank, or a car rental agency.

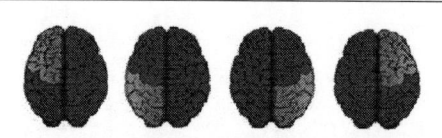

How the Brain's Specialized Types of Thinking See the Same World Differently

QUESTION #7: What's wrong with the world?

LEFT POSTERIOR CONVEXITY: There's not enough food and people don't respect law and order anymore.

RIGHT POSTERIOR CONVEXITY:: There's not enough love. People don't care enough or give enough.

FRONTAL RIGHT: The human race is like a pack of turtles. People are too slow to change. Even now, when we understand the planet's total ecological system and how our past and current behavior is endangering the balance in that system—even to the extent that our own lives are in jeopardy. We need to learn to live as part of the total synergistic system.

FRONTAL LEFT: Distribution is the principle problem. 80 percent of the food is produced by countries with only 30 percent of the population.

The above examples focus specifically on the points of view most often taken by people with only one lead mode. How can we begin to recognize and understand the more complex patterns?

Just as yellow and red blend to make orange, and blue and yellow blend to make green, the four core modes blend together to create new and specialized perspectives. Learning to recognize and relate to these takes time and practice Even so, they will become more familiar to you as you read the remaining chapters in the book.

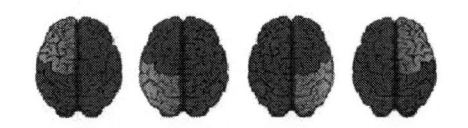

Chapter 4: The Other Key Piece

▲ Introversion and Extraversion

Your preference for one or two highly specialized modes reveals *the type of thinking* your brain does most efficiently, in other words how it likes to process information i.e. sequentially, rhythmically, synthetically or structurally. Of equal importance is your *introversion/extraversion level* that reveals the context within which you are most effective; more specifically, the level of stimulation within the context.

Attending to this context is most important for the 15 percent of the population who are highly extraverted and the 15 percent of the population who are highly introverted. For these people the right job in the wrong context could spell failure. Moreover, because almost 70 percent of the population does not have such extreme needs for high or low levels of stimulation, context is often overlooked or interpreted as a matter of someone's bad attitude or lack of motivation.

Paul's experiences provide an illustrative example. An introverted Frontal Right, Paul had selected and trained in a career that suited his strong Frontal Right lead, long range planning. As faculty positions at universities were declining, he took a recently created position as Director of Long Range and Strategic Planning for a large medical center. Given the changes taking place in the American Health Care System there could be little doubt that Paul's employer needed Paul's natural gifts as a futurist for visionary, innovative planning. Thus, the initial challenge was exciting. Within a few months, however, Paul began to realize that the manner in which the organization was run required him to sell his ideas in order to get support, money and the go ahead. Furthermore, this selling was generally in a high-pressure meeting with several others present. Although Paul did his best, the extraverted context – the high-pressured meetings – in which he was forced to work made it difficult for him to be successful. As well, the pressure to perform as an extravert on the job began to take a toll on his health through the chronic anxiety he developed while attempting to cope.

Paul's solution was to hire a coach (us) and subsequently restructure the situation. By working to meet with each key decision-maker in advance of all decision-making meetings, Paul was able to do the required selling in a more protected, low-volume context. Moreover, by identifying each key player's preference Paul was able to give a sales presentation tailored to each individual's needs. The result – Paul was able to be increasingly successful, while reducing the chronic anxiety he had been experiencing.

Barbara offers another example. An extraverted Frontal Right, Barbara had taken a dual major in college: chemistry and psychology. Her first job had involved cutting edge research in chemistry, something that is typically interesting to a Frontal Right brain gifted at recognizing large scale or visual-spatial patterns. The problem for Barbara was that she was an extravert who needed a much higher level of stimulation around her in order to thrive. Luckily, she was able to find and transfer to a second job as Director of the Human Resources function in the same organization for which Paul worked. As the organization had done little in HR previously, the job required a good bit of creativity and, of course, extraversion to sell the ideas to top management. Not surprisingly, Barbara thrived.

This is how it works. *Extraverts* are most effective in very stimulating situations, situations in which a great deal is going on, in which there is a high volume of input. Obvious examples of the high volume situations on which high extraverts thrive are:

- the football game with a large noisy audience.
- the pit on Wall Street in which trading is done by shouting amidst multiple and rapidly changing visual cues.
- the typical office Christmas party.
- The Boston Marathon
- the front line in a war zone.

Significantly, the volume of stimulation can be achieved through:

- intense and rapidly changing images (visual input);
- loud and diverse sounds or voices (auditory input);
- frequent and impactful physical contact (kinesthetic input);
- intense or high-ticket win-lose dynamics (high risk; high adrenaline).

There are many additional work situations, some less obvious, in which extraverts thrive because they involve a higher than normal level of stimulation:

- negotiating for big stakes (the bigger the better).
- founding an entrepreneurial venture.
- working in a large office with no dividers and multiple phones that ring frequently and loudly.
- selling in a store with heavy traffic or on a sale day.
- working in an emergency room.
- trouble-shooting to turn around a problem division in a company.

Introverts, on the other hand, are most effective in situations with low-volume stimulation, situations in which little or nothing seems to be happening. Obvious examples of the low volume situations in which introverts thrive are:

- the research library.
- the research lab.
- the quiet dinner for two.
- the stroll in a quiet English garden or on the beach at sunset.
- behind the lines in a war zone or better yet, not in the war.

Significantly, the lower volume of stimulation can be achieved by:

- muted and slowly changing images (visual input);
- few and soft sounds or voices (auditory input);
- infrequent or sustained, gentle physical contact (kinesthetic input);
- non-competitive or collaborative contexts (low risk; low adrenaline).

Here are some additional work situations, some less obvious, in which introverts thrive because they involve a lower than normal level of stimulation:

- thinking, creating or working alone, off by oneself.
- a small office with a door that closes, one phone with one line.
- a back-office away from the action.
- organizations in which collaboration, harmonizing and listening are emphasized and valued: a symphony, chamber quartet, church.
- advising or offering service rather than selling.

Importantly, each of these extreme arousal levels, like each specialized mode of thinking, contributes to life and success in special ways. The extreme extravert has an asbestos-like consciousness that enables her to work effectively in situations that are too hot or intense for most of us. These include: fire fighting (literally and figuratively), troubleshooting, innovating, and negotiating in crisis situations. In contrast, the introvert, with his reflective consciousness keeps an individual or culture aware of and connected to its center or core values.

If you are part of the 70 percent who enjoy a balanced level of extraversion/introversion, you thrive in moderate situations – ones that are neither hyper and intense nor sedate and low key. Situations in which you have flexibility to schedule events so that if and when something comes up that requires an extreme response, you can keep yourself balanced by *doing things before and after* each extreme task that provide you with that balance. For example, if you need to negotiate in a win-lose situation, balance yourself by being alone or doing something that uses your natural gifts alone or with one or two people you like and trust before and after. Or, if you find you have to periodically work alone for several hours or longer, plan to balance yourself by being around people and doing something you like before and after each isolating experience.

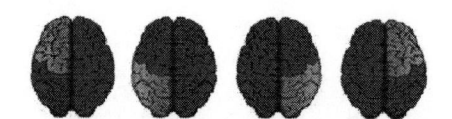

THE EXTREME JOBS
Professional Needing a High Level of Extraversion or Introversion

Preference	Extraversion / Introversion	Matching Professions
Left Posterior Convexity	Extravert	Machine operator or mechanic building or repairing machines on an assembly line, in a factory
	Introvert	Bookkeeping, stocking and inventory, working in a quiet or back office
Right Posterior Convexity	Extravert	Elementary school teacher, athletic coach for children for team sports
	Introvert	Interior decorator, blues musician, nun
Frontal Right	Extravert	Entrepreneur, innovator
	Introvert	Psychiatrist, philosopher, poet, geologist, physicist, jazz musician, composer
Frontal Left	Extravert	CEO (Chief Executive Officer), CFO (Chief Financial Officer)
	Introvert	Mathematician, statistician, actuary, financial analyst and advisor
Double Left	Extravert	COO (Chief Operating Officer)
	Introvert	Design engineer, accountant, operations manager
Double Right	Extravert	Marketing, public relations
	Introvert	Actor or artist, ballet dancer
Double Posterior Convexities	Extravert	Secretary, nurse, teacher
	Introverts	Nun
Double Frontal	Extravert	CEO (Chief Executive Officer), trouble-shooter, turn-around expert
	Introvert	Research scientist, economist
Left Posterior Convexity	Extravert	Journalist
Frontal Right	Introvert	Librarian

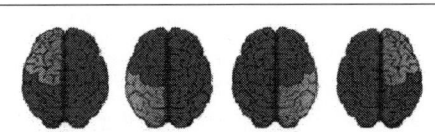

The Benziger Breakthrough

Interestingly enough, because the contexts within which certain professions are practiced are fairly stable, and/or because the profession involves a good deal of internally-focused or reflective thinking, it is possible to identify the types of people who are energized by these professions by overlaying a particular preference with a particular level of extraversion or introversion. **Some examples are given in the chart.**

We'd like to emphasize, however, that this lining-up is not always possible. Nonetheless because the basis of success is actually the volume of stimulation, when considering a career or job the most important thing to do is to look at the specific job or context to determine whether or not it matches you and your extraversion or introversion needs.

▲ Introversion, Extraversion and the Arousal System

According to the work of Hans Eysenck, PhD and Zenith Petrie, PhD, our arousal system establishes the basis for our level of extraversion. Each of us has a natural, stable level of arousal when awake. However, arousal levels vary from person to person. Those who have a very high level of arousal (i.e. they are naturally very alert when they are awake), are seen as introverted because they take in so much information second per second that they typically select environments as optimal that have lower volumes of stimulation occurring (i.e. a library, research lab, nature, a back office). By contrast, those who have a very low level of arousal are naturally barely awake and subsequently seek out sources of stimulation (i.e. a crowd, a front office, the pit in a stock exchange, competition or an argument with another person) in order to achieve an optimal level of inner wakefulness.

Petrie labels introverts *diminishers* because in many situations they need and seek to diminish the intensity of stimulation, to suit their naturally hyper-alert arousal level and preclude their needing to shut down due to being overwhelmed. She labels extraverts *augmenters* because in the majority of situations they need to increase the level of activity or stimulation in order to achieve sufficient wakefulness.

This kind of insight is invaluable. For many years people have had difficulty distinguishing between the interest in people demonstrated by feeling types and by extraverts. Indeed, many people regularly confuse the two to such an extent that many people have taken to calling someone extraverted who showed a keen interest in people. Here, at last, we have a solid, scientific model for distinguishing the two.

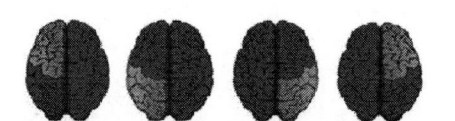

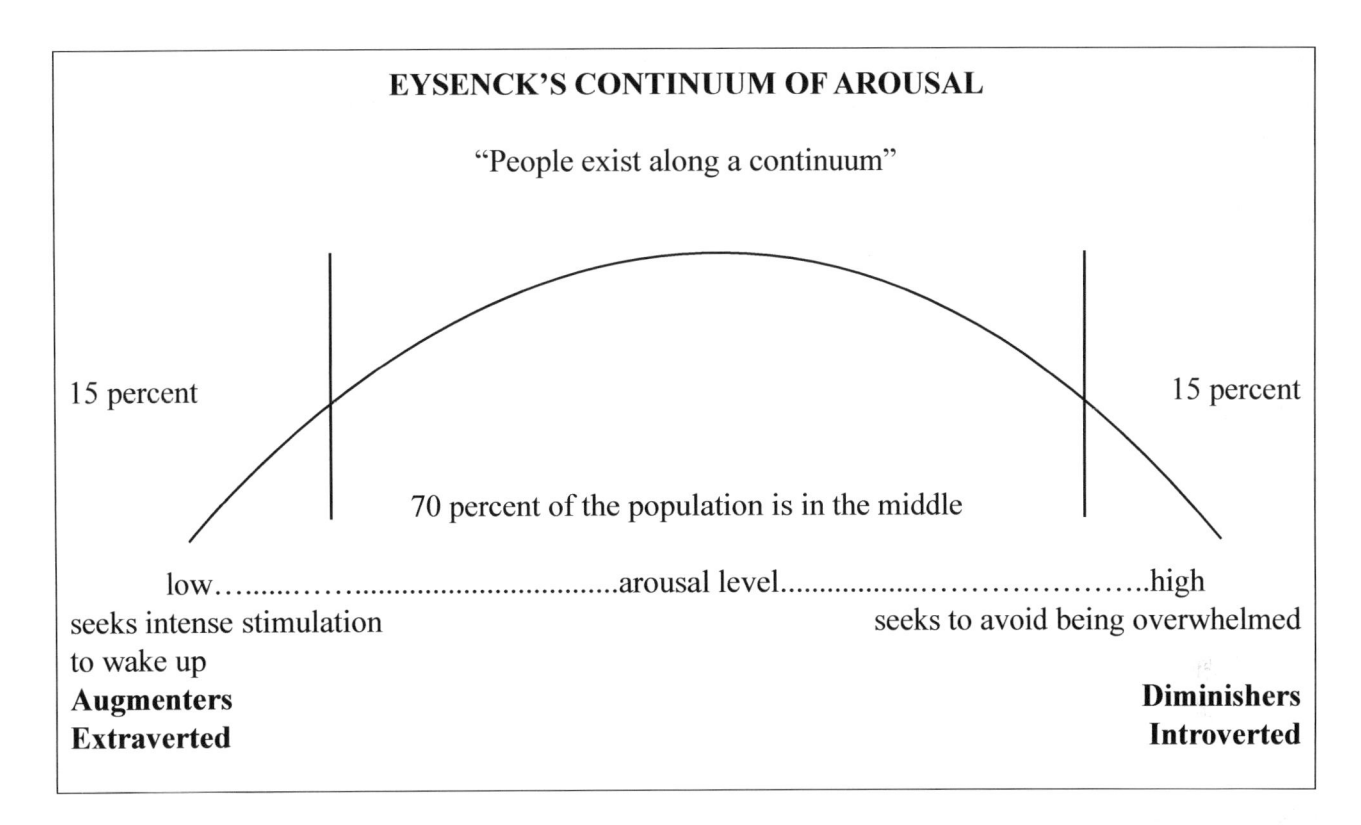

EYSENCK'S CONTINUUM OF AROUSAL

"People exist along a continuum"

15 percent — 70 percent of the population is in the middle — 15 percent

low……………..............................arousal level...............……………..high

seeks intense stimulation to wake up — seeks to avoid being overwhelmed

Augmenters — **Diminishers**
Extraverted — **Introverted**

Another *ah-ha* provided by Eysenck and Petrie's work is the clear understanding that both extraverts and introverts say yes to life. Informally, many Jungians and others have distinguished extra-version from introversion by saying: Introverts say *no* to life; Extraverts say *yes* to life. With Eysenck's new structure, we see that both say yes to life: the extravert in small bites due to the heavy filters their naturally low level of arousal creates; the introvert in big gulps due to the tremendous openness of their arousal system.

As important are the insights concerning the distribution of extraversion and introversion in the population. In recent decades, as counselors and therapists have worked with Jung's model, they have sought to apply Jung's model rigorously, labeling each person as either an extravert or an introvert. How amazing to learn from Eysenck that by far and away the majority of individuals are balanced. His research showed that people are distributed along a continuum of arousal levels, from low to high, based on a normal curve. Thus, only about 15 percent of the population is extremely aroused (introverted) and only 15 percent minimally aroused (extraverted).

This insight actually confirms the experiences of many who have tried to peg everyone as *either* extraverted *or* introverted. Namely, that many people are in between. Eysenck also found that because the arousal system is altered by the experience of fight or flight, prolonged exposure to anxiety-inducing situations tends to raise a person's arousal level causing them to become temporarily more introverted. Later, when the source of anxiety is resolved, the person's natural stable state asserts itself.

Here again is an important breakthrough in understanding. Psychologists observed that under anxiety, people withdraw and also that some people who seem introverted, subsequent to therapy, blossom as extraverts. Subsequently, many wondered if introversion never occurred naturally but only in response to chronic anxiety. At last, Eysenck's research in the area focusing on the role of the reticular activation system showed that both are true. Introversion occurs naturally as a stable state in some people. It also occurs in others as the result of chronic anxiety.

No wonder Jung found himself vacillating in his opinion of introverts: seeing them at first as passive then being struck by the awareness that they were not passive so much as given to forethought; then again deciding that it was not always forethought so much as a habit of *shrinking* that characterized them. Was he perhaps trying to identify and describe both natural introverts and those who were introverted due to heightened anxiety at the same time? Quite possibly.

Indeed, it is easy to see how Eysenck's work and findings are positively healing and uplifting for many introverts who find for the first time in their lives validation for this core aspect of their self.

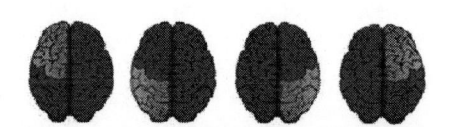

Chapter 5: Working Right, Working Easy

Career Selection and Success: The Basic Principle

Why do people select the careers they do? Why did you decide to become whatever it is you are? These questions have been asked and answered in a multitude of ways ranging from in-depth statistical treatises to Studs Turkel's rambling, anecdotal masterpiece, *Working: People Talk About What They Do All Day and How They Feel About What They Do.* Our fascination with the subject continues. Obviously, our choice of life work is very much a part of *what makes us tick* on some essential level.

Traditional approaches to the subject focus on role models, socio-economic status, learned skills and competencies and access to, or the availability of, higher education as the key factors in that choice. All of these are important factors in the career selection process. What is important is to recognize that brain dominance is also a determining force in our selection of work that *will work for us*. All of us know of an individual who attributes his selection of a specific profession to the family role models: "My dad and granddad were both lawyers. I'm just carrying on the family tradition" or "There's always been a doctor in our family. I simply didn't consider becoming anything else" or "Smith Brothers is a family business. It was just assumed that after college, I'd go to work in the family store". There are also certain career guidelines or assumptions that are generally seen as true and appropriate by many people: upper class kids don't drive trucks for a living; minority kids from lower income families aren't likely to become stock brokers; if you're a girl from a lower-middle class family, you probably should plan on being a teacher, a secretary, a nurse or a nun. Not surprisingly, these cultural assumptions have had a major impact on many people's choice of career.

Nonetheless, for every child who buys into a cultural stereotype or who follows a parental role model, there is another who actively chooses to march to the beat of a different drummer and make his own choice of career. In fact, it is not uncommon for a child to actively reject the path his parents want or expect him to take because "it's just not right for me". Stories like these are common.

> "My dad is a physician and he wanted me to be one, too. But, I just couldn't do it. I'm an architect, which is what I wanted to be."

> "Dad's an executive with Standard Oil. He always tried to get me interested in business, but it's just not my thing. I'm an artist and a painter."

> "Dad was a colonel in the Air Force and he sent me to military school hoping it would motivate me to join up. Well, I guess I'm a real disappointment to him since I was never interested. I was a monk for nine years and now I'm a free-lance photographer. This way I get to travel around the world taking pictures and helping people wherever I can. I did actually co-found a travel agency a few years ago but I turned it over to my partner last year. I need to move around more, have adventures and help humanity."

The Benziger Breakthrough

So, what made these people choose the work they chose? What made certain kinds of work right for them and other kinds not an acceptable fit? Why do they prefer one job to another?

In his book *Callings: Finding and Following an Authentic Life,* author Gregg Levoy seems to grasp the importance of this key, when he tells his reader "What do you love is the question callings pose." After which he reminds the reader that to know what we love, we must listen with our whole body, to discover what it delights in doing. (Harmony Books, New York, 1997, pp 21, 31). Exploring the subject from a very different angle, seemingly, that of neuroscience, Mihaly Csikszentmihalyi in his 1990 masterpiece on , points out that flow is a state in which people who truly love their work find themselves naturally. Flow is the state created by doing something you truly enjoy doing, with enough challenge to keep you interested, but not too much or the challenge you are enjoying could be replaced by anxiety. People experiencing flow reported high levels of inner joy and satisfaction as well as an overall sense of well being. Both Levoy and Csikszentmihalyi suggest flow is a reality anyone can experience. Both offer the reader hope. But neither gives the reader a simple, direct way to identify the activities and situations that will create flow in the reader's life.

The answer would appear to be that, we all can experience flow by choosing to do things that use our preference, or as the grandfather of life-work planning Bernard Haldane says, our *dependable strengths*. It is our preference that determines the kinds of activities that effortlessly hold our attention and energize us. Moreover, how we feel about our work, on a day-to-day basis, and ourselves depends largely on how well that work matches our natural brain dominance. When our work matches our preference, we feel positively reinforced – we feel smart and energized.

When there is a mismatch, when our work draws heavily on skills not managed by our preference, our experience is markedly more negative. We have difficulty concentrating, feel fatigued at the end of the day and often, in the course of trying to learn or do our work, feel dumb. This experience of using and leading with our non-preferred modes for hours a day, day after day, week after week, year after year, is what Dr. Carl Jung identified as *falsifying type*. It is a common and frustrating experience shared by 70 to 80 percent of the population in the industrialized world today. Falsifying Type is made all the more important because, research in the past decade by myself and Dr. Arlene Taylor, supports Jung's observations that over time Falsification of Type leads to illness, depression and collapse.

Given these simple facts of life, it is not surprising we gravitate towards work we believe matches our preference. Whether consciously or unconsciously, this rule guides many of our work-related decisions. We are more attracted to jobs we sense depend heavily on our preference. We try to avoid jobs we sense require frequent use of our non-preferred modes, especially our greatest weakness (the mode diagonally opposite our preference). Once in a job, we prefer advancement opportunities that are even more in tune with who we really are. And if, once we start a job, experience tells us it is going to rely heavily on our greatest weaknesses, we often find or create reasons for quitting.

You may want to remember it as the *Smart-Dumb Rule.* By making career and job decisions based on where your brain is naturally efficient, or smart, you are following the first rule of thumb given in

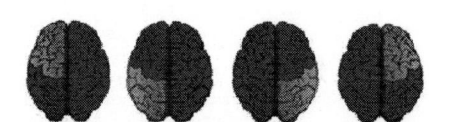

Chapter 1 for ensuring your own success and effectiveness at work:

> **Rule 1:** To develop or nurture your self-esteem, as well as ensure your immediate effectiveness and success, select activities and people that match your preference.

To assist you in using the information about brain dominance to select an appropriate career, or to understand and relate more successfully to someone else in a particular profession, several examples are presented in this chapter that demonstrate the variety of ways people are made smart by the right career choice. It would be impossible to discuss each and every career area. However, the examples that are given from each of four general categories – business, health care, the arts, and leadership – have helped many people. Hopefully they will help you apply the model to your own life and career. As you read through these examples, it may be helpful to begin with the general area that is closest to your own. Feel free to do so since there is no correct order here. As you read each example, think of someone you know in that profession. How well does the information you are reading describe them?

▲ Brain Dominance and The Business Community

Financial Problem Solving, Analysis and Decision-Making including, but not limited to MBAs, CPAs, accountants and financial vice presidents, all of whom focus on how to leverage money, that is, how to make money make money.

Most of these people have a natural preference in the Frontal Left analytic mode and have developed strong competencies in their posterior or Left Posterior Convexity auxiliary. As such they function as double lefts with a lead in the Frontal Left.

This type of thinker enjoys working with data, particularly numbers. They particularly enjoy analyzing numbers to determine "Am I better or worse off than last month? Am I better or worse off than last year at this time? Given what is happening in the national and local economy, in this sector and in others, do these numbers represent a gain or a loss?" This kind of analysis is what accounting is all about. In their own way, accountants are like physicians for both of these groups gather and analyze a body of data about a system. And, when the diagnosis indicates poor health, both prescribe new and different courses of action to take to fix the problem.

Profiles typical of people holding such positions, therefore, would resemble these profiles (which can bee seen on the next page) belonging to three of our clients.

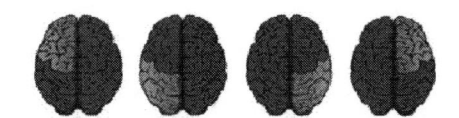

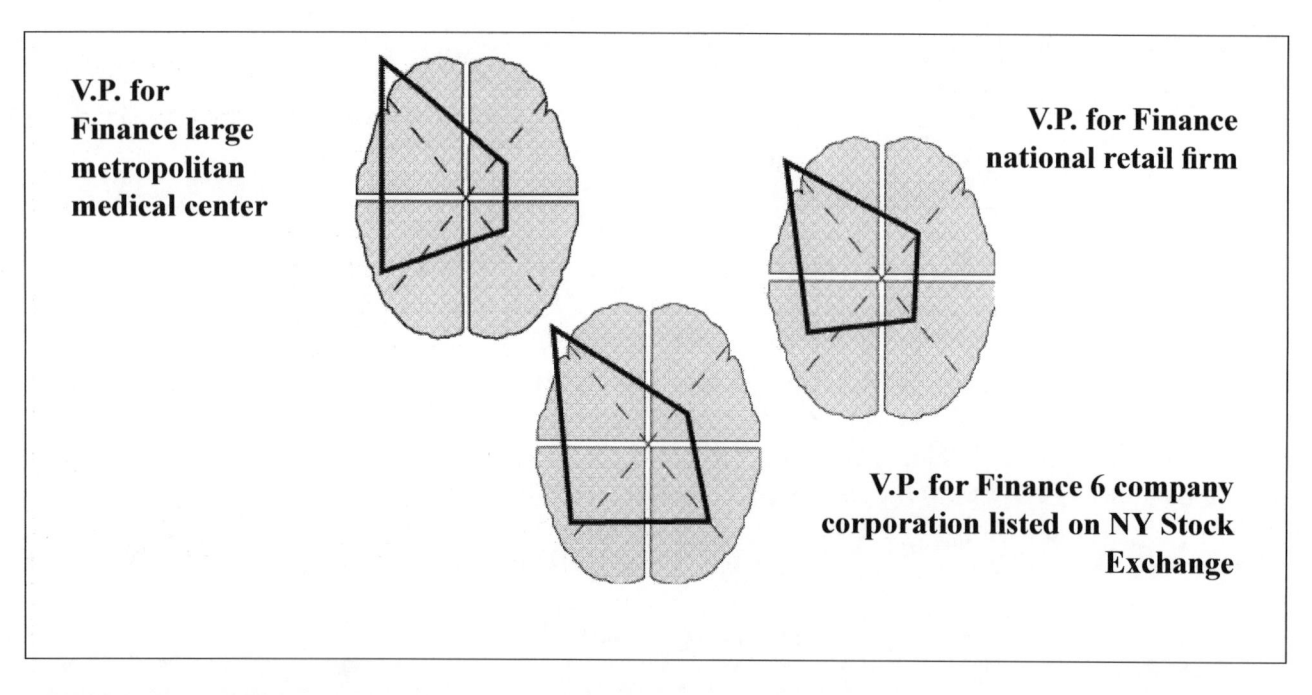

V.P. for Finance large metropolitan medical center

V.P. for Finance national retail firm

V.P. for Finance 6 company corporation listed on NY Stock Exchange

Maintaining Ordered Materials or Sequenced Information in an Organized, Correct and Timely Manner including, but not limited to, file clerks, records clerks, forms processors, bookkeepers, all of whom attend to seeing that the information necessary for the day-to-day operation of the business is kept current and correct.

Although these people often work with the same information as the above group, the diagnostic and prescriptive work done by the MBAs does not interest them. They prefer the Left Posterior Convexity sequential mode, and are often quarter-brain experts, deriving satisfaction from keeping files current and correct, balancing the books and preparing monthly statements. Careful and correct in their work, they have no difficulty in performing the routine tasks that provide the MBA or accountant with the data he analyzes. In fact, they get satisfaction from having and following standard bookkeeping (or recordkeeping) procedures consistently and according to a schedule over time. The more introverted they are, the more likely they are to work alone or with just one or two other persons, in a back office, where their own efficiency and focus will not be disrupted by the noise and production activities of others.

The following sample profiles taken from a few of our clients are typical of people attracted to and energized by work in this field. Note that to the extent that the job also involves being a receptionist, as in many secretarial positions, the profiles indicate additional developed competencies in the person's Right Posterior Convexity auxiliary.

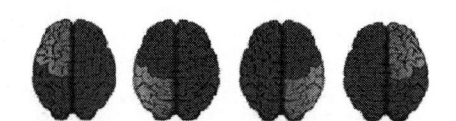

Medical records manager metropolitan medical center

Office manager & secretary in small office

Bookkeeper national research Firm

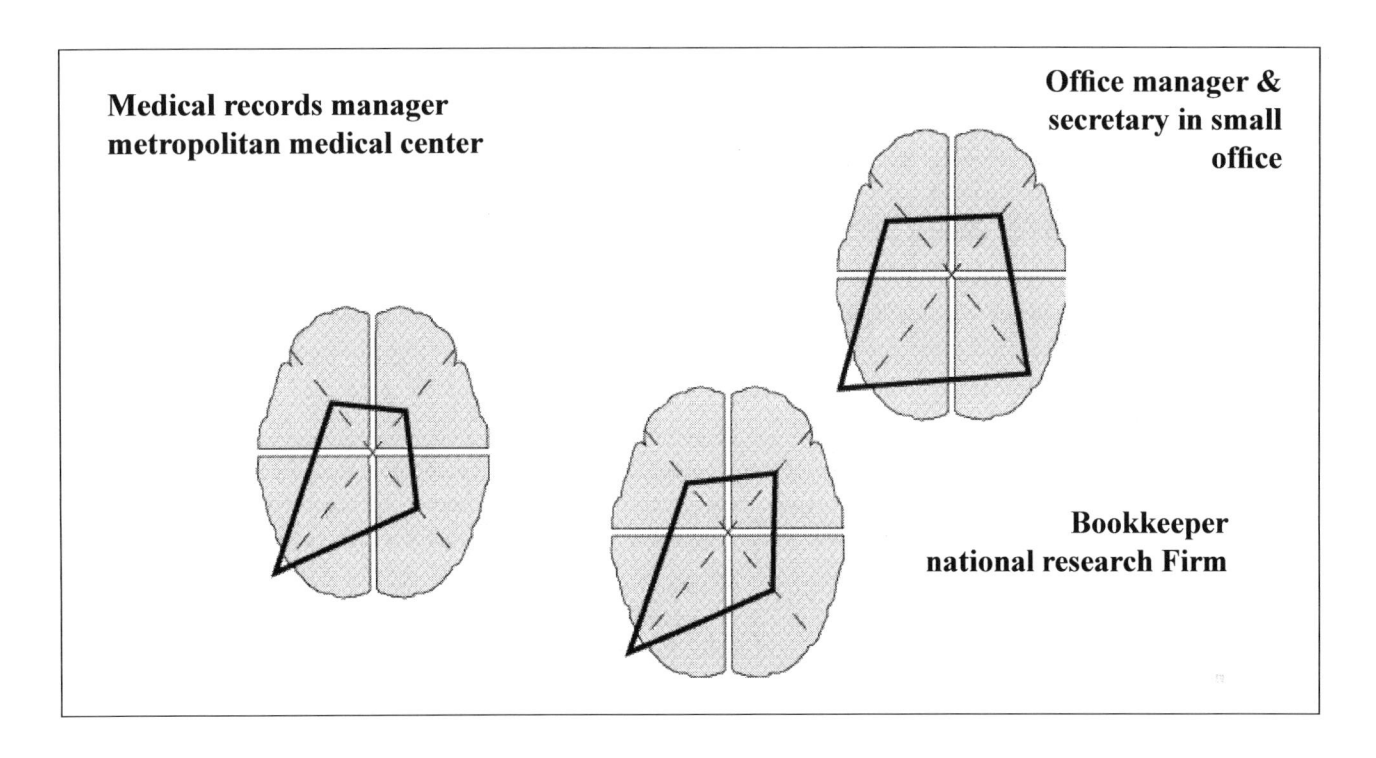

Supervising Others Doing Routine and Procedural Work including, but not limited to, line supervisors and lower to middle management personnel, who are expected to hold the line, meet deadlines, see that performance, service and production are all up to established standards.

Persons attracted to the lower levels of management as a lifetime job tend to naturally focus on and attend to maintaining the status quo more than on technical or financial problem-solving, strategy and issues of growth or expansion. They generally have a strong preference for the foundation-building, procedural mode. Historically, these people have been given the mandate to keep the business moving, keep the assembly line up and operational and keep the workers on task and on schedule. Such a mandate not only requires that the individual excel at working with routines, it also requires that they make the execution of those routines their highest priority. This means they must be able to stay focused on the procedures and not get distracted by people issues or by trying to make improvements in the system. All of which comes quite naturally for a natural Left Posterior Convexity thinker. Left Posterior Convexities who are more extraverted are able to be out where the action is, and often have developed auxiliary skills to assist them in their Right Posterior Convexity. As such, they tend to be highly effective operational managers – when things are running relatively smoothly. An additional trait which seems to be found among those who become operational supervisors – especially early in life – is that they were either only or eldest children in their family of origin.

By way of contrast, people with more frontal access, especially Frontal Left thinkers, with a more analytic focus view lower and middle management positions not as a life goal but as a passageway. As such, these natural negotiators spend only a short time in the middle ranks, moving faster and higher up the organizational ladder as their inherent ability to compare apples and oranges puts them in demand for upper management positions.

Right-brained people placed in lower or middle management positions will tend to be frustrated with all the procedure, which they find inherently difficult to attend to, and will either spend time chatting with others to keep in touch with what's happening (Right Posterior Convexity feeling/connecting thinkers), or developing new ideas for how to do things differently, whether or not the current system needs improvement (Frontal Right, intuitive thinkers). Thus, when and where consistent productivity is the desired goal, Left Posterior Convexity middle managers are both a logical choice and a natural fit.

Entrepreneurs

If a person has a double frontal configuration, with a natural lead in one of the two frontal modes and a developed auxiliary in the other, combining the spatial Frontal Right with the analytic Frontal Left, his options for a satisfying career in business are substantial. Such a person might well turn out to be a company president. Or, if his preference is in the Frontal Right and he is more extraverted, he might become an entrepreneur. By contrast, double frontals who are more introverted are happier as research scientists working in a corporate lab or think tank or as university professors. Regardless, what characterizes this brain configuration is a fascination with new ways of doing things and an ability to visualize goals so clearly that they seem already accomplished.

The profiles below, of entrepreneurs with whom I have worked, tend to be typical of entrepreneurs. Knowing that entrepreneurs have this very strongly developed preference for the Frontal Right, one can begin to hypothesize why they take the risks they're known for and are willing to bet every cent they have on a new idea or business. Simply put, given their brain dominance they are able to picture the successful outcome so clearly and vividly that they may be virtually unaware of the risks involved. Indeed, just as those skilled at a high-wire act focus on a spot at the other end of the wire – not on the audience below – to ensure their balance and personal safety, most entrepreneurs focus on their vision of what they are creating.

This hypothesis is further supported by the entrepreneur's predictably poor sense of scheduling and his difficulty in accurately predicting how long it will take to accomplish a given task or assignment. When asked for an estimate he will quite sincerely say that it "can be done in, oh, say four months", when, in actuality, it will take much longer, perhaps even years. The combination of their already completed vision and their inability to see the total number of steps involved (and the time that will be consumed by each step) makes their estimate miss by a large margin. It's a bit ironic that these thinkers are, on the one hand better than other people at predicting the future and inventing new programs/products which will succeed, while, on the other hand, unable to calculate the amount of time necessary for the project's implementation. In a way it's as though they are, mentally speaking, far-sighted and that, like all far-sighted people, they have difficulty in seeing things clearly as those things come closer. One such entrepreneur once observed that when he envisions a new project, it is very clear but that as he approaches it, it actually begins to blur and he finds his vision going off into the future again.

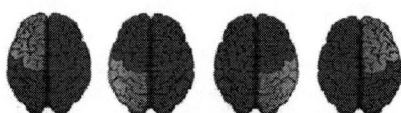

Founder
national retail firm

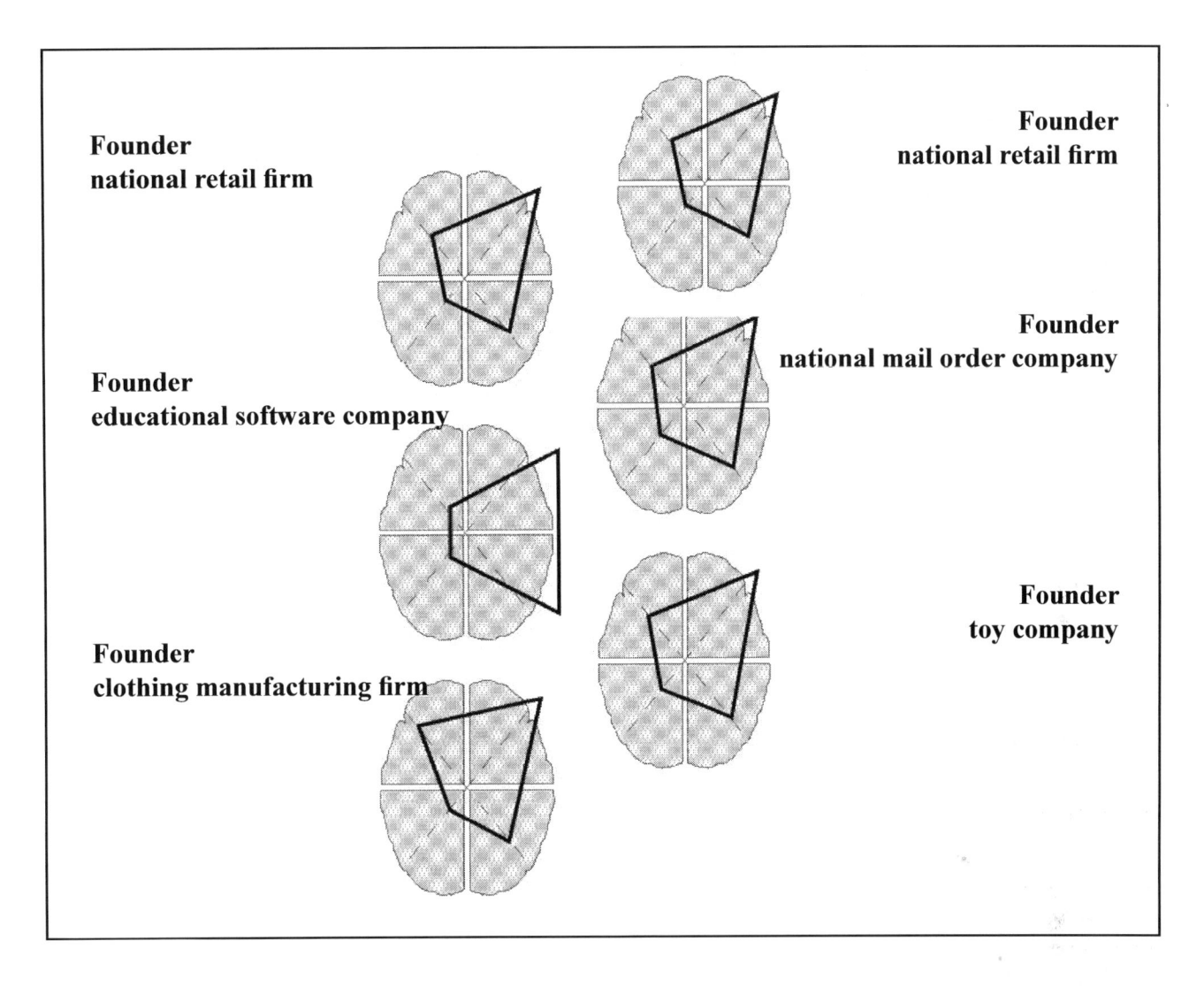

Founder
national retail firm

Founder
educational software company

Founder
national mail order company

Founder
clothing manufacturing firm

Founder
toy company

Another significant point is this: successful entrepreneurs – those who enjoy the challenge of competition; have the drive needed to make a fledgling business a success; are energized by the challenge to find successful ways to get their products to market and get/take a significant share of the market – tend to be highly extraverted.

Balanced or introverted Frontal Rights succeed in business as well, but in positions that don't require them to compete, sell or negotiate as much. They may be expert advisors or research scientists. They too contribute creativity, vision, a willingness to take risks. Just not as company founders or entrepreneurs.

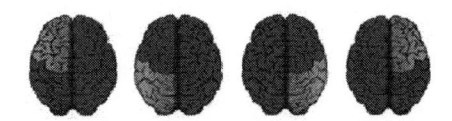

As you will learn later, many more introverted Frontal Rights choose to not enter business. These Frontal Rights find it natural and energizing to travel within, to explore the patterns in the psyche – as psychiatrists, physicists, artists or poets. As such, they are equally important to the development and fulfillment of human life: the extravert's vision of a better product, a bigger company, and a better world created and led by him and the introvert's vision of the self, the universe and their evolving patterns, needs and truths.

Having read through the above discussion and looked at the sample profiles provided, you are probably beginning to see that as a result of the way in which the smart-dumb rule guides career choices, people in the same profession tend to have very similar natural preference. For this reason, from this point on, only the generalized pattern found in each profession is presented.

Engineers

In some areas, such as engineering, it is possible to see the role of dominance most clearly by considering the way in which it affects people's choice of sub-specialty. In looking at the profession of electrical engineering, for example, it is typical to find people with a strong Frontal Left lead and a Left Posterior Convexity auxiliary. These analytic-sequential thinkers prefer precise, detailed work with a physical rather than a conceptual focus, which they can analyze and manipulate.

By contrast, those attracted to chemical engineering share a double frontal pattern, with a natural lead in one mode and a developed auxiliary in the other. When questioned about the reason for this shift and why the Frontal Right would be important in chemical engineering, several chemical engineers responded: "Within the field it is known and accepted that the best chemical engineers work by generating in their mind a three-dimensional, dynamic model of the molecular structure of the chemicals with which they're working. By rotating such images in their mind's eye and observing what happens, they gain insight into possible problems and probable solutions."

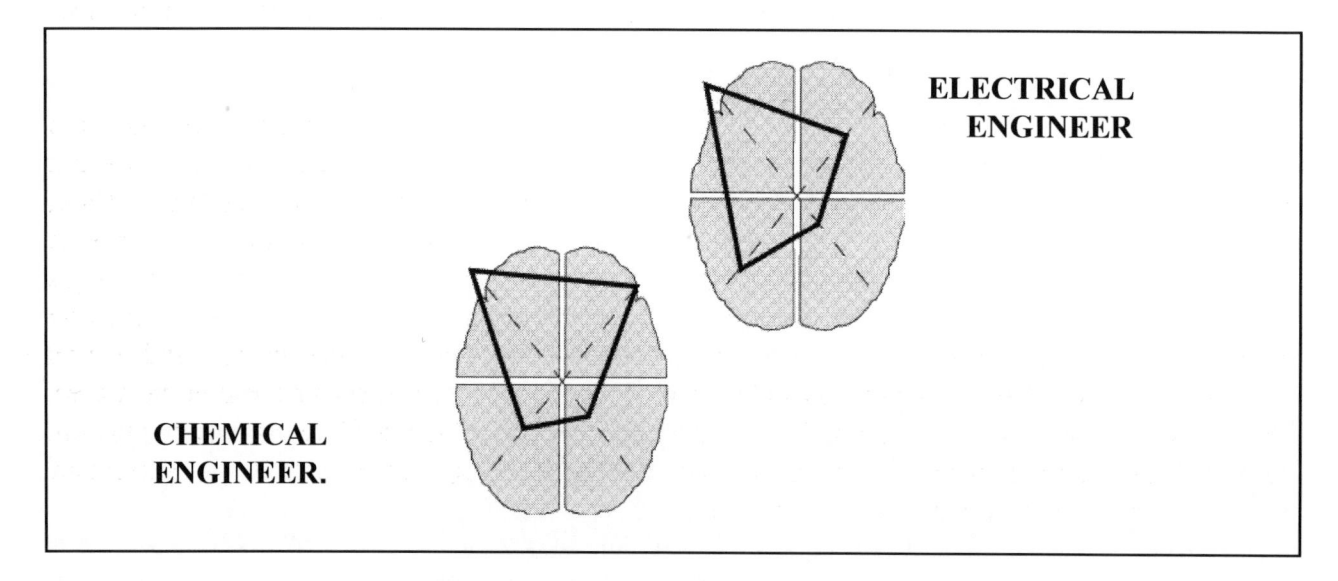

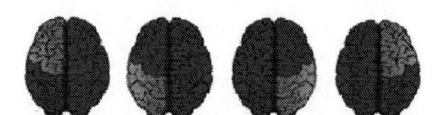

This internal imaging ability is not as necessary for the electrical engineer. Electrical circuitry lends itself to two-dimensional diagrams and does not require the holographic imaging capability of the Frontal Right. Additionally, the focus of electrical engineering is binary (i.e., on/off switching) whereas that of chemical engineering is more fluid and multi-dimensional (i.e., molecular chemical bonds). Chemical engineering students need to learn to visualize the chemicals with which they are working in order to monitor and predict the effect that certain procedures will have on those chemicals. Consequently, the double-left configuration matches the demands of electrical engineering but does not match those of chemical engineering. Unfortunately, the key differences between those individuals who can excel easily in electrical engineering and those who can excel easily in chemical engineering go unnoticed, or at least unappreciated, by those in the field and by the colleges and universities attempting to train engineers. According to the professional engineers interviewed, these institutions teach all engineering classes from a Left Posterior Convexity or double-left perspective.

A key question being posed at meetings of the Society For Petroleum Engineers during 1986-87 can readily be understood once you know about brain dominance. The question was: "Why are engineers so narrow-minded and so unimaginative?" The answer is, of course, when have they ever been trained to be anything else? Most of the petroleum engineers have developed a double-left pattern. All have been trained from the Left Posterior Convexity stabilizing mode. Staying on the path, keeping things in order, doing it the safe way is their strength. They do not use imagination and innovative skills not because they have none but because these skills are a part of the specialized type of thinking managed in our Frontal Right lobe. If one has a natural lead in the Left Posterior Convexity, one can develop auxiliary skills in the Frontal Left on the job – solving real problems. But Left Posterior Convexities do not access the Frontal Right – there are no diagonal bridges. Those engineers who are natural Frontal Lefts theoretically have both the Left Posterior Convexity and the Frontal Right available to them as auxiliaries. As the majority of their training is in the Left Posterior Convexity, it is generally true they have difficulty seeing things differently because their formal training reinforces their biological preference in the left.

Quite the opposite is true for the petroleum geologists who work side-by-side with the engineers in companies like Shell, Arco and Standard Oil. The oil geologist, according to the engineers, is a dart thrower. No one, by which they mean no double-left engineer, can understand how the (Frontal Right, internal image generating) geologists know where to look for oil. According to the geologists, they do so by using data to generate a picture of what must be happening down there. Of course, as soon as you realize that they are Frontal Right thinkers, and you understand how this specific type of thinking works, and how dependable and accurate it can be, what they do seems understandable and natural – rather than impossible or magical. By taking a few pieces of hard data, such as sample measures, which they then combine with their understanding of the pressure and other forces impacting the oil, these geologists can produce an internal movie of the underground process. By watching this film they are able to figure out how and where to drill for oil.

GEOLOGIST

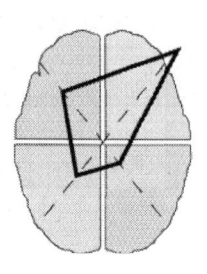

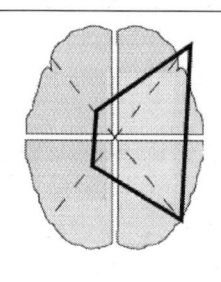

HRD SPECIALIST

Human Resource Development (HRD)

When a person has strong access in the Right Posterior Convexity mode as well as the Frontal Right, however, he needs a job that is more people-focused than the geologist's. Indeed, when double rights, with a natural lead in the Frontal or Right Posterior Convexity, and a developed auxiliary in the other, find themselves in a business setting, their usual way of handling the disparity between their loose, open, nonlinear and interpersonal processing and the generally precise, structured and linear nature of most businesses is to carve out a job for themselves which matches their preference. **Three possible niches are: human resource development, organizational development and teaching communication skills within an organization.**

Journalists & Librarians

While we're still discussing the business community, there are two other professions worth noting - the journalist and the information manager or librarian. Their patterns tend to look very much alike from the perspective of the four specialized types of thinking. Indeed, upon interviewing several librarians, it became apparent that many librarians originally studied to be and/or worked as journalists. What distinguishes them is what distinguishes the entrepreneur from the psychiatrist. The journalist is more extraverted, intent on and interested in the world around him – seeking the activity, noise, crowds, stimulation. The librarian is more introverted and internal.

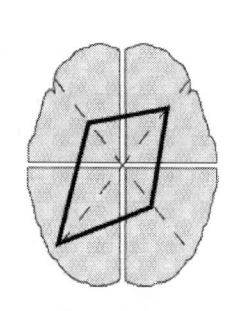

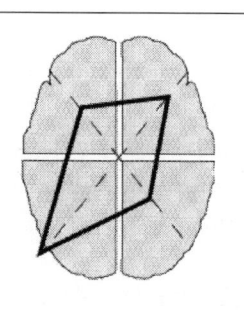

JOURNALIST & REPORTERS

LIBRARIANS & RECORDS MANAGERS

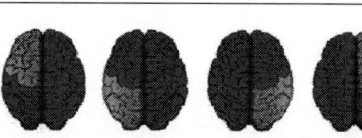

Their similar patterns are interesting because they remind us that although only certain patterns are natural, people do develop and use for some time, unnatural practical dominance patterns. Indeed, there are a surprisingly large number of people with this practical dominance. Further interviewing indicated that some are actually natural Frontal Rights: the war correspondents, adventure-seeking journalists, who force themselves to master their greatest weakness – the Left Posterior Convexity. Some tell themselves that actually writing an article is the price they pay to enjoy their very alive and ever-changing life style. Others turned out to be natural Right Posterior Convexities, who were using both their auxiliaries but not their preference. In sum, all these diagonals were Falsifying Type, either by trying to use their greatest weakness as a regular auxiliary to support their preference or by trying to use both auxiliaries rather than their preference.

If you think about the combination of skills presented in this practical dominance pattern, you will discover that this developed pattern is precisely what's needed to get the job done well. For the journalist, the Frontal Right portion gets the satisfaction of seeing the whole picture quickly (a good use of the visual brain) and, because a different story is covered daily, enough change and variety to keep it stimulated. The Left Posterior Convexity does the writing – reporting what's happening in a detailed, sequential, step-by-step way. Similarly, for the Librarian, the Frontal Right is continually stimulated to look beyond to new and different horizons, to new and different information which might be coming in or which a user requests, while the Left Posterior Convexity sees that all incoming information and publications are cataloged, referenced and shelved according to established, sequential systems.

Another group of persons have been identified more recently who seem to use and like using the other diagonal dominance pattern: the Frontal Left in combination with the Right Posterior Convexity. The clients making up this group tend to be extraverted Frontal Rights who have found that they can succeed well in life, at least for a time working as professional career counselors and business consultants, by using their Frontal Left auxiliary at work and their Frontal Right auxiliary in their personal life – with their spouse, friends and children. Again, they are Falsifying Type and for many of them the sudden shock in their late thirties that they did not want to continue sent shudders through their bodies and souls as they tried to figure out how to let go of their habit of Falsifying Type. These persons with their unlikely profiles make distinct and valuable contributions to the world of business. The only problem is that they are suffering. Thus, the question each one needs to ask is: *How am I Falsifying Type?*

- Is one of the two types of thinking I'm now using my preference? And, if so what is the cost to me of using my greatest weakness so regularly – as I would use an auxiliary? Remember you've learned that a person's greatest weakness is the type of thinking diagonally opposite their preference. It is both inefficient and, as well, not easily available.
- Or, are the two specialized types of thinking I'm now using actually my natural auxiliaries? And, if I feel this is true for me, then which of the other two specialized modes is actually my preference? And, again, what is the cost to me of regularly using both of my auxiliaries instead of my preference.

Summary of Dominance in the Business Community

Although our society offers more left-brained jobs, there are jobs for every lead and as well for every common developed pattern. It's just that when selecting a career, the full range of choices may not be presented as such for workers in transition and for adolescents and young adults selecting a field of study. These people are more often presented with the left-brained opportunities because there are more academic training programs available preparing people for these jobs, there are more jobs available and they pay higher salaries. So, unless you know about brain dominance, directing young people and adults in transition to these double-left jobs, without considering their natural preference makes a lot of sense.

Brain Dominance in the Business Community	
Double Lefts with Frontal Left Leads	Accountants MBAs (masters in business administration), CPAs (certified public accountants) Electrical Engineers
Double Lefts	Lawyers Electrical Engineering
Double Lefts with Left Posterior Convexity Leads	Bankers Machine Operators Machine Repair Personnel
Left Posterior Convexities	Ordering & Purchasing Clerks Record-keepers; File Clerks Bookkeepers; Data Entry Clerks Personnel workers
Double Posterior Convexities	Secretaries
Right Posterior Convexities	Receptionists Communication Specialists
Double Rights	Organizational Development Community Development
Frontal Rights	Entrepreneurs Geologists Architects
Double Frontals	Inventors Chemists & Chemical Engineers Research Scientists Economists
Left Posterior Convexity - Frontal Rights	Journalists Librarians

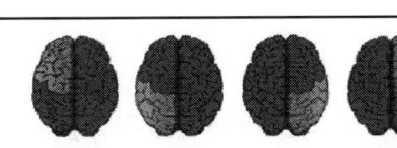

▲ Brain Dominance and The Helping Professions

Like corporate America, health care and the helping professions need and attract a wide variety of preference patterns.

Physicians

A self-selecting process occurs when people choose a career in the field of medicine. With the increased post WWII emphasis on diagnosis (analysis), medicine has become even more strongly a Frontal Left profession. Many, but by no means all, physicians are natural Frontal Lefts. This Frontal Left focus is reinforced and expanded by medical education that is largely double left emphasizing a combination of diagnostic and procedural thinking, reminiscent of the training found in engineering and accounting.

Not surprisingly, there are quite a few similarities between physicians, MBAs, accountants and engineers. All of them have strong Frontal Left leads and enjoy work that allows them to analyze and diagnose. Physicians diagnose the underlying cause of an illness, accountants diagnose the underlying cause of a client's financial problems, and engineers diagnose the underlying weakness in a structure. And, all of them recommend strategies to fix the problem and cure the disease.

Once you realize that most physicians have a practical dominance that is double left, certain legal and public relations problems they are having begin to make sense. From a double-left point of view, a patient's body is a complex, malfunctioning machine that they investigate in the hopes of repairing. They are ready and able to do their job as they see it. But, they are not adept at making their patients feel cared for nor, given their dominance, do they see any logical reason why they should be. Unfortunately, most of us do not like being treated like a broken machine and have difficulty making the doctor's technical skill more important than his lack of personal relations skills.

Although this double-left profile is certainly the most common single profile among physicians, in medicine, as in engineering, there is variation. The range of specialties that abounds demands and provides opportunity for this variation.

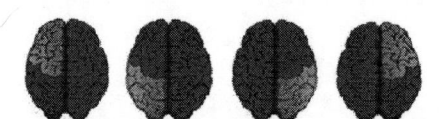

One of the most distinguished specialties is surgery. In the ranks of physicians, surgeons have a reputation for being domineering, demanding and not particularly interested in following the rules. These behavioral quirks are more easily understandable when you realize that as a group, surgeons are not double left (analytic-sequential) but double frontal (analytic-spatial) – with a natural lead in one frontal mode and a developed auxiliary in the other. Although many double lefts want power and control to satisfy their Frontal Left, their Left Posterior Convexity, which values order and stability, keeps them from creating havoc to get their way. The surgeon, on the other hand, combines his analytic/power-focused function with the Frontal Right's disrespect for order and sequence. The result is that within health care, and especially among nurses, surgeons are seen as behaving in whatever way they need to in order to get what they want, including throwing a temper tantrum or breaking the rules.

I had an unforgettable experience working as a candy striper on a hospital nursing ward at age thirteen. While helping to deliver dinner trays, I was suddenly grabbed by the star OB-GYN surgeon who had an emergency in delivery and not finding the help he needed, decided to recruit me. At the time I was struck by the fact that although what the surgeon wanted me to do might help him and his patient, it was certainly non-standard and possibly illegal, facts that didn't faze him at all any more than they faze most Frontal Right's who are trying to get something accomplished.

As fascinating as it is to be able to diagnose and explain these particular behaviors, the question still remains: what attracts these more frontal thinkers to surgery in the first place? To answer this question, consider what happens during surgery when the human body must be taken apart and put back together. Unlike a man-made machine, the human body cannot be taken completely apart in order to be worked on. Nor can it be unplugged, drained of all its fuel and lubricants, steam cleaned and then rebuilt. And, finally, although some surgical procedures go quite routinely, the surgeon must be ready at all times to deal with the unexpected. Translated into brain modes these characteristics of surgery mean the surgeon must have access to both the Frontal Left's diagnostic, problem-solving and the Frontal Right's creative thinking in order to handle the trouble-shooting functions and come up with procedural variations as and when needed.

According to many successful surgeons interviewed during workshops at the American Academy of Medical Directors (AAMD), another reason surgery is so attractive to those with a natural lead in the Frontal Right is that it demands the use of their internal-image generating skills. As is the case with chemical engineers, excellent surgeons use this imaginative, spatial problem-solving part of their thinking to construct in their mind's eye a three dimensional image of the organs and tissues they are operating on. They can then rotate this image and see the places they are unable to see (with their normal vision) and by using this image, continue to use their Frontal Left to operate precisely and effectively.

Although this x-ray vision is considered indispensable by many successful surgeons, it appears to be exclusively a self-taught skill. None of the surgeons with whom I spoke could recall ever hearing it mentioned and all were certain it had never been taught in medical school. In fact, until their conversations with me, they had never even discussed it among themselves out of fear they would be criticized for using a non-rational procedure. The taboo about discussing this skill is so strong that surgeons, who depend on it themselves, still do not talk about it when training residents. When asked by a resident how they had managed a particularly difficult operation in which much was not visible to the naked eye, all of these physicians responded only by saying "Experience, experience".

Psychiatrists

Another medical specialty that has both distinctive and predictable brain dominance is psychiatry.

Almost everyone in medicine appears to know that psychiatrists are the misfits in the world of medicine and, from the perspective of a typical AMA (American Medical Association) member, the psychiatrist is both a problem and an anomaly. On one occasion while on the AAMD faculty, I actually heard a non-psychiatrist physician try to reassure himself that "psychiatrists aren't real physicians anyway". Although his statement may have seemed odd, knowing what you now know, you can appreciate how many standard physicians, with their double-left focus on control and proven/approved procedures would be unnerved by the psychiatrist's looser approach created by their preference for the Frontal Right.

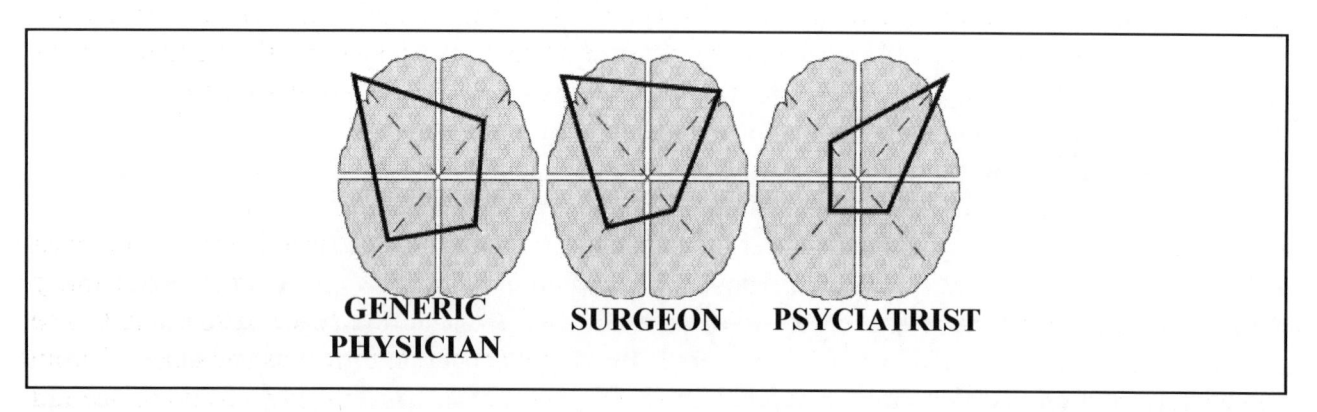

GENERIC PHYSICIAN   **SURGEON**   **PSYCIATRIST**

Unlike the surgeon whose preference is frontal – often but not always with a lead in the Frontal Right and developed auxiliary in the Frontal Left – the psychiatrist tends to be almost exclusively Frontal Right. The behaviors they exhibit which express this focused dominance pattern are their use of metaphor, their sense of humor and their strong penchant for making bizarre comments. Additionally, psychiatry relies on the Frontal Right's ability to perceive patterns. So, it is not surprising that psychiatrists generally test as natural Frontal Right thinkers – and often, as introverts. When psychiatrists work with their clients, they approach their job rather differently than do their analytic colleagues. Although both collect data, much of what the psychiatrist collects is disjointed and not readily measurable. Furthermore, the psychiatrist has to collect the data he works with without being able to isolate it in a clearly discrete system with clear components (i.e. the mental system is not analogous to the circulatory system or the skeletal system). Although to some extent the brain and its physiology are a system – the mind, everyone agrees is more than the brain. And in working with the mind, the psychiatrist is working with something more like the underground oil reserves that the geologist is trying to understand. As such, he works to understand the very undefined subterranean area of a patient's mind. Using his Frontal Right he captures a gestalt of the person's mind and being, from which he creates a picture of their patterned behaviors.

A final word about psychiatrists, in recent years, the increased focus on diagnosis and reliance on drugs and the DSM as the answer, has shifted the day-to-day experience of psychiatrists. Has this shift created work that is more or less appropriate for the Frontal Rights who trained in psychiatry in the past? Has this shift created a job that is better suited to a physician with a preference in the Left Posterior Convexity or Frontal Left? I do not know, but suspect it may have.

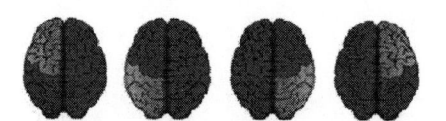

Interestingly enough, many physicians who elect to specialize in Emergency Medicine turn out to have a natural lead in the Frontal Right, although they tend to be more extraverted than psychiatrists. Their initial love affair with emergency medicine is due to their early belief that Emergency Medicine doesn't have all the procedures and routines that characterize much of medicine. What they discover once they have been in Emergency Medicine for a year or two is that it has just as much Left Posterior Convexity routine as the rest of medicine, it is just that the routines differ and the patients are not scheduled. So, what starts out as a fit, deteriorates over time, pushing the ER doctor to use more and more of his natural weakness – pushing him if you will to Falsify Type. One ER physician – who had elected to move from Emergency Medicine to Psychiatry – felt that this misperception of Emergency Medicine might well explain the high burnout rate reported among ER physicians. Based on what's been discovered about the costs of Falsifying Type, his assessment was probably accurate.

Pediatricians

Finally, many Pediatricians have a Right Posterior Convexity preference that leads them to run much less formal practices with generally better patient relations. In the United States, in the 1980's many physicians set up group practices outside of hospitals. Most, originally, included a pediatrician. The idea was to give patients the opportunity to have all their medical needs met in the same place. Within a few years, however, many group practices had asked their pediatricians to leave, as he or she did not generate as much money as their other specialists. Their distinctive manner clearly distinguishes pediatricians as natural Right Posterior Convexities. They charged significantly less than other specialists (cardiologists, radiologists, oncologists). They scheduled fewer patients per day. And, they were prone to talking at length with parents and children. In other words, using standard business criteria, their performance was lacking.

Given the data, each group's decision to drop its token pediatrician was viewed by the remaining partners as a good business decision. What they did not foresee or understand was the big picture in which their practice operated. At the time, the number of malpractice lawsuits being filed against physicians and the amount of the settlement being asked for were both climbing rapidly. Over the next few years, statistical data gathered revealed that although these troublesome and costly suits were increasing virtually everywhere in the USA, there were some group practices which did not get sued. Further interviews brought to light the answer. The group practices that were not sued had pediatricians on their staff. It seems that the Right Posterior Convexity pediatrician's flair for building sound human relationships was not confined to the office. Pediatricians tended to be very active in the community at large – in Scouting, Little League, the church and everywhere making friends and helping people of all ages. The result was that when an attorney approached a person who had suffered medical complications or problems while in the care one of the physicians in the pediatrician's group – the person would simply say: "No, I wouldn't want to sue them. That's Joe's group and I am sure they did their best." So, what was good business in the long run was more whole-brained – including Right Posterior Convexity as well as Left and Frontal physicians.

And so, within the generic category of physicians, quite different brains find a place to enjoy themselves, think smart and contribute.

Nurses

Having briefly explored the world of physicians from the perspective of brain dominance, let's take a look at brain dominance in the nursing profession. Dominance data on two thousand nurses suggests that most nurses are sequential-feeling thinkers with a natural lead in one of the two posterior convexity modes. This profile is not particularly surprising given the fact that for the last several decades nurses have been trained largely as the physician's helpmate – the person who sees that the physician's orders are carried out according to a prescribed schedule (turn the patient this often, give X amount of this medication every four hours, waken him every few minutes, etc.) and who provides the patient with the nurturing care the physician does not have time for. The nurse is both the detail attentive person who sees that the necessary procedures are accomplished and the encourager, the comforter and morale-builder – the posterior convexity complement to the frontal physician.

Within this overall double posterior convexity pattern, individual nurses make choices to find the work that best suits them. For example, there are nurses who have a strongly developed preference for the sequential mode with little auxiliary development in the feeling mode. These nurses gravitate, even in their mid-twenties, to supervisory nursing positions in which they can monitor and correct schedules and procedures. By contrast, those who have a preference for the feeling mode with very little auxiliary competency in the routine mode, elect to remain in staff nursing for decades, even when it means being supervised by professionals many years their junior.

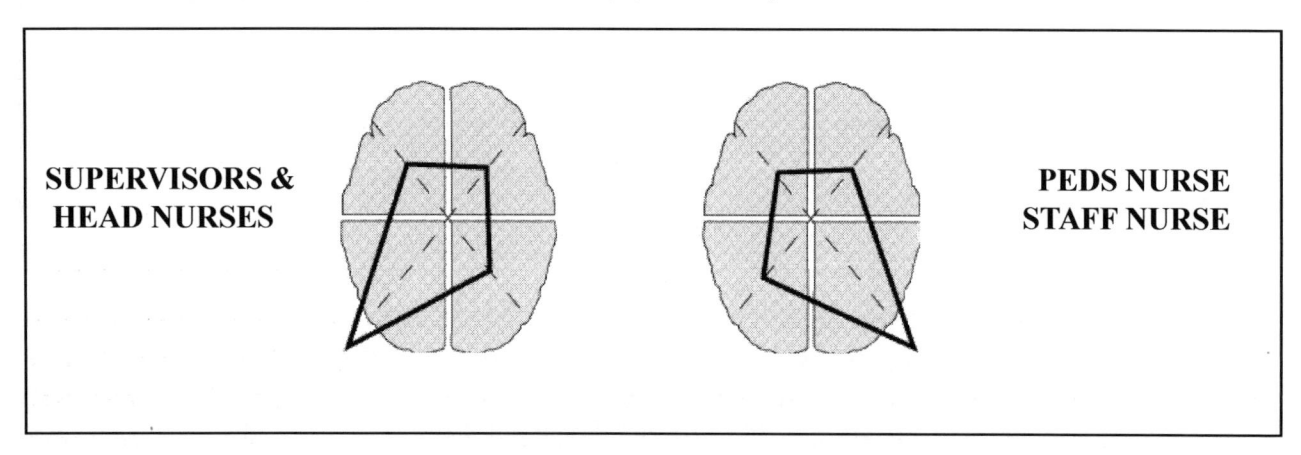

SUPERVISORS & HEAD NURSES   **PEDS NURSE STAFF NURSE**

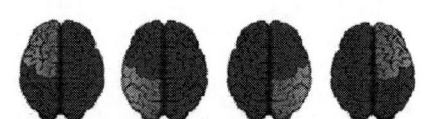

This split in preference between the sequential mode and the feeling mode explains a conflict experienced on many hospital nursing units between nurses advocating the procedure and those advocating a more feeling response. A typical scene recounted to me numerous times by nurses themselves provides an example: A staff nurse is sitting at the edge of a patient's bed talking with the patient. Her head nurse enters and says: "The manual says staff should not sit on patients' beds. Furthermore, we should finish our work before we go around gabbing." The nurse, aware that the patient is in desperate need of attention and nurturing, is at a loss. After all, you can't proceduralize the time and place for appropriate feeling responses. It's something you simply know based on being sensitive in the moment.

Who's right? And what to do about it? Needless to say, a good bit of anger and resentment builds up, as these two different types with their two different and equally important agendas are forced to work side by side. What helps to some extent is that very often, the nurses who have a natural lead in the Right Posterior Convexity feeling mode have developed a substantial number of competencies in their Left Posterior Convexity auxiliary. Just as often, the nurses who have a natural lead in the Left Posterior Convexity routine mode have developed a substantial number of competencies in their Right Posterior Convexity auxiliary. This developing of one's auxiliaries makes one more flexible as a team member – more able to understand and appreciate the gifts of others.

Of course, there are anomalies in nursing just as there are in medicine. One is the intensive care nurse, who works predominantly with unconscious patients and the machines responsible for keeping them alive. These nurses enjoy working in the intensive care unit with the machines. They are generally double-left thinkers with a natural lead in one of the left modes supported by a developed auxiliary in the other left. For these nurses, an opportunity to practice nursing without having to nurture, in the Right Posterior Convexity feeling sense of the word, is often a welcome relief. Some are aware of being more comfortable with the unconscious patients than with the conscious ones with whom they would have to interact. After all, they do not have to talk to an unconscious patient.

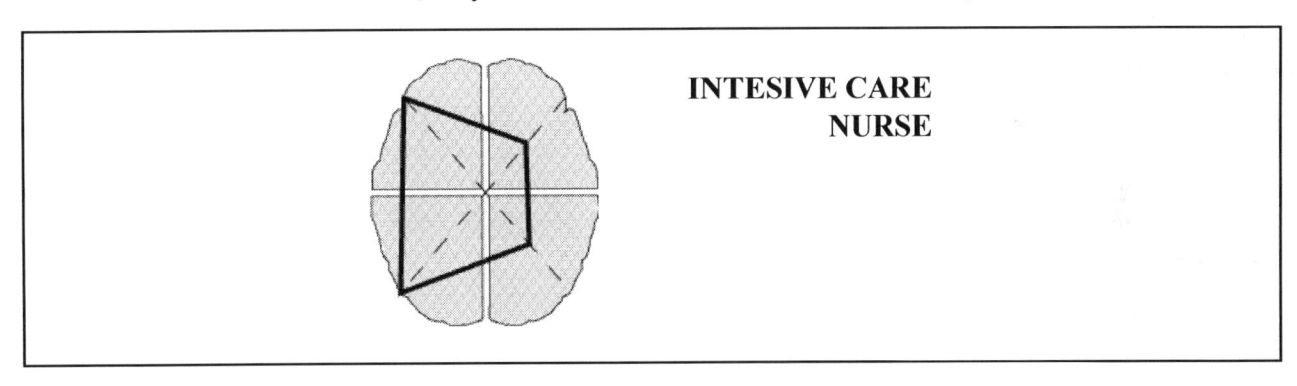

INTESIVE CARE NURSE

Despite the fact that most ICU nurses are left-brained, in one client hospital a nurse with a Right Posterior Convexity preference and Frontal Right auxiliary managed the ICU. This nurse, following a pattern that could be called *tribal*, hired other right-brained nurses to work in her ICU. Some were natural Frontal Rights with developed skills in their Right Posterior Convexity auxiliary. Some were natural Right Posterior Convexities with developed skills in their Frontal Right auxiliary. Although at first glance this might appear to be an undesirable staffing pattern, conversations with the manager revealed that the team had worked out ways of being smart. In their ICU, these nurses used their Frontal Right spatial skills to scan the machines (much like pilots use the Frontal Right to monitor their instrument panels). With their Right Posterior Convexity feeling/nurturing skills, these nurses continued touching and talking to the patients even though they were unconscious. As they said,

"Even unconscious people need to be touched and talked to. It helps their morale and consequently the overall healing process." Others have told me that the ICU is a place that needs Right Posterior Convexity nurses because the nurses in ICU deal with the family much more and the need for the increased communication with and nurturing of patients' families as they face and cope with life and death crises and decisions to take a ventilator off a patient.

If you have trouble believing that barely conscious or unconscious persons benefit from touching and talking, find a copy of the film Lorenzo's Oil. It is a true story. The Right Posterior Convexity mother with the help of a young African did the same thing caring for her son. Talking, touching, singing. And while you watch it, laugh as you recognize her husband, Lorenzo's father, use his Frontal Right preference to actually solve an impossible medical problem – despite the fact that he had no knowledge of medicine.

Turning back to our atypical ICU team, it is interesting to note the tribal pattern in operation and the supervisor's need to be surrounded by people who matched her own natural dominance. It is equally fascinating to notice the ways in which those particular nurses redefined the job in order to use their preference. Moreover, it is possible that things would go quite well – unless or until the very right-brained supervisor left – and the staff nurses found themselves being managed by a more typical left-brained ICU nurse supervisor.

Another specialty within nursing, which seems to attract the atypical nurse, is emergency nursing. These nurses seem to be somewhat sharper and more decisive than the general staff nurse, concerned with precision as and when need be, but otherwise more fun loving than the typical intensive care nurse. When several hundred of them were tested and interviewed over a three year period, what emerged was that on the whole, nurses attracted to emergency room work are developed double frontals with natural leads in the Frontal Right. In other words, their profiles were quite similar to the physicians who went into Emergency Medicine. Although the daily routine and one-on-one intimacy of much nursing care might be very uncomfortable for them, in the Emergency Room or Department, they are indeed smart. They enjoy and are adept at problem solving and seek the opportunity to share this activity with physicians, almost as a peer or equal, an opportunity not traditionally available to them in an office or on the units. Finally, they report being attracted to what they see as the continual novelty and change in Emergency Rooms and the challenge to think on their feet in difficult situations where trouble-shooting is as valued as knowledge and procedural expertise.

Counselors

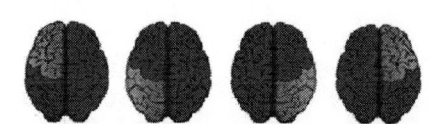

Other right-brainers choose careers in counseling to validate their strengths and make them feel smart. For the double-right-brained individual with a natural lead or preference in the feeling mode, this could mean electing to be a counselor, psychologist or therapist since that career choice provides them with the opportunity to observe patterns of behavior from a perspective grounded heavily in feelings. When such an individual also has access to the Left Posterior Convexity sequential mode, they often choose to be a social worker rather than a therapist in private practice. This choice honors their need for connection and their ability to work well with forms, schedules and procedures – their skill as a therapist with their skill at keeping accounts ordered and complete.

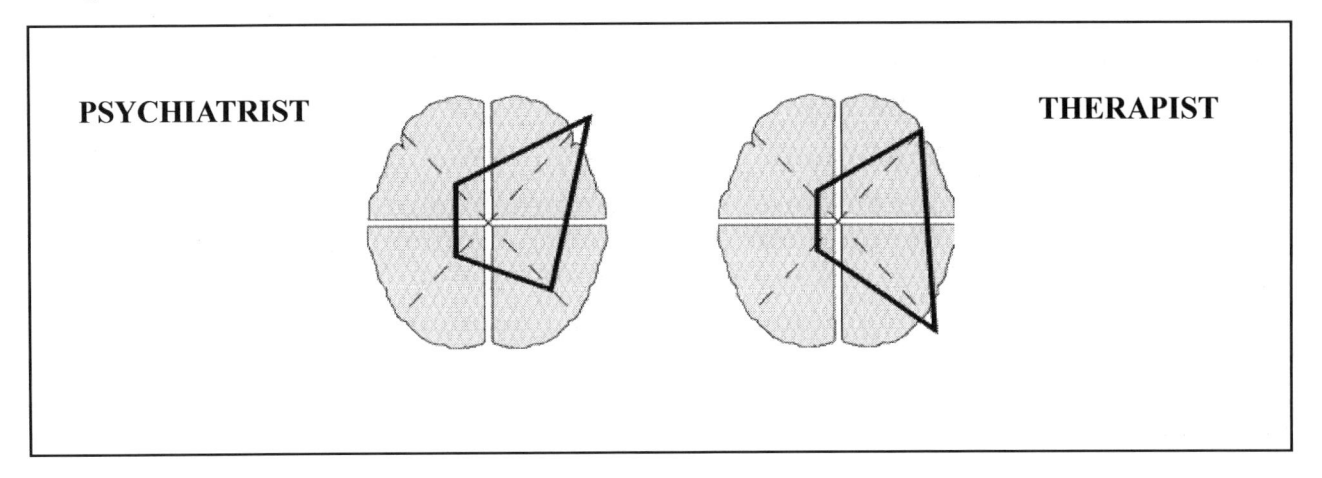

PSYCHIATRIST   **THERAPIST**

A double right with less strength in the Right Posterior Convexity mode, and a preference in the Frontal Right may choose Psychiatry rather than psychology or counseling. Psychiatry is more conceptual, intellectual and pattern-focused than normal counseling. It allows them to use their Frontal Right and removes them from the visceral, personal and connected counseling preferred by Right Posterior Convexities. The difference between the person attracted to being a therapist and the person attracted to being a psychiatrist is particularly evident in the differing approaches these people bring to their work – the therapist or psychologist being more attracted to getting personal and involved with their clients, using empathetic listening, talking with rather than just listening to, touching their clients while listening to them, holding their clients when they cry, possibly even giving advice based on personal experiences or using active techniques such as psycho-drama. By comparison, many psychiatrists are aloof; mainly interested in listening so they analyze a client's patterns of behavior or a dream with its rich display of symbolic and metaphoric information about the client or the client's problem.

Teachers

The most common preference among the elementary and secondary school teachers with whom I have worked is the Right Posterior Convexity. As well, most teachers have at least one highly developed auxiliary that is they function as either a double posterior convexity or double right. This is significant because the schools themselves (their structure, procedures, rules, formats, and administrators) appear to be most comfortable for Left Posterior Convexity students and teachers. If the sample is representative, the time out, which teachers traditionally take each summer, may be necessary for them to recover from each year of Falsifying Type. This would explain the chronic tension within schools between the teachers with their ideas for new and better classes and class structures, and their administrators who are uncomfortable doing anything experimental, preferring the tried and true approaches.

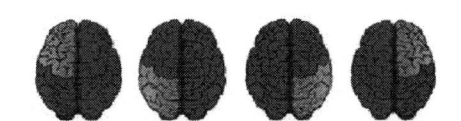

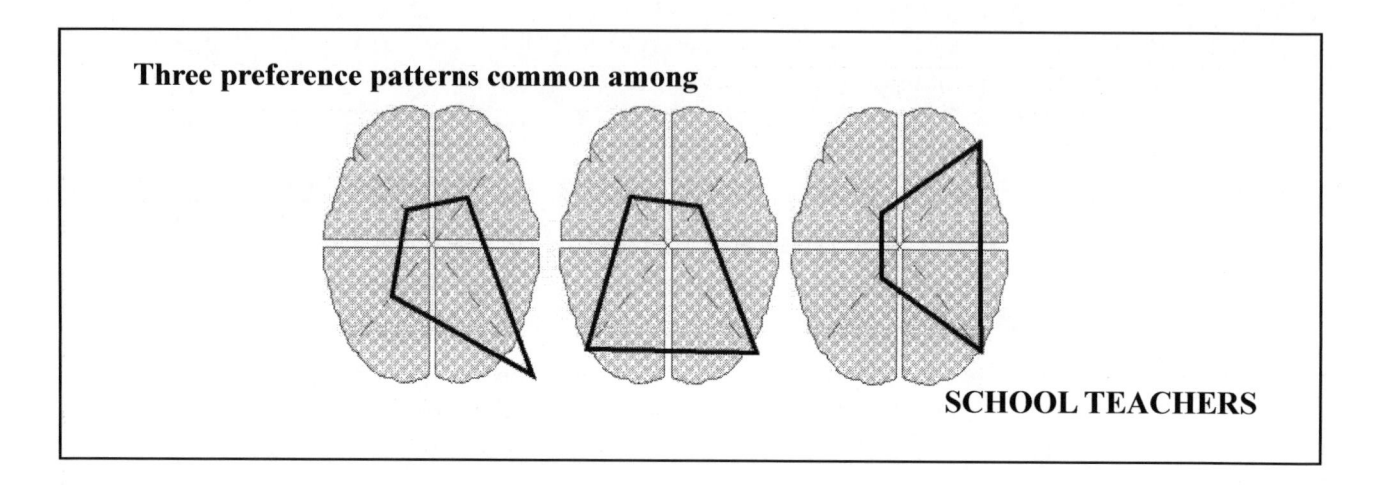

Three preference patterns common among SCHOOL TEACHERS

Another important observation about teachers is that those who elect to work with young children tend to be extraverts who find the noise level generated by a room full of children stimulating rather than straining. Additionally, in recent years as more teachers and administrators have identified classroom management as a major problem in our schools, teachers who are extraverted, seem to be able to handle the growing chaos with grace. By contrast, teachers who are more introverted, who found teaching highly rewarding a decade ago, are now overwhelmed.

Brain Dominance in the Helping Professions	
Double Lefts with Frontal Left leads	Hospital Board of Directors
Double Lefts	Physicians, ICU Nurses
Left Posterior Convexities	Personnel Officers, Hospital Administrators (old) School Administrators
Double Posterior Convexities with Left Posterior Convexity lead	Head Nurses & Supervisors
Double Posterior Convexities with Right Posterior Convexity lead	School Teachers Staff Nurses
Right Posterior Convexities	Counselors, Pediatricians Staff Development Specialists Community and Public Relations School Teachers
Double Rights	School Teachers
Frontal Rights	Psychiatrists Emergency Physicians
Double Frontals	Surgeons Hospital Administrators (new)
Left Posterior Convexity – Frontal Rights	Community Organizers

Summary of Dominance in The Helping Professions

Thus, in the same way that business offers a wide range of opportunities so do the helping professions. Some of the more common ones are listed in the chart on the previous page.

▲ Brain Dominance and The Fine Arts

The data here tends to confirm what many people already suspect: the arts attract predominantly right-brained individuals. However, within that general pattern, there are some profiles of particular interest. For example, many poets and composers have a significant amount of access to the Frontal Left mode. In such cases the Frontal Right appears to be the natural lead. It sets forth a creative vision. Then, the Frontal Left functioning as an auxiliary contributes its skills in support of the Frontal Right goals. To get a sense of how this works, consider if you will the works of Robert Frost and Carl Sandburg.

Certainly Sandburg's "The fog creeps in on little cat's feet" is the kind of highly pictorial and metaphoric thought produced by a Frontal Right area of your brain. Equally visual and metaphoric is Frost's "Two roads diverged in a yellow wood." And yet, what distinguishes both of these poets from many lesser artists is their ability to be precise in measuring their words, in creating meter, in evaluating what to include and what to exclude, all of which are contributions of the Frontal Left analytic mode. Unfortunately, Frost and Sandburg cannot be assessed or interviewed. However, in assessing almost two dozen poets from a Boston area group, a colleague, Chuck McVinney, discovered that those with similar abilities and styles also had Frontal Left support.

This Frontal Left development seems to be common to a number of painters as well and is evidenced in their interest in and ability to use specific painting techniques with *precision*. Some years back, I took the opportunity to talk with to an engraver-artist who at the time was Dean of the Art School at a large university. I shared my observations with him, saying that there seems to be at least two distinct categories of artists: the first made up of double-right artists who have grand ideas and execute them with vitality, color and flair but with no precision; and the second made up of double frontal artists who have visions they can and do execute with tremendous precision, although perhaps with less vibrancy of color. In the first group I included painters like the landscape and flower painters of the Ocracoke Island artists' colony. Many such artists have a Right Posterior Convexity preference, which shows up in their search for community, and need to be connected. Another member of this group might be Robert Rauschenberg. The difference is that his work suggests a preference in the Frontal Right, yet his developed auxiliary in the Right Posterior Convexity encourages him to have a group co-create a communal work of art. The second (double frontal) group was made up of artists like Picasso and Rembrandt. The Dean agreed that one could divide many artists into such groupings, adding that it explained to him where his own ability and precision had come from, and why all artists did not have the patience or ability to work with engraving and lithography.

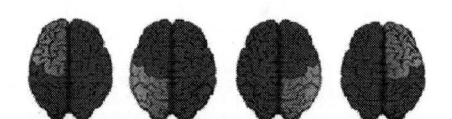

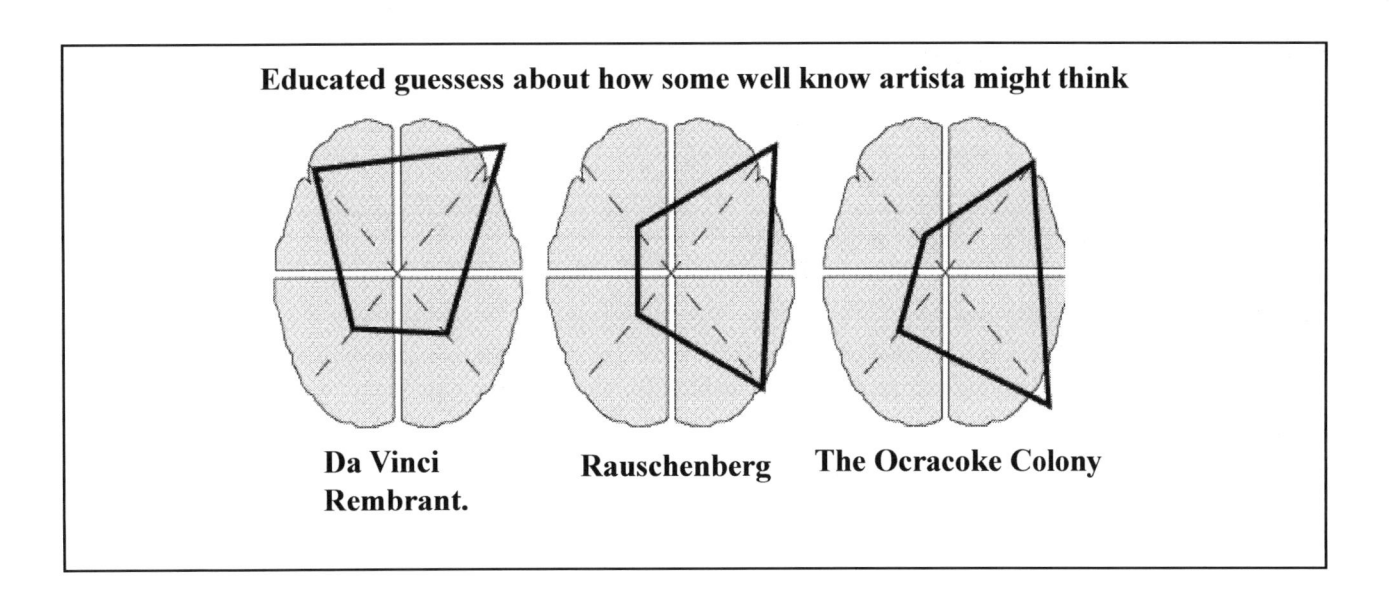

Educated guessess about how some well know artista might think

| Da Vinci | Rauschenberg | The Ocracoke Colony |
| Rembrant. | | |

Thus, even though we associate being artistic with being right-brained, the profiles of artists can be quite diverse, even including some left-brained access if not preference.

Another member of the visual arts community is the illustrator who captures things in caricature. Not surprisingly, such artists tend to be almost quarter brain Frontal Rights.

While working with a large theatre company in The Pacific Northwest, it became apparent that many of the actors and actresses had a Right Posterior Convexity preference. Their favorite way to learn a character was to first observe the nonverbals of a person similar to their character and then to mimic that person's movements. As one acting instructor pointed out, for gifted actors, it is much easier to be aware of the gestures and body stance of a character type (say, a military leader) and to embody these before learning the lines. "Once your body is moving in the right way, it is easier to speak the words in a way which naturally express the character."

In a recent television interview, Michael Caine told a revealing story about his first acting assignment, which supports the idea that many excellent actors are strong Right Posterior Convexities even if their directors are not. His role was that of a military leader. Knowing absolutely nothing about acting at the time, and following his instincts, he looked around for someone to copy. He chose Prince Phillip and noticed in particular the distinctive manner in which Prince Phillip held his hands behind his back as he reviewed the troops. When Caine mimicked this gesture in a rehearsal, the director, who obviously had not noticed Prince Phillip's behavior, commented: "Who is that? Fire that actor, he keeps his hands behind his back all the time!" Obviously, the nonverbal gestures Caine selected didn't match the director's picture of how a military leader should behave.

The method school of acting in which one seeks to get in touch with the feelings and emotions that can be brought to the character (in order to express that character's motivations) also relies heavily on having Right Posterior Convexity feeling access.

Summary of Brain Dominance in the Arts

In summary, the majority of visual and performing artists with whom I have worked show a marked preference for one of the right hemisphere's functionally-specialized types of thinking, as well as often a strongly developed auxiliary in the other. Using the precision and routine functions in the left hemisphere significantly less and generally only enough to give shape to the visions and emotions they seek to express. Not surprisingly, many such artists actually have very weak access (i.e. an avoidance pattern) in one or both left-brain modes.

Given these observations, it is perhaps easier to understand why and how so many performing artists become involved in raising money for good causes such as helping people with special illnesses, helping people in Africa facing starvation and promoting world peace.

Brain Dominance in the Arts	
Double Frontal	Composers Painters Poets Woodcarvers
Frontal Right	Sculptors
Double Right	Jazz Dancers Ballet Dancers Painters[9] Poets
Double Right **with a Right Posterior Convexity lead**	Actors Musicians Interior Decorators

---

[9] Note: remember that painters fall into at least two camps: those who master techniques and whose paintings evidence precision, such as Picasso and Renoir and those whose paintings are more emotive such as EduardMunch, who did "The Scream" and the communal artists of the art colonies such as Ocracoke Island on the Outer Banks.

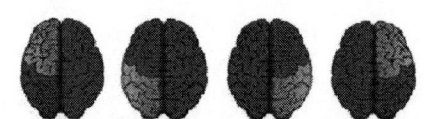

▲ Brain Dominance and Leadership

In theory, leadership is no different from any other profession or job. It attracts a particular kind of person, whose broadly developed, practical dominance enables him or her to execute the full range of tasks embodied in the job of leadership and whose natural preference responds to the needs of a particular time or a particular group of people. What is distinctive about leadership is that because of the range of tasks a leader needs to be able to do themselves, as well as the range and variety of people with whom the leader must be able to connect and build trust, more than most jobs it requires someone who has developed all four modes.

Let's take a minute to explore the job so that we all see why and how this is true. First, as one moves higher and higher in an organization one must think in broader and more conceptual terms much of the time. This involves prioritizing and making complex comparisons and *decisions*, tasks best done by the Frontal Left. It also involves thinking creatively, innovatively and *strategically* – skills managed by the Frontal Right. As yet, leadership is not just a frontal job. Excellent leaders also rely on a range of posterior convexity skills: the Left Posterior Convexity ability to work in the trenches and remain alert to *operational* concerns, as well as the Right Posterior Convexity ability to relate well and reinforcingly with other *people*. In fact, as one moves higher and higher in organizations, it becomes more necessary to work with a wider range of people – the left-brained financial people, the Left Posterior Convexity operational people, the Frontal Right scientists in research and development and the double-right-brained organizational development people. In other words, for the top executive, all types of thinking are needed and none can be sacrificed.

This means the position is ideal, in theory, for those who have developed their natural lead and both their auxiliaries – and are working to integrate their fourth function – the whole-brained thinker.

Another way of understanding why and how the whole-brained skills are required at the top of the organizational pyramid, if a company is to succeed, is found in *cybernetics*, the science of systems. The First Law of Cybernetics[10] (sometimes referred to as the Law of Requisite Variety) states: the unit within the system, which has the most behavioral responses available to it, controls the system. This law comes into play in our lives in many ways. For example, when two people who speak different languages (English and Spanish) use a bilingual translator (who speaks both English and Spanish fluently) to help them communicate and solve problems, in some ways it is the *translator* who controls what happens.

Many expert management systems are designed to identify all the possible obstacles, problems and crises that can arise and to develop an effective response for each. If a competitor invents an unexpected product or if nature introduces an unforeseen disaster, then the companies risk tremendous losses because they did not have the needed requisite variety.

---

10 For additional information on this law and how it impacts human interactions, read *The Magic of Rapport: How You Can Gain Personal Power in any Situation*, San Francisco: Harbor Publishing, 1981.

> **BRAIN DOMINANCE IN LEADERSHIP**
>
> **1975**
> **The Implementer**
>
> **1986**
> **The Visionary**
>
> These patterns were derived from Dr. Benziger's own data, combined with the written work of Harold Leavitt, author of *Executive Styles*, ©1986.

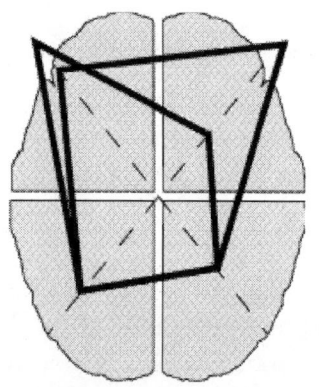

There are two problems with trying to hire a whole-brained thinker to lead your company. First, simply put, there are very few people who have actually developed their natural lead, i.e. their preference, and both its auxiliaries. The second problem with attempting to use this model to select one person to be your company's leader is that even those who have developed their natural lead and its auxiliaries are weak in understanding the needs and challenges presented by their weaknesses. Their success and your company's is limited by how well they understand their own weaknesses.

Thus, if the job of leadership is truly whole-brained, then the best solution is to use a team to fill that job. For this reason, people in leadership positions need to consciously identify and use people whose preferences complement their own to assist them to do their job and where possible to hire and develop a whole-brained team of leaders.

This strategy is, in fact, so critical that it is beginning to be adopted by companies and organizations. In the 1970's the typical company president or chief executive officer had a preference in the Frontal Left. In the 1980's, more and more of the nation's top executives had a preference in the Frontal Right. Both of these groups of leaders had a clear weakness in one of the posterior convexity modes that created problems. The Frontal Left leaders were often blind to problems involving employee morale and public relations until the problems were at a crisis stage. Similarly, the Frontal Right leaders were often blind to problems involving legal and production details until these problems were causing a crisis.

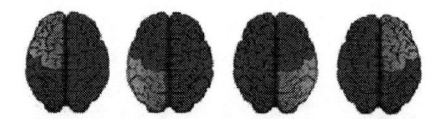

> ## Martin Luther King, Jr.
> ## Visionary Leader
>
> King is a model of the visionary leader. Notice how King, using his Frontal Right preference, created and used metaphor to empower his vision for mankind. These quotes are from a collection of his sermons, *Strength to Love:*
>
> - Our minds are constantly being **invaded by legions** of half-truths, prejudices, and false facts.
>
> - The hard-hearted person never truly loves…he is an **isolated island**. No outpouring of love **links** him **with** the **mainland** of humanity.
>
> - Most people and Christians are **thermometers** that **record or register** the temperature of majority opinion, not **thermostats** that **transform and regulate** the temperature of society. It is better to be a thermostat.
>
> - The **lamp** of independent thought and individualism…

Subsequently, in the 1990's and the beginning of the 21st century, corporations and organizations have begun to choose leadership teams, rather than individuals, in an effort to be certain they have the requisite variety they will need. The earliest such teams comprised a double frontal CEO (chief executive officer), a Frontal Left CFO (chief financial officer) and a double-left COO (chief operating officer). Later teams had an additional team member – a Frontal Right who was the chief architect or chief inventor. What is still lacking on these teams is someone with a Right Posterior Convexity preference to provide the team with a built-in early warning system for problems involving employees and customers.

The reader interested in history and the philosophy of history will enjoy Irwin Thompson's *Archetypes in History,* 1971. With a wide-angle lens looking at history, Thompson tells his readers of four types of leaders adding that the correct or appropriate type of leader comes to the fore in response to the needs of his time. His four types are: the hunter, leader, shaman and fool. The hunter can be a military or business leader and is embodied by General MacArthur and Robert McNamara. Thompson's leader is an administrative leader who excels in stable times. His shaman is a spiritual leader much like Billy Graham, Jesse Jackson and Mother Theresa. And his fool is a visionary-intuitive leader like John F. Kennedy, Martin Luther King, Jr. and Winston Churchill. Of course, the hunter has a Frontal Left preference, the administrator has a Left Posterior Convexity preference, the Shaman has a Right Posterior Convexity preference and the fool has a Frontal Right preference.

Requirements for Being A Successful Leader	
Requisite Variety	Sufficient wholeness so that the leader can communicate and work with all groups within the company or community; and
Appropriateness	The preference that best matches the need of the time or group, so that the specific genius of the leader can be brought to bear on the group's most significant problems or needs.

Combining Thompson's observations with the universal laws from cybernetics, one might anticipate that in the 21st Century, our best leaders will be those whose preference is strengthened:
- by the development over time of both auxiliaries – in service of their natural lead/preference, and
- by a deep appreciation for the value and contributions of his own natural **weakness**.

Summary of How it Works

People are instinctively attracted to work that lets them feel smart, work that matches their innate preference. They can find this congruence in a wide number of areas: medicine, business, the arts or leadership. But, wherever they find it, they will look for the job that fits them best. If a fit isn't available, they may tailor a job to match their mental requirements. Ideally, as we grow older, we become aware of what Bernard Haldane calls *our dependable strengths*. We realize what we do well and in what circumstances. We know whether we work best alone or with other people present; whether we work best when we can delegate, when we can collaborate or when we are directed. In other words, we become aware of our inner roots, our make-up and mental dominance.

And we can also understand and accept any of our life choices that were made in response to family pressure, limited opportunities or available role models that resulted in us Falsifying Type. This realization can empower us to create our own reality, one that will enable us to feel smart and good about ourselves. Our decisions about what job to do, which assignment to take, which promotion to go after will reflect our self-awareness with greater clarity. Our entire life will be naturally and effortlessly brought into alignment with our brain's needs. In the best of all possible worlds the result would be that we would do less of those other things which leave us drained and discouraged and more of those we enjoy and find energizing. And although some may see such a vision as mere fantasy, according to John Naisbitt and Patricia Aberdene in *Re-Inventing The Corporation,* recognizing individuals for the specialized contributions they offer and making the most of those contributions is a must for our society if we are to continue thriving as a nation and world.

Chapter 6: When Work Doesn't Work

▲ Career Shifts Driven by Mismatches

As explained in the previous chapter, we are naturally attracted to careers that match our preference and natural dominance. Unfortunately, all too often this instinctual attraction that is geared to help us find meaningful energizing work, gets derailed. This happens when our perception of a job or career is not accurate – that is when it does not match our actual day to day on the job expectations once we have the job. When this happens, and the individual becomes increasingly aware of the problem, he will usually attempt to remedy the situation by making a career shift – providing his life situation will accommodate the financial setbacks and insecurities that accompany such shifts.

One example of this would be my own early choice to be a long-range regional planner. I made this decision by looking at the scope of the work and its function, as well as at some of the leading role models in the field, and concluded that the work was largely Frontal Right in nature. Five years into my career, I realized that in public planning, where I was then working, a great deal of the work involved processing forms to approve or deny land use changes, variances, conditional uses, and permit appeals – all clearly Left Posterior Convexity tasks. It took me a few more years and a great deal of inner courage to decide I had made a bad choice and to get out. In fact, it was only once my health had begun to suffer dramatically that I got completely out of the field. Headaches, anxiety, muscle tension, fatigue – all indicators that my own brain was Falsifying Type. All these indicators were a part of what Arlene Taylor, Ph.D. has identified as *Prolonged Adaption Stress Syndrome* or PASS. It's just that back then, in the mid 1970's, no one knew about Falsification of Type or PASS. At the time, when I went to a physician for help, he would dismiss my symptoms, telling me it was all in my head – suggesting the chronic severe headaches were imagined. Ironically, he was correct – it was all in my head. Still, as I came to understand, it was not something to be dismissed lightly.

A second example has been occurring with increasing frequency during the past few years in nursing. It seems that despite the smart-dumb rule, over the years, largely because of sociological factors, many non-posterior convexity women have been attracted to careers in nursing. One group of these misfits is comprised of women with a preference in the Frontal Left and whose analytic capability is greater than their skill with either procedures or nurturing. Quite naturally, these women, self-admittedly, have been feeling dumb in nursing. And not surprisingly, when they decide to leave nursing many enroll in law school. The transformation in their lives is tremendous. Many are retained by hospitals needing guidance and advice on issues of risk, malpractice and liability. For these hospitals, their boards and administrators, a lawyer who actually understands what health care is about is a highly valued advisor. Others, once law school is under their belt, find satisfaction and success assisting patients seeking to file malpractice suits. In either case, these women are finally free and empowered to be smart by using their analytical skills to win the day and recognition.

Another example was reported to me, by Anne Sohn, an Oregon therapist, using my work. Her client was a young man who had been trained as a lawyer and was working his way into a position with the firm by doing legal research and writing briefs. When he came to see Anne Sohn, he was in despair. His life lacked all joy. He hated sitting all day in a small office. He hated researching cases and writing positions. He hated never getting to move around, never talking to anyone and never doing anything creative. By having him complete the BTSA, it was learned that he was a highly extraverted man with a preference in the Frontal Right.

You can imagine how uncomfortable he must have been, trying to practice law in a situation that required he work alone and focus on written details. How had he gotten himself into this situation? He said: "My parents wanted me to go into law. They told me it would be exciting and stimulating. They also told me it was a good way to help people and would provide me with the financial security to pursue my other interests – painting, travel and music. And probably with the best intentions, they pointed out that artists rarely make a decent living." Quite naturally, he was worried because he had invested so much time and energy in law and felt trapped. Fortunately, after gaining a better understanding of his brain dominance and his fundamental unsuitability for standard law, this client was able to make the decision to move into a career he would be suited for and which would provide him with satisfaction. He is now doing just that, working for himself using what he learned in law to help and empower others to make changes in their lives – as an artists' representative and trainer leading seminars for artists on "How to represent yourself in contract negotiations". The travel, public workshops and troubleshooting are well suited to his preference in the Frontal Right as well as his natural extraversion. Advocating and teaching allow him to use his Right Posterior Convexity auxiliary skills to promote his vision for himself and for his artist clients. In other words, he has selected work and designed a career that is nourishing and enlivening for him rather than deadly. His decision to change was a good one.

Another colleague of mine, an introverted Right Posterior Convexity, began work as a teacher – a career that was in sync with her natural lead. But when she elected to move to another city, she found herself forced to leave teaching for bookkeeping – to get a job and pay the bills. For almost twenty years she pushed herself to spend every workday Falsifying Type in the Left Posterior Convexity. Naturally, as a Right Posterior Convexity, she made good friends at her place of work, and valued them so much that at times she seemed to forget that she actually hated the work itself. She tended to use as many sick days as she was allowed and to invent reasons to leave early or arrive late. She had mild depression, a lack of joy and fatigue. These are all standard symptoms for someone who is Falsifying Type. So what did she do? She left work quite suddenly to return to her parents home, to care for her father – in other words, she left a place where she felt dumb, exhausted and invalidated, and moved to a place which would allow her to use her Right Posterior Convexity nurturing skills to help someone. For someone else, this returning to help aging parents may be far from advisable, but for this woman, it was the opportunity to stop Falsifying Type and the opportunity to re-embrace her natural lead.

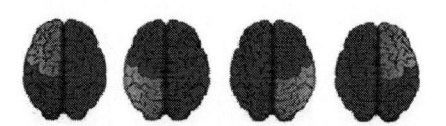

It is not always easy to change careers and to adjust one's life so as to live more in alignment with one's natural dominance. And yet, most who have gone to the trouble to change – to shape a life and career that allows them to embrace and use their natural preference in a context that honors their introversion or extraversion needs - are clearly happier and healthier. Life is too short to spend it chronically stressed, feeling dumb, anxious, irritable, exhausted and/or depressed.

Think about it. Do you know someone who selected a career – possibly one which required them to invest years of their life as well as a lot of money to enter – only to find that once they had gotten there, it wasn't what they'd pictured? Perhaps this describes you. Choosing to change careers to find a deeper level of meaning or satisfaction in a job or career that allows us to use our true self is becoming more common in our society. Our general affluence, longer life expectancy and changing economic patterns and cultural values are opening the door for many of us by giving us more freedom and permission to shape our own lives.

In the last few years this tendency has increased dramatically. Best-selling books both reveal and fuel the trend: Scott Peck's *The Road Less Traveled*; Thomas Moore's *Care of the Soul*, Gregg Levoy's *Callings: Finding and Following an Authentic Life*. As well, a growing number of local and national workshops provide information and empowering support for those who feel they are missing something in life. The University of Chicago's Women's Business Group, a group of more than 2000 women mostly 35 to 45 years old whose members are all alumni from University of Chicago's Business School, sponsored an event for their members in 1999 on how to be true to yourself.

For some, the risks of career change are more frightening than the discomfort they have been feeling on their job. Indeed, Levoy says many people do not respond the first time they hear a call – the fear of change is too great. In such cases, the person will probably not make a life change unless or until PASS – the stress and the deteriorating health it brings with it – force him/her to do so.

If you are feeling unhappy about or unsatisfied with your work-life, it is worth exploring whether your feelings are the result of your work not using your natural lead or not honoring your natural level of introversion or extraversion. If someone you know is feeling unhappy about or unsatisfied with their work-life, it is worth exploring whether the their feelings are the result of their work not using their natural lead or not honoring their natural level of introversion or extraversion

Of course, some people seeking a shift need to make one, not because their current job requires them to Falsify Type, but because their developed dominance is broader than the range of tasks which make up their job – even when some of their tasks use their preference. For example, a woman with a preference in the Left Posterior Convexity, who has developed her Right Posterior Convexity auxiliary, will no longer be satisfied working all day doing just filing and book-keeping. Her natural gift in the Left Posterior Convexity enables her to do the job easily and well. She will be energized by what she does, but feel a pinch that she is not using all of herself. For such a woman shifting to a job that allows her to use both posterior convexity modes, such as teaching book-keeping in a high school, would be both sensible and satisfying.

For such persons – who have developed a wide range of skills in their preference and one or both of its auxiliaries – it is important to understand their mental flexibility and accept that it is not simply a nice thing to have because it means they can always pinch hit, but a practical and psychological reality that demands to be used. For such people, it is not simply variety that is needed, but a special kind of variety that calls upon the full range of their mental skills, their personal *mental toolbox* if you will.

▲ Career Shifts Driven by the Need for Novelty

There is another kind of career shift that needs to be managed differently, and which does not stem from a misperception but rather from the simple fact that our perception of a given career changes as we get to know it over time, from the inside – on-the-job experience, as it were. This shift in the degree of satisfaction provided by a career over time is particularly common for people with a Frontal Right preference. As you recall, Frontal Rights need a lot of change and are unable to maintain, or get rapidly bored with, routines. In fact, for Frontal Rights, two or three years in the same job can be an eternity. For this reason, they instinctively seek work that seems to guarantee a lot of change and a lot of variety on an ongoing basis. Jobs which involve traveling, or visiting clients in the client's place of business, for example. When they fail to find such a thing, they are very likely to deal with their need for novelty by changing jobs frequently.

An emergency room physician came to me for help in figuring out his perennial unease, dissatisfaction and boredom in his chosen profession. As a young man he had considered specializing in surgery, but after looking at emergency medicine, had decided it would be a more challenging and exciting option. Instead by the end of his first year he had already discovered that it was just a set of very routine procedures, most of which he had long since mastered by heart.

He also found that he was having disagreements with other physicians about diagnoses. His personal style of diagnosis was to sense what was wrong with a patient from the doorway. He would observe the patient's energy, body posture, and movement, skin tone and color; then, intuitively, he would synthesize this information into a diagnosis. Although he was invariably correct, his unorthodox (translate: non-analytical) way of approaching things brought him into considerable conflict with the other physicians. Moreover, his feeling of being an outsider and misfit were compounded even more by his Frontal Right sense of humor that was considered by many as bizarre and inappropriate.

Learning about himself in the context of this model, his problem became clear: the boredom and frustration this now middle-aged physician was experiencing with the emergency department was just the natural and normal response of a Frontal Right who has been around for a time. Initially, the unpredictability of the variety and number of patients is experienced as exciting – a kind of troubleshooting, a talent common to double frontals with a spatial lead. Unfortunately, after a short amount of time, when the physician has handled so many knife wounds and so many auto accidents, the kind of procedures he does become predictable and he is likely to think, "I know what's coming. I've been here before". For this strong Frontal Right physician the experience in emergency medicine had become an unexpected and unwanted routine with most of the variables known, predictable and manageable. The career he had seen as full of excitement and variety while in medical school, and actually experienced as exciting and stimulating at the beginning, was now a source of chronic boredom.

Before telling you how he elected to solve his career problem, it is worth mentioning a point he brought out during discussions. It is an established fact that there is an exceptionally high burnout rate among emergency physicians. His theory was that Frontal Right intuitive thinkers self-select emergency care in medical school believing it to be filled with excitement and endless variation (characteristics this type of thinker thrives on). If this is true, then what is being experienced as burnout is simply a growing recognition that appearances in the emergency room are deceiving, and that to a large extent, emergency medicine is simply routine care delivered in a schedule-free context. So what can these physicians do for the rest of their lives? If and when medical schools begin to include dominance in the information they provide to those selecting a specialty, some system-wide answers can be generated. Until then, each one will have to deal with his or her burnout experience in a personal way.

Our emergency physician decided to take the medical board examinations for chemical dependency medicine, a brand new specialty in medicine (he took the very first board exam given), and then began specializing in working with teenagers with substance abuse problems. In making this choice, he is carving out a totally new career (in and of itself attractive to any Frontal Right), which resembles that of the psychiatrist. Although one cannot know whether he will be satisfied over the long haul with this choice, it is clear that working with people's internal problems is vastly more complex than working with cuts and wounds. Thus, perhaps, he will indeed stay interested and satisfied for years.

Of course, this kind of problem also occurs outside health care. Indeed, in the world of business, entrepreneurs who founded their own companies, most of whom are extraverted with a Frontal Right preference, tend to face the same kind of challenge – seeking to find and build a life that continually offers them something new and different. Indeed, many entrepreneurs adopt a lifestyle of founding companies in order to ensure themselves sufficient change and novelty. This is because once they have a concern up and running, say in three to five years, the experience of their own business is much like the ER physician's experience with ER medicine after the first few years. Trouble-shooting gives way to the routine and they find themselves suddenly and profoundly bored, even depressed. To regain their interest and vitality they take (or try to take) some of the company's capital to explore and possibly develop a new project they have been toying with.

Of course if the company has been doing well, it has hired a number of strong Left Posterior Convexities to handle production and to implement quality control measures, to ensure things are manufactured correctly and shipped on schedule. You can imagine the hue and cry that comes from this group when they hear how the boss intends to spend their hard earned profits. The situation typically resolves itself when the founder sells out to a more left-brained buyer, sometimes from within his own firm – freeing himself to move on to a new venture, and freeing his company, its officers and new owners of him!

One of my clients, a California entrepreneur, was in the process of selling his sixth company (which, given his profile, was a smart thing to do). Building a company, especially one that offers an innovative product, enabled him to use and validate his Frontal Right's creative, innovative, change-loving and non-anchored skills. It enabled him to *identify new products,* to use his skill at *predicting* products that were going to be good moneymakers and to *start up* the necessary manufacturing operation. When the new system became standardized, with procedures and productivity quotas in place and specialized machinery developed, the need for his type of thinking became predictably and consistently less until, ultimately, it was replaced by the need for a more rooted, maintenance-focused type of thinking with its own management style. If the Frontal Right thinker and entrepreneur had attempted to stay, he would soon have found himself bored with the work and inappropriately tinkering and meddling with the procedures – just to create some change.

Strong Frontal Right intuitive thinkers need to learn that their ability lies in participating in and leading the *creative* phase of any project. When that phase is over, it is time – for their well being as well as the welfare of the organization or division – for them to move on. Individuals with this preference who are self-aware often market themselves as troubleshooters – selling their services on a project basis to corporations. In larger corporations, they are also able to negotiate being used as an internal troubleshooter, moving from area to area or division to division as the point man with responsibility for solving difficult situations. For example, one oil company makes their troubleshooter's services available to other companies on a fee-for-service basis maximizing the benefit of such troubleshooters. What is important is that everyone involved understands that this dynamic, enthusiastic, Frontal Right thinker will be used only until the project is turned around or up and running, and that at that time, he will, by *pre-agreement,* hire and train his replacement and leave.

One of the drawbacks to having a Frontal Right preference is that those who have it, particularly as they age, may feel they have not completed very much. Since they excel at helping things get started – at birthing new ideas, products, and organizations – they may feel sad or frustrated at having missed the realization and completion phases. They should not interpret this sadness in a self critical way or conclude that it means something is wrong with them. Beginnings are the purview of the Frontal Right intuitive thinker just as endings are the purview of the left-brained thinker who has a preference in either the Frontal Left's Analytical Thinking or the Left Posterior Convexity's Sequential Thinking. It is not a character defect that causes Frontal Right thinkers to move from beginning to beginning. It is the way their brains are organized.

In summary, there is much to be learned about the inter-connectedness of our brain dominance and our career satisfaction. From the examples given, one can see that a significant amount of the re-selection that goes on in midlife can be traced to an individual's desire / need to be smarter, happier, healthier – even if that individual has never heard about brain dominance or preferences. People know when they are doing work they love. They know that work energizes and uplifts them.

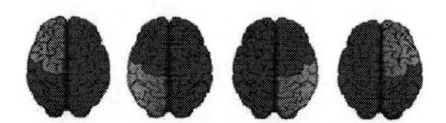

Yet, even when someone has found or created a job that uses their gifts, their preferences and skills in a context suited to their introversion or extraversion, people still find there are some remaining problem areas. The most frequently cited are: procrastination, time management and decision-making. What relationship do the problem areas have with dominance? And, what, if anything, can be done? For fun, and to expand your understanding of how dominance affects our lives, let's look at the answers.

Procrastination

If you are like most people you probably have more work to do each day than you can possibly get done in eight hours. For this reason, you regularly have to decide which tasks to do and which tasks to leave undone. Sometimes the work you decide to leave undone must be completed the next day. Other times you notice no one seems to care whether you do it. In this case, over time, you forget about it completely. In either case, much of the energy influencing your decision to put off doing certain tasks comes from your natural dominance and your own internal desire to do the things that uplift and energize you even if you have not known that these tasks energize and uplift you because:
- these tasks use your preference;
- these tasks match your natural extraversion or introversion; or
- these tasks do both of the above.

In other words, activities and situations that do not utilize our preferences, or don't match our extraversion or introversion needs, or both, are things on which we will unconsciously or consciously procrastinate.

Procrastination in Medicine

In the 1980's I worked with more than five hundred physicians individually, as teams and as workshop participants at the workshops I taught for The American Academy of Medical Directors. The single biggest problem they shared with me was making themselves complete their patient's medical records. For almost all of them the trouble was that they found sitting down to *record* their diagnoses and prescriptions in a meaningful, legible fashion overwhelmingly boring. It is certainly a Left Posterior Convexity task and most physicians are frontal. The task of recording information accurately is a sequential and detailed procedure. The response of 98 percent of the physicians was that of an analytic thinker who appreciates the value and importance of records, but does not have a strong enough sequential thinking pattern to want to do the work himself. As such, they reported finding it an ever-frustrating experience. Analytic skill is basic to being a good diagnostician and physician. But being analytically preferent, when finished with one patient and one analytic-diagnostic task, such a physician wants to go on to another diagnosis, another analytic, decision-making task. In other words, he wants to progress from one smart experience to another smart experience. To write out a detailed, sequential report of what he found, thought and recommended would engage the Left Posterior Convexity more than the Frontal Left and by comparison would not be nearly as mentally rewarding to the physician.

For many physicians, medical records build up throughout the day. Only at the end, when there are no more patients to see and no more opportunities to feel smart do these physicians turn to the task they find so unpleasant. These physicians also reported that during the time they were theoretically focused on completing this task, they were psychologically open to interruptions and distractions – by a phone call requesting a consultation or by another doctor walking by – because they experience these interruptions as more interesting than the medical records. This *lack of natural concentration* is a typical and predictable result of trying to do a task not managed by our preference.

These physicians felt their solution was a good one as they saw only the physician himself being inconvenienced by his staying late. Looked at differently, it may not be as excellent a solution as they believed. It could have had an unfortunate effect on the physician's home life and not just because his lateness upset any mealtime routine with other family members. When we put off until the end of the day tasks that are boring and fatiguing rather than energizing and uplifting for our brain, when we do arrive home, we are often cranky or irritable. Not a good way to begin an evening. It is likely, therefore, that the frontal physician who elects to solve his medical records problem by adding an hour of tedium at the end of the work day may be adding to or increasing the problems in his home life.

The procrastination these physicians are facing and trying to manage is the normal, natural experience we all have when we work at a job we love, but with a non-negotiable part we hate. There is a better way to manage it. In talking with a wide range of people who find themselves in such positions, it seems that the most satisfactory way of dealing with this putting off being dumb is to sandwich these tasks between tasks that are guaranteed highs (tasks that are managed by our preference). It takes a bit of conscious planning but it can be accomplished. This is how it works. We do a task that uses our preference first. It energizes us. We feel strong, solid and generally positive about ourselves as we begin the non-preferred task because we are basking in the afterglow of doing a smart task our brain does easily and efficiently. For this reason, although the non-preferred task drains us, it does not get to us as much. By picking up another preferred task as soon as we have completed the non-preferred one, we are able to regain our general sense of well being by the immediate shot in the arm the preferred task gives us. Using this strategy of *personal energy management* allows us to do a range of work throughout our workday without paying such a high cost. By using it at the end of the day, to structure how we approach any remaining non-preferred tasks, can help us end the day feeling stronger and more positive, ready and available to be with those we love.

Now, let's look back at our physician group. For about 2 percent of them, completing medical records was more than just tedious. For these people, the rational explanations regarding the importance of these documents just went in one ear and out the other. Months went by during which they did not complete a single record. In fact, it was usually only when they were faced with the prospect of being denied privileges that these physicians got motivated enough to sit down and focus intently on their records.

The difference between the first group, the 98 percent for whom it is simply tedious, and the 2 percent who find it nearly impossible is that the 2 percent were all strong Frontal Right intuitive thinkers, with less strength than their colleagues in the analytic mode. None of the physicians in this survey had a natural preference in the sequential mode. None, therefore, were likely to actively enjoy the task of record keeping. Yet those with a Frontal Left preference could *will* themselves to complete the task because they perceived its importance. For these physicians, using the sequential routine function to support an analytic decision was in fact the normal and healthy use of one of their auxiliary modes in the service of their natural lead.

For the physicians with a Frontal Right preference, the situation is entirely different. They do not approach life as a Frontal Left, evaluating every situation to decide what is most important and why, and using their willpower to accomplish those tasks which are a high priority, but not Frontal Left in nature. They lead with vision.

Moreover, for those with a Frontal Right preference, the need to access and use the type of specialized thinking that performs routines is not a demand to use an inefficient, but readily accessible auxiliary – as it is for those with a natural lead in the Frontal Left. It is a demand to use their greatest weakness – the one type of thinking that is both inefficient and inaccessible for them. Understanding the full picture of how their preference makes it more difficult for them to choose to use other less efficient types of thinking makes it much easier for us to appreciate why these Frontal Right Intuitive physicians resisted record-keeping so much, and why most of them found it almost impossible to conceive of completing it.

Precisely how these physicians might learn to consciously and effectively manage their problem, rather than deny or avoid it, is not clear. A variety of approaches are presented in Chapter 11 which discusses Managing Preferences to Maximize Effectiveness. In cases where resistance is this strong, the sandwich technique described above can be used successfully on a once a month rather than a daily basis. It may also help to simply accept that the basic problem with the task is that it is too repetitive for a Frontal Right thinker. As one physician pointed out, although each person is unique, when you have a specialty practice you will often see the same condition and prescribe the same prescription over and over again. Accepting this, one physician created a number of standard paragraphs that he numbered so that all he had to do to complete his medical records was to jot down a series of numbers on each patient's chart. His secretary, whose satisfaction from Left Posterior Convexity activities was predictably higher than his own, typed in the paragraphs that he initialed later. At the time this physician did this, some of his colleagues told me it was illegal.

What is interesting is that in the decade since that happened the addition of computers and specialized computer systems to hospital systems has resulted in charting that is in many ways similar to the system the one physician created. Again the purpose of the system is to save time and ensure that all the medical records are completed. The concern in both cases would be to be certain that where and as needed notes on a patient are added to the pre-written paragraphs provided by the computer's charting system.

Procrastination in a Small Business

Much of the time we procrastinate, we procrastinate tasks, like the physician's medical records, that need to be done on a daily basis. With this kind of procrastination the unpleasant, undone task hovers around us like a gnat or mosquito, putting us in a slightly unpleasant or defensive humor – unless and until we do it.

Occasionally, we procrastinate tasks that only need to be done once, but can, by an adept procrastinator, be left completely undone or go unnoticed for months or years. This kind of procrastination seems, on the surface, to be less of a problem because we often manage to be oblivious to it on a day in/day out basis. And yet, this kind of procrastination can be much more hazardous to our long-term welfare. Such was the case for me when I started my own business almost 25 years ago.

I have a preference in the Frontal Right, intuitive mode, and am highly introverted. At the time I founded my business, I had a number of well-developed competencies in my Right Posterior Convexity Feeling auxiliary that I used effectively to help connect with and help clients. In other words, I used my auxiliary skills to support my preference and my vision to grow a business that helped people thrive, by helping them embrace and use their natural lead function. At the time, my developed strength in the Frontal Left, my second auxiliary, was much less. Given my lack of left-brain access or development, one of the things that simply did not occur to me was the importance of having and using standard contracts to formalize agreements with clients; to guarantee I got paid what was agreed when it was agreed; and to protect me in the event of last minute cancellations. Although a few friends had strongly recommended I implement such a procedure, it was easy for me to ignore these friends and their advice. Then, before I knew it, my business had grown and I was too busy thinking about new program designs and media backup to worry about such things as contracts. I hired an office manager who was wonderful and who took care of all the Left Posterior Convexity administrative functions. She kept all the records straight, processed all the forms with only an occasional query and handled all the client questions and billing. She was a dream come true because with her strong preference for sequential thinking, she would do almost everything that I did not want to do. The business doubled in short order thanks to the detail-sensitive procedures and organized foundation provided by my office manager.

Unfortunately, we only had three-quarters of a brain between us; neither of us was a strong analytic thinker. Because I am such a weak Left Posterior Convexity thinker, I would regularly set fee schedules and then, just as regularly, ignore them so that my office manager was perpetually confused by all these special agreements. Additionally, although I finally did develop a Letter of Agreement that the office manager could use with all new clients, there were old and ongoing clients for whom no such Letter of Agreement existed and with whom there was only a verbal contract.

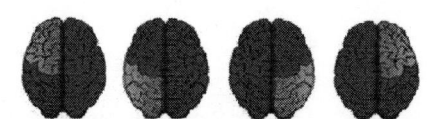

The problems caused by my weaknesses and attendant procrastination will appear quite predictable to those with a preference in either of the left hemisphere's two functionally specialized types of thinking, but to me they were an unexpected source of emotional pain and financial loss. Two of my ongoing clients, organizations which had originally approached her with pronouncements that *"written contracts are unnecessary and we never use them"* and with whom I subsequently had no contracts, began to shift the conditions of their verbal agreements pushing for significantly more service for the same fees.

Obviously, this entire situation was unnecessary. Unfortunately, as simple as it sounds to create and use a contract, it is not so simple for someone with natural preference in the Frontal Right. Moreover, this experience is common. One corporate client with whom I worked shortly afterwards, The CML Group, was highly successful because its extraverted Frontal Right founder had a gift for identifying entrepreneurial ventures that had high potential, but were in trouble because their Frontal Right founders had not managed their left-brained weaknesses well. Most of the founders were Frontal Rights using their Right Posterior Convexity auxiliary. The fact that the founder of the CML Group itself, Charles M. Leighton, was also a Frontal Right made it natural and easy for him to relate well with the founders on a one on one basis. And, the fact that he was about 15 to 20 years older and had developed his Frontal Left auxiliary as well as his Right Posterior Convexity meant that he was able to see and appreciate the needs that the individual entrepreneurs had not identified or managed well.

The moral of the story is: it is important to see and accept where and how weaknesses resulting from our natural dominance cause us to ignore, overlook or procrastinate important tasks because these weaknesses can and do sabotage our success. We will never enjoy the same easy and energizing concentration we experience when using our preference, while doing tasks requiring our non-preferred modes. Yet, when we learn to accept and plan for our weaknesses, we may find we are freer to do and enjoy the things we love simply because we do not have to spend time worrying, trying to cover the bases and back-filling because we didn't do something we would have readily taken care of had our preference been different.

	Everyone Concentrates Easily
Concentration	The natural absorption in a task that accompanies doing anything that uses our preference in a context suited to our Introversion /Extraversion needs.
Procrastination	Turning away from or putting off a task, often one ill-suited to our preference or our Introversion/Extraversion needs. At times it is accompanied by our turning towards what does interest us and what does match our Type.
Lesson	Everyone can concentrate easily and naturally. When concentration is not easy and effortless, or when we find ourselves hoping for interruptions, the chances are high that what we are doing does not fit our preference or our introversion / extraversion needs.

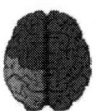

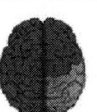

▲ Problems with Time

One of the most interesting places to see the effect of dominance in our lives is by observing how we manage time. A woman manager who had a terrible time getting any work done asked for help in managing time. After conversing with her for a short time the cause of her problem became apparent. As a Right Posterior Convexity feeling type with not very much access to either left mode, she found much of her work (i.e. scheduling and monitoring tasks) frustrating and unsatisfying. As she was gifted at listening to and being sensitive to other's feelings, empathizing with employees who came into her office, being supportive and encouraging when things went wrong, she spent much of her time doing what she and others perceived as socializing instead of working (i.e. scheduling and monitoring tasks). This was made worse by the fact that, once she got someone talking, she did not wish to hurt their feelings by cutting them off. Her problem was not so much with time as with designing a job that allowed her to use her preference and its natural gifts rather than pressure her to Falsify Type.

In the medical community a similar problem arises for many pediatricians. Remember this specialty attracts physicians with a preference in the Right Posterior Convexity. These physicians enjoy working with the more touching clients like kids and moms. Since the *need* to *touch* is most often sublimated into the more socially and professionally acceptable chatting, the pediatrician is more likely than any other physician to dally with the patients regardless of how tight his schedule is. Chatting with the patient or parent, establishing a personal connection and making sure they feel heard are very much a part of his practice. Also, of particular concern and importance to him is making sure not to rush the patient in and out as if seeing them was just business. Although this behavior makes him popular with his patients, it often drives his Left Posterior Convexity administrator into a frenzy.

That both the female manager and the pediatrician have great difficulty staying on schedule and getting work done is a source of frustration and confusion to them and to those with whom they work. Yet, in actuality, the problem is not in managing time, but in scheduling a workday that will be satisfying to the person with a preference for the Right Posterior Convexity Feeling mode.

In the case of the female manager, one possibility could be sharing a leadership position with another, more left-brained manager. The more one understands about leadership, the more one sees it as a complex task requiring a whole-brained package of skills. As this perception spreads and is accepted, it is likely shared leadership will become an everyday way of doing business in organizations. A Right Posterior Convexity manager is not adept at managing schedules and needs someone to perform that function. At the same time, there are numerous left-brained managers who are not at all adept in making employees feel appreciated, helping them resolve conflicts with other employees or helping them with an emotional trauma (as a result of illness, alcoholism or death). For such left-brained managers, having a partner manager who is adept in the area of interpersonal relations could be invaluable.
In the case of the pediatrician, much of the pressure comes from trying to force this Right Posterior

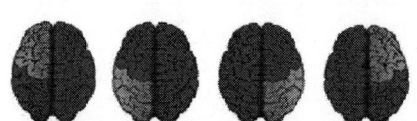

Convexity thinker to move through a schedule that does not allow time for what he feels are necessary conversations. Simply scheduling fewer patients for him would appear to be a poor solution from a cost-effective perspective (which is ultimately how most business decisions are made), but it is not actually that clear-cut a decision. Remember our story of Joe, the community minded pediatrician in Chapter Four: a group practice that has one physician, the pediatrician, who builds goodwill with the community, could well prove to be the cheapest and best liability insurance a group can have.

In other words, in both cases it is likely that the pediatrician and female manager actually actively build positive employee relations, employee trust and good will when they are allowed to do what they do naturally. In companies experiencing low morale and high turnover the contributions of such natural Right Posterior Convexity Feelers might be the missing piece needed to build a strong sense of trust, loyalty and community.

What else happens in the area of time management? What happens for those with a natural lead in one of the left modes?

Those with a natural preference of the Left Posterior Convexity detailed, procedural type of thinking naturally prefer to work by schedules and appointments. Nonetheless, even they have difficulties:
- They get scheduled up so that they have little or no time for impromptu activities or meetings.
- They need more time (and information) in meetings than their Frontal Left colleagues and/or bosses to read and understand new information.
- They have difficulty in applying the 80/20 rule to manage their time.

Left Posterior Convexities believe in attending classes to learn things they need to know. They attend time management classes with the expectation that they will be able to apply the techniques presented in the class. Unfortunately, most time management classes teach a technique called the 80/20 rule which states that 80 percent of the tasks you perform produce only 20 percent of your results; while conversely the other 20 percent of your work accounts for a full 80 percent of your results. Given this formula, the would-be master of time is advised to *sort out* which tasks fall into the 20 percent category and which fall into the 80 percent category. Unfortunately, this theoretically simple task is not so simple for a Left Posterior Convexity, who does not know how to compare apples and oranges. But more about that when we get to decision-making.

By contrast, the Frontal Left is a natural master of time. This person is able to sort readily through tasks, paperwork and information to determine what is worth doing and what should be immediately jettisoned in the wastebasket or circular file. Similarly, when listening to a report or presentation, the Frontal Left is adept at *listening only for key information,* analyzing it quickly and taking immediate, decisive action. Like superman, he or she pushes through work towards the goal of success faster than a speeding bullet.

For the Frontal Right, time management is almost a moot question. For one thing, these people tend to not wear watches or observe clocks. For another, when they are truly interested in a problem, it absorbs their attention for prolonged periods of time during which they block out anything or anyone else trying to get their attention. In such instances they may miss scheduled appointments, meals and even sleep. When interested, they don't need to try to fit everything into an eight-hour day because they never work only eight hours. By contrast, when they are bored they almost never show up at the office and so again may well miss scheduled appointments and meetings.

▲ Dominance and Decision Making

Decision-making is another area in which our work style is strongly affected by our dominance. In decision-making, the general rule that applies is: "You make decisions from your preference unless your environment forces you to do otherwise". In other words, someone who has a Right Posterior Convexity preference makes a decision based on her feelings unless the boss has specifically told her to approach an issue differently. It is interesting to note that although she may comply with this request, she may not necessarily feel right or *comfortable* doing so. In such cases, she is likely to seek out other feeling types with whom she can discuss the problem and from whom she can elicit support.

Feeling types in order to solve or sort out a complex problem use this same seeking of others' opinions. For them, one of the best ways of deciding what to do is to find out what most people want to do. To accomplish this, people with a Right Posterior Convexity preference often amble around, chatting with lots of different people to learn their opinions. Although natural feeling types will listen to logical arguments, they are more likely to be impacted by the person who quietly tells them about a *gut feeling* they have. Although Right Posterior Convexities are known for collaborating, it is more frequently the case that they will let the majority decision stand, provided the agreed upon solution harms no one. Thus, for feeling types, the time required to make a decision is the time required to talk to everyone about it, to collect their feelings and to identify a decision with which the majority feel comfortable. Controversial decisions that seem to be a major source of intense disagreement are decisions Right Posterior Convexities frequently refuse to make at all. In some management books, managers with a Right Posterior Convexity preference are referred to as country club managers because they stay away from difficult issues so that they can keep things running smoothly.

As you can imagine, a strong Left Posterior Convexity procedural thinker approaches decision-making very differently. People with this preference want clear and detailed *guidelines* for all decisions within their area of responsibility. If none exist, they are likely to try to obtain some before proceeding. They'll ask others: "Where has this been done before? How did those people make their decision? What did they decide?" Thus, for procedural thinkers, the time it takes to make a decision is the time it takes to review all the details of the decision, matching them against an approved set of guidelines. Since they can do this by themselves, they may very well spend their decision-making time alone.

Frontal Right intuitive thinkers are equally predictable in their decision-making behavior. In areas of their strength, such as selecting a new approach to solving a difficult or complex problem, they tend to make quick *intuitive* decisions which are often correct, but which they can't easily support with facts or logic. When forced to slow down and consider facts, they often become confused and lose touch with their own internal sense of what's happening. Once this has happened, they are generally easily talked into backing away from their original position. Many successful entrepreneurs, who freely admit to having made major errors because they allowed themselves to be talked out of an intuitive decision by their left-brained colleagues or staff, have reported such experiences.

In areas of their weakness, such as scheduling, implementing quality control or inventory control measures, Frontal Right thinkers are equally predictable. They *avoid* such decisions or make them in such an off-handed manner that they cannot be implemented or tracked. Comments like, "sure, we'll have it done in a month" or "I know we're just getting started, but we'll be in a position to pay you top dollar within three months" are often simply wishful fantasies.

Frontal Left analytic thinkers also have a characteristic style of decision-making. They make their decisions about *consequential* things and don't waste their time on things that will not matter in the long run. They are famous for reminding people of the 80/20 rule, mentioned earlier, which says that 80 percent of the result is obtained from 20 percent of the tasks comprising a job. And, they use this rule to justify their dropping tasks that promise little payback, so they can focus all their energy and attention on the high yield tasks. They call this *prioritizing*. And, it is.

When they are given a problem to solve that they feel is worth their time, natural Frontal Lefts want to study just the key facts. As such, they prefer half-page summaries and charts. Given the key facts, they analyze the impact of each option, and then select the one that will give them the most successful (or occasionally least damaging) outcome as their solution. Frontal Lefts are the founders of the *cost-benefit* school of decision-making.

▲ Work Rhythms, Hours and Speed

Although they are less tied to dominance than procrastination, time management and decision-making, the hours, rhythm and speed at which we work also reflect our dominance.

Where hours are concerned, Left Posterior Convexity and Right Posterior Convexity people work regular hours unless their help is specifically needed. Neither prefers to work long hours.

Left Posterior Convexity thinkers prefer to work regular hours and if they think a job may require them to stay late, they may not take it. Alternatively, if they're in a job in which events are making the hours and working conditions erratic, they may join a union that will fight to get the workers their desired 9 to 5.

Right Posterior Convexity thinkers tend to work regular or even diminished hours so that they can be home with their family. They work long hours at times because they like to help and can be counted on to stay to help out. A frequent reason they stay late is to help a frontal boss. If a Right Posterior Convexity does not have a family, an employer often easily imposes on him or her. If the person has a family, he or she will want and expect the overtime will be returned in the form of flexible time off so that the Right Posterior Convexity can stay home for their child's birthday, for example.

Frontal Right thinkers work in fits and starts and tend to stay late and long. When they get hooked on an idea that is of personal interest to them, they often work non-stop through the night, totally oblivious to time. When they are stuck and can't figure something out, they are just as likely to go for a long walk or to play tennis for hours, much as the chemist John Critch relates doing when stuck in his work on the DNA-RNA double helix.

Frontal Left people work long and hard to get someplace or to gain power and control because they are aware of and buy into the concept of the organizational ladder. These are the people who believe that if you want to be on the fast track you need to demonstrate it by making the commitment to work long and hard hours.

Where rhythms are concerned, the Left Posterior Convexity thinkers tend to be the slowest and the most methodical. Right Posterior Convexities may work equally as slowly, but, in their case, it's because they need to stop for frequent chatting breaks with their boss, their colleagues or perhaps a client. The Right Posterior Convexity's pace also depends more on their mood; if they are sad, they may work rather slowly; when they are happy, they will pick up the pace. Regardless of their mood, they rarely work for a prolonged, uninterrupted period of time alone.

By contrast, Frontal Rights tend to work very quickly. At times, their energy seems to spiral into a frenzy of activity. This spiraling is what tends to separate the Frontal Right from his Frontal Left colleague, who also tends to work quickly but with a sense of control.

▲ Questions and Answers about Work

You say that Left Posterior Convexities are usually picked as supervisors and operational managers. Why is that?

The reason Left Posterior Convexities are well-suited to being operational managers is that they like to attend to routines, details and the necessary procedures in order to keep things running smoothly.

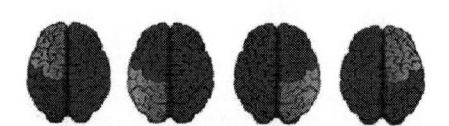

Someone with a preference in the Right Posterior Convexity feeling mode might be distracted by how people are feeling about their work. Someone with a preference in the Frontal Right intuitive mode would most likely interrupt productivity by intermittently designing and implementing improvements in the schedule or procedures. And, a person with a preference in the Frontal Left analytic mode might consider simple operational management beneath his level of skill and try to rapidly move upwards, leaving the position vacant.

What happens when a right-brained thinker is promoted into management?

When Frontal Right research scientists are promoted by their companies into tasks requiring a significant amount of left-brained, operational thinking, significant problems occur. This situation is particularly common in companies like Shell, Dupont and Standard Oil that have all promoted scientists into managerial positions because the non-scientist left-brainers they had used previously had difficulty gaining the respect and cooperation of the scientists in their Research and Development Labs. Unfortunately their solution simply replaces one problem for another. The scientists respect the colleague who is now their manager, but the demands of his new position – the monthly reports, budgets and other control functions of management – cause the colleague who has opted to try management to feel confused, dumb and frustrated. This situation is made worse when the generally more introverted scientist tries to argue with top management for promotions or project money and finds himself unable to sell.

Such mismatched or dominance-crossed promotions may even explain the *Peter Principle,* which has gained so much attention in the past decade, for in every company there are highly extraverted posterior convexity thinkers who seek out top management jobs only to find they cannot follow the abstract thinking involved.

I'm a triple translator. I've developed and use my natural lead and both auxiliaries? Could this be why I've changed careers so often?

It could. It's common for tri-modal individuals to have a number of careers during their lifetime. They initially choose a career that matches their natural lead. Then, as their life and career continue to validate and reward them for being themselves, they expand their range of influence by developing first one and then the other auxiliary. And, as they do, they change their career to match their expanded practical dominance. Again, this happens when someone is rewarded and respected for who they are early and consistently in life.

Are most middle-aged people triple translators?

No, not at all. A person, who is pushed to Falsify Type early in life, often selects their first career because it embodies their Falsified Type. When they encounter an opportunity to embrace their natural lead, which may occur when they are 25 or 45, they tend to leave the first career, embracing instead the one that embodies their preference. Then, they may spend years just reconnecting with their preference before they feel safe and comfortable enough to open to the full use of their auxiliaries. Wounding is funny that way. Sometimes you find a 55-year-old who is a quarter-brained expert. They have been shamed or cast out so often as a misfit and have used so much energy defending who they are that staying true to that lead becomes habitual.

How well I get along with the boss often affects how much I enjoy a job. Is it better to have a boss whose preference matches mine or whose preference is different?

Yes, getting along with the boss is an important part of feeling satisfied and happy at work. How well you succeed is affected by at least ten things only some of which are connected to dominance. Issues of self-esteem and maturity can cloud a potentially terrific relationship. People who have difficulty in relationships in general because they come from a dysfunctional family of origin will have problems at work. Some people who are insecure may try to parent you, even if you are older than they are. Others may try to get you to parent them, even if they are older than you are. Having said that, let's look at the range of ways in which dominance affects how well we get along with our boss.

Ten Factors Affecting How We Get Along With the Boss

Your dominance pattern	Your boss's dominance pattern
How well your own pattern matches your job	How well your boss's pattern matches his / her job
Your self-esteem	Your boss's self-esteem
Your emotional maturity	Your boss's emotional maturity
Your birth order	Your boss's birth order

If you and your boss have the *same preference*, the two of you will probably get along well since you see the world in the same way. In fact, you are likely to really appreciate your boss as a person and enjoy relating to him. You will also tend to give him the benefit of the doubt in difficult situations. Nonetheless, if your boss is hiring only people who think the way he thinks, there will be a problem. Because to some extent all jobs are whole-brained, there will be a part of the job that nobody wants to do since it is outside everyone's dominance. If your boss gives you the problem tasks, you feel dumped on – and over time develop problems from Falsifying Type. If he does it himself – because he does not want to dump on anyone – he is likely to feel irritable when doing the tasks and over time develop problems from Falsifying Type. If the amount of work requiring you to Falsify Type is significant, whoever does it is vulnerable to eventual burnout. The problem with such tribal work teams is that they are not sufficiently flexible to handle all parts of the job well; they do not have the requisite variety.

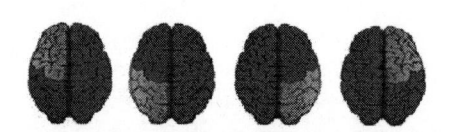

breaks down, your boss is likely to become more crisp, decisive and critical (his analytic Frontal Left preference), while you may become more concerned with the interpersonal ramifications (your Right Posterior Convexity preference). When this occurs, your boss will not understand your feelings-based approach and it will be disconcerting for you to be so out of rapport when you are usually so in agreement. If you want to talk to your boss at this time, you will need to *communicate in his language* – the language of the Frontal Left. You will need to be precise, present key points and argue logically. It will do you no good at all to present things from a Right Posterior Convexity point of view. Having an overlap with your boss gives you a basis for collaboration, but it also leads you to believe you are more completely understood than you in fact are. To do well in this situation you must recognize the differences as well as the similarities between you and your boss.

When you and your boss have *totally different* patterns you will either be a resounding success or a complete failure at working together, depending largely on how mature each of you is and whether or not you succeed in bonding sufficiently well to effectively collaborate. In team building work over the years, it seems that the best product comes out of whole-brained teams. Putting together people with complementary dominance patterns creates a single whole-brained team that can function in place of a single leader or decision maker – as long as they have been helped to value and use each other. According to Naisbitt and Aburdene (authors of *Megatrends and Reinventing the Corporation*), an organizational structure in which more than one person holds the leadership position is emerging in the top corporations around the country and is one of the trends of the future. What makes this difficult to accomplish is that all of the individuals involved need to be sufficiently mature and have sufficient self-esteem to make the collaboration work. If either person is overly invested in his way of thinking and has not accepted that he can benefit from help, the disparity in dominance is likely to cause problems.

In one situation, a division vice-president had been unable to get her budget approved since the arrival of their new chief executive officer (CEO) three years earlier. Although the client understood that the recent years had been a time of severe cost cutting, she believed her division's budget was suffering more than it needed to. A rapid analysis of the situation showed that the vice-president, a strong Frontal Right, was a success because she had a strong intuitive sense for what clients wanted and which new products would sell. Unfortunately, the new CEO appeared to be a strong Frontal Left. Despite her track record, when she went in to request a budget for the coming fiscal year, he expected her to justify her requests in a logical manner that, for her, was almost impossible. Sending her in to negotiate with this new CEO and his new fiscal management team was as inappropriate as sending someone with one year of high school Russian to negotiate a treaty with the Soviets.

When this was pointed out to her, she came up with her own solution almost immediately. The next time she had to present a budget, she would take a strong Frontal Left with her to argue for her position. She herself would present the budget, but her assistant would argue for it when any line item was questioned. With this strategy in mind, she looked to her staff for the strongest natural Frontal Left on her team. Significantly the only team member who had a preference in the Frontal Left was not one of most highly trained members of her team. Nonetheless, bringing this woman with her accomplished the results she wanted. Together, they got every penny she asked for. Each time they were asked a question, the vice-president would turn to Margaret and ask: "Now, Margaret, what exactly was our thinking on this?"

In Conclusion

Almost every aspect of our work life is affected by our internal, physiologically established, mental preference. Regardless of who we are, there are things we will not do well and situations in which we will not get along well with others. This is even true for the whole-brained person, for although they can do almost any kind of job and understand any type of person, focusing for prolonged periods of time in one area or talking at length to a person whose dominance is highly skewed will tire them. Thus, their strength is also their weakness, as is the case with us all.

How can we live a complete life with these inborn limitations? There are many ways. The first step is to learn who we are and to gain a real appreciation for how our dominance has been guiding and influencing us. Once we realize this more fully, then we can begin to be more pro-active about shaping the life we want by managing our own and others' natural dominance more effectively so that we empower them and ourselves at the same time.

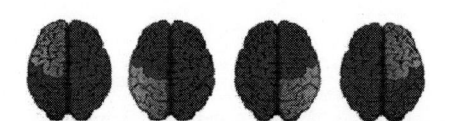

Chapter 7: You've Got to be Kidding

If you have come to the conclusion that dominance affects practically all of what you say, do, think or value, you are well on your way to understanding dominance. Dominance is not the total picture, of course, but it is so close to our core identity that it might be described as part of our genetic roots. Consequently, one might anticipate seeing its involvement in virtually every area of our lives. And although the specific rules that apply to each area of life differ slightly, they are all variations of one of the Two Rules of Thumb which, in this chapter, will be applied to your personal life: your friendships, your marriages and your children.

Friends and Mirrors

Most of us select friends who *mirror*, at least partly, our mental preference and/or our natural extraversion or introversion level. Furthermore, when we meet a person who mirrors us completely, that is, whose preference and extraversion/introversion level *matches* ours *perfectly*, we often feel so comfortable with them that we see them as a best friend. **This then is the basic rule of dominance and friendships: we choose our friends because** *they are like us.* We also call this the *Mirror Rule* and it is an application of the first Rule of Thumb: to develop or nurture your self-esteem, as well as ensure your immediate effectiveness and success, select activities and people that match your preference. At first glance, it might seem very narrow-minded of us to choose friends who see the world as we do. And yet, choosing friends who effortlessly mirror our perceptions and thinking, serves a valuable function: *it fosters our mental and emotional well-being.*

> "A faithful friend is the medicine of life."
>
> Ecclesiastics

Think for a moment of someone you would consider a best friend. Notice how you and your friend are interested in similar things and have formed similar opinions. Notice that your conversations are noteworthy for the amount of agreement between you and the sense of satisfaction you feel following the interaction. Notice how you feel heard and validated. In conversations between best friends this harmony and agreement exists naturally and effortlessly, not because the best friends are trying to make each other feel loved and accepted. This mental congruence is also reflected in their nonverbal signals and the pace and rhythms of their speech.

Having the same dominance allows our best friend to follow our thinking easily and effortlessly which, in turn, gives us the impression that what we think is good, clear, right and of value. Even better, the process is completely natural; we don't have to ask if they are in agreement since their expressed interest and their nonverbals tell us they are. By contrast, someone whose dominance differs from our own will not be able to follow our thinking easily and effortlessly. Despite efforts on their part to express interest (e.g., by asking questions or nodding in agreement), their nonverbal signals will reveal confusion and boredom. Even though they may say, "Yes, I understand", their eyes will be a bit glazed or out of focus and their brow will be wrinkled as they try to understand what we mean or why we value something.

Another thing that happens when we converse with someone who is our mental mirror is that as we begin to express an idea they may begin to smile or nod, even *before* we have finished, because they can already see where we are headed. Contrast the pleasure you feel at this experience with the discomfort you feel when trying to explain something important to someone who does not understand you; you will begin to see the important psychological benefit of mirroring.

> **"A friend is, as it were, a second self."**
> Cicero

A third benefit of talking with such a friend comes not when we are talking but when we are listening to them talk. As we listen to them expressing their thoughts, dreams and concerns, we notice that what they say makes sense to us and that we thought that just the other day. Thus, a best friend is not just a passive, *responsive* mirror (as might be provided by an adept active listener); he is an active *initiating* mirror. He does not simply parrot back to us what we think and feel, he actually agrees with it. We feel connected or as one with him and the gulf between others and ourselves disappears. We belong.

> Friendship is a relation between men at their highest level of individuality. It withdraws men from collective togetherness as surely as solitude itself could do and more dangerously, for it withdraws them by twos and threes. Friends side by side absorbed in some common interest that they had feared only they had. C.S. Lewis, *The Four Loves*

Understanding that this kind of connection comes from an underlying congruence in dominance may provide some insight into why so many of the communication classes offered to adults fail to produce lasting results. The difficulty with trying to make connections and reach out to others is that real and full acceptance comes only once we identify with the other person.

To summarize: in friendship, likes attract and are valuable to each other because being with someone who thinks the way we do enables us to feel connected, accepted, strengthened, affirmed and validated – to develop positive self-esteem. This proves to be most important for people who experience themselves as misfits. Thus, in our society such friendships are most important for: Introverts, Frontal Rights, Right Posterior Convexity males and Frontal Left females, whose self-esteem is otherwise at risk. For these ugly ducklings, finding other swans who model and mirror how they think and who they are is necessary.

Questions and Answers About Friendships

What type of thinker finds it easiest to find friends?

It is easiest for people who have developed and are using one auxiliary in addition to their natural lead to find friends because of the half-brain patterns (double left, double right, double frontal, and double posterior convexity) found most frequently in our society. Furthermore, because these patterns are so numerous, there are many groups that these people could join should they want to find like-minded friends. For example, double lefts, who are often engineers or accountants, frequently belong to business organizations and to clubs that focus on such hobbies as fishing, stamp and coin collecting, model building and model-train operation. Double posterior convexities, often teachers, clerical workers and nurses tend to enjoy church groups and structured organizations that help others. Double frontals, such as chemical engineers, surgeons, architects and research scientists tend to enjoy mountaineering, hang gliding and flying (many actually have their pilot's licenses). Double rights, including some entrepreneurs and organizational development specialists, can often be found involved with community theatre since they enjoy acting, or in art classes or attending exhibits.

If someone has these patterns and they are not finding friends, they are probably not looking in the right places. Of course, they could be having difficulty because they are also highly introverted or highly extraverted and need a mirror who is also introverted or extraverted.

Why don't I have a best friend? Could this have something to do with my dominance?

Indeed it might. Just as those who use two specialized types of thinking have an easier time finding friends who are mirrors for them, because there are so many of them in the population as a whole, those who are quarter-brain experts have a more difficult time finding friends who are mirrors for them because there are fewer people who think the way they do in the population. If you are also highly introverted or highly extraverted it would be even more difficult to find a best friend whose mind mirrors your own, because there are fewer people in the general population who are both quarter-brained and highly introverted or highly extraverted.

For those who function as quarter-brainers and have a balanced arousal level, their difficulty in finding friends can be confusing because on the surface they find many people with whom to talk. After all, the total number of people who have either a preference or a developed auxiliary in each mode is substantial. The trouble arises because most of the people they meet and talk to – with whom they initially get along well – have a practical dominance pattern that is half-brained and have developed strong competencies in another mode as well. And this difference, this lack of congruence in how they think, surfaces over time when the half-brainer tries to shift the discussion – its pace or its topic – to his other developed mode, particularly if it is his natural preference. Unconsciously, the quarter-brainer has a strong interest in keeping the conversation focused in his or her one preferred and developed area. It is not uncommon for this resistance to be experienced as constraint by the half-brainers. So after a time, the half-brainer is likely to abandon the quarter-brainer in search of a broader match.

Of significance is the fact that the quarter-brain individual eventually can find another quarter-brainer who shares his preference and introversion/extraversion level and when this person is found, he or she is a friend for life.

How about people who have developed competencies in both of their auxiliaries, as well as in their preference? Do they find it easier or harder to find a best friend?

Interestingly enough, these people who we might call *multi-dominant* – with a practical or effective dominance incorporating three modes – also have difficulty finding a best friend. In their case it's because *they tend to leave others*. Since there are relatively few multi-dominant people, and even fewer with their specific pattern, such a person may never have a best friend or even understand the term. To satisfy their need for a mirror, multi-dominant people tend to instinctively build *Composite Mirrors*, using one friend to mirror a few of their modes and another to mirror others. Because none of their friends is *completely* comfortable for them, they move back and forth between these partial mirrors to create a full sense of self-acceptance. The results can be troublesome. A multi-dominant person may find giving a party difficult because his friends don't like each other. In fact, they may actively put each other down as they compete for his approval. A multi-dominant person may experience internal conflict about his relationship to each mirror. When they first get together, his experience may be one of delight yet, after a few hours, he may be bored and want to get away. This shift from interest to disinterest is normal and natural for the multi-dominant as his brain tries to balance the attention and time spent in each developed mode. Unfortunately, this pulling away may feel like rejection to the people making up a multi-dominant's composite mirror, so he needs to use tact and finesse in handling his friends.

Multi-dominant individuals tend to make up their mirrors from a series of half-brainers, as the half-brainer's mental flexibility is more in sync with their own. Occasionally they use a quarter-brainer to cover a mode that their half-brain friends don't use. However, this is a difficult relationship since the narrowness of the quarter-brain's focus rapidly becomes uncomfortable for the multi-dominant thinker. Also, one of the problems multi-dominants have in making friends is the time it takes to build friendships. As one strong triple-brainer put it, "Even when you find the pieces, it's difficult to build the friendships because friendships take time and, if you're a multi-dominant, you need three times as much time because your mirror is made of three people. Considered that way, it's almost impossible."

What about trust? How does that fit into brain dominance?

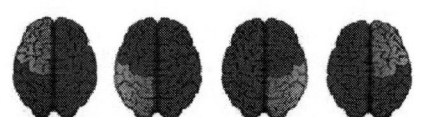

If all else is equal, we are more likely to trust people who share our preference and extraversion/introversion level because they naturally value what we value, understand our fears and weaknesses. And, generally, they affirm rather than discount us when we show them a part of ourselves. This encourages us to feel safe. Contrast the risk we feel sharing ourselves with someone whose preference or introversion/extraversion level differs from our own. In the latter, the chances are great that we feel put down or criticized – if only in their nonverbal signals – making it considerably more *difficult for us to risk* opening up to or sharing ourselves with that person.

Moreover, since it is easiest to build trust with our mirrors, we tend, over the years, to create more opportunities to share with them than with others thereby cementing the bond of trust that exists between us. At the same time, our discomfort with people who are different may cause us to actually avoid many trust-building opportunities with them, thereby reinforcing our initial discomfort. Over time, we may generalize our mistrust of a specific person to include all people with a given preference, or all highly extraverted people. Thus, in time, an introverted Right Posterior Convexity or Frontal Right may come to automatically mistrust all extraverts and most especially extraverted Frontal Lefts. This kind of aversion for one type of thinker often comes from experiences in which we feel we have been rejected or shamed by a representative of that group.

Again, it is those who are most at risk in a group who have the most to lose when they also find it difficult to find and make a best friend. As such, in our general global culture, its introverts have more to lose than extraverts when they do not find a best friend; and Frontal Right intuitives have more to lose than Frontal Left analytic thinkers. People who are members of at risk groups need the validation of an authentic mirror *more* not less than the population at large.

▲▲ Marriage

It's probably no surprise to anyone that the principles that govern how we select our life partner vary dramatically from those we use to select our best friend, although most of us would be hard pressed to understand why. Far from being a perfect mirror for us, thinking as we think, acting as we act and choosing as we choose, our spouse is often as different from us as the day is from the night – often having both a different preference and different extraversion/introversion needs.

This, of course, is something we all know and accept. Our common folk wisdom that opposites attract is reinforced by such lyrics as: "You say tomato, and I say tomah-to. You say potato and I say potah-to. Let's call the whole thing off." It's all very clear. We know we choose to marry unlikely partners, and as the song suggests, we know that our un-alikeness can and does cause real problems. Yet most people don't call the marriage off; most people plunge ahead – desperately attempting to assure themselves that things will be okay and that they do have some common ground with their spouse. After all, the newlywed observes, "We use the same tooth paste. We like the same coffee." And eventually, at a loss for words that would clarify their behavior, most people attempt to explain their selection of a spouse by simply acknowledging "people marry for irrational reasons".

Only recently with the insights provided by brain dominance have we come to understand that our choice of a spouse is perhaps one of the most rational choices we make. The simple explanation, from a brain dominance perspective, is that we marry in order to have the best chance to survive as well as to grow. Paradoxically, this means we marry someone who is very different from us. Someone who can handle those problems in life that frighten, baffle or are otherwise uncomfortable for us.

This then is the Rule of Marriage: *we seek a mate who will complement and complete us* in order to guarantee our survival. You might say we marry to get a whole brain. Importantly, this is more than a mere surface attraction of opposites. It is a deep-seated drive linked directly to our core survival instincts. As such, it is also an excellent example of the second Rule of Thumb which states: to assure your survival, as well as guarantee your long-term effectiveness and success, manage activities and people not matching your preference consciously and carefully, and if possible by enlisting assistance from complementary brains. In other words, we are enlisting our spouse's assistance to guarantee our long-term effectiveness and survival.

You might say that our partnering behavior is another example of the first law of cybernetics, discussed in the section on leadership and leadership teams in Chapter 4. As you may recall, this law tells us "The unit within the system with the most behavioral responses available to it controls the system." Accordingly, when we marry someone whose brain dominance differs from ours, we increase our own ability to r*espond through our spouse* appropriately and thereby successfully to the challenges and opportunities life brings our way – without Falsifying Type.

In many marriages one or both partners seem both aware and appreciative of the wholeness their spouse brings, even if the differences occasionally grate on them. There are the classic stories: the woman who can't balance her checkbook marrying an accountant who can manage money for her; and the crazy inventor with his head in the clouds who marries the practical, down-to-earth woman who sees that groceries get bought and bills paid. In these examples, the individual's *ability to survive* is enhanced by the variety or diversity of skills present in the couple.

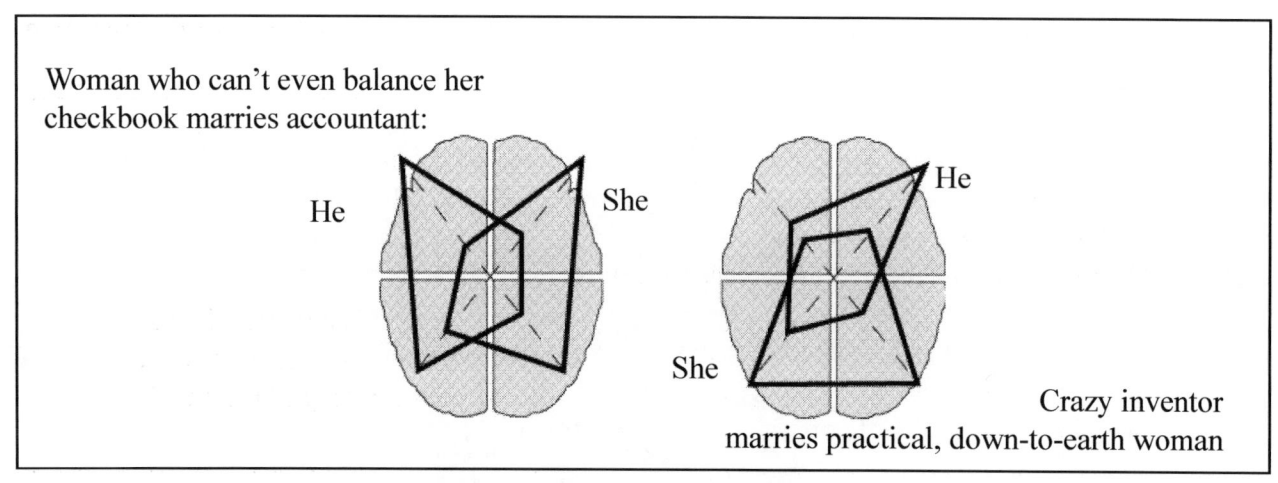

Woman who can't even balance her checkbook marries accountant:

He   She

She

Crazy inventor marries practical, down-to-earth woman

Beyond our need to survive, we all share another need first identified by Abraham Maslow: *the need to learn and grow.* By marrying a person whose brain thinks very differently from our own, we create a learning opportunity for ourselves. We can learn from the brain we marry how to think in ways we may never have imagined. If Carl Jung was correct that the task of life is to develop all four functions within ourselves, then marriage provides us with the opportunity to not only survive, but to succeed at life: to learn and grow on a daily basis and over our lifetime. Thus, in the very best marriages, each person offers themselves as a *loving tutor* to their spouse.

The Problems

Unfortunately, many marriages do not turn out to be positive learning experiences. Although some of the challenges and roadblocks encountered in marriage occur independently of dominance, at least three distinct problems can be linked to dominance. These are: c*onflict, atrophy and miscommunication.*

Conflict occurs when, instead of appreciating our partner's being strong where we are not strong, we get *irritated at our partner's differences*. The two arenas in which conflict arises most frequently are *behavior* (how we do what we do) and *choice making* (where we go and what we do).

An introverted Frontal Left married to an extraverted Right Posterior Convexity might complain: "She always wants to go to parties and be with people. I want to be left alone, to stay home and read." While the Left Posterior Convexity married to a Frontal Right bemoans: "He never follows through with things and is always chasing after some wild idea. Why can't he be more stable and dependable?" These experiences are the natural result of instinctual complementary coupling.

A second problem that occurs in many relationships is atrophy. Here, instead of encouraging our partner to tutor us, and learning from our partner how to become stronger and more competent ourselves, we back off from using their preferred mode. This can occur for two reasons: laziness on our part, or possessiveness on their part. In the first instance, we make our spouse totally responsible for doing those things we don't like to do. In the second, our spouse assumes all responsibility, refusing to allow or accept our help. In either case, the prolonged non-use of our non-preferred mode can mean that what little strength we had in it originally weakens or atrophies.

Conflict and Choice Making

He: "She always wants to go to parties and be with people. I want to be left alone, to stay home and read."

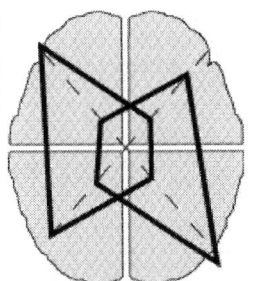

She: "A theatre party? Yes, Sharon, we'd love to come. Tomorrow night at seven?"

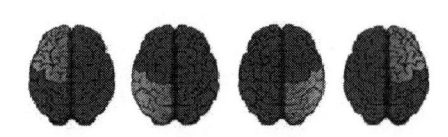

The Benziger Breakthrough

Consider Stuart, a newly divorced forty-five-year-old Frontal Left business man who is unable to socialize and make friends on his own because for the past twenty years his Right Posterior Convexity nurturing wife handled everything. After all, it was she who was so comfortable with people and such a good hostess, why shouldn't she have managed their friendships? Imagine Mary, a fifty-year-old widow who, after twenty-five years of giving her Frontal Left husband all the responsibility for managing their money, does not know the first thing about using a checking account. Clearly, both of these people are paying a high price for having surrendered the competencies they had developed in what was most probably their greatest natural weakness, but could possibly be one of their natural auxiliaries. For even if such surrender felt good and safe in the beginning, in the end it is isolating, paralyzing and tragic.

The third problem with marrying a complementary type is that *expressing ourselves so that our spouse understands us* is likely to be difficult. In fact, many couples report, *"We simply don't communicate."* Actually this is a natural, although perhaps unwelcome, result of marrying to survive. Because the two of you have different preferences, you tend to use different words to convey your thoughts and feelings. A good example of this is a conversation I overheard one morning in a hotel coffee shop. The topic was a short-term loan for which the husband had applied:

Did this couple realize they were saying the same thing? I think not. In fact, I think this is a good example of *does not compute*. She understood only that he did not like the clause. At the same time, he was baffled by the notion that fairness had anything to do with a loan agreement.

Unfortunately, this kind of conversation is typical of complementary brains trying to communicate. Each person feels confused by what the other is saying; each feels misunderstood. Yet despite the fact that neither one is actually getting it, they typically continue to try – to put out signals which say "Go on, I'm listening", because they do value their spouse and do not want to lose them – even if they can't understand them.

Alternatively, they may decide that trying to make sense of what their spouse says is simply too much work. When a person makes this decision, he or she stops listening when the spouse is speaking. This shutting down or avoiding communication may be intentional or unintentional. Either way, it is caused

---

Communications Problems

He: "The penalty clause is excessive."

He: "After a brief pause during which he seemed to be trying to make sense out of what she said. "Well, it **is** excessive."

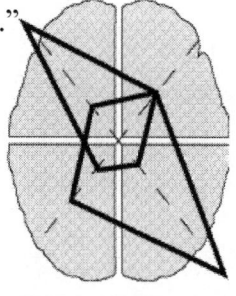

She: "It sounds unfair too."

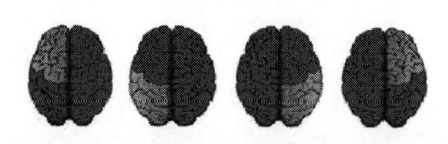

by the discomfort inherent in trying to communicate outside of one's preference.

Let's reiterate the basics. Guided largely by instinct, we tend to marry someone whose mental preference compensates for our weakness, thereby enhancing our chances for survival. Our selection, however wise in the grand evolutionary scheme of things, presents real life problems: probable conflict, the possibility that we will lose what little strength we have developed in our weaker modes and the promise of ongoing communication difficulties. Nonetheless, few people vary from the rule when selecting a life partner, especially a first partner.

Questions and Answers About Marriage

Your theory linking the 'attraction of opposites' to an instinctual, genetically driven need to survive is fascinating. Are you actually suggesting that our dominance could affect our *decision to marry* one lover rather than another?

That's correct. Although we may date people whose dominance patterns are similar to our own, when we get serious and when we actually decide to "tie a knot', we seek out a person whose strengths will compensate for our weaknesses. This is well illustrated by the tale of Kit and Bruce. Kit had a Frontal Right preference, moderate strength in both her auxiliaries, and an unquestionable weakness in the Left Posterior Convexity. She found herself dating and deeply in love with Bruce, a Frontal Left lawyer with a strong avoidance in the Right Posterior Convexity. At first the relationship seemed to work; she felt grounded and secure with his stable Left Posterior Convexity and he felt eased and comforted by her ability to communicate. Since they both had access to the Frontal Left they could spend hours being friends and discussing subjects of mutual interest. One day Bruce was gone; no fight, no explanations, just gone. Some years later, when Bruce did marry, it was according to the complementary rule. Bruce had an avoidance in the Right Posterior Convexity and he instinctively chose a woman whose strength and expertise in that specialized type of thinking would counterbalance his extreme deficiency.

An additional possibility is that Bruce sensed on some level that Kit was more "whole-brained" than he was. In fact, a secondary pattern we've observed is that people tend to select a spouse whose *range of access* matches their own. In other words, people using only one type of thinking marry people who are also highly focused. And, people with competencies in two types of thinking – most often

Bruce and Kit, the woman he dated

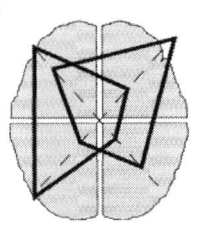

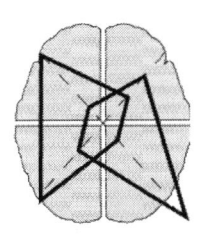

Bruce and the woman he chose to marry

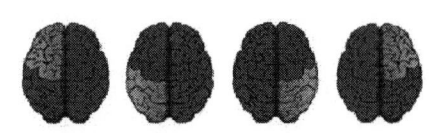

their preference and an auxiliary, tend to marry people who also have competencies in two modes and so forth.

Another wonderful example of how we *instinctively sort out our friends and lovers* is the story of two double-left engineers, Jane and Fred. This marvelous tale began some fifteen years ago when Jane and Fred, both in their early twenties, met at work. They had a lot in common including their dominance patterns. Naturally, they began to spend more time together, talking, eating lunch, and going to movies. This "Bobsey twin" phenomenon continued, as Jane recalls, for five years, during which time they grew closer and closer, although they never discussed marriage.

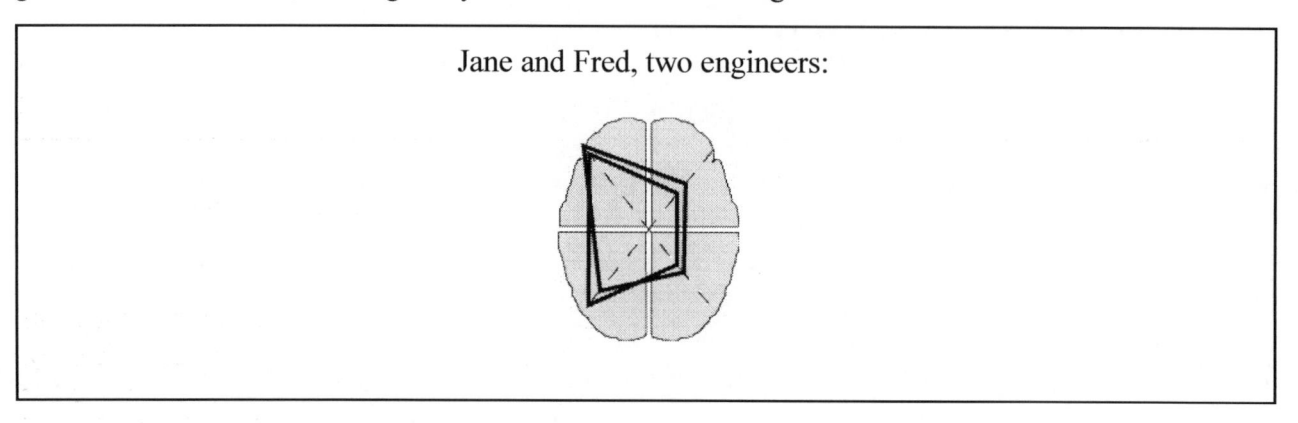

Jane and Fred, two engineers:

Then, things began to happen. Fred met Mary and decided to get married. And, although Jane was quite amenable to Fred's marriage, they stopped spending so much time together as she had nothing whatsoever in common with Mary. Within a few months, Jane met and married someone herself.

From this point on, as Jane tells the story, the two couples have been routinely double dating. Only when they get in a car, instead of following the traditional men in the front, women in the back pattern, Fred and Jane always sit together in the front seat so they can talk about a new computer design, while Mary and Dave always sit together in the back talking about their gardens and the children. "What's more," Jane says, "when we all go to a party, Dave and Mary find each other in minutes and talk for hours. But then of course that's exactly what Fred and I do.... You know Fred and I will always be friends, but I wouldn't have been comfortable married to him. I need Dave and I love him."

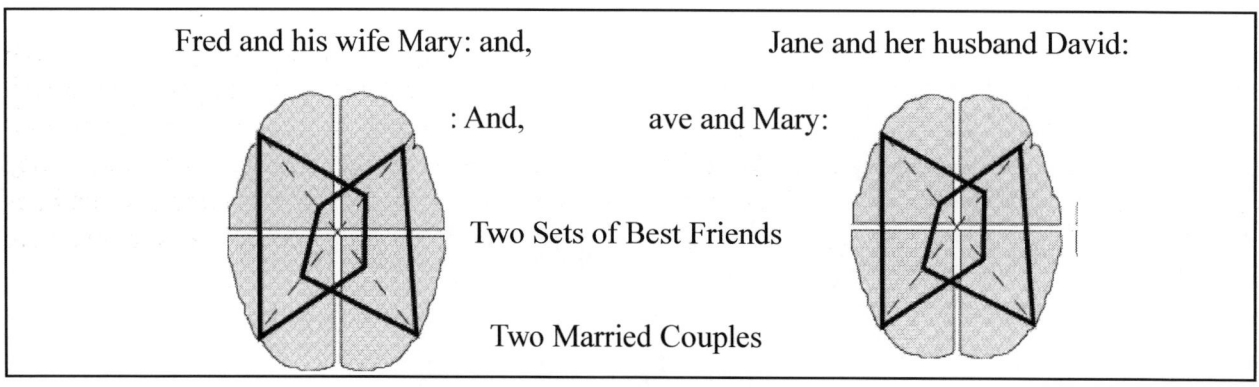

Fred and his wife Mary: and,   Jane and her husband David:

: And,   ave and Mary:

Two Sets of Best Friends

Two Married Couples

Jane and Fred: And,   Dave and Mary:

Two Sets of Best Friends

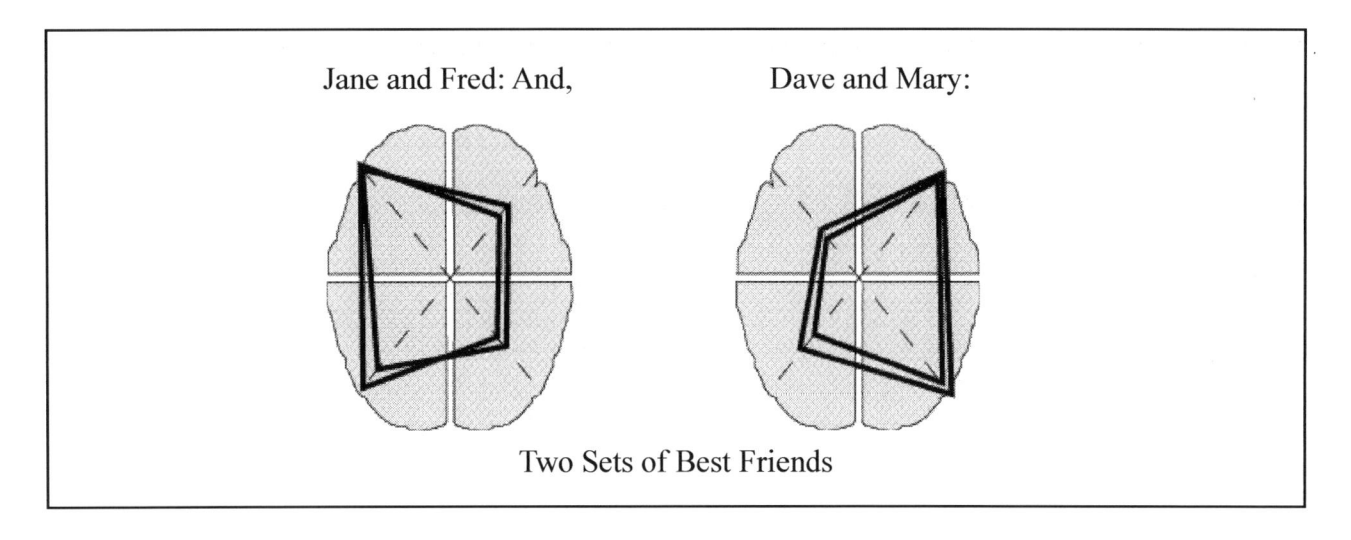

Some people would be jealous of their spouse talking with someone else all the time. What, if any, connection does jealousy have with dominance?

If we marry someone who complements us, we will probably *need* to be with or talk with someone else fairly regularly who is like us and who naturally affirms us. Sometimes this need stimulates jealousy. In Jane's tale, one of the things she shared with us was that some of her female friends had come to her expressing their concern that Mary might be taking Dave away. Her response to her friends showed both strength and understanding. She told them, "Actually, I'm glad they have each other. They're good for each other and they have so much in common – they even worry about the same things."

As Jane told her tale, it occurred to us how wonderfully she put things. Perhaps we should all take care to see that our spouses have a best friend. Not only would it be an excellent strategy for managing their worry (which would preclude our having to listen to them talk for hours about things we don't fully understand or value), it would also help our spouses feel good about themselves. This in turn would help to make our time with them more enjoyable and rewarding.

You've shown how our dominance affects our selection of a spouse, but what happens *once we're married*? How does dominance affect the way in which we relate or get along?

Let's begin by looking at how complementary couples that are happily married manage. In one such couple, the husband is an orthopedic surgeon, with a Frontal Right preference, developed Frontal Left auxiliary and avoidance in the Left Posterior Convexity. The wife, a grade school teacher, had Left Posterior Convexity preference and developed Right Posterior Convexity auxiliary. In other words, they complement each other almost perfectly – he is strong where she is weak and she is strong where he is weak. Given their preferences, she naturally manages most of the routine tasks, including the bill paying, while he provides the element of novelty and adventure.

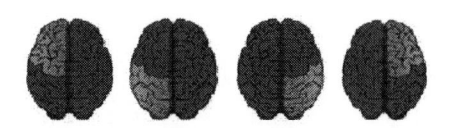

> Orthopedic surgeon married to a grade school teacher

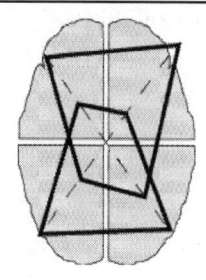

What is interesting is that early in their marriage, while he was in medical school, her strength in the Left Posterior Convexity was a Godsend to them both. Being so weak in the Left Posterior Convexity mode, he had great difficulty with much of the medical school curriculum that required a tremendous amount of memorization of facts and details. His wife, with a mind made to manage detail, helped him not only by drilling him repeatedly before tests but also by making sure he stayed on task to complete the more left-brained assignments which he would have otherwise walked away from. He recalls, "Without her, I never would have gotten through." His choice of words is quite revealing when you consider the second Rule of Thumb that we select a spouse who complements us to help us survive.

Another example of *how the happily married* do it is offered by Jeff and Margaret. Jeff is also a Frontal surgeon. His wife is a Posterior convexity. Happily married for 25 years, they began to manage their complementary patterns early on by establishing *territories*. His territory, *being a surgeon,* enabled him to use his preference and favorite auxiliary regularly, which helped him feel smart and good about himself. Additionally, it brought in enough money to support them and the children they eventually had. At the same time, Margaret's work around the home enabled her to feel smart, performing lots of posterior convexity tasks while contributing to the family. For Jeff and Margaret the territories of *work* and *home* made perfect sense during their first two decades of married life. As they began their third decade together, and as their children left home, Margaret found less and less to keep her busy. There were fewer groceries to buy, less laundry to do, no kids to chauffeur around or take care of.

How Margaret solved her problem is a wonderful story. She went to a secretarial school for training in typing and general business procedures, and then took over as her husband's office manager, enabling the couple to continue functioning as a *team*. An interesting point is that Margaret doesn't see herself as invading her husband's territory because she doesn't consider herself a part of the work world. She is just helping out, seeing that her husband's office runs smoothly, in the same way she made sure everything at home went smoothly. In other words, the shift in setting doesn't affect the basic structure of their relationship.

What about this idea of establishing territories? Is that a useful way to manage the differences in a complementary marriage?

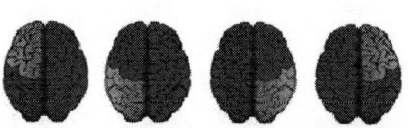

Territories can be useful. However, they need to be created to match the specific dominance patterns of persons involved. It is worth mentioning that the general territories that Jeff and Margaret found so useful, work and home, worked for them because of their particular dominance patterns – and who they were as people. For another couple, say a husband with a Frontal Left preference and a developed auxiliary in the Left Posterior Convexity with a wife who has a Frontal Right preference an auxiliary in the Right Posterior Convexity, the same division could be disastrous. The husband would be satisfied with work (possibly a career in engineering or accounting), but the wife would constantly be experiencing *mixed feelings* about her role at home. When asked to be nurturing to her husband or children she would feel smart, and yet when asked to perform the routine tasks of shopping, meal preparation, laundry, etc. she would feel tremendously drained and fatigued, or even *dumb*.

You've given examples of how complementary coupling can work, but I know a lot of couples who can't seem to make it work. Would you give some more specific examples of marital problems that can be directly linked to dominance?

Of course, not all complementary couples succeed. Terri and Mark found living together meant one problem after another. Terri lived as a "right-brainer" – her preference in the Right Posterior Convexity supported by a developed auxiliary in the Frontal Right. Mark lived as a left-brainer – his preference in the Frontal Left supported by a developed auxiliary in the Left Posterior Convexity and an avoidance in the Right Posterior Convexity. Terri was working with the Chamber of Commerce, and Mark, as a mechanic, when they came to Anne Sohn for marital counseling.

Terri expressed an inability to comprehend why her husband got so hostile and angry when she met or chatted with her friends and acquaintances. It seems that whenever and wherever they would go out together, Terri would invariably meet lots of people she knew. Of course, this was understandable, given her job with the Chamber and her Right Posterior Convexity gift for connecting with people and making friends. However, one thing would lead to another and Terri would end up getting engrossed in a lengthy conversation or, alternatively, would invite whomever she had run into to join them at their table. In either case, Mark would become furious – refusing to talk with anyone and demanding that they leave immediately. Later, once they were headed for home, he would say, "I don't know why you have anything to do with those people. You don't really mean anything to them. And they don't really care about you at all." At which point, if Terri tried to explain her point of view (her interest and delight in people), Mark would retreat into a gloomy silence that would last for days.

Mark the mechanic

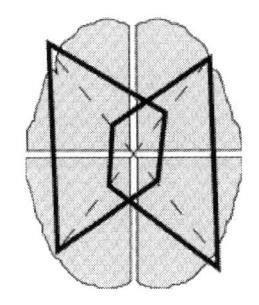

and, Terri with the Chamber of Commerce

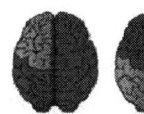

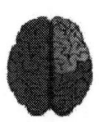

Ironically, due to his extreme avoidance of the Right Posterior Convexity feeling mode, Mark couldn't tolerate in Terri the precise thing he had married her for: her warmth and friendliness. Having no usable Right Posterior Convexity function himself, many social situations left him feeling uncomfortable and inept, and needing his wife's support. When he saw her giving attention to others, his discomfort would grow into feelings of rejection, invalidation and jealousy. Since Terri's Right Posterior Convexity nurturing skills were not being directed at Mark to help him through his discomfort, Mark's inability to process his feelings ultimately exploded in rage and a vehement devaluing of Terri's other relationships. Of course, it is also likely that she was very extraverted and that he was significantly less so, even if he was not an introvert.

Mark's retaliatory punishment of his wife – his anger and prolonged pouting – were especially difficult for Terri, who as a Right Posterior Convexity was particularly sensitive to disharmony with her husband. In fact, as she realized, she found herself in a no-win situation. She hated being cut off from her husband during his periods of silence and withdrawal following each incident, but on the other hand, the choice he was giving her, to isolate her from all others, to disconnect from her friends and acquaintances with which she shared a range of experiences, was no more tolerable or acceptable for her. Thus, eventually, Terri and Mark were divorced.

Sadly, the problems that tore apart Terri and Mark are common ones that many couples face, particularly when one or both members of the couple haven't developed sufficient emotional maturity to handle and appreciate their partner's differences. Where psychological immaturity coincides with an avoidance pattern, many couples don't make it. And, it would be a mistake to say their problems were all caused by brain dominance. More often, our maturity carries more weight than our dominance in determining our ability to succeed as part of a happily married couple.

Discussing maturity raises the issue of psychology. Is it brain dominance or psychology that makes us try to *control* our spouses?

Both are powerful factors. And it is unlikely that dominance alone causes one person to try to control another. What is more likely is that someone who is insecure and has high control needs would select a person who is used to being controlled and accepting.

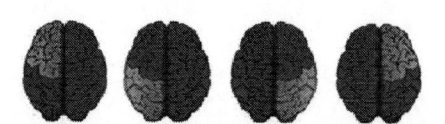

The following story provides a useful example of how a highly expressive, extraverted Right Posterior Convexity elementary teacher found herself being controlled by her husband who, from what she said, had a lead in one left mode and an auxiliary in the other – and an avoidance in the Right Posterior Convexity. She explained that whenever she got excited and enthusiastic about something, her husband would come up to her and, taking hold of her wrists, move her arms down to her sides where he would hold them while instructing her to calm down. Would every left-brained man do this to a Right Posterior Convexity wife? No. Would any Right Posterior Convexity accept this being done to her? No. Why did her husband do it? The answer is unclear and complex. Possibly feelings and expressiveness were not only foreign and unfamiliar; they were, due to his avoidance pattern in the Right Posterior Convexity, a source of real fear. Again, what is amazing is that on some level it is just possible this man married his wife because of her expressiveness!

You've mentioned *avoidance* as a common problem in marriage. What do you mean by avoidance and how does it work?

Avoidance is intentionally or unintentionally turning off or spacing out on your partner because he or she is talking about or focusing on content you aren't interested in or have difficulty understanding due to the difference in your dominances. Here are some examples of what we mean.

A group of corporate lawyers and accountants, all working for the same petroleum company, had a shared weakness in the Right Posterior Convexity feeling mode. When asked to write an article about a car accident that would interest a Right Posterior Convexity reader, the group seemed perplexed. After 10 minutes they had written the following: Pregnant woman killed in car accident this morning. The group had been able to identify a situation that would interest Right Posterior Convexities, but had been unable to write in the *language* Right Posterior Convexities would understand or use. As well the brevity of the group's article was more typical of direct, no-nonsense Frontal Lefts than of the more expansive, conversational Right Posterior Convexities. To help, they were instructed to each imagine returning home at the end of a day to be greeted by his wife, who immediately begins to tell him about a terrible accident she has seen. They were then asked: *What would your wives say?* All six men began talking at once. For a moment it seemed I had found the key to helping them learn to speak and use a mode other than their natural lead. But then, the men all stopped talking. The reason they stopped was that, although they all knew the first sentence that would come out of their wives' mouths, none of them knew the second. Over the years, finding their wives' chatter uncomfortable, they had taught themselves to tune her out, paying just enough attention to give her the impression they were actually listening. Their approach was, as they explained, much more effective than trying to stop their wives from talking. And, it was *avoidance*.

Another example of avoidance happened one night as I was returning home from a long weekend. My companion was an accountant I had been dating. It was late and he was driving while I relaxed. Suddenly, he began talking about the stock market, a subject of great interest to him as he had a Frontal Left lead. Since I actually did care about him (if not the stock market), I tried to pay attention. Sadly, after only a few minutes, I noticed I had not heard much, if anything, he'd said. Instead, my awareness had shifted to noticing his face, his smile, and the curve of his dimples – all his nonverbals. In other words, without doing anything consciously to make it happen, my brain had shifted its attention away from what it could not easily understand (the left-brained information about stocks) to what it understood best (his Right Posterior Convexity's nonverbals). I, or more correctly, my brain was *avoiding*.

Avoidance is a way of staying smart and screening out those things that make you feel dumb, incompetent and irritated. Since we are all likely to feel this way when asked to process in our weakest mode, some avoidance is probably an inevitable part of any relationship. Too much, however, can lead to distance between the partners and set the stage for divorce or a marriage in name only.

Would it be helpful for a couple to know each other's dominance pattern?

One couple put it this way: "It's not that the differences go away. It's just that we see them and ourselves differently. It *helps us to be less irritated* and to not take things so personally or seriously. We used to get irritated by each other's quirks. Now we just recognize them for the natural behaviors they are. In fact, we even laugh about them – together. We also don't feel the need to try to change each other anymore."

Knowing their brain dominance has freed this couple to laugh more and control less. We think that's a considerable improvement. Author and psychologist Sheldon Kopp, in his second book *End of Innocence*, said that he grew up the day he accepted not only that his mother didn't love him, but as well that, "It wasn't personal," in that his mother would have had difficulty loving any child. In a similar vein, you might say that understanding each other's dominance helps couples to grow up – to learn to not take personally the apparent slights and misunderstandings that result from their differences – the differences that are in fact the basis for their mutual attraction.

In another situation, learning about brain dominance actually saved a marriage by helping the client learn her problem with her husband was *physiological* (caused by dominance) rather than *psychological*. Mary was a woman who had already been married and divorced numerous times. According to the psychiatrist she had been seeing for the last fifteen years, her problem in making her relationships work was that she had a *father complex*. According to the psychiatrist, this complex was evident in the fact that each time she married she chose a man who behaved just like her father. From his perspective, in order for her life to improve, Mary would need to work through this complex. Mary never fully accepted the psychiatrist's diagnosis. Yet, since she kept marrying and divorcing the same kind of man, she had begun to assume, "He must be right."

When Mary became familiar with the work I am sharing with you in this book, she realized two things. First, she and her father had complementary thinking styles. And, second, it was completely natural for her to marry men whose brains complemented her own. That these men coincidentally thought just like her father may have been confusing but it did not mean her choice of husbands was wrong. Following the workshop Mary arranged to have her current husband's profile done to confirm her analysis. She also stopped seeing her psychiatrist, deciding instead to spend the money on fun activities she and her husband could enjoy together. At last report, Mary and her husband are happily entering another year of marriage.

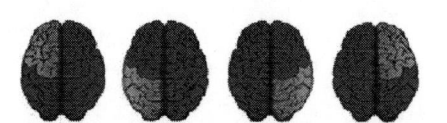

Of course it is certainly possible that Mary had some real issues with her father. Most of us have areas of pain and sensitivity where our parents are concerned. But did that make her choice of husband *wrong*? Once Mary was able to understand the reason for her selection of these men and to make sense of the difficulties she was having with them, she could separate her childhood issues with her father from her adult relationship with her husband. This in turn freed her to enjoy him for what he was and what he brought to her present life.

You emphasize the phrase: *marrying to get a whole brain*. Do all couples that marry to get a whole brain actually get one? Don't some couples end up with only half or three-fourths of a brain?

In many couples the husband and wife have a combined strength in only two or three modes. This is true for a few reasons. For one thing, the younger the couple, the greater the chance that one or both have only one truly strong type of thinking – their natural preference. You can imagine that a young person without a highly developed auxiliary might sense the need to marry – to expand their chances of survival quite early.

Then, sometimes, people marry whose preferences are side by side and who have an auxiliary in each other's preference – again; together they have access to only two of the four specialized types of thinking or, if one of them is using both auxiliaries, to three types of thinking. Sam and Jennifer's marriage is an example. Sam is an advertising executive with a diagonal practical, developed pattern using the Left Posterior Convexity and Frontal Right. Jennifer, a typical entrepreneur, has a double frontal pattern tilted to the far right, where she has a natural lead, and an avoidance pattern in the Left Posterior Convexity.

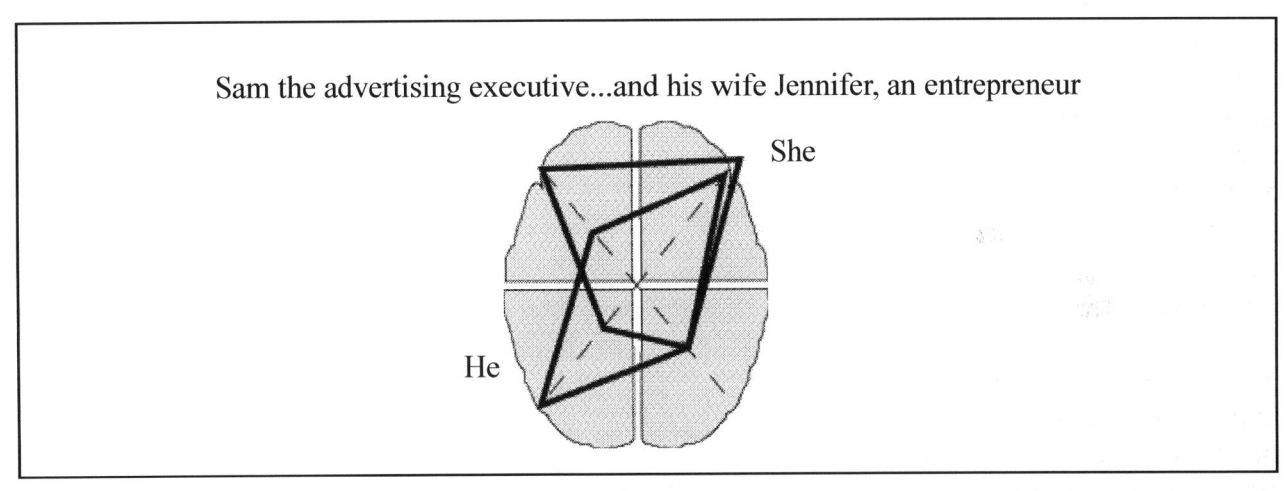

Sam the advertising executive...and his wife Jennifer, an entrepreneur

As a couple they have strength in the Frontal Right and both left modes. As individuals and as a couple they are not really adept at using the Right Posterior Convexity. And although they enjoy each other and are prone to sharing flights of fancy, their mutual deficit in the bridging/nurturing mode has caused some predictable problems, particularly now that they have children. Children, as we all know, need nurturing, which neither Sam nor Jennifer do a lot. Thus, although they both love their children, their way of caring for them is to teach them to take care of themselves and each other.

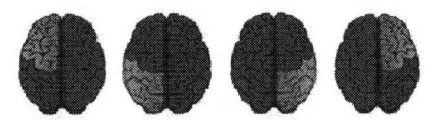

Another problem that Sam and Jennifer have faced is the result of her avoidance in the Left Posterior Convexity stabilizing mode, coinciding with their mutual strength in the adaptive Frontal Right. Over time, to compensate for Jennifer's weakness with routine and details, Sam has increased his use of his own Left Posterior Convexity, at the expense of his Frontal Right. Although they both have developed strengths in the Frontal Right, Jennifer's is so much greater than Sam's that he has backed off so as not to suffer in comparison. Subsequently, Sam is spending much more time in Left Posterior Convexity activities than is healthy or appropriate for him, given his pattern at the time of their marriage. The costs would depend on which specialized type of thinking is actually Sam's preference. If his true natural preference is in the Frontal Right, as is Jennifer's, then his backing off behavior from the Frontal Right, over several years, could make Sam a good candidate for midlife crisis and the range of mental – emotional problems found to result from Falsifying Type.

Discussions and coaching on how to get in touch with his body's biofeedback about which specialized type of thinking was his preference helped Sam discover that his preference is in the Frontal Right. Subsequently, he took steps to re-own his Frontal Right preference and his self-perception as a creative person. Jennifer, who made a conscious effort to not go into competition with him in the Frontal Right, encouraged him. Jennifer also explored her own avoidance problems in the Left Posterior Convexity and began to build some competency there. Again, personal maturity and responsibility are important in the happily married scenario.

Barbara and Michael are another couple with a combined strength in only three modes. Barbara, a therapist, is a strong double right with a preference in the Frontal Right and avoidance in the Left Posterior Convexity. Michael, a journalist, has the practical diagonal dominance pattern that accompanies the profession, combining the Left Posterior Convexity and Frontal Right. Barbara and Michael's matching Frontal Right enables them to share a good bit of amusement and an enthusiasm for adventure. Their mutual weakness in the Frontal Left means they have ongoing, predictable problems making decisions and managing money. Additionally, Barbara and Michael tend to have sudden conflicts when Michael unexpectedly shifts from his spontaneous Frontal Right way of doing things, which Barbara also enjoys, to his more careful Left Posterior Convexity approach that is planned and organized. Since Barbara has so little Left Posterior Convexity, she does not understand why her husband suddenly wants to be places on time, or put the house in order, or be asked to whom she has written checks and for how much. As strongly right-brained as she is, Barbara is most comfortable with her husband when he is in his Frontal Right. When he does go left, she often gets upset, even though his Left Posterior Convexity strength, which offers her a sense of safety and stability, is part of why she chose to marry him.

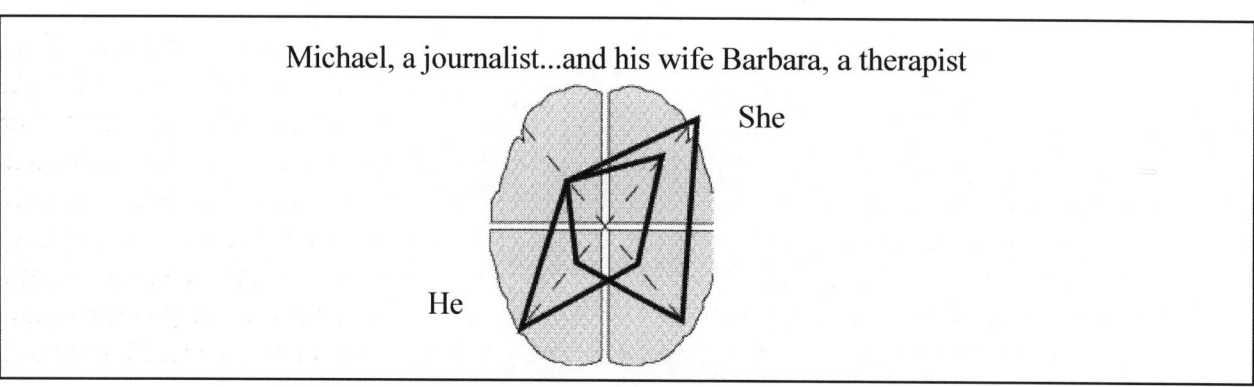

Michael, a journalist...and his wife Barbara, a therapist

Significantly, how this couple manages over time will depend in part on which type of specialized thinking Michael identifies as his preference. If he is a Frontal Right, he will eventually collapse from the fatigue and stress of so many years of Falsifying Type, using his greatest weakness as a lead. And, as he recovers he and they will have to accept that he can no longer do all the Left Posterior Convexity things that he carried for years. If his preference turns out to be in the Right Posterior Convexity, Michael will still crash again from years of Falsifying Type, trying to use both of his auxiliaries instead of his preference. But, as he recovers, the couple will benefit from his contributing Right Posterior Convexity relating skills from his preference, and to some extent he will still be able to use his Left Posterior Convexity – but as an auxiliary – not as a preference.

Intriguingly, many of the marriages in which couples share a lead or auxiliary are between someone who is clearly self-identified as a Frontal Right and a partner who has a highly developed Frontal Right and has a preference for either the Frontal Right or Right Posterior Convexity. Dr. Frank Farley, at the University of Wisconsin, noted this atypical pattern of spousal selection by Frontal Rights in the 1990's. Farley's 20 years of research on people he labels *Big T's* (thrill seeking individuals), who seem to be extraverted Frontal Rights, suggests that most highly creative people seek the high level of stimulation derived from thrills. As an aside he notes that, whereas most people tend to marry people substantially different from themselves, Big-T's tend to marry each other. One explanation for this might be the low level of social tolerance for many Frontal Right behaviors, such as day dreaming, laughing inappropriately, leaving things in stacks and generally not following the organized procedures that underlie so much of our educational and professional activities. Possibly Frontal Rights seek some validation by marrying each other.

This may be even truer when Frontal Rights are selecting a second spouse or marrying for the first time, late in life. Again, when two people with similar preferences marry, they are likely to enjoy each other very much and to have a tremendous, initial friendship. However, over time, the incompleteness of their combined access, the fact that they are not whole-brained as a unit, will begin to produce problems that neither of them can handle. How well they cope with those problems largely depends on whether or not they anticipated the problems going into the marriage and made provisions for handling them. A conscious decision to violate the rule is preferable to an unconscious one, as you will see from the following anecdotes.

One such couple attended a Brain Dominance Workshop for Families sponsored by their church. They had virtually identical double right dominance patterns – with a Frontal Right preference and Right Posterior Convexity auxiliary – with which they had lived as a couple for some twenty years. Our questions revealed that the husband's first impression of his wife (19 years earlier) had been that she had a dominance quite different than his own. As he tells it, "I still recall the night we met. I was only 18 and my buddy John and I had gone to the drug store to get an ice cream soda. She was working behind the counter and 15 minutes later I told John 'I'm going to marry that girl.' You see, what I remember is that when she was making our sodas she was so neat and clean and orderly. She had this way of making sodas just so and everything was tidy. I figured she was the one for me. You know, I also still remember how surprised I was when we started dating and we turned out to be like two peas in a pod. Neither of us ever paid any attention to time, which meant that we were both usually late. We both laughed a lot. We both enjoyed simply wandering along the country roads. I think if the term best friend has a meaning, we were best friends."

As we talked to the couple it became clear that they were, in fact, a two-person mutual admiration society and authentic best friends. The children, however, were shocked at their father's description. For although they agreed that he was nearly off the scale in his own tilt to the right, they saw their mother as a strong Left Posterior Convexity thinker. In their eyes, she was the detail-oriented planner, organizer and administrator of the family.

We then turned our attention to the mother. How could it be, we asked, that your husband sees you as a carefree, fun-loving, spontaneous person and your children see you as factual, cautious and planned? She was silent for a moment, as if lost in thought, and when she finally spoke she said something we have never forgotten: "That explains it. Twelve years ago I had a massive hemorrhage of the left cerebral hemisphere for apparently no reason at all. What I recall about that time is that I simply didn't want to do any more left-brained thinking. Of course, I didn't have a label for it then and I couldn't explain it well, but in a way, my hemorrhage was a way of saying 'Stop making me do this.' After all, now that I'm damaged, they can't make me do it because I'm not able to." This is an amazing and revealing story of Falsification of Type and its costs.

Raising children, making house payments, doing laundry for four, planning and preparing meals all require the use of the left brain's skill in prioritizing and in handling routine tasks. The husband, not a skilled left-brain thinker himself, had selected his wife for those particular abilities and never stopped to consider that his initial assessment might not have been accurate. The wife, who did have some learned competencies in the left, (such as soda making, which she had learned from her grandfather, who owned the drugstore) decided order was preferable to chaos and so began Falsifying Type using her non-preferred types of thinking to run the household and do what needed to be done. For eight years her falsifying continued except, of course, when she was alone with her husband. During those times she would revert to her preference and be the happy, fun loving, double right he described. Unfortunately, most of her time was spent in her weak areas and, if she is correct, the result was a stroke. Since she was unable to verbalize her dilemma, she made a nonverbal statement and damaged her left cerebral lobe so that everyone would know it was her weakness, not her strength.

Such a story is an excellent example of what can occur when one or both members of a couple misperceive the other's dominance. What is wonderful about this case is that both people were able to hang on to the love they felt for each other. More often, love is eroded by the problems, depression and anger that occur when a person Falsifies Type by performing for long periods of time in one of their non-preferred areas.

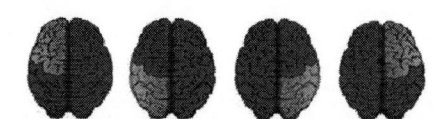

A second example of how like-brains manage in a marriage concerns Norm and Jean who also have virtually identical double right profiles, each with a Right Posterior Convexity preference and Frontal Right auxiliary. In explaining their situation, Norm pointed out that this is a second marriage and that their children, all from their previous marriages, live on their own. In other words, many of the Left Posterior Convexity and Frontal Left pressures of raising children and running a complex family structure (that caused so much trouble for the preceding couple) are not things that Norm and Jean have to manage. As such there is little need for either to Falsify Type.

And yet, they still have a problem. They have to be careful not to *compete* over who's best at working with people and who's the best photographer and who's the most creative. Norm recalls that in his first marriage (to a very left-brained woman), he enjoyed the position of being the artist in the family. In this second marriage he has to share the glory and figure out how to not compete.

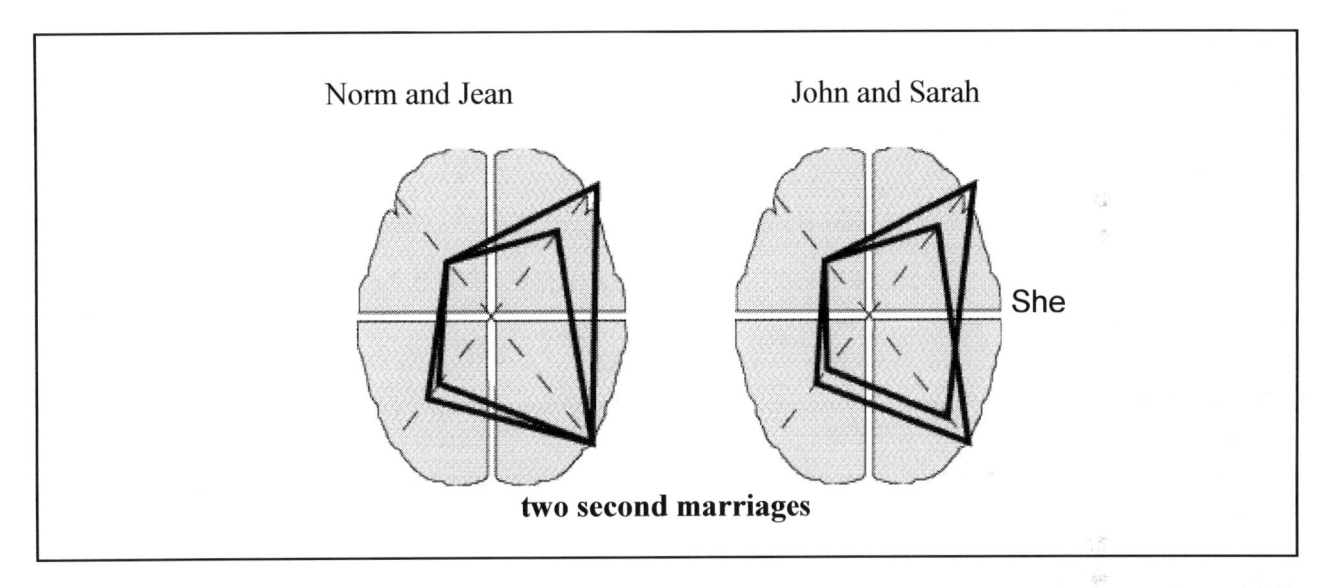

Norm and Jean   John and Sarah

                                              She

two second marriages

In John and Sarah's relationship, another marriage of like-minds, the couple learned about brain dominance prior to making their decision to marry and determined that they would have to both consciously cope with the areas neither partner wanted. To protect their love and guarantee that no one would get stuck with these problem jobs or feel resentful because their spouse was not taking care of it for them, John and Sara made a list of the left-brained tasks that neither of them really had the competency to handle. They then reviewed their list to separate the tasks into three categories: ones they could do together, ones they could alternate handling and ones they would need to hire someone else to do. To date, their strategy appears to be working for them and they have a happy marriage. They both have developed a bit more competency in the left modes, but neither is abandoning their natural lead and neither is Falsifying Type.

If more couples were aware of their dominance going into their marriages, they might develop *conscious strategies* for handling the problems and avoid unnecessary conflict and disappointment as well as plan together how to manage any mutual area of weakness so that neither is forced to Falsify

The Benziger Breakthrough

Type in order to stay in or save the marriage. This thought has occurred to many people with whom we work. One psychiatrist designed a pre-marital counseling service to assist couples to deal effectively with each other's dominance and manage their shared pattern of strengths and weaknesses. Again, such approaches can be very helpful. Indeed, for any couple, sorting out how their similarities and differences need to be honored or adjusted is an important part of getting along well over time. The key is that the couple – and counselor if they use one – understand the nature and costs of Falsifying Type and begin their joint effort by each focusing on themselves to discover and affirm their preference. This is the mode we must not abandon in our efforts to empower our spouse and our marriage.

You've told several tales about right-brainers who have married each other rather than live with a lefty. Do left-brainers ever marry each other?

We have some examples from second marriages. In these examples, one or both members of the couple have had bad experiences in an earlier, more traditional complementary relationship and shared that their decision to marry their current spouse was in part rooted in a desire to avoid a repeat performance of their first marriage.

One such marriage is between Fred, an executive with a Frontal Left preference and developed Left Posterior Convexity auxiliary, and Martha, a bookkeeper with a Left Posterior Convexity preference and a developed Frontal Left auxiliary. The couple describes themselves as content. And, according to Fred, they get along well, although their marriage lacks something. When questioned further, he'll speculate that the *something* that it lacks is the fun, enthusiasm and sense of adventure – which are, of course, typically provided by the right brain.

Another left-brain couple observed that although they enjoy being together very much, their mutual lack of people skills is causing problems with their social life. It seems that more than once, after putting months into building a relationship with another couple, they suddenly find the other couple not calling them or returning their calls and they have no idea why. Furthermore, lacking the Right Posterior Convexity ability to recognize hurt feelings early and re-establish harmony, they do nothing. That someone else might know what to do, or have done something already, is a mystery to him or her.

If most of us marry to get a whole brain, do people who developed both their auxiliaries need to get married at all?

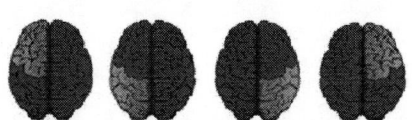

Interestingly enough, such high functioning individuals, if and when they marry, tend to do so later than their friends and contemporaries. As one of them put it, "I knew all along that I wanted to get married but the men I met simply didn't believe me." This tends to suggest that their whole-brainedness makes them less likely to be viewed as available partners by prospective mates. As one married whole-brained woman told us, "It's certainly true I got married late in life. What's also true is that I have a very hard time convincing my husband that I need him. He doesn't see it and neither do the children. My boys have told me again and again 'Mom, you don't need anyone'. You know, it's the oddest feeling to be told that by your sons and husband. I can't explain to them how and why I do need them in a way they understand and accept."

When asked why they marry, they usually say that it is for the connection – that no one can really thrive alone and isolated. Furthermore, just because they don't *need* to be married as a biological imperative, doesn't mean they don't *want* to. Their main problem seems to be in convincing potential mates that it is okay to marry someone who doesn't need you in order to survive (particularly since the mates are probably not whole-brained and the survival role *does* apply for them). And it may be that on some level they sense they are relating from a one-down position, i.e. their spouse offers four modes while they only offer two. We assume it takes a fairly secure person to handle such a situation.

In Summary

Differences in dominance lead us to the altar and provide us with opportunities to learn and grow. They also lead us to inevitable conflicts about how things are going to be done as well as pressure to Falsify Type. If the conflict gets bad enough, or if we are not mature enough or skilled enough to handle it, our differences combined with our expectations may eventually lead us to the divorce court. Alternatively, likeness in dominance may lead us to be friendly spouses. But it can, just as naturally, lead us into anger and resentment if one partner is forced to Falsify Type; to do for both what neither one can really do for him or her self.

In the final analysis, therefore, there are no right or wrong choices in marrying. What one chooses spouse-wise is a matter of personal choice. Whether one does it by instinct or for comfort, in the end it is really a matter of deciding which lessons in life you want to take on and choosing accordingly.

Family Life With Children

We have seen in the preceding section how people who marry to get a whole brain learn to cope with and, in some cases, fully accept their spouse's very different thinking pattern. Although it is common for each partner to feel somewhat disappointed that their spouse doesn't fully understand them, each also knows on some level that this difference is something they need – that it is a strength undeveloped within themselves, without which they would be less prepared to meet the full gamut of life's challenges. We also noted the differences between our selection of a spouse who often has a preference in our area of greatest weakness and our selection of a best friend whose mental preference is almost identical to our own, and who therefore can and does effortlessly affirm our self-esteem. When children enter the picture or join the family, these two ways of relating come together. While the parents continue in their relationship with each other to seek complementary modes, all family members, including the parents, in the context of the total family, seek the affirmation and companionship that comes from being fully accepted and comfortable.

Thus, with and in our families, we are generally likely to feel:

- Most comfortable in a family in which there are others with our preference and our introversion-extraversion level;
- Most comfortable with and closest to the family members whose preference and introversion-extraversion level are the same as ours; and
- Less comfortable if and when something happens to shift the balance.

The multiple concerns and issues involved in understanding children and parenting well relative to brain dominance are addressed below.

Questions and Answers

Does Brain Dominance run in families?

This question is perhaps better restated as: If two left-brained people marry, do they have left-brained children? And, if two posterior convexity people marry, do they have posterior convexity children? And so on.

First off, this is a difficult question to answer because the drive that causes most people to marry to get a whole brain precludes our having the kind of data we would need in order to answer it. There simply aren't that many instances in which two right-brained people marry, or two left-brained people, or two posterior convexitys or two frontals. And, when this does occur, it is most common in second marriages that frequently do not include children.

Given these constraints, it is possible to say that indeed if and when two people of like dominance marry, there is a greater possibility that they will have children of similar dominance. A greater possibility is, however, not the same as an absolute rule.

At least two cases have come to our attention over the years that suggest this. In the first, two double lefts (presumably each with a preference in one of the two left modes) married and had four children, three of whom had a preference in the left and one of whom had a preference in the right. In the second, two double right parents, one with a Frontal Right preference, one a Right Posterior Convexity preference, had three children, two of whom had a preference in the Frontal Right and one of whom had a preference in the Right Posterior Convexity – and all three of whom had a double right practical dominance.

What happens when one child has a distinctly different dominance from the other family members?

One cartoonist calls this *The Enigma* effect. And, naturally, how it is experienced depends on whether you are a part of the majority or the one who is seen as different, the enigma, the weird kid, the *misfit*.

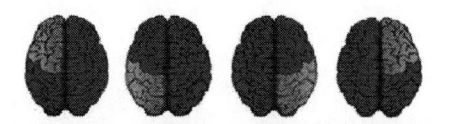

Those who think alike clearly set the tone for how *things get done around here*. This tends to mean that they see the problem kid as a misfit who isn't trying and isn't cooperating – the child responds by Falsifying Type so that he at least appears to fit in. It is typical in such situations for the parents to develop a strong sense of "Where did this child come from?" Sometimes they may even joke about the difference by suggesting that the hospital must have switched babies on them. Another frequent comment involves one parent suggesting that the child is "a throw-back to some long deceased relative on their spouse's side of the family."

It is worth noting that the individual who has the distinctly different dominance tends to be and feel invalidated by the family. Because no one in the family structure values the same things and thinks in the same way, he may have difficulty building his self-esteem. To the extent that he feels pressured by the family to adopt their way of thinking by Falsifying Type, he may also feel resentful and angry.

In our competitive, modern post-industrial and now global society the two kinds of people who report being seen as and seeing themselves as misfits are introverts (see Appendix F) and those with a Frontal Right preference. In many classrooms and offices highly creative Frontal Rights are regarded as odd, weird, strange and or goof-offs. In the family, however, there are no rules. Someone with any preference, whether extraverted or introverted, can be an outcast. It all depends on the preferences and introversion/extraversion of the other family members. Let's look at a couple of examples.

In the first, which we refer to as The Case of Miserable Martha, Martha, Right Posterior Convexity, found herself in a family of two double frontals (her father and her eldest brother) and two double lefts (her mother and her older brother). Although we do not know each person's actual preference it is safe to assume that she was an isolate in her family of origin that was clearly more frontal and more left

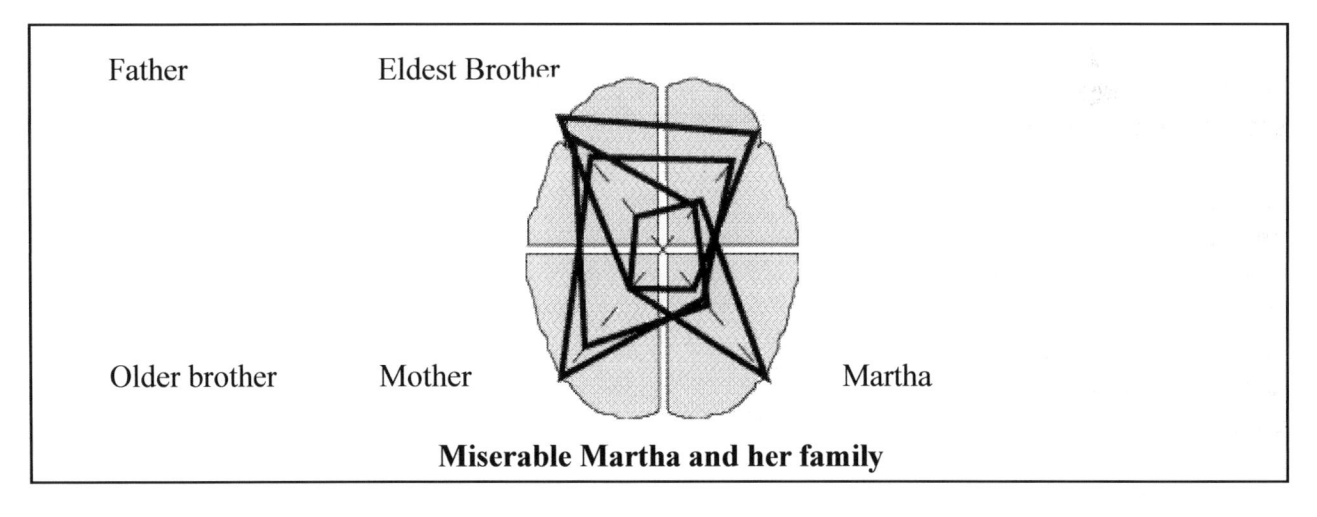

Miserable Martha and her family

Martha's father was a career diplomat so, by the time Martha was fifteen, she had already lived in eight different countries. This constant moving around and lack of roots, combined with the repeated loss of friends, seemed not to affect anyone else in the family, but for Martha it was a terrible experience. Each time the family would be uprooted, Martha would find herself seriously depressed and in heavy grief. Unable to find any emotional support or comfort from her family, who saw her behavior as childish and self-indulgent, Martha increasingly isolated herself in her room where she would cry for hours.

As if this weren't enough, the father, who was a high-achieving Frontal, constantly put pressure on Martha to be a success like her brothers (one of whom eventually got his Ph.D. in physics, the other who became an engineer). To make his point, he would bring her articles about successful female executives, bankers and lawyers stressing that this is what he expected of her and that it was the only level of performance he would consider adequate. Since this was totally impossible for Martha, given her dominance pattern, every attempt she made to excel in the academic areas that would lead to such careers resulted in failure. This led the family to conclude that she was stupid and lazy and they let her know it (along with the fact that she was an embarrassment to them). Finally, when she was 15, the family solved its problem with Martha by shipping her off to a boarding school. And during the three years she was away at school, no one from her family wrote or visited her nor was she ever invited home for holidays.

Ironically, Martha had one special talent, which, though obvious, was never acknowledged or appreciated by her family. Of all the family members, Martha had the greatest aptitude for learning to speak foreign languages quickly and easily using her gift for picking up and expressing tonal information (which is consistent with her strong Right Posterior Convexity profile). Unfortunately, she did not do as well in the classroom study of the language, where more emphasis is put on writing, spelling and grammar (Left Posterior Convexity), and so it did not change her family's opinion of her academic incompetence.

Now an adult, Martha has spent years in therapy trying to undo the damage to her self-esteem caused by her upbringing. Learning about brain dominance has helped her understand that she was the wrong person in the wrong family and to appreciate the person she is. Unfortunately, it cannot take away the pain of those years of rejection and invalidation. But it is opening the door for her healing.

The second case that illustrates the enigma phenomenon is that of Norman, a strong Left Posterior Convexity thinker brought up in a family of "crazy right-brainers".

When Norman tried to establish rules and schedules so he would know when to be where and what to do, the rest of his family – his inventor father, his interior decorator/entrepreneur mother, and his artistic and musical siblings ignored Norman and persisted in their own, more spontaneous behavior.

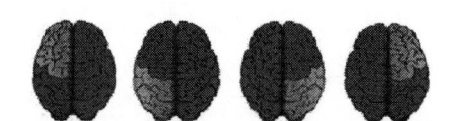

Norman and his family

His Brother

Norman

His Father

One Sister

His Mother

His Other Sister

If they were all home and happened to eat at six, great. If not, well, no matter. If someone felt like going out to get pizza, those who were there and wanted to go, would go, and those who were not, would fend for themselves. If dirty laundry was turned in somewhere near the weekend, it might be clean by Monday morning, and then again, there's nothing wrong with retrieving a dirty shirt from the hamper. To make matters worse, Norman's right-brained family, so very interpersonal and gregarious and interested in helping, would try to help Norman by suggesting that he have some fun, take an art class or laugh once in awhile. Indeed their efforts although well meant, showed no understanding that they were asking Norman to violate his deepest nature, to Falsify Type.

As the years passed and Norman's differences remained – in spite of repeated attempts by the family to rescue him from himself – Norman's parents began to feel that although they had been successful parents with their other two children, they had most decidedly failed with Norman. Their growing sense of powerlessness to help Norman turned into total despair shortly afterwards when, following his 18th birthday, Norman enlisted. After all, to right-brained parents, voluntarily joining the army can only mean our son wants to kill people. This is not at all how left-brained parents perceive the same reality. For them, joining up means a cost effective way to pay for one's college education, an opportunity to travel and see the world before settling down, and last but not least, a way to sow one's wild oats away from home.

Fortunately, just days before Norman left for Boot Camp, his father learned about this model. Excited and relieved at the same time, he rushed to find his son and wife to share the good news – that Norman was normal and healthy. Norman's very right-brain family was actually able to see, accept and be happy that Norman was choosing, after 18 years of being a misfit and enigma in the family, to join an organization that recognized and valued his gifts.

Can the sense of isolation and feeling of being a misfit, occur to family members who aren't children?

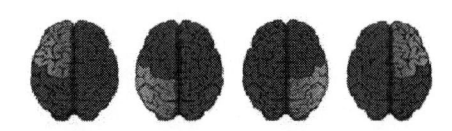

Most definitely. The key point here is to look at the context. Anytime anyone is in a situation in which his preference or his natural extraversion or introversion differs from the group's, he is at risk and vulnerable to the pain of not belonging, not being good at what's important, not being wanted or not being loved.

An excellent example is Jeanette's – The Misfit Mother. The family's profiles revealed Jeanette to have a Left Posterior Convexity preference.

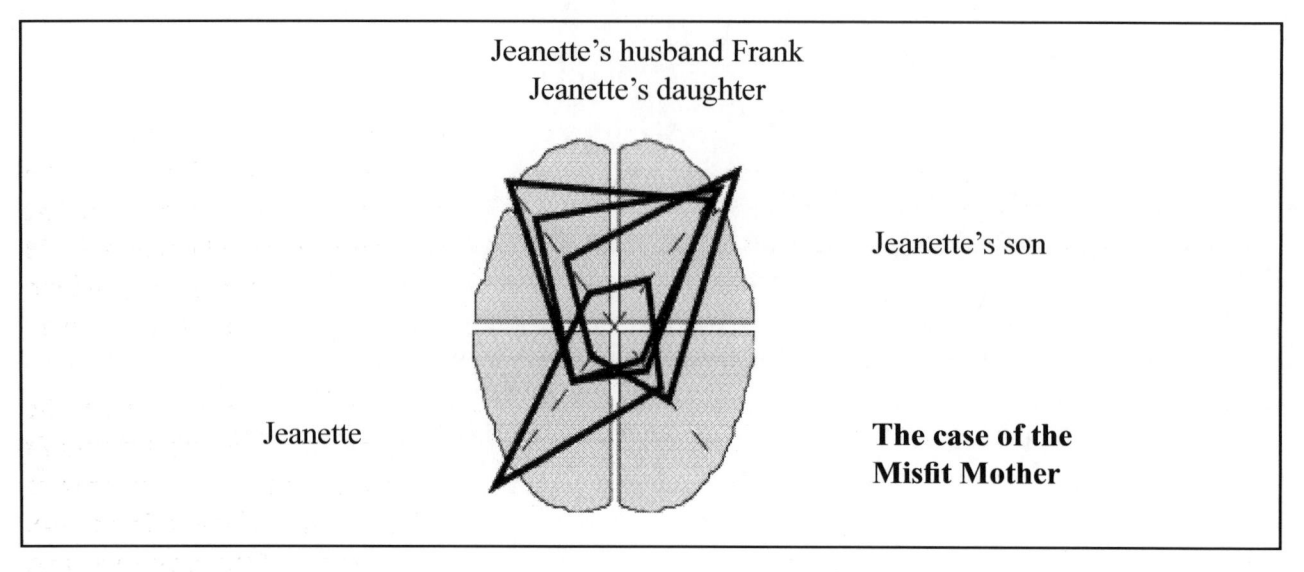

Jeanette's husband Frank
Jeanette's daughter

Jeanette's son

Jeanette

The case of the Misfit Mother

While her husband Frank and both their children had Frontal preferences – one, her daughter, had an actual avoidance in the Left Posterior Convexity. The disparity between Frank and Jeanette's preferences (Frontal vs. Posterior Convexity) wasn't a problem when the couple first married. They had their differences, but then so did every couple. When their children were seven to ten, the age during which the frontal lobes mature according to Luria and Piaget, Jeanette found herself becoming a misfit in her own family.

Although Jeanette was attentive and dedicated as a wife and mother, the children, who were coming into their own with respect to their Frontal preferences, began to prefer and seek out their father's company, and at the same time, actively resent and reject their mother's Left Posterior Convexity. This dislike for the way their mother acts led the daughter to develop a set of gotcha games the kids could play on mother. For example, since they knew it was important to her that they are on time, they went out of their way to make sure the family was always late. And because Jeanette wanted them to have dinner together at a regular, fixed time, they purposely arranged their extracurricular activities to conflict with the dinner hour. In addition, whenever they were having a discussion with their father and their mother entered the room, they would stop talking until she left.

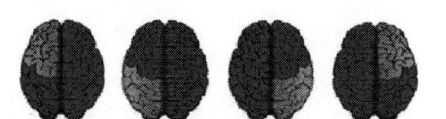

Although it seems incredible that Jeanette's husband didn't notice and put a stop to this behavior, it appears that his own relationship with the kids was so good, it never occurred to him their jokes and behaviors might bother his wife. Since he thought her rules were silly and that she couldn't really understand the things they discussed anyway, it may have made perfect sense to him that the three of them acted as they did.

From interviewing Jeanette, it became clear that she had known for years that she was an outcast in her own family and that her children didn't like her, but she had never been able to understand why. When asked how she coped with the emotional pain of being rejected, she responded in a very Left Posterior Convexity way: "I just did the things I knew I was supposed to do as a wife and a mother and I kept the family together. After all, that's what's really important, isn't it?"

Not everyone can respond with such stoicism to being ostracized by his or her family. In another case, a Right Posterior Convexity mother became severely depressed and suicidal by being cast in the *role of the misfit* (her husband and both children all had preferences in the left). For her, the fact that her children preferred their father's company was proof of her failure as a mother (which to a Right Posterior Convexity is a terrible thing indeed). Only after she learned about brain dominance and her family's profiles was she able to stop blaming herself and move beyond her near suicidal depression.

Here again, Sheldon Kopp's insight in the *End of Innocence* (that he finally grew up the day he understood that although it was true that his mother didn't love him; it was also true that it wasn't personal) is very helpful. Kopp's wisdom is something from which we can all benefit. Learning to accept that the seeming rejection of another may not be personal is an important life lesson. Of course, the lesson is easier to learn when you also know the *reason* the rejection occurs. Martha, Norman and Jeanette all learned that in their lives and in their families, their feelings of being an outcast and failure were caused largely by the fact that their preference really was different and that this difference was okay. Learning this helped each reevaluate their experience and accept that the rejection they felt was not personal. As such, it freed them to accept themselves.

Again, when someone is a misfit, they tend to suffer. Those who are misfits and seek to diminish their suffering by Falsifying Type may diminish their sense of isolation. The cost of such Falsifying Type is, however, so tremendous that Falsifying Type is not to be undertaken or encouraged lightly. People are healthier when they understand and value their own gifts and have role models, mentors and friends who share and value their preference and introverted or extraverted needs.

What about the situation in which no one feels particularly isolated, yet one parent clearly feels uncomfortable with one of the children?

You can be uncomfortable around one of your children for one of two reasons. First, it may be the child's preference is so different from your own that indeed the child is an enigma – to you. If you have a Left Posterior Convexity preference supported by a Right Posterior Convexity auxiliary, you might feel this way about a daughter with a Frontal Right preference. She is likely to think so differently from you that you are uncomfortable around her and feel you don't know what to do with or for her, or even how to spend time with her so that you both enjoy being together. Your sense of unease and perhaps even nervousness with this child may be quite similar to the way you feel in the presence of adults with the same preference. It's just that with an adult you can say that one doesn't have to understand everyone, but you feel guilty when you don't enjoy your own child.

There is another explanation, which at first may seem odd. It's possible to feel uncomfortable with a child because he is just like us. In this instance, the discomfort stems from our not having accepted a part of our self – most likely our preference. This happens most often when a parent has been Falsifying Type for years consciously or unconsciously. The tale of David and his son, Martin, illustrates this. David, the father, had a Frontal Right preference and a Frontal Left auxiliary. Over the years David learned that no one appreciated his creative contributions. He was put down as a useless roving prankster. Not surprisingly, David chose to Falsify Type by using his Frontal Left auxiliary as his lead. This allowed him to fit in and as well to hold a regular job so that he could support his family. When he began to realize that his son reminded him more and more of himself when he was young – David grew uncomfortable and pressured his son to Falsify Type as he had, to fit in. When his son refused, David became angry and frightened for his son.

It is actually quite common for parents who have been Falsifying Type for years, because their true preference was a source of trouble or pain, to encourage a child who shares their preference to Falsify Type as they have done.

Whether the child's preference is completely different from our own, or too much like a part of us, the discomfort we feel tends to be tied to an aspect of our self we haven't fully accepted, resolved or integrated.

In some families one child seems to mediate problems between the parents. Some books say birth order is involved. Is there any evidence that brain dominance might be involved as well?

A Right Posterior Convexity child may seek to mediate in order to create more harmony around her. Mediation is a skill that is easily mastered by Right Posterior Convexities. It takes advantage of their ability to connect with others and build trust as well.

What if any relationship exists between birth order and dominance?

Based on what is known, birth order has no role in determining preference. Remember, dominance is a biochemical reality that has genetic roots. However, birth order may play a role in reinforcing or discouraging a child's use of their preference. Only and eldest children tend to be socialized to develop and use the Left Posterior Convexity as children and the Frontal Left as adults – to be responsible. If a child has a preference in the left, then this impact will reinforce their preference. If a child has a preference in the right, the impact of their birth order will be to encourage the child to Falsify Type. But again, birth order is only one consideration. If the parents support the child's natural preference, the tendency to Falsify Type will be less. If one of the parents models the healthy development and use of the child's preference the tendency to Falsify Type will be lessened rather than reinforced.

Another example of how preference and birth order interact involves those who are the youngest child in their family of origin. Just as eldest and only are reinforced to be leaders and to develop and use the Posterior Convexity and Frontal Left, youngest children tend to have more difficulty in leading and developing and using auxiliaries in the left if their preference is in the right. Indeed, some male children with a preference in the Frontal Left have difficulty as managers because they make good decisions, but have difficulty being the boss – telling others what to do.

What about twins and brain dominance? Would *identical twins* have the same preference?

Yes, certainly. And yet, as they grow older, one twin may make a choice to abandon her preference to develop a different specialized type of thinking – to create a sense of herself as a separate person. Because this involves Falsifying Type, the twin, like anyone else who Falsifies Type, is vulnerable to fatigue, irritability and depression and is also in line for a mid-life crisis unless and until she re-owns her preference.

Why does a child gravitate towards a particular relative or family friend?

When a child finds an adult whose preference and introversion/ extraversion level matches their own, they are likely to find themselves drawn to spend time with that adult. Indeed, if it weren't for the age difference, they would fast become best friends as the delight is often mutual. For the child, an adult mirror – especially if they are the same sex, is a positive role model and potential mentor.

It seems from all you've said that it's important for parents to reinforce and validate their child's preference. How can I identify my child's preference?

A child's preference is generally visible at about age two. These brief descriptions identifying habits of mind that typify children with each of the four types of thinking will help you identify your child's preference.

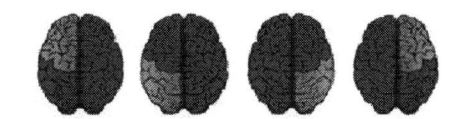

Identifying Your Child's Preference

The child probably has a **Left Posterior Convexity** preference if she or he:
  seems to need more routine,
  prefers to eat at the same time daily,
  prefers to have the same food for the same meal,
  prefers to be told what to do and how to do it,
  likes train sets that go around on a track,
  likes to read books about the real world,
  prefers true/false tests,
  wants his/her room kept "just so."

The child probably has a **Right Posterior Convexity** preference if she or he:
  likes to change clothes often and play dress up,
  is chatty,
  knows everyone in the neighborhood,
  is known by everyone in the neighborhood as friendly,
  touches and likes to be touched,
  enjoys and often wears bright colors,
  likes to read biographies, romances and animal stories,
  likes and remembers to take care of pets,
  giggles or is silly often,
  likes to help or to share experiences,
  likes to be in the same room with others rather than alone,
  isn't particularly good at tests.

The child probably has a **Frontal Right** preference if she or he:
  wanders off or explores,
  daydreams,
  draws a lot, often expansively covering entire page,
  is good at visual or spatial games: (i.e. pick-up pairs),
  moves and gestures when talking,
  prefers to run, jump and climb, while making loud noises,
  may not read as a young child,
  when exploring is limited may read voraciously about new and
  different things,
  is good at geometry,
  prefers essay tests in which there is no one right answer,
  seems to have a shorter attention span,
  may know answers in school without knowing how or why,
  may often be "ahead of the teacher."

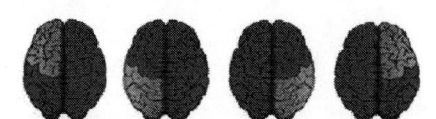

Identifying Your Child's Preference continued.

The child probably has a **Frontal Left** preference if she or he:
  gravitates towards tools and machines,
  tries to take apart small machines such as portable tape players,
  is articulate, but not *chatty*,
  likes to construct things using tools,
  is good at math,
  seems to prefer multiple choice or essay tests,
  likes to argue,
  sets "goals" for himself.

If you have difficulty identifying your child's preference, try backing into the answer by figuring out what your child is not. Then, once you have identified your child's probable preference take time to verify it. Increase the opportunities and time your child has in his or her preference while decreasing the opportunities and time in his or her three other types of thinking. If your child seems to be happier, more content or more comfortable when you do this, you are most likely correct about his or her preference.

It's important to note that you can't verify a child's preference if you don't offer them a variety of opportunities – several for each specialized type of thinking – in both introverted and extraverted settings.

Remember, some homes have few or no "stage props" for certain types of thinking. If this is true of your home, find a way to fill out the range of options before testing your child's preference. Then check to see what your child naturally chooses to do. One way to handle what may be missing in your home environment is to find an adult with a preference not represented strongly in your home environment. Invite that person to come over with some stage props to spend time with your child. Sometimes this filling out of the options occurs naturally when the child notices that they really enjoy hanging around or helping a particular neighbor. In fact, before trying to adjust your own situation, you might check to see if your child has a habit of going over to a particular adult's home regularly. It may be that your child has found his own role model.

Once you are certain about your child's preference, you can help your child develop by finding ways to validate that preference. If the preference is one often seen as a misfit, or if your child is introverted, it will be even more important for you to find emotionally healthy adults with your child's preference who can and will spend time with him.

How can I reinforce and validate my child's preference?

The following chart will help you identify ways you can reinforce and validate each of your children. As you read, notice what you are already doing that's right. Next, look for new ideas – things you can do to validate each child. Finally, notice what if anything you are doing with the intention of "helping" your child may be damaging or invalidating to your child, given his or her preference.

▲ **How to Validate Your Child's Preference**

Here are some ways to validate your **Left Posterior Convexity** child,
Create 3 or 4 step procedures for doing as many things as possible, then be sure to go over each procedure slowly and in a step-by-step manner with your child.

- Compliment your child for his or her ability to do things on time.
- Compliment your child for his or her ability to do things according to the procedures he or she was given.
- ask your child to teach a houseguest the procedure for something (i.e. washing dishes or feeding the cat).
- Tell your child that everyone has things they do to contribute to the family, and ask him which of the tasks he has learned would he most enjoy doing regularly as his contribution. Then reward him for doing it with a *thank you.*
- If you want something done differently, make a point of telling your child, You and I will be changing procedures, let's learn or load the new procedure and be tolerant of any emotional discomfort he or she feels around the changes you introduce.

Here are some ways to validate your **Right Posterior Convexity** child:

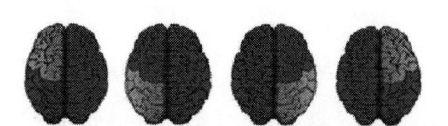

- Spend time with your child just playing.
- Ask your child to guess what someone is feeling. Then have them tell you why they think that might be true and what about the person's stance suggested it.
- Ask your child to come with you to do a favor for someone.
- Ask your child to come with you to take a gift to someone.
- Suggest your child make or find a gift or card to give – a pinecone or a magic pebble or seed make an excellent gift.
- Ask your child to plan or help you plan a party.
- Provide your child with soft and interesting brightly colored fabrics with which to play.
- Provide your child with clothes and costumes for "dress up".
- Hug your child often and make a big deal of the joy it gives you when they hug you.
- Encourage your child to have a pet and to take care of it. The best pets for a Right Posterior Convexity are those that can be touched and petted.

Here are some ways to validate your **Frontal Right** child:

- Allow your child to be, act or dress differently.
- Compliment him or her for his imaginative choices.
- Remind your child that he or she does not have to join in.
- Encourage him or her to explore.
- Be sure your child has options for exploring safely – a bike, access to a bus or train.
- Tell your child that daydreaming is okay, that some of the world's most creative people have been and are daydreamers.
- Create a wall for your child's art.
- If at all possible, be sure your child has a room or area of his or her own in which being neat is not necessary.
- Read to your child about the lives of Nikola Tesla and Edmond Halley.

Here are some ways to validate your **Frontal Left** child:

- Help your child learn to reason.
- Practice the art of critical analysis with your child.
- Encourage your child to develop strong logical arguments for things he wants to have or do.
- Create and play a debating game with your child.
- Be sure your child has machines and tools with which to play/work.
- Be sure to comment positively on your child's skill in these areas.
- Give your child lots of opportunities to make his or her own decisions every day.

An imaginative Frontal Right parent helped validate his very left-brained three-year old son by going to the junkyard to find an old typewriter and giving it to his son with a set of tools. For many months when his dad and mother would go to work or go out, Adam would work on his typewriter, which essentially meant he worked at taking it apart.

I understand that you believe in validating people. However, as a parent, I want my children to learn to get along and become contributing, successful members of society. Based on what you've said, my son appears to be a Frontal Right. He's a real problem at home and school. He doesn't do the things we ask him to. He doesn't do his homework. What can I do to help him?

Typically, a child who resists as much as you are suggesting does so because he has to *defend* who he is because he has not been given opportunities to succeed by doing what comes naturally for him. Your best bet is to study your child to confirm what comes naturally for him. You may find he is a Frontal Right. You may also find he is highly extraverted or highly introverted. Once you know for sure, give him plenty of opportunities to develop and use his preference in a setting that matches his introverted or extraverted needs. If possible, find things that allow him to win (if he is extraverted) or be recognized and/or rewarded. Once you are giving him the chance to succeed at being himself, consistently, his dysfunctional behaviors will stop. For more on defensive behaviors see the next chapter.

▲▲ Kids and School

In order to understand the impact schools have on our children, it's helpful to understand their structure. For example, the following generalization is true of most schools in the industrialized world. The type of thinking that's used the most, given the most support and greatest opportunity to develop is the Left Posterior Convexity. Our schools and their curricula, like the majority of American, European and global businesses, were developed in the 1800's, during and in response to the industrial revolution. For almost 150 years, during most of the 19th and 20th centuries, the world needed an abundance of workers who were adept at performing routines dependably on assembly lines and in offices. Our schools were designed to fill that identified need.

Today, at the beginning of the 21st century, life is very different! With the popularization of computers, globalizing of the economy and e-commerce, manufacturing and distribution are becoming increasingly automated. There is less demand for Left Posterior Convexity workers and more demand for a diverse work force that includes new and different types of workers. Today's businesses want more workers who contribute vision and creativity to invent new and better products, help them anticipate trends and embrace change; as well as more workers who are gifted at relating to customers and building good will. Similarly today's world needs innovative, creative problem-solvers who can solve the new and complex global problems we are all facing, i.e. global warming, air and water pollution. As well, the world needs those who are adept harmonizers who can facilitate the healing of the widespread, deeply felt emotional and psychological wounds left from centuries of war so that our global village will be safe for all.

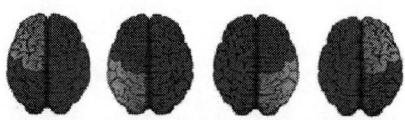

In summary, today's schools need to catch up. They aren't providing the kind of education our modern, evolving global economy and world needs. It's appropriate, timely, even critical for schools everywhere to re-invent themselves, to change as rapidly as possible, so that they can produce the new diversity of workers and global citizens our world needs. Business is shifting to become more whole-brained. So should education. Those who question the reality of these large scale social changes and demands, and hence don't see the need for our schools to change, might want to read John Naisbitt's and Patricia Aburdene's second book, *Re-Inventing the Corporation.* Naisbitt and Aburdene marshal enough evidence to prove their existence to anyone. The good news is that many, many teachers, administrators and politicians as well as parents want to improve our schools so it will happen soon.

For the present, to help children attending our existing schools, it's wisest to assume these children are attending a school in which most of the curriculum is structured to suit the Left Posterior Convexity: the classes are taught by teachers with a Left Posterior Convexity preference or a Right Posterior Convexity preference and a strongly developed Left Posterior Convexity auxiliary; and the school is run by administrators with Left Posterior Convexity preference or strongly developed Left Posterior Convexity auxiliary.

Having laid the groundwork for discussing what is happening with our children in today's schools, let's look at some of the topics that concern all of us.

How does each type of child respond to school?

Given the right school, any and all children can respond to school with excitement and passion. All children can develop a love of learning. All children can actually learn. Tragically, given their history and structure, most of our schools today are not right for all children. Given their predominantly posterior convexity structure, posterior convexity children are obviously and quite naturally the most comfortable.

Children with a Left Posterior Convexity preference find these schools enjoyable and satisfying. They are able to read well, complete the majority of true/false and multiple choice tests and value a high school education and diploma as the way society does things.

Children with a Right Posterior Convexity preference enjoy the same schools because these schools give them the opportunity to meet and spend time with lots of other people and lots of different people in classes, through extra-curricular activities and in the hallways. This positive attitude towards school is especially true of Right Posterior Convexities who are more extraverted and have a developed Left Posterior Convexity auxiliary. For such children, school can actually be fun. Of course, very few of the courses aside from music, art and dance actually teach content that helps these children develop their Right Posterior Convexity gifts. The exceptions are peer counseling and mediation both of which were introduced on an experimental basis in the 1990's to help children cope with conflict and violence. These courses are terrific and empowering for Right Posterior Convexities because they help them develop and use their natural gifts.

Children with a Frontal Left preference are, by contrast, bored in and by the schools and yet they stay in school. They are bright and the Left Posterior Convexity is, after all, one of their auxiliaries. Indeed, until puberty, it's their most favored accessible auxiliary. So, doing what the system wants them to do is not that difficult for them. They sit at the back of the classroom doing something unrelated to what's being done in class. And, if you ask, they'll tell you, they don't pay attention because they don't need to. They already know what is being covered and ace their exams. Moreover, they see their teachers as slow, even dumb, in comparison with themselves. They have analyzed society and life. They know what it takes to win. And, they intend to win. So, they stay in school to get their high school diploma, often graduating early and/or going on to obtain one or two college degrees. They are the ones everyone knows will succeed in life. They may not be at ease at a party, but they'll do well in life especially if they have a balanced or extraverted need for stimulation and especially when do well means to succeed in business.

Children with a Frontal Right preference are also bored. However, they lack the ability to easily and dependably access and use the Left Posterior Convexity that causes them to be and feel invalidated in school.

Additionally, Right Posterior Convexities with a Frontal Right auxiliary also report school is boring and invalidating. Speaking about the kids on his adolescent psych unit at a Chicago hospital, one physician shared: "You know, more than 85 percent of the kids we see here have a preference in the Right Posterior Convexity or Frontal Right. They're confused and irritated by the facts and figures they are asked to memorize in school. Yet, they excel in dancing and acting."

Why are certain children *problem children* at school?

The problem child at school is most often highly extraverted and/or has a Frontal Right preference. Each is a problem for slightly different reasons.

Extraverts need a high level of stimulation – noise and movement – to stay awake, to attend, to think and to learn. Sadly, most classrooms put extraverts to sleep because they've been designed by well-intentioned educators to be quiet learning environments in which noise, talking and movement – all of which help the extravert stay awake enough to learn – are discouraged. Not surprisingly, extraverts who get into trouble for talking, passing notes and fooling around are quite often simply trying to keep themselves awake.

Frontal Rights are a problem because they need to regularly be given the big picture and communicated with in a manner that allows their abstract, metaphoric, pattern-sensitive brains to grasp what is being taught. And, sadly, few classes communicate effectively with their preference. Most are structured to speak to their greatest weakness – the Left Posterior Convexity, because that is how classrooms have been run for two centuries and because most elementary and secondary teachers and administrators have a Left Posterior Convexity preference or auxiliary that guides most of their behavior and communication.

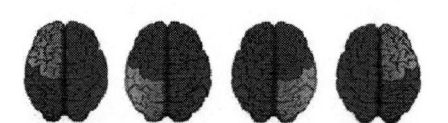

As a result, Frontal Rights frequently have difficulty in both concentrating and learning when focusing on content designed to speak to and develop their greatest weakness, the Left Posterior Convexity. This type of thinking is located diagonally across the brain from their preference, the Frontal right, which is the area of greatest natural efficiency and in which their own gifts are based. To put this differently, the learning environment in most schools is all too often enriched for Left Posterior Convexities, but impoverished for Frontal Rights – abundant with Left Posterior Convexity stage props, but empty of Frontal Right stage props.

According to Paula Englander-Golden, who co-authored Virginia Satir's last book, *Say It Straight* [11], and is presently head of the Say It Straight Foundation that works in schools with problem kids, the following is true:

> The majority of problem kids identified by schools are either natural Frontal Rights or natural Right Posterior Convexities with a Frontal Right auxiliary who feel the existing system treats them as though they are *irrelevant*. When they are related to authentically in a manner that accepts and validates who they are, i.e. their natural preferences, their disruptive, acting-out behaviors cease and they begin to relate normally.[12]

Indeed, when: they are in the right school or classroom where and when Frontal Right teachers are used; when and as the content focuses on abstract patterns or trends and ideas; when they are not asked to read before the portion of the corpus callosum bridging their frontal lobes has myelinated (approximately puberty); Frontal Rights tend to learn readily. Indeed, they are often identified as gifted or geniuses.

Which children are most likely to become dropouts?
Some years ago, I worked work with a Washington State Senate Commettee created to develop an educational system for the street kids who had dropped out of the system. At that time, our study suggested that two types of kids are most likely to become drop-outs: kids with a Frontal Right preference; and kids with a Right Posterior Convexity preference and Frontal Right auxiliary. Interviews with drop-outs in Washington State and Wisconsin both indicate most drop-outs are adept at fine arts, frequently being excellent dancers, musicians, and/or actors – in other words, they have a preference in the Frontal or Right Posterior Convexity and a developed auxiliary in the other. These kids find the traditional school to be a source of invalidation and lowered self-esteem. Many are labeled by it as "learning-disabled" with respect to language and reading. Moreover, they lacked the analytic skill (enjoyed by kids with a Frontal Left preference) to appreciate the long-term value a high school diploma could have so they drop out.

What about violence in the schools? There seems to be more and more of it. Why is it increasing so much and what can we do about it?

---

11 Paula Englander-Golden and Virginia Satir. *Say It Straight*. Published by Science and Behavior Books, Palo Alto, California. 1990.
12 Paula Englander-Golden, a colleague and friend of Dr. Benziger, in multiple conversations with the author in the 1990's, made these observations. The observation about the normalization of disruptive behavior has been substantiated by multiple research projects conducted by Dr. Paula Englander-Golden and Dr. David Golden.

Yes, the violence in schools does seem to be increasing, disturbingly so. In fact, it is increasing in schools around the world according to a Special Report in the International Herald Tribune, February 14, 2000, on the problems and trends in International Education. Leaders in many nations, including Japan, the United Kingdom, France and the USA have been trying to understand the problem as well as identify effective solutions.

Notably, among the most effective solutions found thus far are the peer counseling and mediation programs that were introduced on an experimental basis in the 1990's to help children cope with conflict and violence. According to this global report, when used in France, the United Kingdom and USA, these programs have been highly effective. Significantly, these courses or programs develop and use the Right Posterior Convexity's gifts for building connection, trust and good will. They build on and use the Right Posterior Convexity's ability to sense non-verbal signals indicating that someone is feeling cut off, unwanted, or invalidated and reach out to contradict their pain and isolation. They are powerful, highly effective programs that unwittingly made these schools more right and meaningful for Right Posterior Convexities because they have identified and used the contributions of the Right Posterior Convexity.

Related to these programs are courses and programs based on Daniel Goleman's *Emotional Intelligence*. These courses were not covered in the special report however. Goleman's book has done a great deal to identify the need for having and developing emotional intelligence. It does not however actually help the reader develop that intelligence. Nor does Goleman understand that different aspects of what he calls *emotional intelligence* are based in different aspects of our physiology. For this reason, Goleman's work which has attracted attention around the world – his book has been a best seller in Hong Kong and Argentina as well as in the USA and Europe – can be used to sell key influentials (the school board, the superintendents, principals as well as teachers, parents and kids) on the need for programs that develop and educate our emotional intelligence. Then, once there is some agreement that this is needed, the peer counseling and peer mediation programs can be introduced to actually educate and develop everyone's emotional intelligence. Ultimately it is these Right Posterior Convexity training programs that offer hope that actually lead to a reduction in violence.

Possibly the most successful peer counseling program is based in Seattle, Washington and is known as Co-Counseling or Re-Evaluation Counseling (RC). The program is global and was created more than 30 years ago by Harvey Jackins, author of *The Human Side of Human Beings* and many other books introducing and clarifying the art of co-counseling. You can learn more about this powerful technique, that has been proven to work effectively with several minority groups as well as straight, white people.

- Visit and read material on the Re-Evaluation Counseling Home Page www.rc.org
- Take an introductory or Fundamentals Course and begin using the techniques.
- Contact Rational Island Publishers, Seattle.

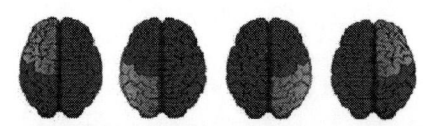

Significantly, co-counseling is something children and adults can learn and practice. It is direct, immediate, experiential education of our emotional intelligence using our Right Posterior Convexity's abilities to recognize and process emotional information in a connecting, healing and trust-building, community-building manner.

As mentioned earlier, at least two other programs, both used globally, have been proven to decrease violence. The first is the school-based program known as *Say It Straight (*SIS) created by Paula Englander-Golden and Virginia Satir and The Say It Straight Institute. The key to this program is its focus on helping adults and kids in the school environment create positive, authentic connections. To accomplish this, it teaches adults and kids to not blame anyone, not invalidate anyone and not make anyone irrelevant. This program offers workshops for teachers, parents and kids and has been found to have long-term results in reducing violence as well as drug usage and criminal behavior. In the USA its implementation is being funded experimentally in some cities and school systems.

Where and when SIS is used, it makes a real difference. The difficulty seems to be that it does require the entire class or the entire school to participate. And, it does not offer the individual student a global network of other adults and kids. By contrast, the peer counseling training and community offered by Jackins provides the individual with a global support group as well as a long-lasting set of life skills the individual can take with them in life and use effectively even when things around him are not fair and/or a boss or colleague is not talking straight. As such, *Say It Straight* might be a complementary program to peer counseling programs that helps explain the big picture of what is needed to relate in a healthy manner and, like Goleman's *Emotional Intelligence*, does more to confirm the need to accept, honor and train our emotional intelligence than actually develop it.

The second program that has been shown to decrease violence significantly, in schools and elsewhere in the world, is the family of Transcendental Meditation techniques offered globally for more than thirty years by Maharishi Mahesh Yogi. The impact of TM on violence is so clear and measurable that the Journal of Conflict Resolution has published two very different studies in the past ten years, reporting the impact of TM and the TM Siddhis program on the level of violence in schools, urban crime and wars. Again, to learn more about the power of these 5000 year old techniques and what they offer us today in the 21st century, visit the following web sites: www.natural-law.org (the web site for the Natural Law Party); and www.alltm.org (the web site for the International TM organization).

Finally, on the subject of violence, a Chicago-based Jungian, John Giannini has written a book, *The Compass of The Soul,* in which he suggests that the violence in the USA and industrialized world today is the predictable result and expression of our society's left-brain, extraverted bias and represents the manifesting of our public or social shadow. For non-Jungians, John is saying: the fact that our culture values and rewards extraverted left-brained behavior so highly, almost to the point of denying the reality of any other way of viewing the world, causes some who are introverted right-brains to rebel or resist this cultural position in a primitive, violent and anti-social manner. Hence much unexplained violence is actually the acting out of angry, alienated introverted Intuitives (Frontal Rights) or angry, alienated, introverted Feelers (Right Posterior Convexities). John may be right. From a systems approach, many violent kids are the right-brain kids whose need for validation and belonging has warped their ability to **create** into killing and their **need for authentic spiritual connection** into devil worship.

Based on what you've told us, we need to look for and adopt strategies that will help us create whole-brained classrooms that are healthy, empowering and effective, along with strategies that are effective with right-brained kids. Are there any existing programs you would recommend, in addition to those you talked about above?

The good news is there are many good programs because many good people have been trying to help solve the problem of violence and improve our schools for many years. Here are some that I recommend personally.

- Jean Houston's books and workshops have been around for more than 30 years. Jean teaches people working with kids who are having difficulty in learning to read – many of whom are Frontal Rights – to do the following: imagine then read. My own experiment with this approach suggests the following order or procedure works very well when teaching reading to Frontal Right kids:

  - Ask the child or children to first imagine (Frontal Right activity) a tale or story, then after you have given them a few minutes to do this, with their eyes closed, have them open their eyes.

  - Draw a picture with colorful crayons on big news print of what they imagined (Right Posterior Convexity activity). Then when they have completed their drawing.

  - Have them tell you the story they imagined, using their drawing.

  - Ask them to write the story.

  - Finally, have them read the story they wrote.

- Research completed at the University of Edinburgh, announced in January 2000 that the use of color overlays for reading improves reading by 25 percent. This information was presented in a January 2000 BBC report. The children have pastel colored, clear overlays to hold over each page. Understanding brain dominance, you can see that it helps Right Posterior Convexities read by adding Right Posterior Convexity input (the color) to the otherwise Left Posterior Convexity task of reading. This technique can help Frontal Rights as well because they, too, can get this additional information by using their Right Posterior Convexity auxiliary, in the same way the drawing of the imagined trip or story above helps the Frontal Right.

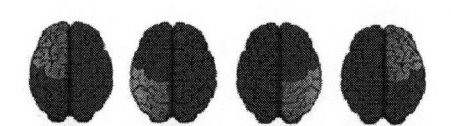

- Workshop Way and the Five Freedoms is an amazing program developed by Grace Pilon, a nun, working both in Philadelphia's inner city and on Native American reservations almost 30 years ago. Because of Workshop Way's success, the international director of Workshop Way, Kathleen Gallagher, asked me to study their approach to determine why they are so successful to the extent that their program raises a child's readiness for school and their IQ. My own study of their work revealed that this program is tremendously powerful and indeed brilliant. Rather than worry about translating every course into a language that each child can understand, Workshop Way structures a classroom and climate in which each type of child is free to approach learning in the manner that suits their dominance. It is powerful and successful.

First, Workshop Way is based on what Grace Pilon identified as the five freedoms. Significantly, Grace believed the purpose of education was to teach all people (children and adults) to solve problems and differences with their minds rather than their fists. Grace herself intuitively invented the Five Freedoms when trying to educate kids in very difficult environments and it is these Five Freedoms that are the key to its power and universal value. All schools could be easily and rapidly improved to be more effective places of learning for the full diversity of kids by honoring and implementing these Five Freedoms. Here's why:

- The Freedom to Move, which is built into all Workshop Way classrooms, allows especially Frontal Right kids who need to move to see the pattern or big picture, to do so as and when they need to. Many Frontal Right adults know that when they are stuck, moving helps them. They may not always talk to others about this peculiar fact of life as a Frontal Right, but they know it to be true. To provide kids with this same opportunity seems to have empowering results. They learn and like learning.

- The Freedom to Decide or Choose is helpful to all kids but it is most important for two types of kids. The Frontal Left kids like to be able to decide what to do and why as well as when. After all they are *decision-making machines*. And, the Right Posterior Convexity likes to be able to choose to study or work on an assignment with another child rather than alone, so that they can use their natural gifts in the Right Posterior Convexity, even if the assignment is in the Left Posterior Convexity.

- The Freedom of Location and Position is another Freedom. It is vital for many children. Right Posterior Convexities need and use it to sit close to others with whom they connect. Left Posterior Convexities need and use it to stay in their seat at their desk. Frontal Rights who tend to need to move and stretch a good deal will use it to move and to perhaps sit on their desk rather than at it. Frontal Lefts need it to implement or act on any choices or decisions they have made. Extraverts need and use it to be in a group or be where the stimulation is greatest. Introverts need and use it to be out of the way, where they can comfortably focus, even in a separate room or an alcove if too much is going on and they are beginning to feel they are overwhelmed by the noise or activity level.

- Amazingly and significantly, the Freedom to Talk is built into all Workshop Way classrooms. Understanding brain dominance as well as you do at this point, you will appreciate that it helps Right Posterior Convexity kids learn and like school because it allows the child to talk with the teacher and classmates as often as they like, which is generally most of the time, in a non-intrusive manner, one which does not disturb others, but which allows the

Right Posterior Convexity child to use their natural gifts – monitoring and responding to facial expression and non-verbal communication and connecting.

- The Freedom from Fear is intriguing. It is most helpful to the Left Posterior Convexity kids, especially early in their schooling when school itself is new, or later, whenever they are exposed to something completely new. In these situations this Freedom helps empower the Left Posterior Convexity to not be overwhelmed by anxiety, to stay, to learn until he is comfortable with the new material.

In addition to the Five Freedoms, Grace Pilon invented and articulated a number of powerful strategies or techniques that make a tremendous difference in the learning climate for all types of children. Two of the most powerful are:

- One powerful technique that Workshop Way teaches teachers to use is Cushioning. It is a powerful and a brilliant technique that is useful for all children. One example of cushioning would be to remind students before they answer a question that it takes courage to volunteer to answer a question. Validating the courage whether or not the child's answer is correct. Noting that children know different things because they come from different families and have had different experiences. And they can all learn.

- Another, the Precious Smile, ensures that each teacher connects and validates each child each morning before lessons actually begin. It is a brilliant and very powerful strategy that helps children to feel they belong and feel cared about in school. It involves the teacher smiling at each student as that student talks with the teacher. Radiating approval, acceptance, love and validation.

To learn more about Workshop Way, the Five Freedoms, and strategies such as Cushioning and The Precious Smile, contact a Workshop Way consultant (www.WorkshopWay.com) After more than four decades dedicated to public education, Grace Pilon died in 1995 at age 88, and Kathleen Gallagher retired, but other Workshop Way consultants are still available. You can begin by contacting:

- Susan Harnage, the executive director of Workshop Way and veteran teacher, can be reached at: 001-602-961-3670. **SHarnage@aol.com**

- Anne Marie McMahon, a Workshop Way consultant and school principal, based in Yonkers, can be reached at 001-914-423-2429. w574@adnyschools.org

Also, if you wish to order the audiotape program of a workshop I gave a few years ago to the Workshop Way Consultants, who were all active educators and mostly teachers, at their international conference that year, contact our office. The 2-tape program addresses:

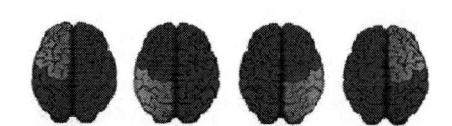

- the link between teaching and brain dominance; and
- the link between Workshop Way's Five Freedoms and brain dominance.

Summary

Families and school classrooms are the smallest and most intense experience we have of communal living. Most of what we experience in other groups later in life can be tied to the patterns we learned and roles played out in our family of origin and our school. When we seek affirmation and validation by choosing to spend time with family members who think the way we do, we foreshadow our behavior at work and in our community at large, where and when we seek friends to affirm our way of thinking and being. When we are affirmed and applauded for using our preference in our family and to participate in and contribute to the family, our self-esteem is strengthened. When we are affirmed and applauded for using our preference in school, our self-esteem is strengthened and a positive feeling for others and our community is fostered. We grow mentally and emotionally happier and healthier. The way is paved for us to live a life in which we are true to ourselves, energized and impassioned by the work we do and life we lead because we are living a life in which we are acting true to ourselves and we are accepted.

By contrast, if we are rejected in and by our family or school, are shamed or forced to Falsify Type, our self-esteem and mental health suffer. If we learn at home and in school that the only way to belong is to Falsify Type, the tone is set for a life disconnected from self and defensive (hostile or resentful) towards others – a life in which we, our natural self, do not belong.

If there is a lesson to be learned from studying brain dominance in families and schools, it is that *context* is all-important. In order to determine what someone might be experiencing, we need to look at their preference and introversion or extraversion, the preferences, introversion or extraversion of those around them, and finally what activities they are being asked to do. When a person is not thriving, there is a good chance the context in which that person is living, studying or working is not validating

Chapter 8: Your Whole Brain Over Your Lifetime

Everyone is born with a set of preferential patterns around which they must live their lives. And, whether one is discussing handedness or brainedness, the rule is the same: first, *"know thyself"* and *"to thine own self be true"*, then seek to grow and become more. In real life, this simple rule is not as easy to follow as one might hope.

▲ Being True To Yourself

For some people, being true to themselves by living *True to Type* to their preference and introversion/extraversion needs is easy and effortless. These are the fortunate ones. They have the opportunity to develop, use and be rewarded for using their preference in an environment matching their introversion/extraversion from an early age. Hence, they develop a set of energizing and enlivening competencies using their preference and, along with it, a coherent and positive sense of self. For these people, life flows smoothly. From an early age, their self-esteem and life-direction are strong. By age 20 or 25 they're doing what comes naturally, in a socially-approved position in the home or on the job, often using the most socially acceptable of their auxiliaries to support their preference as and when necessary. Their use of these two specialized types of thinking – their preference and one auxiliary – is stable. Their persona is generally stable as well – for almost two decades. And, because they are using and being rewarded for using their preference so much of the time, they are energetic and enthusiastic about life and in good heath. They regularly experience *Flow* – that optimal mental-emotional condition reported by Mihaly Csikszentmihalyi in his book by the same name, and exude abundant joy and hope.

Later, around age 45, they begin to experience an inner need to grow. At this point in their lives, these normal healthy people adopt and begin developing their second auxiliary. They take a class in something different; do something outside their range of expertise, while on a holiday or vacation or apply for a job that will open the door to opportunities to develop and use their second auxiliary. When asked, they tell you it isn't that they're dissatisfied with themselves or their lives; it's just that they're curious about these new areas. One might describe what these people are experiencing as *mid-life spread*.

These people are living their life *over center*, leading with their preference and supporting that preference with one or both auxiliaries. The term *over center* is apt. It emphasizes that the person's weight (leading) is in the preference, not in an auxiliary. And it reminds us that in the brain, the auxiliaries for any mode are located on either side of that mode. So when a person uses their auxiliaries appropriately, they are putting some weight in each of two arms or lever arms but keeping most of the weight over center in their lead. In fact, many people get off center by trying to lead with an auxiliary or their greatest weakness.

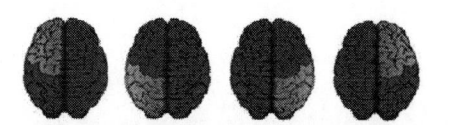

▲ Falsifying Type

For people who are not born into a family and/or community that accepts, understands and welcomes who they are, life doesn't flow so smoothly. Many children, as well as adults, find themselves under pressure to Falsify Type to fit in. Right Posterior Convexity boys are shamed and teased by their peers as sissies and told to toughen up by adults. Frontal Left girls are told that arguing isn't feminine. And Frontal Right children of both sexes are both teased and punished as fanciful daydreamers. Somewhat

> "This above all: to thine own self be true"
> Polonius

later, the Right Posterior Convexity man is discouraged from entering a female profession; the Frontal Left woman is told she's an aggressive bitch; and the Frontal Right is told he or she needs to be practical and make long-term commitments.

To make the above situations worse, in our present society introverted children and adults are rarely comfortable with who they are, because they are regularly invalidated and shamed for not being enthusiastic about competing, negotiating or selling, which are the three hallmarks of our extraverted global business culture. For those unfamiliar with the manner in which our culture effects introverts, Elaine N. Aron's *The Highly Sensitive Person: How to Thrive When the World Overwhelms You,* first printed in 1996, is enlightening. This harsh fact of life means that the people who are most at risk are those who belong to one of the above groups and are, as well, introverted: introverted Right Posterior Convexity males, introverted Frontal Left females and introverted Frontal Rights of either sex. These three types see themselves as ugly ducklings that without public or well-known role models have difficulty discovering they are swans.

Faced with such non-nurturing environments, an adolescent misfit might choose to adapt by Falsifying Type by matching in chameleon-like manner the coloring and pattern of the environment. This option is appealing to a child misfit as the judgment and rejection of others threatens his still developing self-esteem, which is intimately linked to his sense of belonging. Indeed, a child misfit has only two options:

- to Falsify Type in order to fit in; or
- to resist and remain an outsider or misfit.

It is important to notice that later as adults we have a third, more empowering option – to change our environment. However, children are limited typically to the first two options.
If the child chooses the first option or path, to Falsify Type, he will over time, often decades, learn two powerful lessons:

- when one Falsifies Type to fit in, one's sense of self-esteem is weakened rather than strengthened;

and
- using non-preferred competencies over extended periods of time brings fatigue, boredom and possibly depression but not joy.

Initially, I observed and reported the costs of Falsifying Type in *Falsification of Type: Its Jungian and Physiological Foundations & Mental, Emotional and Physiological Costs*, 1995:

- the short-term results of Falsifying Type are increased irritability, headaches and difficulty in mastering new tasks, and
- the long term results of Falsifying Type are exhaustion, depression, lack of joy, a homeostatic imbalance involving oxygen, increased anxiety, increased introversion, the premature aging of the brain and a vulnerability to illness.

In the same year, in an article on *Rethinking Stress, Depression and Midlife Crisis,* I identified the link between Falsifying Type for years and mid-life crisis as well as depression. The article synthesized my work on Falsification of Type and its costs with my earlier work on *Overcoming Depression* in 1992. It emphasized the role of what has been identified as our number two-crisis response, Conserve/Withdraw, in triggering depression. It suggested the massive and systemic impact of Falsification of Type prompts the pituitary to repeatedly trigger Conserve/Withdraw. Physiologically, Conserve/Withdraw is an important alternative your body can use to cope with stress. Conserve/Withdraw is an alternative to Fight or Flight that has been largely overlooked by the medical community; possibly because Hans Selye had identified Fight or Flight as *the* stress response, a term that caused many to believe Fight or Flight was the only response to stress. In fact, Conserve/Withdraw's vital role was identified as early as 1987 by Blair Justice in his wellness treatise: *Who Gets Sick: How Beliefs, Moods and Thoughts Affect Your Health.* Both responses are designed to help us survive stress. Both are managed by our autonomic nervous system. And, both are functionally specialized responses designed to do very different things. Fight or Flight, managed by the sympathetic portion of our autonomic system, is designed to help us get on top of a manageable problem. It provides us with more energy so that we can conquer the problem by mastering it or outrunning it. Conserve/Withdraw, managed by the parasympathetic portion of our autonomic nervous system, is designed to help us survive problems that are larger than life, problems that are too big for us to solve or cannot be solved now given our life situation. The key to Conserve/Withdraw's success in helping us is that when we emerge from it, our reality has changed such that the problem is now solvable. Let's look at a few examples of when and how Conserve/Withdraw helps.

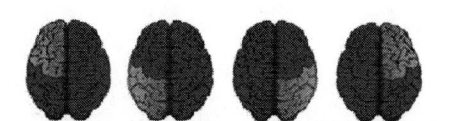

> **Examples of Conserve/Withdraw**
>
> A starving adult in Ethiopia. The lack of food caused her body to automatically trigger Conserve/Withdraw. The result: her body automatically shut down, conserving her existing internal resources – water, oxygen and energy – so that she would live longer. When food was airlifted in, she was still alive. Without the unconscious automatic help from our number two-crisis response, Conserve/Withdraw, she would not have been alive when the food arrived.
>
> A child is trapped in a mineshaft and lives for a week without food or water. The child's body automatically triggers Conserve/Withdraw. The result: his body automatically shuts down, conserving its existing internal resources – water, oxygen and energy – so that the child will live longer. When the child is discovered, he is still alive. Without the unconscious automatic help from our number two-crisis response, Conserve/Withdraw, the child would not have been alive when he was found.

For this automatic survival mechanism to be successful the problem has to be resolved, the hopeless situation has to be transformed, within a given amount of time. In other words, its ability to help us conserve our internal resources is not infinite – help must come and bring with it a change in our reality.

Dr. George Perdrizet[13], Director of Research for Hartford Hospital's EMS/Trauma Program, uses Conserve/Withdraw on a regular basis in transplant surgeries. His findings show that Conserve/Withdraw triggered prior to a transplant surgery helps people survive and recover more rapidly from major surgery with fewer complications! The key he adds is not only that the surgery changes his patients' (to date all animals) objective reality, but as well that when they awaken following the surgery, they are given hopeful uplifting information. Perdrizet's breakthrough findings on the value of Conserve/ Withdraw to stress management are so impressive that he was invited to present them at meetings on stress in the United States, France and Switzerland in 1999 and 2000.

Significantly, Perdrizet's findings support my own observations that Conserve/Withdraw triggered continuously brings about a mind-body condition that we recognize as depression because when the individual emerges from Conserve/Withdraw his world has not changed. He is still invalidated and rejected for who he is and subsequently withdraws once more.

In November 1999, Arlene Taylor, Ph.D. and I co-authored an article in which we reported the findings of her decade-long study, *The Physiological Foundations of Falsification of Type and PASS.*

---

[13] Information about Dr. Perdrizet's work may be obtained by contacting him at Hartford Hospital. The information presented here is from conversations between Drs. Benziger and Perdrizet in Dillon, Colorado, December 1999.

The Benziger Breakthrough

The findings corroborated my own findings and identified PASS, the Prolonged Adaption Stress Syndrome, as a previously unrecognized factor in chronic fatigue and depression. The complete family of symptoms that Taylor's work identified as linked to extended Falsification of Type, were:

1. fatigue
2. hyper-vigilance
3. immune system alterations
4. memory impairment
5. altered brain chemistry
6. diminished frontal lobe functions
7. discouragement and/or depression
8. self-esteem problems.

Not surprisingly, when someone persists in Falsifying Type for decades, using his inefficient, non-preferred types of thinking almost exclusively, he is likely to experience what is known among life-career counselors and therapists as a mid-life crisis. In such cases, this crisis may be created by a complete collapse of the personality, sometimes referred to as a mental breakdown, or by some other constellation of mental, emotional and physical problems created over time by the profound and unavoidable physiological stress brought on by Falsifying Type. In either case, the crisis can be seen as an opportunity, not as a tragedy. Through such an internal re-evaluation, the adult who has abandoned his preference can:

- remember who he is; and
- choose to embrace and re-own his original preference.

And, if he is introverted as well, the crisis / opportunity if supported by an understanding of the work presented in this book, can help him accept, understand and value more deeply his natural introversion. And in turn, it may lead him to seek more introverted friends to serve as empowering and validating mirrors.

Of course, re-owning one's natural preference is not a simple act. It often involves making changes in one's work and personal life. These changes may be in the work we do, in the environment in which we do it, how we manage our responsibilities as a partner, spouse and parent as well as our hobbies.

Sadly, many opt not to heal the first time they become aware of what has been going on in their lives. Many middle-aged individuals resist hearing what their bodies and minds are trying to tell them. They continue to resist the on-going biofeedback that is saying: *stop!* For these people, the fear of having wasted so many years of their lives is compounded by confusion concerning two quite different things: their financial security and how to develop skills in the preference they have not used for years. When you remember and allow for their weak and eroded sense of self-esteem from years of Falsifying Type, it is easy to understand why they don't act to take care of themselves and why they persist in coping by consuming large amounts of alcohol or mind-sedating drugs.

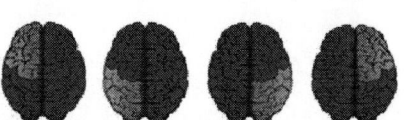

Defending the Self[4]

If, on the other hand, the misfit elects to follow the road less traveled, to hold fast to his own sense of self regardless of the feedback from his environment, a completely different set of learning awaits him. First of all, he will learn that he must always be prepared to defend himself for as an avowed misfit he will always be under attack. In response to the chronic hostility his environment directs towards him, he will probably develop and depend on a set of defensive behaviors. These may be either active and aggressive or passive. If he develops an openly hostile pattern, he will probably be known as an angry young man. If he develops a passive strategy, often that of avoidance, he will most likely be known as a difficult young man who keeps to himself a lot and is perhaps a drop-out or a run-away. Either way, his defensive behaviors will begin to cause trouble. In the first instance, he may get into trouble with the law or with the organization for which he works. In the second, he will find himself repeatedly isolated without the support of friends and colleagues. And, typically as well, every now and again, he will swing *briefly* from his position of passive hostility into one that is openly aggressive or violent[14], for such a person, the pre-eminent need becomes finding a place where he can be true to himself without being rejected so that there is no longer a need for the defensive behaviors.

Most of us know such people. The key is that people trapped in such an angry, resentment-burdened life can transform and heal their lives by finding and moving to the place where they can be true to themselves without being rejected. A Frontal Right man known to be an angry and difficult employee leaves the company and within two years is renowned as an innovative, successful entrepreneur in fabric manufacturing or computing. A Frontal Left woman known to be an angry and difficult nurse, leaves nursing, attends law school and finds herself five years later a happy, well-liked and respected attorney sought out for her ability to make excellent decisions.

Again the question of introversion arises. For introverts experience the regular unremitting hostility, but not the option to Falsify as extraverts. It simply is not something their physiology allows. So it is more likely than not that introverts will be found to be more defensive, not because they are naturally defensive, but because they are living in a world that attacks them. As such, when working with or trying to empower introverts, it is vitally important to help them find a place where they can be true to themselves without being shamed or humiliated so there is no longer a need for their defensive behaviors.

Bringing It All Together

And so, the paths that seemed so different meet. Whether we are accepted for who we are and subsequently grow and prosper in our early years, reaching out in mid-life to grow further or are rejected as a child and spend years attempting to deal with what it means to be a misfit by Falsifying Type or developing defensive strategies or both, it seems we all move ultimately towards the same wholeness. Carl Jung spoke of individuation as a highly personal process that sought to involve

---

14 For those unfamiliar with the tendency for habitually passive resistors to swing briefly into open resistance, the reader is forwarded to *The Path of Least Resistance* by Robert Fritz 1984, Part 1 Section 3 on the Reactive Responsive Orientation.

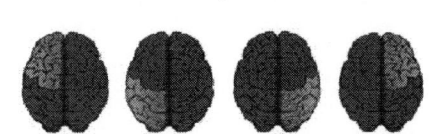

the development of all four functions. Abraham Maslow spoke of self-actualization. Both men held highly energized inner visions of mankind growing and evolving. When they are brought together, their visions are perhaps even more powerful for Maslow's insights explained why so many people seem to ignore their inner compass while Jung's vision clarified why actualization seems unattainable for so many people. After all, if you have been Falsifying Type for decades, it is really quite easy to achieve or satisfy any of the needs below self-actualization. But we cannot self-actualize unless and until we stop Falsifying Type. Self-actualization is the joyous expression of the developed self and its gifts that includes its preference and its natural level of introversion or extraversion. You might say that just as PASS is the predictable outcome for someone who Falsifies Type, self-actualization is the predictable outcome for someone who lives True to Type.

▲ Questions and Answers about Falsification of Type

I'm still unclear about why anyone would deny his or her preference. Is Falsification of Type conscious? Why would anyone choose to Falsify Type given how much more enjoyable and rewarding it is to use our preference?

There are at least six distinct reasons – some more conscious than others – that appear to lead people to abandon their preference. Many, but not all, of these often begin to affect us in childhood.

Reasons People Falsify Type
...or abandon their natural preference

- their need to feel accepted, to belong and to fit in.
- their need to avoid punishment or shaming for being different.
- their need to establish a separate identity.
- the absence of the stage props required by their natural preference.
- the absence of role models.
- their need to ensure that something that needs to get done gets done in a marriage or partnership where neither person has the required preference.

Let's take a moment to look at each of these. First, there is the need to feel accepted. You might think that this need to belong is the same as the need to avoid punishment for being different. But in truth, they are distinct. For a young child, one who is still dependent on the actions of the adults in the family for survival, being different can be uncomfortable. Furthermore, as a child begins to mature, the drive to look to his or her sex role model for behavioral cues is strong. Although there is evidence that all children are vulnerable to such a need during their first dozen years, it is the child with a Right Posterior Convexity preference who is most sensitive to the disharmony created when they are different. For this reason, Right Posterior Convexity children experience the most pressure to Falsify Type to fit in.

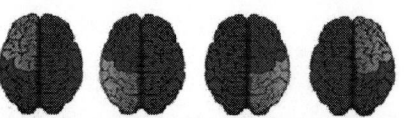

Looking at an example of this kind of Falsification will help us to understand it. Sunny, the daughter of my then office manager, Jean, was a bright energetic eight-year-old when I first met her. From watching her and listening to her tales of discovery as well as her mother's tales of woe, it was easy to spot Sunny as a highly extraverted Frontal Right. Sunny's mother was aware of her daughter's preference and like any loving parent tried to help Sunny feel good about herself. And yet, as she was an introverted Left Posterior Convexity, validating Sunny's behaviors was not easy for Jean. By the time Sunny turned ten, she was showing signs of Falsifying Type. In an effort to harmonize and connect with her mother, Sunny would parrot the rules and dicta she had heard her mother state. Moreover, at school she experienced even more pressure to change who she was. By the age of twelve, Sunny began skipping school, telling her mother she was so different from the rest of girls at school that the other girls regularly teased her and called her names. If she were going to attend school, she would either have to cope with the pain of being different or begin Falsifying Type to fit in. At this point, her mother acted to resolve the problem by sending Sunny to a boarding school where she hoped she would find other bright Frontal Right girls.

As I watched Sunny suffer, I recalled being made fun of by my classmates for my boundless curiosity and enthusiasm for learning. I also recalled the glares on the faces of classmates because I always knew the answers, always asked questions that took the content further and always got good grades – all rather typical behaviors for introverted Frontal Rights. I did not know if this were also true of Sunny, but probably. It was painful being so different. I recall purposely flunking art class, to prove I was like my classmates.

Punishment and invalidation often come from the adults in the misfit's environment. These include: being given extra homework or assigned extra study hall time for daydreaming or doodling (both natural patterns of thinking for a Frontal Right) or for passing notes and talking in class (typical ways in which Extraverts try to cope in the quiet classroom) and being grounded for not keeping one's room neat and orderly or not doing routine tasks in good Left Posterior Convexity form. Ironically, in this era of renewed interest in creativity, one of the single most disturbing punishments still being meted out comes from the art teachers who, in the interest of Left Posterior Convexity correctness, label a drawing in which the roses are colored green or brown as wrong or no good.

In considering the above information on childhood and adolescent adaption, it is worth noting that because of the current structure of our society and its role models, four natural dominance patterns are rejected or attacked more frequently than others. This is important because it suggests that children with these natural patterns may require more help and understanding than their peers in building a positive sense of self-esteem.

A description of each of these four at-risk groups of children follows.
- The young Right Posterior Convexity male is more likely to be made fun of by his peers and seen as a child to be developed by his parents and teachers than a naturally left-brained boy. Over and over this child is likely to be told that he needs to learn to fight back and act like a man and that he should remember that big boys don't cry, as he hears himself being labeled a sissy and a cry-baby by his classmates.

- The young Frontal Left female is likely to be receiving messages that her excellence in math is fine but that she should be learning to baby-sit, to cook, to sew, to be a girl scout, all the while hearing herself labeled unfeminine by her peers.
- Frontal Right children regardless of sex are generally seen as a behavior problem because, although they are quite bright, they get bored quickly and tend to disrupt class, even if only passively by doodling. It is also true that young Frontal Rights are often punished for not being sufficiently social and for preferring to go out exploring on their own. The name that these children most often hear is *weirdo*.
- Introverts with any preference regardless of sex are so highly invalidated that when introversion occurs along with one of the above three it is well to consider the individual is at risk.

Trying to fit in, to be loved and trying to change to avoid being punished or shamed are common. And yet, there are other reasons people Falsify Type. People also Falsify Type to establish a separate and distinct identity. This kind of Falsification occurs most often with identical twins who naturally have the same preference. During their formative years, this sameness may be seen as a problem because others cannot tell the twins apart. And yet, during these years the natural bonding between the twins appears to hold them together. For some twins, reaching adulthood brings the challenge to establish a separate identity. To meet this challenge, one or both twins may begin to dress differently, live separately, and/or establish a distinct set of skills. It is this last step that can result in a twin Falsifying Type. As one twin, Sandy, put it: "We were both good at music, but I had to have my own identity, so I stopped playing the piano and began to study accounting. It was as far away from music and my sister as I could get." Initially, and throughout her twenties and thirties, this decision to assert different abilities was seen as helpful. Sandy felt strengthened by this choice. Then suddenly in her forties a peculiar thing happened. Although her twin continued to live comfortably and happily, Sandy began to feel uneasy. Her work with a therapist helped her understand that what she was going through was a mid-life crisis. The upshot was predictable: Sandy realized that she had to re-embrace music and her Right Posterior Convexity preference. Even though the earlier Falsification had been consciously chosen for an important and valid reason, and had indeed helped Sandy establish self pride and achieve an identity of her own, Sandy had to return to find her original self and her preference in order to be ultimately happy, healthy and fulfilled.

Others who abandon their preference in order to establish a separate identify are doing so for slightly different reasons. A Right Posterior Convexity girl, raised by a Right Posterior Convexity alcoholic mother may opt to identify with and develop one of her auxiliaries simply to distinguish herself from her mother. Again, the pressure to be different from someone one does not trust or respect is powerful. It can lead to decades of Falsifying Type before the person's own inner nature begins to reassert itself.

A fourth reason people Falsify Type is that their environment lacks the stage props needed to fully develop or use their preference.

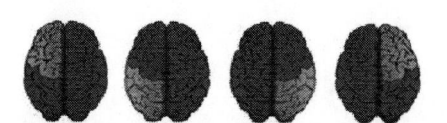

As adults we notice the importance of such stage props when we are in an environment that doesn't speak to us. The difference is that as adults, we have options: we can change the environment so that it feels right or we can leave the environment and go somewhere better suited to our brain. One common example adults encounter is the traditional office, which is well stocked with Left Posterior Convexity sequential forms and files but devoid of any Right Posterior Convexity or Frontal Right stimulation. When forced to work in such an office, Right Posterior Convexities try to adjust the environment so that it speaks to them by bringing in photos of their spouses and children, plants and/or flowers, which they place on their desks. Frontal Rights might try to adjust the same environment by painting the walls white and adding more shelves for their stacks.

Children don't have the same flexibility to alter or leave an environment. If a child is born into a family where he is the only person with his preference, that child must live and try to actualize himself in the environment designed and controlled by his parents – an environment that is unlikely to speak to his brain. If there are no paints, you can't paint. If there are no musical instruments, you can't learn to play one. If there are no machines or tools, you can't learn to work with them. Many Frontal Rights report being forced as children to keep everything orderly and never being allowed to be creative, to play with ideas or to move things around. Mozart was musical but he also benefited from an enriched musical environment as his mother had instruments in the home and played them for hours a day. Being born into an environment that suits your brain is more important than people realize. Imagine being born a gifted swimmer – in the desert. At what point does the child in the desert discover swimming is an option?

The fifth reason people Falsify Type is that they have never seen or known a role model who embodies and models their preference and its full scope of gifts. Such an absence has a clear impact on children. A number of our Frontal clients report being raised in Posterior Convexity homes. These people generally recall the first time they actually met someone, as an adult, who had their natural preference. One man, raised in Posterior Convexity home, in the rural south, with a Frontal Left preference, didn't discover what logical thinking was and that life could be interesting until he attended a course for officers in the military. The speaker, with his clear, articulate and powerful command of logic, was like no one this man had ever met. He was, for him, a role model.

As an introverted Frontal Right, I was probably luckier than most. My father and many of his colleagues were natural Frontal Rights. As a result, I was given both opportunity and modeling. In fact, my childhood environment could be described as an enriched environment for any young Frontal Right: my parents both spoke and read in several languages; the family traveled widely in the USA and Europe, I was allowed to go to Italy for three months at age 12 and to France alone at age 16, graduate students from many nations lived in our home with us and mother allowed me to come home from school and spend hours in the living room – turning the furniture upside down to build and explore space or alternately playing with a huge set of large blocks. And in the summer, beaches were a perfect place to build sand castles. I had many opportunities to imagine, create, and play with space and to spend time with Frontal Right adults who served as role models. Dad shared his own spatial and metaphoric thinking, modeling creative intuitive thinking in how and where he chose to drive or hike as well as through his landscaping, sketching, make-believe story telling, architectural skill and, his choice of career focus, the God-Concepts of the Romantic Poets. Other Frontal Right adults who were neighbors and friends served as uncles and mentors for me, including Buckminster Fuller and a number of his futurist design professors.

Although I was probably dyslexic, no one noticed. They all accepted that I did not like to read. So I learned by listening to conversations between highly educated adults more than by reading. And, as well, by having my parents read to me such works as C.S. Lewis's *Perlandra*. So it was that my childhood environment provided me with a healthy foundation for life – a set of skills in my preference, positive self-esteem and a certain knowledge that Frontal Rights belong and contribute. As I have met and spoken with other Frontal Rights in the past decades, I am reminded again and again of the importance of my childhood environment. The lack of such an enriched environment in childhood, structured and organized for the individual's preference and complete with stage props and role models, is what seems to have made it difficult for them to know themselves. Indeed, many have never learned to actually think spatially or metaphorically or actively look for patterns. Many seem to live with what Jung might have called an "immature Intuitive Function" – despite the fact that it is their preference. They make changes in their own lives but they don't master change and use vision to help themselves and others to make change. The possible exceptions are those who have taught themselves to use their spatial gifts, in combination with their imagination, as surgeons and chemists and chemical engineers and geologists.

Our schools and teachers talk about providing an enriched environment. They are well intentioned. They just lack the understanding and insight needed to provide a flexible environment that can function as an enriched environment for children with all four preferences whether they are extraverts or introverts.

Finally, the sixth element that pressures individuals to Falsify Type is being in a partnership, personal or business, in which tasks that need to be done require the use of a specialized type of thinking that neither partner prefers. In this case the partner who has a penchant for being responsible, due to having been the eldest child in his or her family of origin, will Falsify Type in order to see that the task (paying bills, for example) is done. Or, alternately, the partner with a natural preference for the Right Posterior Convexity will adapt to do the job, motivated by a need to keep the peace.

Of course going outside one's area of natural efficiency occasionally is not the kind of adapting that causes problems. The problems arise when someone accommodates by spending hours and hours a day in one's inefficient and inaccessible weakness. If it goes on for months or years, the cost is such that the person accommodating may lose all sense of joy in life. They want the partnership, but at what cost? How do they explain the cost to others?

From all you've said it would seem that almost everyone adapts. Is this true?

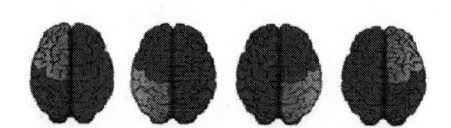

Everyone adapts but not everyone Falsifies Type. As discussed earlier, many people are born with a preference that causes them to be consistently and strongly rewarded. For males with either a Left Posterior Convexity or Frontal Left preference and females with either a Right Posterior Convexity or Left Posterior Convexity preference, life in our culture is validating and affirming. Those with these preferences are generally rewarded for being themselves and doing what comes naturally. These people adapt throughout their lives by developing and using their auxiliaries to support their preference, not replace it.

Not surprisingly, these same people tend to have the strongest and most positive sense of self-esteem from an early age and seem the most baffled by the fact that other people are not as at home with themselves and are plagued by shaky self-esteem, depression and other mental or emotional problems.

What makes you so sure that Falsifying Type is so dangerous?

It is worth looking at the anecdotal evidence on this basic fact of life. Jung himself related stories of persons who were exhausted and neurotic as a result of Falsifying Type in the 1930's. Working with hundreds of clients in the late 1980's and 1990's I discovered that when a person uses a preferred competency (i.e. a competency developed in their natural preference), they are energized internally so much that they want to do more of the same type of work because they want to feel those good feelings. Some people laughingly say I would pay you to let me do that. You might say using a preferred competency is eu-stress (good or beneficial stress) as defined by Hans Selye. This is very different from what happens when someone uses a non-preferred competency (i.e. a competency developed in any of their three non-preferred modes). When using a non-preferred competency, the person experiences fatigue, irritability and boredom. Pressure to do more of such non-preferred competencies is experienced as anxiety or tension producing or stressful.

Finally, remember the work of Arlene Taylor, Ph.D[15],[45] who in 1999, after working with Falsification of Type for more than ten years, announced her findings to the medical world. It was definitive. Using non-preferred competencies to Falsify Type over time is a major stressor that impacts both our minds and bodies.

Would you explain more fully the costs of Falsifying Type, identified as PASS – the Prolonged Adaption Stress Syndrome?

According to Arlene Taylor, Ph.D., eight commonly observed symptoms may be present in varying degrees in individuals who have been Falsifying Type. This collection of symptoms, called PASS, can include:

1. Fatigue - prolonged Falsification of Type requires the brain to work up to 100 times harder, which

---

[15] The answer to this question was taken from The Physiological Foundations of Falsification of Type and PASS, written by Dr. Arlene Taylor and Dr. Katherine Benziger. December 1999. It is available at www.benziger.org.

quite naturally creates fatigue. This may be noticed as:
- a growing fatigue that is not alleviated by sleep;
- interference with the quality of sleep obtainable;
- decreased dreaming;
- exhaustion;
- a tendency to crave specific foods and/or ingest high fat/high sugar snacks in an effort to get quick energy. The result can be a weight gain with all the stressors that being overweight can generate;
- a tendency to self-medicate in an attempt to try to alter brain chemistry – neurotransmitter ratios – and make oneself feel better. This is often accomplished through some kind of addictive behavior (i.e. caffeine, nicotine, alcohol).

2. Hyper-Vigilance - prolonged Falsification of Type can create a state of hyper-vigilance as the brain goes on protective alertness. This is a safety mechanism that can show up in a variety of different ways.
    - The brain can be temporarily pushed toward introversion. As indicated by data gathered using the BTSA, this is evidenced as a decrease in the individual's natural extraversion level. It requires tremendous energy to maintain this state of protective alertness and can further increase the person's fatigue level.
    - There can be a temporarily increased sensitivity to environmental stimuli (i.e. light, sound, odors) that can impact relationships, both personal and professional.
    - There may be an observed change in the kinds of activities the individual gravitates toward. Previously enjoyed activities may be discarded in favor of less gregarious situations. Sometimes the individual appears to be isolating the self from others, perhaps in an effort to decrease the amount of stimulation that the brain must process.

3. Immune System Alteration - Falsifying Type can be thought of as the individual living a lie at some level. Lying can suppress immune system function (i.e. can temporarily shrink the Thymus gland) that can negatively impact one's health. Symptoms that can be seen include:
    - slowed rate of healing (i.e. following a cut or abrasion);
    - an exacerbation of auto-immune disease symptoms;
    - an increased susceptibility to illness (i.e. colds, flu);
    - an increased risk of developing cancer.

4. Memory Impairment - Cortisol, released under stress, can interfere with memory functions. In 1994, in *Why Zebras Don't Get Ulcers*, Robert Sapolsky summarized the impact of stress on memory as:
    - Decreased ability to lay down a memory, to store data in long-term memory or access/recall the memory at a later date. This can involve a decreased utilization of blood sugar by the Hippocampus, which, in turn, can create an energy shortage.
    - Diminished neurotransmitter function. Metaphorically, the "phone lines are down." This can

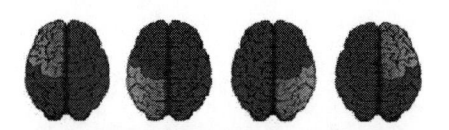

reduce effective neuron communication. The mind becomes muddled and there is often a concomitant reduced ability to concentrate.
- Increased production of free radicals that can actually kill brain cells from within.

Sapolsky's findings, reported in his 1994 book, on stress-induced cortisol impairing memory function, were corroborated in March 2000 in a report released by Dr. James McGaugh, Director of the Center for the Neurobiology of Learning and Memory at the University of California, Irvine. McGaugh said stress-induced cortisol depresses memory for a short period of time. McGaugh's findings explain why when you are exposed to a stressor, such as a job interview, examination, combat or courtroom testimony, you can't remember a lot of things you should remember very well. The connection, of course, is that Falsifying Type over time is a chronic stressor that would continuously produce excess cortisol and thereby impair memory.

5. Altered Brain Chemistry - prolonged Falsification of Type can interfere with hypothalamus and pituitary function that, in turn, can interfere with hormonal balance. This may be appear as:
   - decreased growth hormone;
   - decreased insulin secretion;
   - decreased production of sex hormones (estrogen, progesterone, testosterone);
   - decreased reproduction functions (ovulation, building up of the uterine lining, menstruation);
   - an increase in the production of gluco-corticoids (that can prematurely age the Hippocampus); alteration in the permeability of the blood brain barrier.

For women, these abnormal and imbalanced changes in their brain chemistry tend to produce a variety of symptoms related to their cycle including: headaches, mood swings, worsening PMS, early menopause, lowering of the libido, skipping of periods all together and/or difficulty in conception. What has happened is that the stress in their life (produced by falsifying type) has caused their nervous system to produce mineral corticoids and gluco-corticoids rather than androgens and estrogens – the sex hormones they need to have a normal, healthy, sexually in tune body.

Importantly, other stressors can bring about these same problems; it is just that until Dr. Taylor's 1999 identification of PASS, Falsification of Type was generally an unrecognized, unacknowledged stressor. Women with these problems seeking help did not know and were not told that Falsification of Type was a stressor and that one way to help themselves was to stop Falsifying Type.

6. Diminished Frontal Lobe Functions - prolonged Falsification of Type as a significant stressor can interfere with functions typically associated with the frontal lobes of the cerebrum. Symptoms can include:
   - a decrease in artistic/creative endeavors (i.e. writer's block);
   - a reduced ability to brainstorm options;
   - a reduced ability to select the best option in a critical situation;
   - interference with the ability to make logical/rational decisions;

- increased injuries due to distraction and/or making mistakes;
- slowed speed or diminished clarity of thinking.

7. Discouragement or Depression - prolonged Falsification of Type can lead to the repeated triggering of the Conserve/ Withdraw reaction to stress. This can be especially true for high introverts, although it can be observed in extroverts who, as years go by, continue to perceive a mismatch between who they are as individuals and societal expectations and/or repeated episodes of failure. This can lead to discouragement, especially as fatigue increases, and can contribute to the development of depression or to the exacerbation of existing depression. Estimates suggest that upwards of 20 million individuals in the USA are depressed, 15 percent of whom are suicidal. Prolonged Falsification of Type would appear to be a key factor in at least some of these cases.

8. Self-Esteem Problems - any or all of the other symptoms can contribute to a perceived diminished overall success in life. In turn, this throws one's self-esteem off balance. Problems in this area can appear as low self-esteem or inflated self-esteem or flip back and forth between them. Examples include:
   - low self-esteem problems resulting in an individual taking on victim characteristics and/or trying to be all things to all people;
   - inflated self-esteem problems resulting in an individual becoming defensive quickly as a result of years of invalidation;
   - the individual may swing from one extreme to another. This can be seen when the individual is invalidated professionally, but validated personally with a small group of friends. The resulting dichotomy can be puzzling, unnerving, and even disconcerting as the individual strives (unsuccessfully) to be viewed as successful in both arenas.

So what does it all mean?

That's an excellent and important question. To make sense of what we are learning, it is necessary to understand a little bit about stress and stressors, as Falsification of Type has been identified as a significant stressor. Generally speaking stressors have been found to interact with us in two ways. Part of its impact or effect on us is due to the stressor itself and part of its impact or effect on us is due to our perception of the stressor.

When the stressor is outside us, the accepted formula suggests:
- 20 percent of the effect on us is due to the stressor itself;
- 80 percent of the effect on us is due to our perception of the stressor.

Understanding this formula[16] can be helpful when the stressors are environmental and situational –

---

[16] There seem to be many 80:20 rules. One refers to the way in which people prioritize work and teaches us that 20 percent of the work we have to do accomplishes 80 percent of the results while 80 percent of the work accomplishes only 20 percent of the results. The second 80:20 rule has to do with the oxygen distribution in our brain and states that the body needs 80 percent of the oxygen and the brain needs 20 percent of the oxygen we breathe in to function effectively. This then is the third such rule and has to do with breaking down the impact of a stressor into the stressor itself and our perception of the stressor.

outside us. It helps us learn to value and use re-framing. Earlier in the book, you read about the nurse who managed a physician's temper tantrums by seeing him as a small child. The image that she created of the physician's actual head on a small raging child helped her to not get frightened. Although the image was a Frontal Right metaphor for his behavior, the words she used were at the same time a re-framing. Re-framing is very powerful when the stressor is external. When a stressor is inside us, however, and involves a mismatch between who we are and expectations of society, school, church, and family *and* a non-negotiable and significant misuse of the brain, then re-framing is less helpful. When considering Falsification of Type, we have to re-evaluate the formula for how a stressor impacts us. To say that only 20 percent of the impact is due to the nature of the stressor given its objective impact on our brains is to inflate our capabilities. Falsifying Type has a huge impact on us and will continue to have an impact on us, even when we seek to alter our perception of the situation. This simple truth combined with the fact that almost half of us are Falsifying Type means those seeking to improve their own and others' mental health need to know about, and be prepared to educate others about, Falsification of Type and its costs.

	Frontal Left Thinking	Left Posterior Convexity Sensing	Right Posterior Convexity Feeling	Frontal Right Intuition
WHO'S FALSIFYING TYPE[17]				
Men:	22%	65%	48%	43%
Women:	31%	43%	41%	47%

Education, understanding, empathy, emotional support and re-framing of one's individual experience are powerful psychological tools. In the face of Falsifying Type, however, these tools are basically powerless because the individual spends hours and hours each day in activities that require their brain to work up to 100 times harder and the living of life throws their body systems into distress. As Jung himself said in Psychological Types, the only thing that can make a difference is the individual's re-owning of their preference. Individuals who exhibit symptoms of PASS may be evaluated for possible underlying physiological illness and in the case of PTSD, or Post Traumatic Stress Disorder, for a history of previous trauma. They also need to be evaluated for the presence of prolonged Falsifying Type. **If this is found to be present,** they need to be helped to identify their true preference and strategies that can reduce their **falsification.**

The ideal, of course, is for the individual to stop **Falsifying Type** as soon as possible. In our society, however, this can be easier said than immediately accomplished. In the meanwhile, understanding **prolonged Falsification of Type as a significant stressor** can help individuals deal with it more efficaciously.

---

17 The data in this chart comes from *Falsification of Type Its Jungian and Physiological Foundations & Mental, Emotional and Physiological Costs* by Dr. Benziger, 1995. KBA, Dallas. Page 56.

I am disturbed and a bit confused by your reference to Falsifying Type altering our brain chemistry specifically in a manner that worsens PMS. Could you say more about this?

The key is to understand the link between stress and PMS. Possibly the best book on this subject is *What Your Doctor May Not Tell You About PreMenopause*, by Dr. John R. Lee. Reading this book will help you understand the link and understand that many women, as a result of stress, are having tremendous hormonal imbalances from age thirty on. Once you fully understand this link then it is simple to understand that Falsifying Type is a contributing cause to these problems because Falsifying Type produces stress.

In my own case, I began missing my period as soon as I went to boarding school at age 16. Our family doctor, in 1964, was wise enough to tell me the missing periods were stress induced and could be brought back by my taking tranquilizers. He had me take these for one month to prove his point then took me off them so I would not be using drugs. His understanding of my body and its reaction to stress was helpful and his wise approach to tranquilizers healthy. However, he did not really understand that absent periods were occurring because the stress was causing my brain to produce corticoids rather than estrogen and progesterone. Sadly for me, the stress in my life, including Falsifying Type, caused me to miss my period frequently throughout my 20's, 30's, 40's – worsening the PMS, despite the fact that actual bleeding was often minimal, and often triggering depression. It was all very confusing and no one understood or explained that the stress that was causing my brain to produce so many corticoids was not producing estrogen or progesterone. And that it was the lack of these hormones that was causing me to feel so badly, plagued by both depression and PMS.

Thus far when you've talked about adaption, you've cast it in a negative light. And yet, many people see being flexible and able to adapt as a positive trait. Isn't some adaption positive?

Yes, of course, in some cases, *adaption is positive*. Essentially, there are two kinds of adaption: additive adaption, which is positive; and Falsification of Type or *replacement adaption* that is negative.

For those who have been validated for their natural preference, additive adaption is common. In fact, we've looked at it already in the context of people developing and using their auxiliaries to support their preference rather than replace it. We have been focusing on the negative costs of Falsification of Type simply because many people suffer from it and have no idea what is happening to them and why they are having so much difficulty. Let's look at a story that illustrates how and why additive adaption is positive.

Michael was born with a preference for the Frontal Right. As a young male, whenever he would ask his father, a physician, for permission to take the family car or stay out late, his father would ask him to explain to him why he should allow his son to do these things. Through trial and error, Michael learned that when he answered his father using sound logic, his father's preferred mode, his father gave permission. In fact, one of his clearest recollections from his teen years is of the night when he finally developed an argument that was completely acceptable to his father. On that night, his father responded by saying: "You have given me an answer that demonstrates you know how to think. Now that I know this, you don't need to ask again. You may take the car and stay as late as you decide you want to." What Michael learned from these evening encounters with his father was not that he needed to totally give up his Frontal Right preference, but simply that in particular situations he could be more successful by using his Frontal Left auxiliary. Thus, as Michael matured and entered the job market, he held on to his sense of himself as an intuitive, image-directed thinker, but *added* to it his ability to respond analytically where appropriate. By age 30 he was a bank vice-president earning an excellent income. The fact that the bank was more conservative than he was did not cause him particular problems. Nor did he have trouble handling the analytical, Frontal Left loan decisions he was called upon to make. Since his own sense of himself was so firmly intact, he was able to use the competencies he had developed without conflict. And, when the time was right, he was able to leave the bank and set up a business of his own in which he could use his preference more without creating problems or feeling like a failure. Thus, for Michael, additive adaption, developing and selectively using an auxiliary to support his preference, enabled him to be more successful without diminishing his self-esteem, confusing his sense about what he needed to be happy or severely impacting his health.

Could you please give some additional examples of people who have turned away from their natural preference early in life?

One client with a Right Posterior Convexity preference, Joan, came from a family that owned a drug store. Her story was told earlier as an example of couples with similar dominances marrying. As the store was seen as a family enterprise, everyone in the family helped out from an early age. Joan's job was to work at the soda fountain where she learned from her grandfather the specific procedures for making sodas, floats, shakes, etc. One of the things that were emphasized frequently was the importance of keeping the counter clean by wiping it with a towel after every customer had finished and gone. Working at the soda fountain was fun for Joan because it meant sharing time with her family and helping out, which her strong feeling function delighted in doing. Although she wasn't naturally interested in keeping everything neat and clean, if this was what would bring praise from her grandfather's lips, a clean counter could be managed. In such a contained situation, Joan's use of her Left Posterior Convexity auxiliary to support her natural lead's desire to increase good will and community was actually appropriate. It represented only a few hours of her week and, as well, was done in a situation that allowed her to use her Right Posterior Convexity at the same time to greet and chat with customers.

When Joan and her husband met me, they had been married for 20 years and had two teenage children. They saw themselves and each other as very right-brained. Their children, however, as you may remember saw their mother as a Left Posterior Convexity, since she had almost single-handedly run the entire household and been the one responsible for stability and routines. Given that her husband's original perception of his wife was as neat and orderly, Joan's husband simply left all the Left Posterior Convexity routine tasks for her to do. What also came out was that Joan did this tremendous amount of Left Posterior Convexity work knowing full well it was not her thing. Recall that after years of Falsifying Type, Joan had a massive hemorrhage of the left cerebral hemisphere for no apparent reason at all.

And, although Joan had suffered tremendously by the time we met, this story is one of triumph. She did, after all, stop Falsifying Type and re-owned her natural preference and together, with her family, found ways to get the routine tasks necessary to the running of a four-person family accomplished without depending on Joan's competencies. By doing these things, Joan was validating and honoring her true self.

Joan's experience is not unusual. Many Right Posterior Convexity women, who love home and family and enjoy and excel at nurturing, find them-selves asked to do an ever-increasing amount of Left Posterior Convexity work. Whether they are able to keep the amount of Left Posterior Convexity work contained enough and at the same time hold on to and actively use their Right Posterior Convexity is a question each must face. Many, motivated by their preference to please, find themselves moving more and more out of balance, as their lives shift from one in which the Left Posterior Convexity activities support a still strong Right Posterior Convexity, to one in which the Left Posterior Convexity activities dominate and the Right Posterior Convexity becomes less and less used. This is particularly true when these women are trying to manage all the Left Posterior Convexity tasks alone at home for hours a day. In such situations, the lack of other people around makes it more likely that they are not using their Right Posterior Convexity most of the day. By contrast, if there are other members of the family, aging parents or an uncle in the home all day as well who help with the chores and offer regular opportunities for the woman to relate, nurture or nurse using her Right Posterior Convexity skills, the woman may find she can manage the Left Posterior Convexity load more comfortably.

How do we know if we're Falsifying Type? That is, if we were born with a preference for a specialized type of thinking which we don't identify with now?

That's an excellent question. The simplest answer is to:
1. notice whether your life indicates you've been Falsifying Type;
2. notice whether you truly enjoy doing what you do every day;
3. discover as much as you can about yourself as a young child.

When you have gathered as much information about yourself as a child as you can, stop and review everything you have learned about yourself, while keeping in mind the following question: which mental strength or weakness does this information about me suggest? Usually, by the time you have completed this self-analysis, you will have a pretty good sense of your natural preference. Also, a more detailed set of suggestions that you might find helpful are in the box below. And, if you have not already done so, consider taking the Benziger Thinking Styles Assessment (BTSA) and reviewing your results within a personal coaching session[18].

How To Get In Touch With Original Dominance
- *Remember* your earliest years. How did you like to spend your time? What activities did you

---

18 Information about the BTSA as well as how to take the electronic version of the assessment can be found at www.benziger.org.

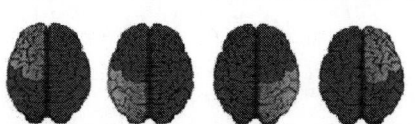

enjoy the most and what about them specifically did you find so enjoyable? How did you fill your leisure time when what you did was totally up to you? Did you prefer to be alone or with others? Who, in particular, did you seem to enjoy the most and what do you think their preference was? In developing a data base about yourself, you might wish to include memories of kindergarten through fifth or sixth grade – what classes or projects you enjoyed and which you disliked and why.

- *Ask* family members what they recall about you as a child.

- *Remember* specifically which *classes you enjoyed* and did well in: were you good at mathematics (Frontal Left) or geometry (Frontal Right) or spelling (Left Posterior Convexity) or art (Frontal Right) or in intermediate or high school foreign languages and singing or playing an instrument (Right Posterior Convexity). Did you enjoy team sports (extraverted) or individual sports (introverted)?

- *Remember* how you did and felt when you had to take *tests in school*. Did you prefer and do best on the true and false tests (Left Posterior Convexity), the multiple-choice tests (Frontal Left) or the essay tests (Frontal Left and Frontal Right)?

- *Look* at the specialized types of thinking you believe might be your actual preference. Identify the activities and tasks you do, which rely heavily on each type of thinking. Then consider while doing those things, are you energized and happy, feeling comfortable and satisfied? If you enjoy the tasks and are energized by the tasks regardless of the setting, the chances are greater that these are natural strengths. If instead you feel slowed and blah either during or after completing a task, the chances are greater that this area is not your preference, but rather an area of learned competency.

- *Look* at the tasks above again, but this time consider whether how you feel when doing each task is because of the task itself (the type of thinking being used) or the fact that you are with others in a noisy, busy or competitive place (an extraverted setting) or alone in a quiet non-competitive place (an introverted setting)?

What do you say to a 45 year old adult who realizes she abandoned her preference as a kid, and wants to re-own it now?

It is a good deal easier to re-own a type of thinking than to develop a type of thinking you have never used. Generally, all one needs to do to re-own any type of thinking is to follow the instructions for developing and strengthening competencies given in the next chapter.

There is, however, another consideration. When we as adults approach re-owning our area of childhood preference, we do so *in context*. Because we are now also a spouse, parent and worker we may run into some resistance from our family, friends or colleagues. If we have been acting like a good Left

Posterior Convexity doing all the family chores and bills, we can expect that our spouse has a vested interest in having us continue to do these. Indeed, if we had begun to Falsify Type before we met them (as happened with Joan), it is probable that what originally attracted our spouse to us was the belief, based on our behaviors, that we were a Left Posterior Convexity thinker who would attend to all the details of their lives. In such cases, special attention will need to be given to helping those we live and work with to accept our new identity and to minimize their resistance.

Geri, a Frontal Right, offers an example of how this happens. Over the years she Falsified Type by replacing her preference with first one auxiliary and then both. As a young woman to be accepted as a female, she adopted and developed a wide range of Right Posterior Convexity feeling skills. Later, as a professional, she adopted and added to her falsified pattern Frontal Left skills. Her resulting Frontal Left/Right Posterior Convexity pattern worked well in that she used her Frontal Left at work and her Right Posterior Convexity at home. The problem was neither type of thinking was her preference. When Geri realized that her feelings of emptiness and her lack of self-confidence came from the fact that she had rejected her natural preference early in life, she opted to stop Falsifying Type and re-own her Frontal Right preference. Geri's teenage daughter was openly antagonistic to Geri's efforts to change, going out of her way to criticize her mother for not trying to be the Right Posterior Convexity nurturer the daughter wanted her to be. To the daughter, it was of no importance that trying to be Right Posterior Convexity was making her mother miserable. It was the way mothers were supposed to be and that was that. One can only hope that as Geri's daughter matures her concept of what it means to be a mother will become more flexible. For, in reality, mothers come in all shapes, sizes and preferences.

You mention that those who Falsify Type at an early age go through a mid-life crisis. How does this relate to the crisis identified by Gail Sheehy in *Passages*?

This is the same crisis simply described from a different perspective.

Not everyone experiences a mid-life crisis. What would you say about these people?

They probably didn't abandon their preference and subsequently haven't been Falsifying Type for years. As already noted, these people enjoy a more stable life and experience that they describe as a mid-life spread. This spread is motivated by a desire to grow and expand, but lacks the urgency of a mid-life crisis.

You mention Sheehy's *Passages*. What about her *Pathfinders*? Is there any particular preference that correlates with being a pathfinder?

Given the way in which Sheehy used *Pathfinders* as another name for the creative geniuses of life, it is probable that all Pathfinders have a preference in the innovative, change-making Frontal Right supported by at least a moderate competency in one auxiliary. If their auxiliary is in the Frontal Left, they may be seen as a pathfinder in science or business. If their auxiliary is in the Right Posterior

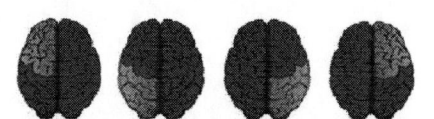

Convexity, they are more likely to be found developing new and better, ecologically sensitive ways for people and/or living organisms to live together.

As long as we are looking at other books and authors, what is your opinion of Leonard Shlain's 1998 book *The Alphabet Versus the Goddess: The Conflict Between Word and Image?*

Shlain's thesis is an important one. Namely that since the advent of wide spread literacy with the invention of the printing press about 400 years ago, modern civilizations have required those who read to learn to use the left hemisphere. Robert K. Logan, in *The Alphabet Effect: The Impact of the Phonetic Alphabet on the Development of Western Civilization*, presented a very similar thesis equally powerfully in 1986. According to Logan, the printing press only reinforces what the phonetic alphabet had put in place – namely the requirement that an educated person use the Posterior or Left Posterior Convexity. Both authors offer powerful arguments.

- the left-brained individual does not need to adapt to read and write and think using the phonetic alphabet and printed word; but
- the right-brained individual with a preference in the Frontal Right or Right Posterior Convexity must adapt to read, write and learn using the phonetic alphabet and printed word.

These implications are significant because it means that people with these gifts live with more internal, physiological stress than had been realized. Again, it suggests those identified here as at risk may be further stressed out trying to participate as responsible, literate members of society.

You talk about the importance of developing one's auxiliaries. Could you give us an example of someone who has managed to develop and integrate both of his auxiliaries?

A physician friend selected hematology as his specialty in medical school. Once out of medical school, he went to work as a researcher at a large hospital connected with a well-known medical school. For about five years, he taught and did his research quite happily, developing an excellent reputation as he did so. After all, he was a highly educated man using both frontal modes. He had a Frontal Right preference he used, supported by a Frontal Left auxiliary. Life was good.

One day he learned his mother had cancer and for several agonizing months, he watched her become increasingly ill. When she finally died, our friend was devastated. He was an expert in cancer research trying to find cures for the dreaded disease and yet for all his expertise, he had been powerless to help his mother in any meaningful way during her final months and weeks. The existential and spiritual pain he felt motivated him to redirect his life and career. He began practicing actively as an oncologist and working directly with cancer patients and their families in hospice settings.

Because of his motivation, and because the Right Posterior Convexity was actually his second auxiliary, he managed to develop a real competency in caring and nurturing – the skills demanded by his new career focus. Within a few years he had developed a reputation as one of the finest oncologists in the

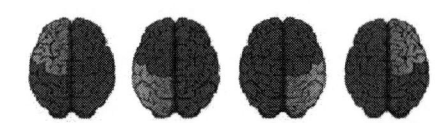

Los Angeles area. Even more importantly he felt better about himself. During this phase, he essentially stopped using his Frontal Left auxiliary. In other words, he did not become a Frontal Right using both auxiliaries but one who had swapped one auxiliary for the other. As well, later on in this phase, his very heavy hospice patient load forced him to Falsify Type functioning more as a Right Posterior Convexity with a Frontal Right auxiliary than as a Frontal Right with a Right Posterior Convexity auxiliary.

When I last spoke with him, he was beginning a third phase of his career, leading a group of professionals, at the hospital with which he was affiliated, to develop new solutions for some of the pressing organizational and delivery problems facing health care. The new task was much more Frontal, requiring skill in logical and spatial-intuitive thinking. What was most interesting was that as the months passed and he became more and more engrossed in this new direction he was able to observe: "My old energy is back. I am excited and alive." As you now appreciate, what he was noticing is the natural and normal result of being smart and doing a task that matches his natural preference.

Upon reflection, he realized that during the decade he had been working full time with oncology patients, developing and exercising his auxiliary in his Right Posterior Convexity feeling function as much as possible, he had never felt the surge of energy and natural high using his feeling skills that comes from doing what you are physiologically built to do. On rethinking his experiences, the following is likely: when he first began to get into oncology and hospice everything was new to him as everything is new to the ER physician during the first few years. Thus, it is likely that during the first few years of the decade he focused on hospice work, this Frontal Right physician was using his preference to get a comprehensive overview of the field, understand how things were done and what worked and didn't work. Even creating conceptual and theoretical links between the nurturing and connecting skills he was developing and other things that he knew about the human mind-body system. After the first few years, the novelty would have worn off and he, like the ER physician, would have found himself using his preference less and less and his auxiliary more and more. In other words, over time he would have shifted from using his auxiliary to support his preference to using his auxiliary exclusively.

What is important is that he chose to grow and develop to be a more complete person. When, months later, he phoned to tell me how he was doing, I was deeply moved that after considering an offer to go into full-time management, he had decided against it. He would work in management, but he wanted to maintain his oncology practice, too. Seemingly, he understands he has three distinct sets of competencies – one in his preference and two in his two auxiliaries – and that his life is better when he uses all three, allowing each to do the things it does best. His first auxiliary, the Frontal Left, makes him a top-notch researcher. His secondary auxiliary, the Right Posterior Convexity, serves him well as a spouse, father, grandfather, friend etc. It is fair to say he has significantly integrated his feeling function.

In the example you just cited, the man's motivation to develop his Right Posterior Convexity

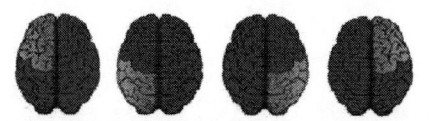

came from the trauma surrounding his mother's death. Do traumatic events generally play a key role in a person's decision to develop an auxiliary?

Not always. Many people who have grown up with both adequate validation and opportunity in their preference move naturally in mid-life to explore their second auxiliary. Where trauma seems to play a key role is when the traumatic event highlights the area of weakness and the person is still too young to have already developed their second auxiliary. The physician was in his early thirties when his mother died of cancer and the specific nature of the trauma was such that had he already developed his Right Posterior Convexity, he would have been able to respond more meaningfully and more satisfactorily to his mother's needs. Her death simply made him painfully aware of an area of personal weakness.

Another traumatic event that often prompts the development of an auxiliary is divorce. Typically, when a couple divorces, each person becomes painfully aware of the things that the other person handled, which they themselves either never knew or no longer know how to manage. It is not uncommon, following a separation, for a man unskilled in making friends and getting along with people to read widely in that area and even take evening classes in communications or for a recently divorced woman, inept at the mechanical work her husband had always handled, to take a class in automotive repair or electrical wiring. Each of these acts helps the recently divorced person gain a sense of balance and wholeness, a sense that although alone they can cope effectively. Each also reflects an opening or expanding into a heretofore undeveloped or weak mental mode.

What happens if a person ignores one of their non-dominant functions – one of their auxiliaries, or their weakness?

As you know, Carl Jung recognized that we all have a natural weakness – the diagonal mode from our preference – that he termed our *inferior* or *shadow function*. According to Jung, ignoring the shadow function can be dangerous. A person with an undeveloped Right Posterior Convexity/feeling function may tend to make enemies, or at best not make friends, and tend to repress rather than process their hurt and rage over life events such as rejection by a lover or the death of a loved one. A person with an undeveloped Left Posterior Convexity routine function will predictably get into trouble with details, suffering because a bill wasn't paid or a clause in the contract wasn't noticed. Such a person will have difficulty keeping track of the papers that seem to accumulate in life: tax forms, bank statements, appliance warranties. The person with an undeveloped Frontal Left/analytic function will have tremendous difficulty when they have to make difficult decisions. And the person with an undeveloped intuitive function will tend to take fewer and fewer risks as they age, staying closer and closer to home and the routines they established early in life.

Although these problems may not appear so dreadful, Jung's observation was that the longer a function was ignored, the more troublesome it became. The following two examples will serve to illustrate how right he was.

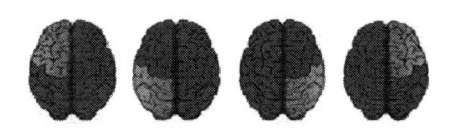

The first is of a man with a natural Frontal Left preference and an almost total avoidance of the Right Posterior Convexity. As a youth the effects of this weakness were barely noticeable, visible only in the fact that he had few friends and that those he had were limited to his social circle and had simply been a part of his life for years. Then, as a young man he was sent to Viet Nam as a captain. Each day he would decide whom to send out where and each night he would sit and write the pro forma letters to the parents of the men who had been killed in action. When he returned from Viet Nam, he would talk with no one about what had happened and how he felt. He simply went to work day after day and long into the nights at his uncle's legal firm, accruing accolades by the dozen for his excellence in the profession. Throughout this time he did not date. Then his father died and he was left to live alone in the house he had been raised in. And still he spoke to no one. Ten years later, now an even wealthier and more successful lawyer, he began dating a woman he had met several times at the home of childhood friends. But things did not go smoothly. She suggested they try going together to see a therapist she knew. He went twice and reported it was the single most frightening thing he had done in his life. As sometimes happens, even with the help of a therapist, they were not able to resolve their differences. Five years later he was still single and not dating. When discussing his life with a friend of many years he commented: "My feelings are like Pandora's box. I don't want to open the box. I cannot cope with it. I prefer to live as I am." Such a story is heart-rending. It bespeaks of a terrible waste of human life and energy. Yet it is actually quite typical of those who cannot face developing their shadow function.

Another example is less tragic but equally illustrative of the impact ignoring a weakness can have over time. This is the story of a Frontal Right woman who had successfully developed and integrated both of her auxiliaries but continued to deny her inferior function, the Left Posterior Convexity. The weakness began to show up early in her life as a tendency to spell poorly (even though she had a large vocabulary) and a tendency to make addition and subtraction errors (even though she liked math and understood calculus). In graduate school the principle effect of her weakness seems to have been her insistence in doing a major paper and taking an extra three-credit course instead of doing a thesis. Her understanding of the difference between the thesis and the major paper was that the thesis had to be typed correctly according to a form, with all references noted in footnotes and with a bibliography, but that the major paper required much less procedural correctness. During her early career, her lack of tolerance for procedure began to rear its head as she grew resentful of all the bureaucratic procedures she was supposed to follow. Then for a few years things seemed to improve. She was awarded a personal secretary whose natural lead in the Left Posterior Convexity enabled her to attend to the details of report writing (spelling correctly and catching typos) and accounting (adding correctly), which came so hard for her. Soon, however, her entrepreneurial tendencies took hold. She opened a business of her own and because she was operating on a shoestring, the ultimate responsibility for attending to the details returned to her. The tales of woe were amusing, if costly. In the first few years her lack of attention to detail and lack of tolerance for forms meant that she did not see that all clients were sent contracts to sign, which on occasion resulted in a client canceling at the last minute. It also meant that when a client or colleague said: "Oh, we don't need a contract, a hand shake is enough," she went along with their suggestion, which ultimately led to two major disagreements as to what exactly she was supposed to do for each and for how much money. Later when she moved her office to a larger location, this same weakness cost her again when she failed to realize that although she had gotten bids from four moving companies and a second bid from the lowest in order to confirm its accuracy, the bids were in no way binding, and she was, therefore, legally bound to pay the movers the full moving bill (which amounted to 300 percent of their estimate). It would be easy for her to accuse others and life of being unfair, but in truth, the beginning of the problem lies in her own preference. If, and when, she can use her Left Posterior Convexity routine function when it is called for, she will find many of the complications in her life disappear.

An important step for anyone having difficulty as a result of their inferior or weakest function is to recognize and begin to value its contributions to life. If a person can do this, they can choose to enlist help from others who have a preference for that function or type of thinking. This teaming up with a complementary brain, which has been identified as appropriate in both work and marriage, is just as important for our personal inner growth.

I'm interested in the work of Jean Piaget, who believed children develop certain mental capacities at a specific age when their hormones and physiology open the door. Is there other evidence to suggest that our access to specific types of thinking is physiologically orchestrated?

That's an excellent question. Although there is not enough evidence to say you are 100 percent correct, there are scattered bits of information, which taken together, point towards some such phenomenon. And although what is known is mostly about children, it is worth reviewing.

- According to Jean Piaget, there are physiological windows in all children, from age two through age six, when the child is geared to acquire language. The window to which he refers involves only the Left Posterior Convexity (vocabulary) and probably the Frontal Left (language structure). During the time the window is open, the child can pick up one, two, three and possibly more languages. The key is regular exposure and the opportunity to use the language. After this window closes, due to a shift in the biochemistry, the learning of a new language becomes markedly more difficult. This dove-tails with other research that suggests that foreign languages learned in high school (when the window is closed) are not learned in the left where our native language is learned but rather in or by the Right Posterior Convexity, which learns by picking up and matching rhythms.

- Another piece of this puzzle comes from the work of Joseph Chilton Pierce, *The Magical Child*, who believes reading should not be taught prior to the age of eleven or twelve. If he is correct, it may be because reading involves the ability to think conceptually which requires both frontal lobes. Moving back and forth between the left and right frontal lobes is not easy to do until the portion of our corpus callosum, which connects these two areas, has begun to mature. This happens with the onset of puberty. For female children this may happen as early as age of six or seven. For male children it occurs somewhat later, around the age of eight or nine. Whether or not Chilton Pierce is correct about reading, this doorway to conceptual thinking and adulthood is clearly physiologically orchestrated.

- Another possible window has been identified by studies of young babies who seem to recognize the human smile (and frown) before they can see and recognize anything else. This ability is located in the Right Posterior Convexity. Is this early recognition orchestrated by physiology to improve the baby's chances of surviving?

- Another window occurs in women who give birth to their child without being cut or drugged. Within minutes of the birth, a neurochemical shift occurs that seems to boost the new mother's access to the Right Posterior Convexity where nurturing is housed. The studies, done by midwives, indicate that God and Nature want every woman to be a good mother even if she doesn't have a natural preference in the Right Posterior Convexity.

- Finally, another window occurs shortly before death, again in cases of natural death. As the brain dies, from front to back, in the final hours or sometimes days, the dying person experiences an increased activity in the Right Posterior Convexity, again the area of the brain that produces and values spiritual experiences. This may explain the commonly reported ability of dying people to see and communicate with angels and those who have already died. It is a beautiful example of the Grace of God for it guarantees each person that although they must die they need not fear death. When seeing and communicating with angels, people report they feel loved and safe. All fear is gone.

Taken together these facts begin to form a strong if not fully developed argument for a series of physiological triggers that might assist people in walking around their medicine wheel. It is highly likely some such system exists as an overlay to the basic theory and structure of brain dominance.

One final question, there are three positive experience-based concepts that people value: direction, integrity and joy. How does Falsification of Type relate to each of these?

Having a sense of direction and being self-motivated is a wonderful human trait. Those who have it seem to bring energy with them and enliven their world. Is this coveted experience linked to Falsification of Type? Most certainly. As John Giannini reminds us in his book The *Compass of the Soul*, only when we are living true to type – true to that aspect of our self that expresses itself in our natural lead function as our preference, is our sense of direction solid and dependable as well as energizing. This is characterized by the reality of *flow*, identified by Mihaly Csikszentmihalyi: "The optimal experience of *flow* is when psychic energy flows effortlessly. This occurs when the information that keeps coming into our awareness is congruent with our goals, working at top performance the experience is so enthralling" (p.39). This is direction and motivation at its finest – self-motivating, self-rewarding structure. As such those Falsifying Type are more likely to be lacking in coherent direction.

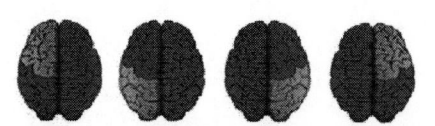

In her related work on *Sacred Contracts Awakening Your Divine Potential*, Caroline Myss, observes that finding things we enjoy is key to living the life. Identifying the archetypes that, according to Myss, are part of our archetypal wheel not surprisingly brings forth archetypes that match and embody our natural preference and the way in which we want and need to use that preference.

With respect to integrity, I am reminded of John Beebe's observation in his very powerful and helpful book *Integrity In Depth*, 1992. "Symptoms of integrity go by clinical names like anxiety, depression, … and seem to be founded in what Jung called a *justified doubt in oneself*" (p36). It puts these symptoms in, I feel, the proper perspective: they are trying to help us save ourselves by drawing attention to the fact we have abandoned ourselves and that we are in trouble because we have been Falsifying Type rather than living and being true to ourselves.

And, joy, that uplifting energy that opens the door for each of us to do more and be more, to be generous of spirit because we are ourselves overflowing. There is certainly a link for those who Falsify Type rarely if ever know joy. *In Joy, Inspiration and Hope*, 1991, Verena Kast reminds us an autobiography of joy (e.g. our own recollections of when and where we experienced joy) may be helpful in understanding ourselves. Kast is correct in this, for when we are in a situation that uses our natural lead – our preference, in an environment that matches and honors our introversion/extraversion, we are most likely to experience *flow* and therewith joy.

Summary

Our mental preference affects us throughout our lifetime. Most especially, it affects our self-esteem and success. When our natural mental preference is rejected or shamed, our self-esteem is at risk. If and when this occurs, many of us have a tendency to Falsify Type in order to fit in and receive the validation we need. Unfortunately Falsifying Type causes more problems than it solves. Falsifying Type leads to:
- chronic low self-esteem, as the acceptance and validation we receive are for a false *self*, not us;
- the experience of PASS;
- and a mid-life crisis unless or until we re-embrace, use and validate our original and natural mental preference.

Thus, modern neuroscience would echo the wisdom of the ages. To live a vibrant life, to thrive, *know thy self and to thy own self be true*. Indeed, living in balance, over center and True to Type, could be the best way to apply the principles of Integrative Medicine as explained by Dr. Edward Taub, the founder of Integrative Medicine, University of California, Irvine. According to Taub "The human body is an energy system and energy systems function optimally with efficient fuel. Homeostasis keeps it together. Disruption of that energy, by whatever means, is what we call disease."[19] Falsifying Type is, as we now know, a huge disruption of our energy system.

And, yet, at the same time, for long-term survival and success we must learn to appreciate and use those types of thinking in an empowering yet safe way. The key to pulling off this magic trick is to not forget your true preference while learning and using non-preferred competencies. For this reason, it is

---

19 The quote is from a foreword Dr. Taub wrote to Fit for Life by Harvey and Marilyn Diamond. Warner Books, New York 1985. Page xiv.

always wiser to learn about, develop and validate your natural lead prior to developing competencies in other specialized types of thinking.

With these pointers in mind, in the next chapter, let's look at ways you can use your whole brain by developing competencies in other types of thinking and learning to communicate clearly and effectively with others.

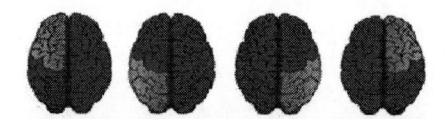

Chapter 9: Developing Competencies

Although both Carl Jung and the Native American Plains Indians believed each of us is born with only one preference that would always be who we are, both also believed the task of life is to grow, to travel around the medicine wheel, to accept and develop all four specialized types of thinking.

▲▲ Competencies

And, while it is true that we can't change our preference, we can develop competencies in our non-preferred modes. This is because competency in any mode develops naturally as a result of repeated usage. The more you use a given mode and the more often you actually participate in activities that require that kind of thinking, the more competency you are likely to acquire. Unfortunately, this process takes time and, when working in an area of non-preference, may be fatiguing and stressful. Consequently, you may be tempted to abandon the effort early on. If you want to increase your ability to use and depend on a non-preferred mode, you will have to resist the temptation to quit. Additionally, when developing new competencies, withhold judgment about how you're doing, give yourself permission to feel dumb and make mistakes and give yourself plenty of time in which to succeed. Having a *tolerant and supportive attitude towards yourself* while working to develop a competency in a non-preferred type of thinking is the first and most important step towards achieving your goal. Once you have adopted the appropriate attitude, try using the following plan.

▲▲4-Step Plan for Competency Development

1. **Find a role model or mentor** who has a preference for the specialized type of thinking you want to develop and begin hanging out with them. Ask them to talk about their thinking. Have them share with you their approach to problem-solving and decision-making. Get them to talk about their interests, values and worldview. Then practice seeing the world through their eyes. To the best of your ability, see things as they see them. Use the Perspectives Chart in the next few pages to help you select the best person.

2. **Use the quadrant** you want to develop by involving yourself in a variety of activities that depend on it. See the *Activities for Developing Competencies* following the Perspectives Chart for ideas on what to do.

3. **Read** material that would interest someone with a natural preference in the specialized type of thinking you are seeking to develop. This means material that is about something that is generally of high interest to that type of thinking and people with a natural lead in that mode. And it means material written in a way that the mode itself readily understands. (See the suggested readings later in this chapter.)

4. **Find a way to become a contributing member to a Whole Brain Team**. Your participation will enable you to fully see and appreciate the contribution of your non-preferred modes.

Questions and Answers

The general strategy sounds great. But how do I find a quadrant expert? How do I know the person actually has strength in the type of thinking I want to develop?

Finding a mentor or advisor demands you recognize the behaviors characteristic of the specialized type of thinking you want to develop. To develop a clear picture of the person you want as a mentor, read the Perspectives Chart. If you are still uncertain, re-read the section in Chapter 3 describing that type of thinking.

A Perspectives Chart for Recognizing the Brains Around You

LEFT POSTERIOR CONVEXITIES

Descriptors:	Cautious, conservative, detailed, procedural, sequential
Skills:	Holding to deadlines and schedules, monitoring, performing routine or procedural tasks, whether operational or administrative, proof-reading
Typical Phrases:	Let's go by the book, look in the procedures manual, it's better to play it safe, law and order are important, we've always done it this way, there's no reason to change, it's important to establish good habits, self-discipline, what's the right sequence or order?
Self-Perception:	Industrious, productive, reliable, thorough, dependable
As Seen By Others:	Boring, grinds out the task, stuck in the mud

RIGHT POSTERIOR CONVEXITIES

Descriptors:	Musical, rhythmical, sensitive to nonverbal behaviors, makes eye contact, speaks with their eyes, spiritual, intuitive about people
Skills	Bridging, encouraging, harmonizing, nurturing, teaching, welcoming, writing personal notes and letters
Typical Phrases:	Caring, family, human spirit, participation, meaningful, personal growth, sharing, teamwork
Self Perception:	Deeply caring, concerned person (if extraverted), a deep-feeling person (if introverted)
As Seen By Others:	A non-stop talker, a soft-touch, touchy-feely

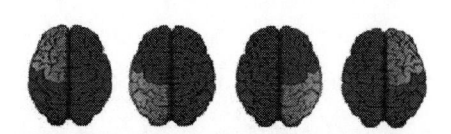

A Perspectives Chart
for Recognizing the Brains Around You

FRONTAL RIGHTS

Descriptors: Artistic, creative, expressive, holistic, intuitive, innovative, spatial, synthesizing, dreaming, metaphoric, pattern sensitive, sees the biggest picture, is a stacker and/or doodler

Skills: Creative problem-solving, design, making change, seeing the big picture, seeing the trends and synthesizing ideas and patterns, discovering, inventing, innovating (if extraverted)

Typical Phrases: Conceptual block-busting, being on the cutting edge, playing with an idea, finding something new, synergistic, all-encompassing, systems

Self Perception: A visionary leader (if extraverted), a visionary thinker (if introverted)

As Seen By Others: A space cadet with his head in the clouds, a dreamer, unfocused, a fool

FRONTAL LEFTS

Descriptors: Analytical, decisive, directing, evaluating, factual, logical, mathematical, quantitative, precise

Skills: Decision-making, precision, weighing and measuring, evaluating, prioritizing, calculating, negotiating, financial problem-solving, technical problem-solving, functional and structural analysis, using precision tools

Typical Phrases: Understanding the key factors, doing a critical analysis, knowing the bottom line, breaking it down or taking it apart, using leverage, weighing all the variables, maximizing the Return on Investment (ROI)

Self Perception: A strong, decisive leader (if extraverted), an expert resource (if introverted)

As Seen By Others: Critical, unemotional and uncaring, power-focused, calculating and manipulative, hard, cool, distant, intelligent (if introverted)

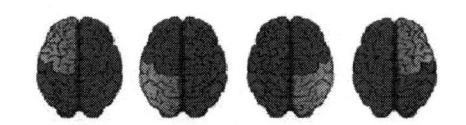

OK. Now, suppose I have found a mentor and have been hanging out with him or her, learning by osmosis. What about the second step – doing things that require me to actively use the type of thinking I want to develop? Can you give us some suggestions for developing each type of thinking?

The following lists of activities for developing competencies in each of the modes should provide you with some ideas.

▲▲ Activities For Developing Competencies

To develop competencies in the **Left Posterior Convexity:** begin valuing forms, planning and organization, along with brown, dark gray or black (colorless) objects that are solid and square and have a function then. Then continue by doing several of the following.

- Select an activity that you really want to do (because it uses your preference and matches your introverted or extraverted needs), then figure out how you could make time to do it by doing something else that you *have to do* more efficiently. Create a routine for doing the have to, and do it regularly, using the time you save to enjoy the want to.

- Identify a luxury, something under $1000, that you want to buy, but for which you do not have the spare cash. Next, make a personal budget that will save you $5, $10 or $20 a week. Then follow the budget, being certain to spend the money you save on the luxury you selected.

- Make a deal with your partner that if you do certain housework on a routine-basis (i.e. every Saturday morning you do laundry or every evening you do dishes before relaxing for the evening) you'll get an extra long hug and cuddle from him/her each time.

- Make a list of your most frequently purchased groceries, toiletries and household cleaning materials, make 20 copies of the list and keep one on your refrigerator at all times. Whenever something is almost out, go to the refrigerator and circle. Then, once a week or whenever you go shopping, take the current list from the refrigerator door. After several weeks, notice whether you have fewer occurrences of getting to the grocery store and wondering what else it was you wanted.

- Go through your home and look for things that would be more helpful if they were ordered, alphabetized or organized, then once a week choose one and organize it. Find and alphabetize your recipes; label and alphabetize all the manuals for your appliances, sound system, TV, computers; sort the hand tools, putting them in boxes or drawers that make them available.

The above suggestions are all opportunities to value and use routine thinking for its efficiency. Once you are more receptive to this contribution of the Left Posterior Convexity, you can begin to develop your appreciation for its relationship with details, its respect for details and its ability to focus on and take care of the details in life.

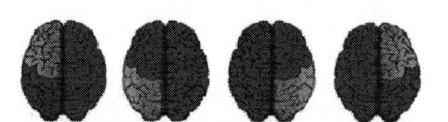

- Go through your home, making a list of the little tasks you've been meaning to get around to, i.e. a broken latch, a squeaky door, a pile of papers needing to be sorted and filed. Choose one and take care of it immediately. Then, notice how you feel having taken care of that problem – your relief, sense of increased safety, delight or pride.

To develop competencies in the **Right Posterior Convexity**: begin valuing feeling, body responses and intuitions about people, along with bright red, yellow, blue and green, colorful circular, spherical or egg-shaped objects, which help you connect with others or harmonize. Then continue by doing several of the following.

- Keep a daily journal of your feelings.
- Practice observing other's non-verbal communication.
- Listen to rhythmic music and move your body with the beat.
- Practice sharing your feelings regularly with a friend you trust.
- Practice making eye contact when you are sharing your feelings.
- Take an acting class.
- Join a choir or singing group.
- Practice harmonizing the colors in furniture in one room.
- Practice harmonizing the colors in your clothes by combining.
- Play with children and let them direct the play/game.
- Take a Feldenkreis movement class or massage workshop.
- Collect natural objects (shells, rocks, pinecones).
- Then, use several to remind you of special people and experiences.
- Get and give regular massages.
- Take a Reiki class and learn to heal with touch.
- Experience your spirituality in a prayer circle.
- Get and give 10 hugs per day.

Notice that the suggestions for the Right Posterior Convexity are not as detailed as those for the Left Posterior Convexity. That's because this type of thinking isn't as detailed as the Left Posterior Convexity. You don't have to perform an entire routine. What is important, when developing the Right Posterior Convexity, is to stay with your feelings about the harmony in your environment – is it present and real? Or, is it missing? What might you do to increase the harmony in your environment? Experiment until you actually feel that something is in harmony. Not in order, but in harmony.

To develop competencies in the **Frontal Right:** begin valuing spontaneity, creativity and intuitive thinking, spirals that are open and dynamic, and very large work surfaces and ivory or pastel walls which invite you to create your own reality and be different. Then, continue, by doing several of the following.

- Create and use metaphoric descriptions for people, things or relationships.
- Design a personal symbol, mask or logo using symbolic shapes, forms and materials. Then explain

its meaning to someone else.
- Daydream.
- Take 300 photographs just to see what happens.
- Invent a gourmet dish and eat it!
- Go for an adventure in a part of town you don't know, consciously entering at least two parks, streets, paths or alleys that strike you as unpromising to see if you can discover something thought provoking or idea-generating in each.
- Keep a diary of your dreams and work with someone to interpret or analyze their symbols and symbolic content.
- Go to the library and select 7-10 books about things you know virtually nothing about. Bring them home. Then, each day open and read a different book. Open the book randomly, scanning for less than a minute, then read three pages in the book. At the end of the week notice what you've learned from reading in this manner. Has anything you've read unexpectedly helped you or shed light on something else in your life?
- Do the same type of exercise using a search engine to find and download 7-10 articles about things you know nothing about.
- Attend a Frontal Right Coaching and Skill Training Weekend[20].

To develop competencies in the **Frontal Left:** begin valuing facts, analysis and rational thinking, along with black (colorless) objects which are highly effective, precision tools, which you use to excel in solving some kind of problem - communicating, calculating, nailing something down. Then:

- Take a logic or debate class.
- Practice prioritizing using rational reasons rather than feelings. Remember, you can prioritize anything, even your grocery list!
- Play logic games or chess.
- Find out how one of your home appliances works.
- Become active in an investment club.
- Take an auto repair class.
- Learn to program a personal computer.
- Play devil's advocate in the next group discussion.
- Analyze an intuitive decision for rational components.
- Write critical reviews of your favorite books, movies and radio or television shows.
- Describe an important project entirely in quantitative terms (using numbers).
- State your current goals and objectives in one short paragraph (1/2 page maximum).
- Learn how to use tools and measure precisely.

Now you know the kinds of things you can do to develop a non-preferred type of thinking. Remember, when actually choosing an activity, unless you have been using your preference and both your auxiliaries for years, it is best to develop or further develop one of your auxiliaries rather than your greatest weakness.

This sounds wonderful. But I've tried developing competencies outside my preference and all

---

20 For more information go to Dr. Benziger's web site www.benziger.org

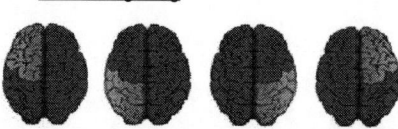

that happens is I get upset, angry and frustrated. How can I succeed at developing the new skills I've selected?

Actually, almost everyone experiences these negative emotions when they start to develop a type of thinking other than their preference. Remember, these other types of thinking are all naturally highly inefficient. That means using them is hard work. All the same, the following 7-Step Success Strategy will help you.

▲▲ 7-Step Success Strategy

1. Select two activities that require the use of one of your non-preferred areas. The activities you select should both use the same non-preferred area. Pushing or pulling yourself in too many directions at once can be more confusing and frustrating than conducive to growth.

2. Spend time thinking about the activities you have selected. Why do you want to learn to do these things? Make a list of all the positive benefits. Then, make another list of all the difficulties you have had in the past few years because you have not known how to do these two things.

3. Determine what stage props you will need in order to learn or practice these activities. See the suggestions for stage props in the next few pages.

4. If you have to buy the props, buy all the necessary stage props and don't scrimp when you do so. If you need something, buy it (even if it does cost more than you usually spend).

5. Create a space just for these activities and props that reflects or speaks to the specialized type of thinking you have elected to develop and *avoids* stimulating other types of thinking.

6. Practice the activities you've elected to develop. It is best if you practice daily and at the same time every day. It is also best not to schedule more than two hours on any given day.

7. Finally, remember that although you are learning to develop a new skill, you need to continue validating yourself for your preference. So, whenever possible, *follow each competency practice session with an activity that uses your natural preference.*

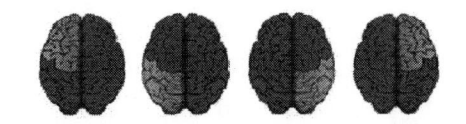

You mentioned stage props when talking about our childhood environments and again here in the Strategy for Success. What do you mean by stage props?

Stage props are those objects or tools that stimulate the area of the brain and functionally specialized type of thinking you wish to strengthen, or alternatively turn down parts of the brain that might interfere with the type of thinking you are attempting to stimulate. Hot pink speaks to the Right Posterior Convexity. It is colorful. And, it is useful when you want to use either right mode, as it tends to tell the Frontal Left that nothing important is happening, which in turn causes the Frontal Left to turn itself down to idle. Here are examples of stage props and how you might use them.

POSSIBLE STAGE PROPS

For the Left Posterior Convexity
Create a very organized space decorated in subdued tones, possibly two-toned (white and brown or grey) striped or checked wallpaper with:
- A filing cabinet with empty files to put things in
- A computer or word processor
- An accounts ledger and accounting software
- Other machines that are productive and efficient – the specific machines you use will depend on where you want to develop your Left Posterior Convexity. Remember, many home cleaning and cooking machines are designed to do tasks efficiently and have different cycles and tools to be used for different jobs. Home office machines offer the same opportunity. Getting familiar with all the machines you own and how to use them and reading the instruction manual for each is a terrific way to grow your appreciation for the Left Posterior Convexity.
- A calendar
- A timer
- A *Pert Chart*
- A *To Do List*
- A dictionary
- Procedures manuals
- Instructions manuals
- How-to books
- A daily hour-by-hour schedule
- A desk set with containers for paper clips, pencils...
- Rectangular no-nonsense furniture
- **Marching music.**

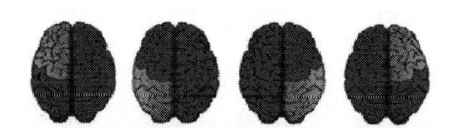

POSSIBLE STAGE PROPS

For the Right Posterior Convexity
Create a sense of abundance or the cluttered effect decorating in bright happy colors possibly with wallpaper that has small flowers or hearts or circles on it with:

    Seashells, pinecones, seed pods
    Green plants and fresh flowers
    Photographs of your family
    Photographs of smiling people
    Paper with crayons or markers of many colors
    A fragrance source that stimulates positive feelings for you (incense, candles, scented potpourri)
    Comfortable chairs with an afghan or blanket
    Inspirational books (with pictures): *Jonathan Livingston Seagull, the Bible, The Prophet, Gift From the Sea*
    A book of your favorite poetry
    Clay with which you can play
    Something connecting to children or infants (a child's drawing, their baby shoes)
    A favorite, very soft stuffed animal
    Ethnic or folk art, Native American, Mexican
    Lots of personal mementoes
    Your high school yearbook
    Gifts from loved ones
    Rhythmical music as well as
    Natural sounds: waterfalls, the sea, rain falling, a breeze blowing...

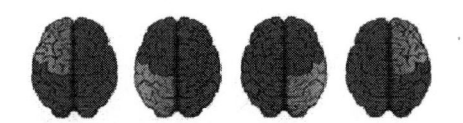

> **POSSIBLE STAGE PROPS**
>
> **For the Frontal Right**
> Create a spacious and airy area with high ceilings decorated in light tones, off-white, like an artist's studio, with natural lighting if possible and with:
> - Lots of flat available surfaces for stacking and working
> - A flip chart with lots of flip chart paper
> - Push pins to tack up things
> - Walls you can tack things onto
> - Lots of magic markers in many colors
> - Caricatures or line drawings
> - Photographs of abstract patterns and spirals
> - Geometric shapes to play with
> - Symbolic shapes or objects
> - A reading corner with magazines, reference books and articles on a wide range of topics
> - Lots of space with no structure
> - Pillows on the floor
> - Baroque music or jazz.
>
> **For the Frontal Left**
> Create a space with minimal clutter, decorated in black, white, or navy.
> - Photographs of arrows hitting the bull's eye on a target
> - Precision tools
> - Scales and or a gavel
> - A calculator
> - A statement of your goals and objectives
> - Charts with numbers and percentages
> - Framed awards, diplomas and certificates
> - A five-year plan

I like the Strategy for Success you outline, but I'm afraid when I try to do Step 6 in which I'm supposed to actually do something, I'll feel bored, frustrated and uncomfortable and I'll find myself getting up and walking away.

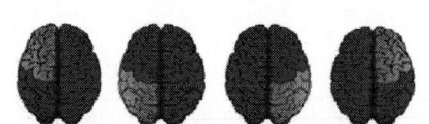

When developing a non-preferred competency, it is sometimes necessary – as part of creating the optimal climate – to shut off a competing part of your brain. For example, many people find it easier to get in touch with their right brain if and while they have turned down the volume and activity level of their left hemisphere. They might accomplish this by adding hot pink balloons to their environment to discourage the left hemisphere from paying attention and/or by avoiding spoken or written language for a time (because speech and vocabulary centers are located on the left) and by making an agreement with themselves that while they are practicing thinking right, they will not do any prioritizing, analyzing or clock-watching. Then, with the stage set, they begin to focus on input and thinking processes native to the area they want to develop. If they want to develop competency in the Frontal Right, they may attend to shapes, patterns, line drawings, abstract forms, sculpture and negative space. By looking at photographs or art or by walking through their own neighborhood looking at it differently. If they want to develop competency in the Right Posterior Convexity, they may attend to rhythms, colors, feelings and the sense of their own body moving through space.

In other words, the process for getting in touch with and developing a new type of thinking is a three-step one.

And, although you might think it makes more sense to do step two first, in reality, it is easier to stop

---

Three Steps In the Dance

1. Add anything that will turn on the part of the brain you want to contact and/or turn off the other parts.
2. Stop doing things that are known to activate other parts of the brain.
3. Engage the area and type of thinking you want to develop.

---

doing things you usually do that use one type of thinking if you have already added things to your environment that don't make sense to the part of the brain that manages that type of thinking.

At first, structuring your thinking and awareness in this way will seem and feel unnatural. And, remember, we are extremely susceptible to interruptions and distractions when using our non-preferred modes. So, assume any boredom, discomfort or resistance you have while getting into this new type of thinking is part of your brain's way of reminding you it is being asked to think inefficiently. This is particularly true during the first *20 to 30 minutes* when we are still trying to settle down so that we can use the non-preferred area. During this time we often have or notice impulses to abandon the task for something else. If we can hang in for the entire 20 or 30 minutes, however, our resistance settles down and we can begin to develop new competencies. Unfortunately, this 20 minutes of discomfort is not a one-time phenomenon; we are likely to feel this way each time we begin working in a non-preferred type of thinking and will have to make ourselves work through it again and again if we are to gain real competency in that area.

I'm a reader, so Step 3 of your Competency Development Plan interests me. Could you recommend books that are relevant for each of the four specialized types of thinking?

You might explore some of the following books.

For the **Left Posterior Convexity:** Find and read three procedures manuals cover to cover. Read all the instruction manuals for your appliances.

For the **Right Posterior Convexity:** *The Language of Feelings* by David Viscott, *The Angry Book* by Theodore Isaac Rubin, *Focusing* by Gedlin, *The Emotional Hostage* by Cameron-Bandler and Lebeau, *The Dance of Anger* and *The Dance of Intimacy* by Harriet Lerner, *Rebirthing: The Science of Enjoying All of Your Life* by Jim Leonard and Phil Laut, *Vibrational Medicine: New Choices for Healing Ourselves* by Richard Gerber and any book on nonverbal communication.

For the **Frontal Right:** *Drawing on the Artist Within* by Betty Edwards, *Creative Dreaming* by Patricia Garfield, *The Right-Brain Experiences* by Marilee Zdenek, *Brainstorms and Thunderbolts* by Carol O. Madigan and Ann Elwood, *The Path of Least Resistance* by Robert Fritz, *The Intuitive Edge* by Philip Goldberg, *Higher Creativity* by Willis Harman, *Jamming: The Art and Discipline of Business Creativity* by John Kao, *The Death of Competition: Leadership and Strategy in the Age of Business Ecosystems* by James F. Moore, *New Traditions in Business: Spirit and Leadership in the 21st Century* edited by John Renesch, *Order Out of Chaos: Mans' New Dialogue with Nature* by Ilya Prigogine, *The Holographic Paradigm and other Paradoxes* edited by Ken Wilber, *The Artist's Way: A Spiritual Path to Higher Creativity* by Julia Cameron, *The Idea Fisher* by Marsh Fisher.

For the **Frontal Left:** *How We Know: An Exploration of the Scientific Process* by Martin Goldstein & Inge F. Goldstein, *The Prince* by Niccolo Machiavelli, *Thinking Physics* by Lewis Carroll Epstein, *The Wall Street Journal, Brain and Perception: Holonomy and Structure in Figural Processing* by Karl H. Pribram, books on chess strategies. Additionally, you might want to ask your mentor what he or she reads and read that.

What if you feel you should develop a particular type of thinking, but don't really *want* to do it?

You are not alone in having this feeling. An individual's psychology can indeed impact their willingness and ability to develop competency in a quadrant. This is particularly true when someone feels angry, resentful or invalidated with respect to a particular type of thinking. Here are two examples that may help you see how our psychology affects our success. These two examples are common. They also are examples of people having difficulty with their greatest weakness. For example, a Frontal Right who has been heavily invalidated and shamed by people committed to doing things the right or correct way often resents having to learn and use the Left Posterior Convexity at all. For such a person, the first step is to make peace with the type of thinking around which they have emotional wounds. Learning to value (but not use) that type of thinking, in the present, and making a distinction between people in his or her past and the way in which they modeled this type of thinking and the ways it can be and has been used by others to help humanity.

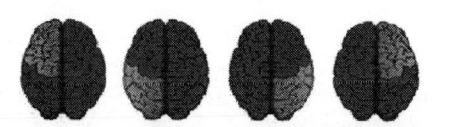

The second example would be a Right Posterior Convexity who wants to access the Frontal Left but who has been wounded by Frontal Lefts. If this is your situation, to free yourself from your anger, you might make a list of all the ways the Frontal Lefts in your life have used their analytic skill to put you down. After you have completed your list, ritually burn the list while singing "We Shall Overcome". Then, if possible, write a new list identifying any times in your life when an analytic Frontal Left has used his or her ability to prioritize and evaluate to help or support you. And as a last step, work on increasing your validation of yourself as a Right Posterior Convexity before you begin working on developing competencies elsewhere.

No one should develop competencies from the position that "There's something wrong with me" or "I should be different." This form of adaption ultimately damages an individual's self-esteem. And, it may also cause the area you are seeking to develop to be permanently colored with resentment and negative emotions. For this reason it is a good idea to carefully consider what is motivating you to change. In terms of dominance, there is no good, right or best pattern. It is not better to be frontal or posterior convexity, right or left-brained. If you are motivated to develop competencies out of dissatisfaction with who you are, consider instead devoting your energies toward developing more competencies in your preference, validating your preference and building your self-esteem. When you have achieved these then moving on to acquire non-preferred competencies will be easier and more rewarding.

Having spoken about how our psychology affects our willingness and ability to develop a particular type of thinking when that is in fact our greatest weakness, it is worth taking a few minutes to notice how it can also affect our use of one of our auxiliaries. A typical example here might be a Frontal Right woman who is rewarded for developing non-preferred competencies in the Right Posterior Convexity, but shamed as masculine or wrong for developing her Frontal Left auxiliary. Although this may not be a problem for her in the first 45 years of her life, when she is seeking a husband and having a family, it may suddenly become a problem when she is divorced and on her own at 55. Again, what helps when we have been wounded is a three-step process. First, identify and name the source and nature of the shaming or invalidation that is causing us to feel uncomfortable using or not wanting to use a particular type of thinking. Second, release the history as past and behind us. Third, begin to value the manner in which this type of thinking can and does contribute to all life, including our own.

Summary

Competencies take time and energy to develop. This is especially true when the competency is in one of your non-preferred types of thinking. Nonetheless, they are empowering and helpful. They help us take care of ourselves and they help us take care of others. As such they bolster our self-esteem but not if we abandon our preference to develop them. So always remember: a competency in a non-preferred type of thinking does not change that type of thinking into a preference. All it does is give us a new non-preferred skill that we can use to help ourselves.

> ## ▲▲ Life's Two Rules of Thumb
>
> **Rule 1** To develop or nurture your self-esteem, as well as ensure your immediate effectiveness and success, select activities and people that match your preference.
>
> **Rule 2** To assure your survival, as well as guarantee your long-term effectiveness and success, manage activities and people not matching your preference consciously and carefully and, if possible, by enlisting assistance from complementary brains.

The developing of any non-preferred competency is something that from our Two Rules of Thumb we know will not generally energize us nor bring us immediate joy. And yet, developing such competencies may help us survive and may help us help our family survive. So, knowing how and when to develop them can make us a stronger, more self-reliant person as long as we don't abandon our preference in the process or use these non-preferred competencies in the wrong time or place causing us to be chronically fatigued and or cranky.

For guidelines on when and how to best use these non-preferred competencies, see the final chapter of the book. The chapter tells you how to both leverage your preference and manage your non-preferred competencies so that you enjoy the highest possible levels of energy and health along with increased effectiveness.

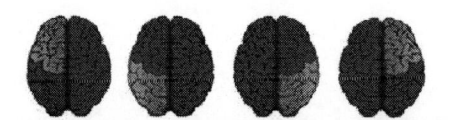

Chapter 10: Getting Along and Communicating Clearly

Many people don't want to develop lots of non-preferred competencies now or later. What they do want is to be able to communicate with people who see things differently than they do. Luckily, there are things you and they can do to improve how you communicate with someone whose preference differs from your own. Let's explore them.

Communicating

The most important thing to remember if you want to communicate effectively with someone whose preference differs from your own, is that you must be willing and able to speak *their language*. For example, if you are a Frontal Left boss working with a Right Posterior Convexity employee, and each of you have developed your Left Posterior Convexity auxiliary, things will go smoothly as long as you're both using the Left Posterior Convexity. When a problem occurs, however, it's likely you will go to your Frontal Left to solve it, while your employee moves to his Right Posterior Convexity also with the hope of solving the problem and discord. To effectively communicate then, you will both need to move to the Left Posterior Convexity or one or both of you will need to adopt the other person's language.

In theory, it doesn't matter who switches to match. In reality, however, many people are either *unwilling* to make the effort (since they believe the other person should be the one to do it) or they are *unable* to do so (since they are unaware of the problem and ignorant of how to solve it). For this reason, if effective communication is important to you, assume it's your job to switch modes. Spending a lot of time trying to figure out whether it's a case of unwilling or incapable probably won't accomplish much. Furthermore, as you practice talking to different brains you will increase your own personal power and ability as a communicator (which won't happen for the person who simply hangs out in their preference and demands that everyone else come to him).

To help yourself, read through the following guidelines for communicating with employees, bosses, as well as friends and family members with whom we have personal relationships. As you do so, remember that these guidelines are for dealing with quarter-brains (which make up only 25 percent of the population) and that you will need to blend them when dealing with more complex practical dominance patterns. Also remember that each of us, including the person you want to communicate with, has only one preference. If you can determine what their natural lead is, use it.

Communicating With Employees at Work

When You're the Boss

Employees come in all shapes, sizes and dominance patterns. Below are some guidelines you can use when you're the boss to help you manage each type of thinker when they are your employees.

To manage an employee with a **Left Posterior Convexity** preference:

- Give clear, specific, and detailed, step-by-step instructions for each task or project. If it is a complex project, be sure to break it into sub-routines and steps. Teach each sub-routine separately. Do not be afraid of being too specific during the learning phase.

- -Provide your Left Posterior Convexity employee with an orderly workspace in which they can have a place for everything and everything in its place. It is important that they have files and other devices for organizing their working materials and minimizing clutter. Do not expect them to share space with a Frontal Right.

- Remember that your Left Posterior Convexity employee wants approval and recognition for and gets satisfaction from matching established procedures. He/she will want to know if they did the right thing and if what they did was what they were supposed to do. To be successful, you need to take time to give them these kinds of feedback. For example, tell them you noticed that they have been doing something just as you asked them to and that you want them to know you are glad they are so dependable.

- Left Posterior Convexities do not know how to improvise or deviate from standard procedures and feel extremely uncomfortable doing so. If you want them to make exceptions to the rule you will have to design a procedure for handling exceptions.

For example, a friend of Anne Sohn's, who owns and operates a gardening business, came to her for advice on how to handle a problem with a Left Posterior Convexity worker. The young man would do well on all standard tasks but would become resistant and unhappy when asked to do special things for a client, often forgetting to do them at all. When asked what was going on, he would say he didn't know why anyone should get special treatment and that it wasn't part of the standard procedure. To get him to do these tasks, his boss had to redefine and restructure his concept of what was standard procedure. So, she created a standard procedure checklist for each client that made the extras simply part of the standard procedure for that client instead of extras. She also defined a new overall standard procedure; namely, that it is standard procedure to check and follow the standard procedures for each separate client. Once she did this and her worker had time to adjust to this new arrangement, things improved. He no longer had to deal with exceptions; he had a standard procedure for everything (even if those procedures varied from client to client) and he completed all the tasks.

- Left Posterior Convexities want to work regular and predictable hours (and take their breaks and lunch at predictable times). If you ask them to deviate too much from their routine, they will become frustrated and difficult. Do not expect this employee to work much voluntary overtime unless you have and use a clear procedure to request it. Even then, don't push it.

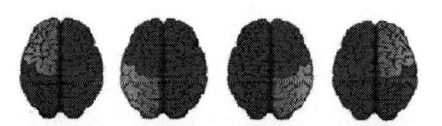

- Left Posterior Convexities work at a slow and thorough pace and will not respond well to being pressured or hurried up. They need to know what their deadlines are in advance and be able to be sure they have time to meet them. They also need to work with a minimum of interruptions (since interruptions break down their routines).

- Do not ask Left Posterior Convexities to handle crisis situations unless there is a prearranged procedure for dealing with that particular crisis (these are the people who actually paid enough attention during the fire drills to know where they are supposed to go and what they are supposed to do). When managing Left Posterior Convexities, be sure to have specific procedures for all the emergencies they are likely to encounter and cover those procedures with them in advance.

To manage an employee with a **Right Posterior Convexity** preference:

- Give them work that uses their interpersonal expertise (counseling, teaching, encouraging, nurturing). Do not expect them to be highly attentive to repetitive tasks, statistics or work that takes analysis.

- Understand that the Right Posterior Convexity needs to like the people he works with and will often stay on a job he otherwise dislikes or is not suited for because he likes the people. Interpersonal problems on the job are a major source of stress and dysfunction for the Right Posterior Convexity and should be taken seriously by their manager (since the Right Posterior Convexity is not likely to get much productive work done until the problem is handled).

- Provide your Right Posterior Convexity employee with a warm and friendly work environment. Harmonious colors, plants, a comfortable chair, their own coffee mug and space for personal mementoes (pictures, sentimental objects) on their desk are necessary for their sense of emotional well-being. Doing a task they don't like, which doesn't match their dominance, can be made easier if they have a photo of their child to look at. Each time they look at the photo it brings up in them warm, loving feelings they have for their child and energizes them to continue doing the task they have to do. If the photo is one taken at an important event or joyous moment in their child's life, the effect will be even more powerful. Doing this to help your employee be more effective would be using sandwiching / packaging (See Chapter 11: Strategies for Managing Weaknesses.)

- The Right Posterior Convexity seeks to belong and needs to feel they are a part of the team. Activities that encourage group sharing and that include everyone are important to keeping the Right Posterior Convexity worker happy and productive. Right Posterior Convexities do not respond well to hierarchies or to the idea that some people are more important than others. They need to feel that they can have a dialogue (in which their feelings and opinions are valued and respected) with their supervisors and managers.

- You can get your Right Posterior Convexity employee to work overtime asking him personally to do so (preferably as a favor) and by emphasizing either how much he is needed or that it's part of being a good team player (which to a Right Posterior Convexity means filling in when and where they're needed).

- Right Posterior Convexities rarely work for a long time at a stretch and they need to take frequent relationship breaks (which means that they need to stop what they're doing to chat and relate for awhile). To effectively manage a Right Posterior Convexity, you will need to see these breaks as normal and natural. Trying to stop a Right Posterior Convexity from taking his/her relationship breaks will only result in less productivity during the time when they are doing other things. Gently steering them back to work (without criticism) after such a break is probably the best approach. In some situations, Right Posterior Convexities can actually be very effective if they are encouraged to sit together (so they can see each other) and chat (relate) as they all do the same non-dominant, routine task. This would be using packaging to increase their performance (See Chapter 11: Strategies for Managing Weaknesses.)

- If you're going to manage Right Posterior Convexities, you should realize that they use feeling comfortable and connected as their standard for evaluating the success of their day and the way their job is going. If they feel good and connected with their co-workers, work is going well; if they feel badly or there is a lot of stress and tension in the office (which they will notice more readily than others), work is going badly. Thus, it is important to check in with them regularly to find out not only what they've been doing, but also how they feel about it. If they are not feeling good about what they're doing, ask them if they have any suggestions that would make a difference.

- Right Posterior Convexities tend to have trouble staying on a production schedule and being punctual since they will always prefer interpersonal activities to impersonal tasks and will readily interrupt work to deal with people problems. To help them stay on task you will need to connect their timeliness or the deadlines (whatever you want them to attend) with the effect it has on other people. Most Right Posterior Convexities will try to be more timely when they can see that by doing so they make another person's life easier and by not doing so they make it more stressful.

- Right Posterior Convexities work for approval and appreciation (positive strokes, compliments, hugs, tokens of appreciation, recognition of their contribution) rather than just for money or promotion. In fact, many Right Posterior Convexities have talked themselves out of promotions because they wanted to stay with the people they liked. You will bring out the best in your Right Posterior Convexity worker by being generous with your praise and your attention.

To manage an employee with a **Frontal Right** preference:

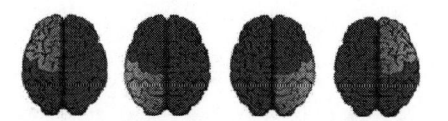

- This employee is best used in a creative, research and development or trouble shooting capacity. He will become bored quickly doing repetitive tasks (like processing forms) or working with details. He is best used in the innovation phase of any project and then moved on once the project is up and running. If you leave him with a project that has become routine, he will begin to tinker inappropriately with the procedures and make a lot of unnecessary work for you (and everyone else).

- Whenever possible allow the Frontal Right employee to *work alone* and to *set his own hours*. He will tend to work for long periods of time and then need to take long periods of time off. Do not under any circumstances expect him to fit himself into a standard 9 to 5 schedule.

- While at work, the Frontal Right employee may appear to be doing nothing as he sits staring out a window or resting with his eyes closed. In actuality, this daydreaming is the Frontal Right's way of incubating and processing the information he is working on. As a manager, you will have to allow him his doing nothing (incubation) time or give him two or more projects to work on simultaneously (so he can incubate one while working on the other) if you want his brain to work the way it's designed to.

- With his passion for innovation, the Frontal Right employee spends a lot of his time trying to find ways to alter and improve work procedures (even if nobody has asked him to or is in the least bit interested). You may want to exploit this natural tendency of his and have him put his ideas in writing, turning them in to you as he writes them. Some of them are likely to be quite good.

- Provide the Frontal Right employee with a large workspace in which there is plenty of room to stack and spatially arrange things and many surfaces available for displaying visual cues (walls, boards, shelves and counters).

- Realize that the Frontal Right employee is terrible at meeting operational deadlines and at estimating the amount of time necessary to complete a task and adjust all his time projections accordingly. Remember that as a strong Frontal Right, his mind sees the project already done. It also neglects to notice all the steps needed to get there. Everything takes longer than he thinks (sometimes much longer).

- Frontal Rights prefer to work unsupervised and with as little intervention in their process as possible. The best thing you can do for them is give them a problem to solve and then leave them alone while they solve it. You may want to check in with them every once in a while to see how it's going. When you do so, they may not tell you (because they don't exactly know how it's going). You need to remember that a great deal of Frontal Right work is unconscious and try not to worry.

- Frontal Rights prefer to be given instructions that leave a lot of the details open and up to their own discretion. This is the kind of person who will appreciate it if you tell them to just wing it and figure it out any way they can.

- Frontal Rights (particularly those with very few Right Posterior Convexity skills) tend to offend others without knowing they are doing so. As their manager, you may need to explain that they aren't being rude when they doodle in meetings (a moving pencil helps them to think) and they aren't being disrespectful when they don't follow the rules (they just don't follow rules) and they weren't making fun of you when they laughed inappropriately during the budget review (they were just looking at their own internal pictures). Don't expect the Frontal Right to handle these interpersonal disputes. His strategy will be to withdraw to avoid the conflict altogether. Besides, he isn't known for his ability to articulate why he does things. Of course, you could introduce your Frontal Right to the whole brain thinking model and, while validating his identity and your appreciation of his creative abilities, help him understand how his behavior affects others.

- When giving your Frontal Right employee a task or project, be sure to provide him with an overview of how the work you're giving him contributes and fits in. He needs to see the big picture and is not satisfied just doing his part because you tell him to.

- Your Frontal Right employee wants money or special equipment for a project he is working on. Don't expect him to be able to sell it to Frontal Left management. He's counting on you to do that for him. A good manager to a Frontal Right is one who gives him the space in which to be creative, sees he has the equipment he needs and makes sure nobody bothers him while he's working. When you're managing a Frontal Right, it is sometimes difficult to remember exactly which one of you is the boss since they certainly don't treat you that way. Try not to take it personally. They don't follow rules either.

To manage an employee with a **Frontal Left** preference:

- Give directions and present information in a brief, direct, logical manner. Stress salient facts and highlight key points. Remember this individual is interested in knowing the bottom line, not the process you used to get there or how you feel about it.

- Provide them with a functional workspace in which they have access to all the tools they need to do their job. Whenever possible give them exclusive use of those tools (Frontal Lefts dislike sharing their tools with anyone else). If you don't know what such a workspace would look like, ask your employee.

- Give them specific goals to meet but allow them to decide what process to use to accomplish the goals. Don't be surprised if they delegate part of the task to someone else. They will not necessarily do all the work themselves, but they will consider themselves ultimately responsible for seeing the goals are met.

- Expect them to be competitive and to jockey for position in the organizational hierarchy. Frontal Lefts believe in the fast track and will do whatever they can to leverage their way up the organization. If it looks like one of your Frontal Left employees is going to be promoted over you, do whatever you can to help him. By furthering his success instead of resisting it, you make it likely he'll take you with him.

- Do not expect them to participate in social functions unless it increases their chances of promotion or advancement. They tend to be social only for political reasons.
- Plan to give them specific rewards (money, promotion, increased power) for a job well done. Frontal Lefts work to get ahead. They do not work for approval, belonging or emotional strokes.
- Give them work that uses their strong evaluation and decision-making skills. Do not give them work that is highly repetitive or that requires strong interpersonal skills.
- Your Frontal Left employee values effectiveness and rationality. He will have extreme difficulty dealing with anything that looks like incompetence, redundancy or emotionality and will probably manifest that difficulty by becoming critical or contemptuous. So, it's helpful to remember that Frontal Lefts are often oblivious to the messages conveyed in their non-verbals and their tone of voice. They often sound like they're giving orders and may be perceived by others as cold, critical and uncaring. It will probably be necessary to help a Frontal Left's co-workers to come to terms with him since he is not interested in (or skilled at) working out interpersonal differences. This doesn't mean you let him walk on or abuse his co-workers. However, they need to learn that his non-verbals, while distinctly different from theirs, are just his way.

Finally, for all employees, introduce them to the whole brain model so they can learn to work smart as well as to value the function, style, needs and contribution of each of the other specialized types of thinking.

Getting Along With the Boss at Work
When You're an Employee

We've all had a lot of different bosses over the years, some of whom we got along with better than others. And, some of how well we get along with them has to do with brain dominance. In fact, how well we get along with a particular boss largely depends on at least 10 distinct factors:

our own dominance pattern	our boss's dominance pattern
how well our own pattern matches our job	how well our boss's pattern matches his job
our own self-esteem	our boss's self-esteem
our own emotional maturity	our boss's emotional maturity
our own birth order	our boss's birth order

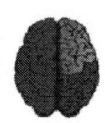

All these factors need to be taken into consideration when trying to understand the dynamic relationship between boss and employee. Obviously, it is important for you to know your own dominance pattern – your preference, your developed auxiliaries and your weaknesses. And you need to know how well it matches your job. It is also important for you to consider your boss's pattern, not only in relationship to your own, but in relationship to his job as manager/supervisor. If there is a poor fit between his job and his pattern, he may be frustrated or angry and as such he will be more likely to procrastinate about (or avoid altogether) many of the tasks you need him to do as your manager. As well, your self-esteem and how well each of you handles your emotions are particularly important when one or both of you is under pressure. Also, birth order plays a role. Eldest and only like to be the boss. Youngest have difficulty taking the lead even if they would like the status.

It's also true that what we want in a manager depends on who we are and what we expect. Before we go into the specifics of dealing with each of the different brains as bosses, look at how some other people define their best and worst managers. Paul, an engineer and quarter-brain Frontal Left (shown in black), working for a large international oil company, identifies his best manager (solid line) as a quarter-brain Frontal Left like himself, and his worst manager (dotted line) a quarter-brain Right Posterior Convexity. When asked why the Frontal Left manager was the best, his response was: "He was like myself, logical and methodical. He liked numbers and he left me alone." When asked why the Right Posterior Convexity manager was the worst, Paul's response was that "He wasn't interested in numbers."

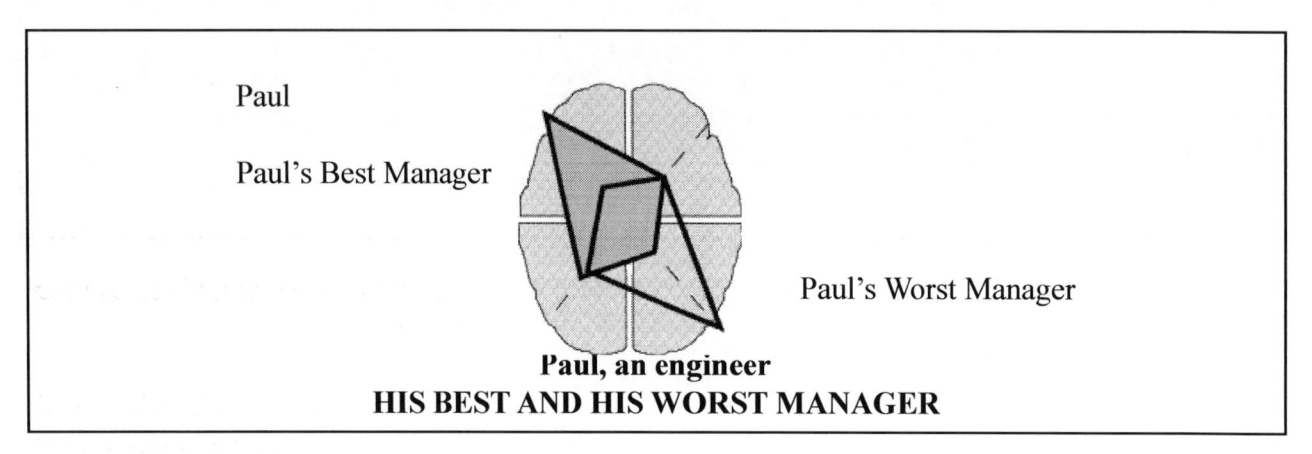

Paul

Paul's Best Manager

Paul's Worst Manager

Paul, an engineer
HIS BEST AND HIS WORST MANAGER

Another example shows how differently employees identify what they need in a good manager. Jill, a double right works in Marketing. Her best manager was a Triple Translator (double left and Frontal Right) who was best because, as she put it, "He had more of my semi-strengths. We complemented each other." In contrast, her worst manager was a quarter-brained Frontal Right. Her explanation of this was that "He offered less than I did in other areas. He was very creative, but that didn't wash in a work environment."

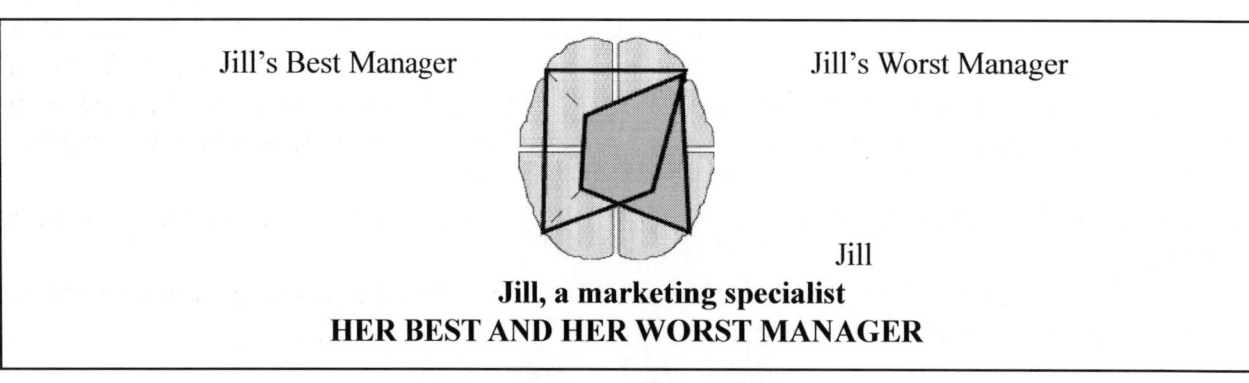

Jill's Best Manager

Jill's Worst Manager

Jill

Jill, a marketing specialist
HER BEST AND HER WORST MANAGER

Our final example illustrates how we can dislike a manager even if we both share the same lead function. For George, a double left, his worst manager was a quarter-brained Frontal Left (even though that was George's own lead mode). His explanation: "He was difficult to work with, very financial and detailed and constantly checking. He refused to listen and he had the interpersonal skills of a rock – not even a pet rock."

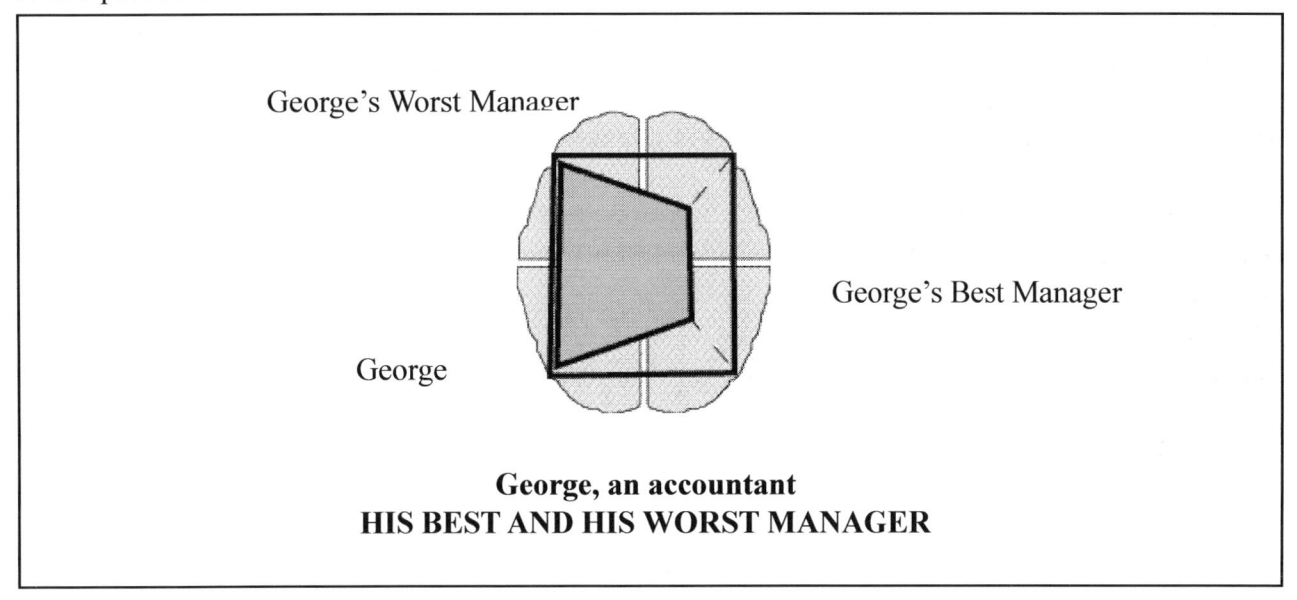

George, an accountant
HIS BEST AND HIS WORST MANAGER

For George, his best manager was Whole Brained. In describing this manager, George told us, "He was a combination of a lot of things. He also had an ability to operate in all areas."

As you can see, everyone has a way they prefer to be managed, and it is not necessarily by a boss with a matching brain profile. Before you go any further, you may want to think about how you like to be managed and what you expect from a boss. As well, if you are or have been a manager, think about how you like to manage others. Then compare your personal preference with the information that follows on how each of the different brains likes to manage.

These charts on Getting Along with The Boss cover each of the four specialized types of thinking in two different ways: first, by giving you an overview of that particular type of boss and then by giving you some guidelines for dealing with them. Please remember that these are quarter-brain descriptions and must be blended for the more complex patterns. Also, remember that *a boss's area of weakness will be almost as important as his area of strength.* A double left with an avoidance in the Right Posterior Convexity and a double left able to use the Right Posterior Convexity will manage very differently.

- Expects you to be familiar with the procedures manual, the dress code and the rules and to follow them.
- Takes a long time to make a decision and generally makes his decisions based on precedent (Has this been done before? What happened then? Who else has already done this?)

Guidelines for Getting Along With The Boss

The Left Posterior Convexity Boss

First, check to be sure your boss is Left Posterior Convexity. A Left Posterior Convexity boss:

- Most highly values consistency, loyalty and reliability in an employee.
- Actively dislikes change and resists innovation. Prefers to stick with established procedures and the way things are done here.
- Expects staff to be punctual.
- Expects staff to meet all deadlines.
- Expects you to be familiar with the procedures manual, the dress code and the rules and to follow them.
- Takes a long time to make a decision and generally makes his decisions based on precedent (Has this been done before? What happened then? Who else has already done this?)
- Is most amenable to answering informational questions (how-to's) or explaining procedures.
- Has difficulty understanding work areas such as Research and Development and Organizational Development.
- Expects workers to stay on schedule and to complete all their tasks in a neat and orderly manner.
- Is poor at handling crisis, troubleshooting or revising procedures that no longer work.
- Evaluates his personnel using a standard form and by checking to see if they've completed all their assigned tasks in a thorough and timely manner.

If you decide you have a Left Posterior Convexity Boss, here's what to do and not do to get along with your boss:

- Be punctual. Be neat. Be appropriate.
- When you have something to discuss, schedule a formal meeting.
- Whenever possible, send a memo and an agenda in advance of your meeting or presentation.
- Talk slowly.
- Use words carefully.
- Emphasize security, guarantees, safekeeping and ways to limit risk.
- When using audio-visual aids in making a presentation: show a lengthy, step-by-step action plan that indicates who will be affected and how they will be affected by this change or project.
- When making a project proposal, provide lists of other companies who have done similar work or used a comparable system. List all the research that backs up your proposal (a lengthy bibliography) and the names and positions of those who support this type of work, system or approach. Come up with as much supportive and historical documentation as possible.
- Play by the rules. You may think a dress code is ridiculous; your boss probably doesn't.

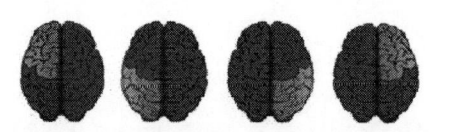

- Don't hurry him through decision-making. He needs time to review all the historical data before he will be willing to decide.
- Going through correct channels is very important to Left Posterior Convexities. Find out the correct procedure for asking for a raise, getting time off or making a complaint and do it that way first. Many people don't get what they want from Left Posterior Convexities because they don't approach them the right way.
- Pay attention to details. When you work for this person, how you do something and in what order matters as much as the final result.

The Right Posterior Convexity Boss

First, check to be sure your boss is Right Posterior Convexity. A Right Posterior Convexity boss:

- Uses the consensus method for decision-making and will need to know how everyone feels about it before proceeding further.
- Actively avoids making unpleasant or unpopular decisions which is why some Right Posterior Convexity managers are known as country club managers
- Has difficulty setting up or creating schedules.
- Is supportive of personal growth and activities that improve employee morale or develop their skill at team building.
- Resists hierarchy and authority. Wants everyone to be part of the team and the department to be one big happy family.
- Puts people's needs ahead of production schedules, often making exceptions to the rule.
- Will be supportive of your need for personal time and understand that your moods can affect your job performance.
- Expects personal loyalty and has personal relationships with staff. Is not particularly effective lobbying for change or money.
- May play favorites on the basis of who he or she likes best.
- Is highly sensitive to interpersonal conflict. Will try to resolve it and, if that is unsuccessful, suppress it.
- Evaluates personnel by how well they fit in, how enthusiastically they participate and whether or not they have a good attitude.

If you decide you have a Right Posterior Convexity Boss, here's what to do and not do to get along with your boss:

- Get to know them before doing anything else.
- Listen to and reflect their feelings back to them.
- Make eye contact with them when you are talking with them.
- Respond to their feelings and feelings of others. With a Right Posterior Convexity feelings are actually more important than the facts.

- Talk in terms of 'We'.
- Use symbolic metaphors, especially ones that deal with life cycles, family, and spiritual truths i.e. birth, seeds, parenting.
- Talk in terms of the contribution you, this project or the department can make. Express your concern for others and your desire to be of help or service to them.
- Present ideas and requests in personal, informal conversations.
- When using audio-visuals in a presentation: make them up as you go along, use pictures (especially of people smiling), and avoid references to numbers, percentages or money.
- When doing handouts, use color (especially rose, light blue, light yellow, light green or pink). If you include a bibliography, be sure to include some information on the people (who they are, where they are, etc.).
- To sell them on an idea, show them how they can use it to build morale, facilitate personal growth or help or empower others.
- When you want something, ask for their help in getting it.
- Relate personally. Take the time to build rapport.

- Be social and participate fully in group processes and events (potlucks, retirement and birthday celebrations)
- Be enthusiastic.
- Use plenty of eye contact.
- Be physically expressive. Use touch to make your point or establish connection If the situation permits it.

The Frontal Right Boss

First, check to be sure your boss is Frontal Right. A Frontal Right boss:

- Wants his/her employees to supervise themselves.
- Prefers to give his staff an overview (the big picture) and have them take care of filling in and handling the details.
- Makes his decisions intuitively and becomes confused when asked to justify the decision logically.
- Often uses metaphors to describe what he wants to accomplish or how he wants someone to act.
- Likes innovation, novelty and ideas that are on the cutting edge.
- Is far more interested in concepts than in things or people.
- Actively avoids conflict and will not get involved in personality problems or interpersonal disputes. Will give the impression of being oblivious to what's going on. Telling him what's going on will not change the situation in the least (he'll still refuse to get involved).
- Often changes things (procedures, the office layout) just for the sake of novelty.
- Actively dislikes paperwork and may be chronically late in getting it completed even when it has to do with promotion or his own budget.
- May be extremely vague when giving directions or explaining what he wants. He sees his own

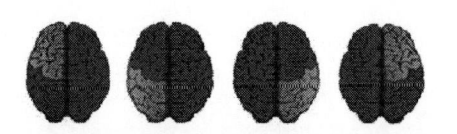

internal pictures, but tends to forget his staff can't see them.
- Will have difficulty lobbying with Frontal Left management for budget, equipment and extra staff even when he is extremely excited about a project.
- Hates doing personnel evaluation (he dislikes both the form and theprocedure) so you may not know where you stand with him (or the job) for months on end. When he gets around to it he usually evaluates by considering whether or not the person has interesting ideas and makes a creative contribution to the department.

If you decide you have a Frontal Right Boss, here's what to do and not do to get along with your boss:

- If you are not a strong Frontal Left yourself, find a strong Frontal Left to help your boss lobby or negotiate support for your project with management.
- Handle all personnel disputes yourself.
- Communicate ideas in informal, personal conversations (don't expect him to sit through meetings).
- Talk more rapidly than you usually do.
- Show how your ideas relate to the cutting edge, the latest research, etc.
- Create word pictures when presenting information to him. Remember he's a highly spatial, visual, pattern-sensitive thinker.
- Show how your idea parallels theories in other, non-related fields.
- Use words and phrases like: vision, perspective, the big picture.
- Use humor and play with ideas.
- When trying to present a concept, use metaphors. A few examples might be:

Concept:	**Metaphor**
value of diversity	most card games use more than one suit
people united by shared values	aligned they're stronger, even magnetic
people acting without questioning	lemmings

- Draw pictures emphasizing symbols and shapes (circles, spirals, squares, wings, pyramids, wheels); draw on a flip chart or napkin or scrap of paper as you talk.
- Encourage your boss to doodle or draw as you talk.
- In preparing handouts, cite references to concepts and ideas that link to what you want him/her to understand.
- Be prepared to handle all the details and paperwork for proposals yourself. If you need something signed, carry it in to your boss and watch while he signs it. He may have a visual filing system, but it's only for papers he considers important and your forms probably won't be important to him. So, don't just leave the papers on his desk.

- Don't move his stacks or clean up his workspace. You will destroy his whole filing system and he'll hate you forever.
- Be amused. It will endear you to your boss and its better than the alternative.

The Frontal Left Boss

First, check to be sure your boss is Frontal Left. A Frontal Left boss:

- Most highly values effectiveness and productivity.
- Likes making decisions and tends to do so quickly.
- Makes decisions on the basis of the effect such a change would have on the entire system or by using a cost-benefit analysis.
- Is results oriented. Evaluates success by the bottom line or Return on Investment.
- Is goal oriented.
- Is interested in moving up the organizational ladder.
- Tends to delegate well and often.
- Likes being on top of a hierarchy.
- Will probably be possessive of his territory and/or authority.
- Dislikes handling personal or personnel problems.
- Uses his employees' and division's performance as a way of moving ahead   personally.
- Respects a competent arguer and a strategic negotiator.
- Expects his workers to make logical presentations when they present information or ask questions.
- Tends to give orders rather than make requests.
- Is often perceived as cold, critical and uncaring due to his lack of awareness of his own non-verbal signals and his tone of voice.
- Prefers to have information presented in a concise manner with the key points expressed in miles or percentages and emphasized by the use of bullets.
- Evaluates his personnel by: cost-benefit, their personal effectiveness, their productivity, and their promise/potential for long-term gain to him and the organization.

If you decide you have a Frontal Left Boss, here's what to do and not do to get along with your boss:

- Be brief. Know what you're going to say before you say it. Stress the key points and provide half-page written summaries when possible.
- Learn to do critical analysis and present material in that form.
- Use precise numbers (42.5), percentages (15 percent), and dollar amounts ($150,000) whenever possible.
- Cite recent research when making your case for a project.
- To score points, show how the policy or product you are endorsing will give the organization or a key person leverage or the better or surer Return On Investment.
- Prepare handouts that are: precise, concise, in black and white.

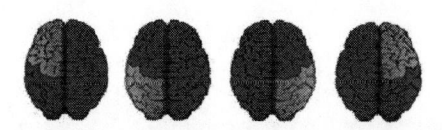

- When using audio-visual aids in making a presentation: use prepared charts showing bottom line numbers or numerical research, restrict data to the key points, use straight lines and angles, use black and white, and make sure the charts and diagrams are precisely drawn. Also be sure the technical aspects of your presentation come off without a hitch.
- When requesting something, be specific and state logically its functional value.
- Don't take his tone of voice or his order giving personally.
- Realize he actively dislikes incompetence, inefficiency, redundancy and emotionality. Don't waste his time and don't let him catch you wasting yours. Also keep your personal life out of the workplace.

Personal Relationships

Quite naturally, the information you've read about getting along and communicating with someone whose dominance differs from your own also applies to relationships away from work, relationships with friends, neighbors and family. In fact many people find they use the information in their private lives even more often than at work with wonderful and healing results. For this reason, in the next pages many ideas and suggestions are presented. Some may be easier for you to implement than others.

Now, before getting into the suggestions for each type of person/ thinker, let's look at five tips to consider when dealing with anyone at home whose preference differs from your own.

Tip 1: Remember that variety is the spice of life and that even though we are all created equal, we are not all the same. Learn to appreciate the differences between yourself and others as not merely amusing, but necessary. And, give up any ideas you have that your way of doing things is the only way or the right way. Your preferred way is just one of the ways.

Tip 2: Be patient with yourself and others. Relating is hard work and you're not going to do it perfectly (no matter how much you know).

Tip 3: Practice, practice, practice. Then practice some more.

Tip 4: Realize that disappointment usually comes when we expect a particular behavior and get another behavior instead. It is important to learn not to expect a Frontal Left to behave like a Right Posterior Convexity (and vice versa).

Tip 5: Have fun reading through these guidelines and associating them with the people you know. Just because this is important doesn't mean it has to be serious.

Now, with these tips in mind, consider using the following guidelines in your personal or home life.

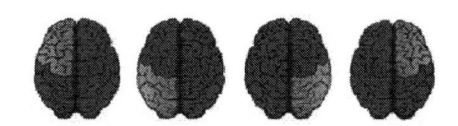

▲▲ Guidelines for Communicating At Home

About the **Left Posterior Convexities** in your life:

- Left Posterior Convexities prefer to plan and schedule activities and outings in advance. If you are dating a Left Posterior Convexity, he or she will be happiest if your date always falls on the same day of the week so they can predict what will happen on that day and plan for it. On the other hand, Left Posterior Convexities dislike surprises and resist doing anything spontaneously or on the spur of the moment. They will often decline to go on an outing (which might have been fun) because they didn't plan for it or know about it far enough in advance.

- Left Posterior Convexities prefer to have every day filled and scheduled so they can predict what will happen and build routines around it. So, arranging to meet a friend who has a strong Left Posterior Convexity can sometimes be difficult because they have no free time (Wednesday is my dance lesson, Thursday I clean my house, Friday I go grocery shopping, and so forth). What's more, they won't be comfortable deviating from their routine to fit you in.

- Left Posterior Convexities value consistency and predictability in their friends. If you want to get along with a Left Posterior Convexity, you'd better do exactly what you said you would exactly when you said you'd do it. You'd also better be on time (for everything).

- Left Posterior Convexities usually have and stay on a budget. Don't expect them to be comfortable deviating from that budget even if something is a good buy or a wonderful opportunity (unless they have a procedure for handling such a situation). They like to plan their spending, keep their checkbook balanced, and know where their money goes (down to the last penny).

- Left Posterior Convexities value tradition and the way things have been done in the past. Your Left Posterior Convexity will probably want to observe the same holidays every year in exactly the same way (eating exactly the same food). A friend of Anne Sohn's discovered this fact (to her great dismay) when she tried to introduce a new way of preparing green beans at their Thanksgiving dinner. Her Left Posterior Convexity husband became extremely upset by this change and promptly explained to her at length that "this is NOT the way green beans are prepared." If you're trying to change a Left Posterior Convexity's habits or routines, do so gradually and expect resistance and some emotional upset along the way.

- Left Posterior Convexities often have difficulty making friends so they often get involved in structured group activities, like dance classes or bridge clubs, that have the social element built in. If you want to meet a Left Posterior Convexity, those are good ways to do so.

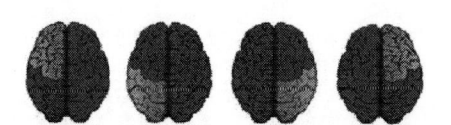

- If you're going to live with a Left Posterior Convexity as a lover or a roommate you had better learn to be neat, orderly and regular in your routines. Left Posterior Convexities have a place for everything and they want everything in its place. They have right ways for doing just about everything and adhere to them faithfully. For many Left Posterior Convexities, there is one and only one way to bake a cake, make a bed, decorate a Christmas tree, clean a bathtub, etc. and if you don't do it their way, you're wrong. If you need to live in a less structured way, try arranging it so you each have private space. That should make it easier to keep your communal space his way. Or, you can try a scheduled rotation of how the space is kept; one month in your companion's way, one month in your own.

- Since Left Posterior Convexities need to build everything into habitual patterns and are anxious about change and the unknown, they tend to date for a long time before they marry. If the Left Posterior Convexity in your life is taking a long time to pop the question, it's probably because he's not used to you yet. Be patient, emphasize the ways being married is going to be just like what you're already doing.

- For a Left Posterior Convexity, half the fun of going on a vacation is planning it in advance. When they sit down and work out a detailed, step-by-step itinerary of where they're going and what they're going to see (preferably minute by minute) what they're doing is loading their routine. Next, during the weeks (or months) before they leave, they get the pleasure of anticipating the successful execution of that routine. And finally, on the vacation, they have the pleasure of actually running their pre-loaded routine (and the closer they are to being perfectly on schedule the happier they are). Left Posterior Convexities like planned, scheduled, organized vacations; they like packaged tours, they like using guidebooks, and they like going all the way through the museum or the chateau (or whatever they happen to be touring), making sure they see what they are supposed to see. Those who prefer a spontaneous approach may want to vacation with someone else.

About the **Right Posterior Convexities** in your life:

- Right Posterior Convexities like to have favorites - their favorite food, favorite song, favorite color, favorite restaurant, etc. - and they will probably want to know what your favorites are (so they can give them to you). If you are not the kind of person who has favorites, it will probably suffice to give them a list of things you really like (but don't be surprised if they ask you which of those things you like most).

- The Right Posterior Convexities in your life will want to share and process feelings. Consequently, they will always want to know more than just what happened; they will also want to know how you feel about what happened and what it means to you. Then they will want to tell you how they feel about it and what it means and so forth. Conversations that only give information are not considered real talking by Right Posterior Convexities.

- Right Posterior Convexities are sentimental about holidays and anniversaries and they expect to observe and celebrate them. (Forgetting a Right Posterior Convexity's birthday is practically a mortal sin.) If you're trying to come up with a present to give them, remember that it doesn't have to be large or costly but it does have to be personal, something that reminds you of them. You can also give them flowers since most Right Posterior Convexities are extremely fond of them and like to have them around.

- One of the things that often amazes non-Right Posterior Convexities, is the sheer number of friends, acquaintances and people to relate to that many Right Posterior Convexities have in their life. What amazes them even more is how much of their time Right Posterior Convexities devote to staying in touch, whether chatting on the phone or by sending cards and writing notes. If you're going to be in a relationship with a Right Posterior Convexity you better get used to all the people and not feel jealous because you don't get all of their attention.

- Remember that Right Posterior Convexities value touch and are therefore likely to want to give and receive lots of hugs. Hug them often (and not just in a sexual context).

- Right Posterior Convexities prefer to live in a warm, cozy and harmonious environment, usually filled with plants, sentimental objects (pinecones, shells, a dried corsage) and pictures of places they've been or people they love. They need to have their things around them – it's what makes it feel like home.

- For a Right Posterior Convexity, a vacation is an opportunity to visit friends or family or to have the time to re-connect with significant others. Once again, people are the primary focus rather than places or activities.

- Many Right Posterior Convexities are hypersensitive to tone of voice and nonverbals. Since their brain monitors for disharmony, they tend to interpret any movement to increase the physical distance between you and them as a kind of rejection and any sharp, curt or abrupt tone of voice as criticism. Remember, with Right Posterior Convexities, how you say something is probably more important than what you actually say.

- Right Posterior Convexities tend to spend money impulsively and emotionally particularly when they are buying things for other people. Don't expect them to manage their money (or even to be clear where it went).

- Right Posterior Convexities value homemade gifts and are likely to give presents they have made themselves (a pie they baked, a sweater they knitted). They also like to do potluck dinners because, at a potluck, everyone gets to contribute something they've made. If you want to be disapproved of by a Right Posterior Convexity, bring store bought stuff to a potluck. (Obviously your life must be terribly out of balance for you to need to do such a thing.)

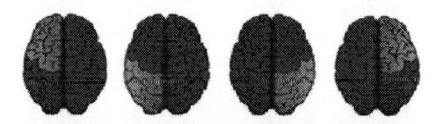

- Right Posterior Convexities who have children may bring them along to social events whether or not it's appropriate for the children to be there. They seem to do this because they are more worried about leaving their children in someone else's care (who may not treat them as the Right Posterior Convexity wants them to be treated) than they are about inconveniencing others by the children's presence.

- Lastly, many Right Posterior Convexities want to believe that it is possible for people to get along all of the time. This notion causes them a lot of disappointment and tends to lead to rather unrealistic expectations about their own and other people's behavior. Not liking someone (or not being liked) is hard on a Right Posterior Convexity and is likely to upset them emotionally.

About the **Frontal Rights** in your life:

- Frontal Rights don't attend (graciously) to mundane details like paying bills or remembering to buy groceries. For many Frontal Rights, these things only come to mind at the last minute and so they often have to scurry around trying to get the problem handled. If you're in a relationship with a strong Frontal Right and having bills paid on time is important to you, you probably better plan on handling them yourself. Alternatively, you can try putting up signs all over the house that say "Pay the Bills!" This will probably get them to pay them (but it still won't make it matter to them).

- Frontal Rights avoid conflict in relationships and tend to handle it by withdrawing physically and emotionally. They also tend to actively resist wanting to talk about it (unless their Right Posterior Convexity auxiliary is strongly developed). If they are going to express hostility, they are most likely to do so through passive aggressive acts. If you push a Frontal Right long enough, his strategy of withdrawal and avoidance will ultimately break down. At that time he will go into one of his back-up modes (usually rooted in his most developed auxiliary: Frontal Left, Right Posterior Convexity) and do his fighting from there, which can surprise you if you aren't prepared.

- When a Frontal Right becomes preoccupied with a creative problem his environment tends to become messy, cluttered and completely disorganized. Then, all of a sudden his spatial sensitivity will kick in and he will rush about straightening things and restoring visual order. You should not confuse this Frontal Right penchant for visually pleasing space with a desire to keep a clean house (they're not into cleaning). You must also learn not to move their stacks or try to clean up their mess when they're working on something. Those stacks are part of their thinking process and need to stay where they put them until they're done working.

- Frontal Rights like to do things spontaneously; they like impromptu, spur of the moment activities and outings and their favorite approach to a trip is to just pick up and go. They want their friends to take as much pleasure in this approach as they do and will be hurt if you don't want to drop everything and pursue this new idea they have.

- Because play and humor are important to them, they are likely to eliminate anyone who is always serious from their circle of acquaintances. Although this may not seem like a good reason to cut someone, for a Frontal Right, not being interesting is a serious character defect.

- Similarly, because they thrive on new ideas and concepts, they may eliminate someone who is very pleasant but never really has anything interesting to contribute from their circle of friends.

- Many Frontal Rights tend to resist formal commitments and may date or even live with someone for years without taking steps to more specifically (or legally) define the relationship. They may also date a number of people simultaneously without feeling any conflict about doing so. One very Frontal Right research and development engineer found that when he first started to date someone, and that relationship was in the innovation phase, he wanted to spend quite a lot of time working on that project. Once the relationship was established and had become more routine, although he was still interested in continuing to relate, he would tend to pull back and find another project to give his attention to. This was very hard for his partners to handle, since they interpreted his shift of attention as rejection. In actuality, he was just behaving like a typical Frontal Right innovation or start-up junkie.

- Frontal Rights like to be alone and tend to require lots of physical and emotional space, except possibly those who are extremely extraverted. They need the time to think their own thoughts and look at their internal pictures, especially when they are working on a project. At such times, give them a wide berth.

- Frontal Rights don't like to spend too much time doing any one activity. For them, variety is the spice of life and a little of something goes a long way except when they are caught up in solving a problem in which case they may work non-stop for days with very little sleep. So, in general, expect them to need to get up and move around after they've been talking for a while. Expect them to want to vary their activities. And expect them to always have more than one book going at the same time. And, don't necessarily expect them to finish anything.

- Frontal Rights see vacations as opportunities to explore and adventure. They may go white water rafting or off to explore some culture that intrigues them. In either case they will do the minimum amount of planning necessary to get them there. While on vacation they will want to keep their days open and unscheduled so they can go off in any direction that intrigues them. They should never vacation with a Left Posterior Convexity.

- Frontal Rights spend money impulsively and may not necessarily know where it went. They manage money by a kind of gestalt awareness of about how much they have and about how much they owe and about how much is coming in. Unlike Right Posterior Convexities who tend to spend lots of money on others, Frontal Rights tend to spend money on other people only when they are actually with them and they are feeling good about themselves and the interaction. The key phrases for their style of gift giving are spontaneous and unplanned.

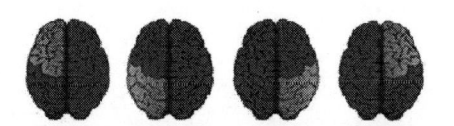

About the **Frontal Lefts** in your life:

- When dealing with a Frontal Left you need to remember that feelings are not something they want to deal with. So, don't expect them to pay attention to your feelings. (They won't.) Don't expect them to notice their own feelings. (They won't.) And don't expect them to willingly spend any of their time sharing feelings, processing feelings or relating on a feeling level. (They won't.) Also remember that Frontal Lefts actively dislike emotional scenes and will go out of their way to avoid them. So, if you're thinking of throwing a fit or telling them how you really feel (in order to clear the air or convince them to do something), give it up. It will only convince them that you are someone to be avoided.

- Frontal Lefts see vacations as a time to unwind, relax, be alone, or do nothing. Going fishing is a perfect Frontal Left vacation activity. If you require more fun, socializing, excitement or variety, you probably should not vacation with a Frontal Left.

- Frontal Lefts tend to be workaholics and may only participate in social activities that somehow advance their careers. To get them to go to social functions you will have to demonstrate how doing so will help them get ahead. Telling them "It'll be fun!" is not a recommended strategy

- Frontal Lefts tend to decide that they are ready to marry (and then very systematically go about finding a partner). They also tend to choose their partners for functional reasons, based on their assessment that the person they have selected will handle certain tasks well (like raising the children) or fulfill certain roles (being a hostess). Romantic love is not a necessary prerequisite. Please remember that when a Frontal Left marries he is not doing so in order to have someone to share his deepest feelings with. It is more likely that he is marrying in order to have someone to handle all the feeling functions so he won't ever have to be bothered with them.

- Frontal Lefts see their homes as private places where they can have peace and quiet and relax and unwind. They do not necessarily see them as places to relate. Many a Frontal Left spouse prefers the evening paper to a friendly chat. If you're going to be married to a Frontal Left, you're going to need to remember they don't particularly like to talk. Leave them alone; they're not intentionally rejecting you.

- Frontal Lefts want to be the prime decision makers and to control the major purchasing decisions for the household. They also tend to delegate certain areas of responsibility to their partner (like managing the grocery budget, making the food buying decisions). The areas they delegate tend to be either things they don't want to handle (like dealing with social situations) or things they consider too unimportant for them to waste their time on (remember the 80/20 rule).

- When subjected to chronic stress, Frontal Lefts often have Vesuvius tempers (which means they unexpectedly blow up), since they don't vent their feelings easily or on a regular basis. When this happens, the best thing to do is notice the anger, but don't react to it. The Frontal Left is frightened that his anger will be dangerous and destructive. If you attend to it without reaction, it will pass more quickly and will probably soon be forgotten. (Note: this pattern actually occurs due to a weakness in the Right Posterior Convexity and as such may occur as well in strong Frontal Rights and occasionally Left Posterior Convexities.)

- Remember Frontal Lefts argue and play devil's advocate for the pleasure it gives them (and because it sharpens their analytic skills). Try not to take it personally if they are curt and abrupt and don't get your feelings hurt because they are badgering you or ordering you about. They don't do it to hurt other's feelings. They are just oblivious to the effect it has on other people's feelings.

- Frontal Lefts want to live in a functional environment. They want their tools and appliances to be well maintained and in good working order and, if they have time, will gladly do home improvements and repairs. They also like to spend their time tinkering around in their workshops. If you want to have someone help you fix your plumbing, ask a Frontal Left.

- Frontal Lefts tend to buy quality products using the rationale that when you amortize their cost over time they are the best value for the money. Since Frontal Lefts are so critical of poor workmanship, they tend to inspect the things they buy carefully and at length. Let them buy their own tools, clothes, etc. unless you are absolutely certain you know exactly what they want.

- Lastly, Frontal Lefts tend to become unreasonably annoyed at anyone who wastes resources. They expect you to turn off the lights when leaving a room. They expect you to regularly attend to the maintenance of your automobile so that it performs well and lasts as long as it should. They are appalled if they think you are wasting your money or are doing a poor job of managing it. These may not seem like big deals to you, but they are to a Frontal Left and you can expect to be criticized when you fail to act responsibly in these areas.

Summary

In the preceding pages you've been introduced to many ideas on improving how you communicate and get along with others in your life. Because of its detailed and specific nature, you may have found yourself skimming over much of this chapter. Indeed, it contains too much information for most people. Nonetheless, it is excellent reference material. When you do have someone with whom you want to get along better and/or communicate more clearly, open the book to this chapter for help.

As well, keep in mind that these guidelines for communication are for situations in which the second Rule of Thumb for long-term success and survival applies. They are to help you manage activities and people not matching your preference consciously and carefully so that you can enlist and benefit from their assistance and support.

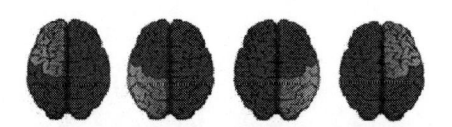

> **Life's Two Rules of Thumb**
>
> **Rule 1** To develop or nurture your self-esteem, as well as ensure your immediate effectiveness and success, select activities and people that match your preference.
>
> **Rule 2** To assure your survival, as well as guarantee your long-term effectiveness and success, manage activities and people not matching your preference consciously and carefully and, if possible, enlist assistance from people with complementary brains.

To be happy and healthy you will need to continually seek a balance between such long-term strategies and your need to nurture and reinforce your self-esteem as well as enjoy immediate success and satisfaction. To achieve these, the first Rule of Thumb is still the best way to care for yourself through the validation and use of your natural preference. One way to help yourself achieve this balance is to learn and use the final set of guidelines in the next chapter. These teach you to leverage your preference and manage your weaknesses to keep your energy higher and your joy fuller. Using them, you can orchestrate your days so that the two rules of thumb are dynamic simultaneous themes that combine to create the song of your life.

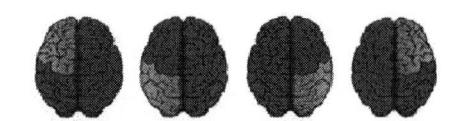

Chapter 11: Managing Preferences to Maximize Effectiveness

In the preceding chapters you have learned a lot about your brain and how it responds to the world. Now it's time to learn how to put all that you've read to use so that you can be more effective, feel better and more energized. The first part of this chapter will show you how to help yourself by using two different but complementary approaches to managing your preference:

- leveraging your preference (i.e. preferred type of thinking); and
- consciously managing tasks using any other type of thinking.

Each approach can enhance your personal effectiveness and well being. Maximum benefits come from using both.

Then, once you've learned how to help yourself, later in this same chapter you'll learn how to help other individuals and work teams so that they can be happier, healthier and more effective.

▲ Leveraging Your Preference

From the perspective of brain dominance *"Know thy self"* means know your preference and your stimulation needs as defined by your level of introversion/extraversion. And *"To thine own self be true"* means use and leverage your preference in an environment that satisfies your need for low, moderate or high stimulation. The best and surest way to do this is to energize or charge yourself by starting each day over center using your preference in a context that provides your brain with the stimulation it needs to function optimally. You'll know when you've got it right because you'll be experiencing that sense of *"flow"* Mihaly Csikszentmihalyi wrote about.

Remember, *self-charging* is an important life-skill. It is as critical to our well-being and success as self-soothing. Those who do well in life use it regularly, consciously or unconsciously. If we haven't learned to self-charge then we must teach ourselves. Not surprisingly, different people need to engage in very different, highly specific activities to ensure this self-charging. Moreover, certain types of thinking seem to almost naturally self-charge doing their morning routine i.e. the habitual things a person does from the time they wake up until the time they leave for work or school, while other types do not. As all of us benefit from self-charging, understanding this point can be very important especially for those who do not generally self-charge doing their morning routine. (To remind yourself about morning routines, see The Left Posterior Convexity Sequential Mode at the beginning of Chapter 3.) Now, let's look at some examples of self-charging.

Examples of Self-Charging

- A person with a Left Posterior Convexity preference will be energized by attending to something that allows him to think/act in a proceduralized manner sequencing, organizing things that lend themselves to being sequenced; or by using well-organized materials to perform a routine. Almost all morning routines provide some self-charging for Left Posterior Convexities.

- A person with a Right Posterior Convexity preference will be energized by attending to something that allows him to focus on the presence or absence of harmony and act to maximize the authentic sense of connection and harmony between people, voices, instruments and/or colors in the environment. Some morning routines either because they involve connecting with and nurturing others or because they involve music or meditation, achieve some self-charging for Right Posterior Convexities.

- A person with a Frontal Right preference will be energized by attending to something that allows him to use his visual-spatial imagination in combination with metaphoric thinking to be creative; generate a positive vision for the future; or invent a new solution, strategy or product. A few morning routines seem to charge the Frontal Right – those that involve running or jogging outdoors in a scenic area with natural beauty and panoramic views. The length of time actually spent self-charging the Frontal Right is often less than half an hour.

- A person with a Frontal Left preference will be energized by attending to something that allows him to use his logical skills to evaluate and prioritize options or make decisions concerning complex but known problems. Morning routines that involve reading a morning newspaper such as the Wall Street Journal or watching CNN to catch up on critical business and economic information can charge the Frontal Left. The length of time actually spent self-charging the Frontal Left is often less than half an hour.

- Highly extraverted persons will be energized by doing an over center task in a noisy, crowded, fast-paced or competitive environment, especially one that is open and with 3-foot high dividers or cubicles maximizing interaction and stimulation.

- Highly introverted persons will be energized by doing an over center task in a quiet, out of the way, non-competitive or slower environment with fewer distractions or rooms/offices with floor to ceiling walls and doors that close, maximizing privacy.

- The 70 percent who have a balanced level of inner wakefulness will be energized by doing an over center task in a moderately stimulating environment that does not require the person to function at either of the above extremes.

Individuals and teams who use self-charging report their whole day goes better. These people start their day over center, using their natural preference for at least an hour (preferably two) in an environment appropriate for their stimulation needs. So, for the best results do what these people do. Structure your day so that during the first two hours you are using your preference in an environment suited to your introverted, balanced or extraverted needs, without interruptions.

Let's stop for a moment to look at how and why self-charging is so effective and compare self-charging with what happens when we start the day *randomly* doing non-preferred tasks simply because they present themselves when we walk in the door. The box immediately below gives you a key that will help you understand the graphs we are going to be looking at. Take time to read it first.

Key for Illustrative Graphs

The three vertically stacked, horizontal bars in each graph indicate how someone is feeling. Movement from bottom to top, from darkest to lightest shows movement from less energy to more energy, from negative feelings to happier feelings. Movement from top to bottom, from lightest to darkest shows the reverse, from more energy to less energy, from happier feelings to more negative feelings.

White	indicates feeling energized and terrific
Gray	indicates feeling happy and comfortable
Dark Gray	indicates feeling drained, fatigued and irritable

The two letters identify tasks and whether or not a given task uses one's preference:
   A   indicates a task that uses one's preference
   B   indicates a task that does not use one's preference

Look at the first graph and notice the effect self-charging has on a person's energy and mood. This is why self-charging is so important and why it is a valuable tool for managing your energy. By using self-charging, you can ensure that your energy is increased and uplifted. In this three-hour example, the person has three tasks to accomplish: two A tasks that use his preference and energize him and one B task, that uses a type of thinking other than his preference and drains him. To charge himself (i.e. to *self-charge*) he does both A tasks before doing the B task.

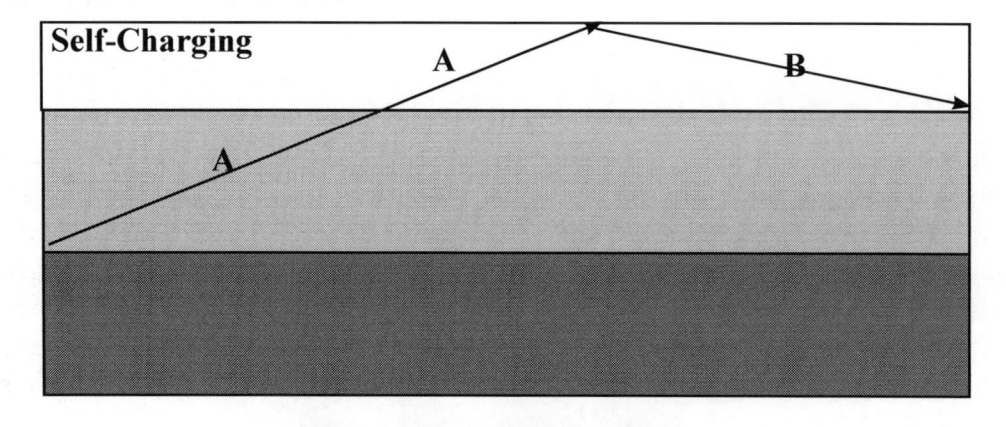

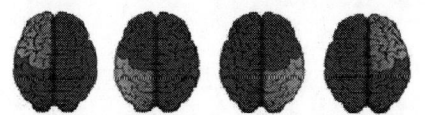

Self-Charging

The result is that he raises his energy and mood substantially prior to doing the B task, providing himself with a cushion of abundant energy and good feelings. When he does do the B task, which drains him, it brings him down, but only from feeling terrific to feeling good and comfortable. To understand the value of the cushioning, look at the next graph showing what happens when someone starts his or her day randomly.

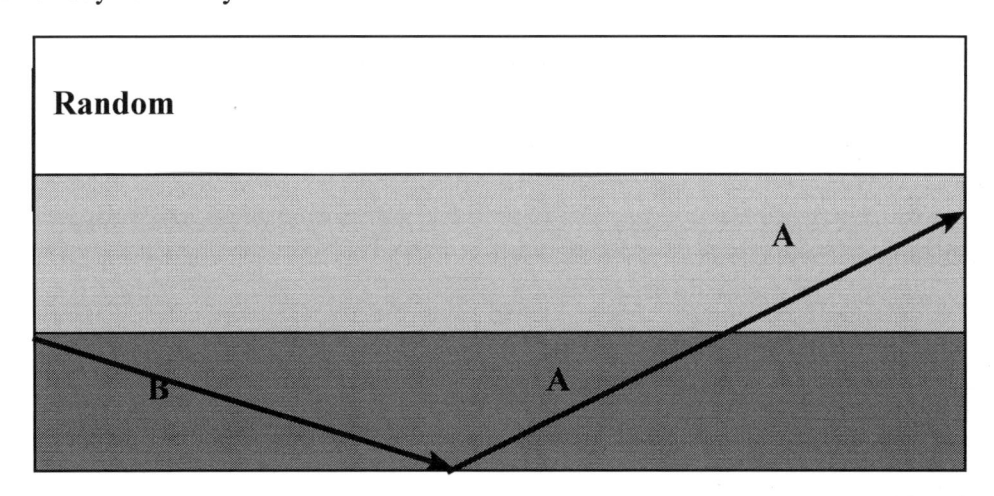

Random

Random, unplanned scheduling of tasks often results in our starting the day off doing non-preferred B tasks. As such, it's often more harmful than we realize. In this example, the person does the same three tasks – two A tasks which use his preference and energize him and one B task which uses a type of thinking other than his preference and drains him. The difference is that he does the one B task before doing either A task. The result is that he drains himself so much immediately that the energy he gains doing one of his A tasks merely brings him back to neutral. And it is not until the third hour when he does the second A task that he begins to really feel and be energized.

Take time to compare these two very different approaches to getting the same work accomplished. If you look closely you'll notice that both examples end up in the same place. After three hours the person is feeling good and comfortable. The difference is that in self-charging the person is feeling good for all three hours and actually very highly energized for two of the three. By contrast, the random approach leaves the person never really feeling terrific, feeling okay for one hour and actually rather badly for two hours. Clearly taking time to start the day off on the right foot by using your preference for a few hours makes a real and significant difference in how you feel throughout the day.

When teaching these techniques to a group of salesmen some years ago, their manager, an extraverted Right Posterior Convexity male, said that he found doing the B tasks at the beginning of the day worked very well. He did them first, got them out of the way and was free to enjoy the rest of the day. On the surface this man's account appears to be in contradiction to the personal energy management approach being recommended here. A brief discussion with the manager however, revealed that at the time he had been using his approach, he and his wife were happily married with four school-aged children. Their morning ritual was to all get up two hours before they had to be at work or school and have breakfast together around a large kitchen table, telling each other jokes, laughing together, sharing and talking. In other words, the reason the extraverted Right Posterior Convexity sales manager had been able to come to work and start the day off with B tasks was that he had just spent two hours at home self-charging himself – using his Right Posterior Convexity preference to nurture and connect with his family.

As you look at these graphs, again think about what you do and have done in the past. Was there a time you began every day by self-charging yourself and using your preference for a couple of hours? Have there been times when you felt forced to start the day doing B tasks that left you drained and feeling irritable?

It can be helpful to think of your brain as a battery. When you use the battery to start and drive your car, your car runs well, your battery remains strong and you can use it while you're driving to provide power for the car's lights. But, if you use your car's battery to operate your car's interior or headlights when it's not on or you aren't driving, your car's battery is drained – sometimes so much that you can't even start the car. Driving your car charges its battery. Using your car as a source of light drains it. Using your brain to do things that use your preference charges your brain. Using your brain to do anything else drains and fatigues it.

So, as you move through the day, try to consciously structure your time so that at least 50 percent of what you do uses your preference in situations that satisfy your need for high, moderate or low stimulation. When you do, you'll find you feel stronger and happier. And, finally, see if you can manage to end your workday using your preference. You will be self-charging so that you're energized and ready to enjoy or make the most of your evening – whether you spend it alone or with friends or family.

▲▲Managing Your Weaknesses

Our only true strength is our preference. All other types of thinking – both of our auxiliaries as well as our greatest natural weakness – are relative weaknesses. Each requires our brain to work very hard even where we've developed significant competencies in them. Even if they appear to be comfortable because they satisfy our introverted or extraverted needs, in reality, tasks requiring our non-preferred competencies drain us because they force our brain to work extremely hard.

So when planning your day, week and life it is best to remember that regardless of how much you develop or use a skill, if it doesn't use your preference, it is more draining than energizing. This means evaluating your job to determine which of your activities use your preference and which use another type of thinking and then consciously managing when and how you attend to the tasks that require you to use a type of thinking other than your preference. Note that communicating clearly with someone whose preference differs from yours should be treated as a non-preferred task as it often requires you to consciously structure and or edit how you express yourself, in order to speak that person's language. (Look back to Chapter 10: Getting Along and Communicating Clearly.)

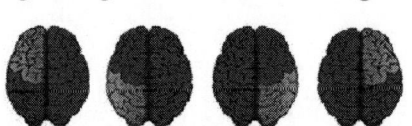

Fortunately, several strategies have been identified and proven to be highly effective when managing tasks that depend on a non-preferred type of thinking. Not all are equally appropriate or even possible in a given situation. However, taken together as a set of tools they provide us with an empowering alternative to being frustrated and exhausted and/or doing a less than an optimal job. Significantly, most of these strategies fall into two categories or approaches: redesigning our job and requesting help. You may be more comfortable with one approach than the other. By being familiar with both approaches and all seven strategies you will increase your options.

Redesigning Jobs and Tasks

Generally speaking there are two kinds of redesign possible: formal and informal. When an evaluation of your job has revealed that the fit between your preference and the tasks you are expected to perform is poor, it can be a good idea to consider a formal redesign such as a job or career change.

Three real-life examples illustrate when and where formal redesign is helpful. The first is the technical wizard, an Introverted Frontal Right, who has been promoted to management. His new position has many benefits and one significant cost. It forces the wizard to use his Frontal Left auxiliary and his Left Posterior Convexity weakness more than his preference most of the day. When he is helped to understand why his new job is so frustrating, he decides to request a demotion back to research so that he can be true to himself and enjoy both his work and life. The second example is the Extraverted Frontal Right entrepreneur who, although his company has been highly successful, has to do more administrative and operational work. Both of these require her to use her Frontal Left auxiliary and her Left Posterior Convexity weakness more than her preference most of the day. When she learns why being a success isn't all it's cracked up to be, she decides to restructure or sell out so that she's free to pursue new interests compatible with her Frontal Right preference. Finally, a Right Posterior Convexity nurse, who entered nursing to help people, moved up the career ladder to a supervisory position to increase her income and status. Her new position has several benefits and one significant cost. It forces her to use her Left Posterior Convexity auxiliary and her Frontal Left weakness more than her preference – most of the day. When she learns why her life has lost its zest, she chooses to request a demotion to staff nursing or switches to a career in Human Resources or Public Relations. All of these are formal approaches to redesigning how an individual spends their workday. They are powerful and empowering strategies for dealing with jobs that don't or no longer match who someone is.

If you are in a situation in which most of what you do does not use your preference and you cannot for some reason formally redesign what you do soon, do as much as you can to increase the how and when you use your preference away from work, in the evenings, at home and on the weekends. This will not accomplish as much as formally redesigning your job but it will help you until you can make a more powerful and empowering change in what you do most of the time.

When the degree of fit is moderate or better, the necessary redesigning may be accomplished through one or more less formal means. These three strategies, along with the four for requesting help are the even strategies we recommend people use to manage their auxiliaries and natural weakness on a day-in, day-out basis.

▲▲ Strategies for Managing Weaknesses

Redesign the Task
1. *Sandwich* it between two tasks in your preference
2. *Package* it with a task using your preference
3. *Schedule* it at a peak energy time

Request Help
4. *Select* and use a modal Mentor
5. *Trade* the task to a modal expert
6. *Delegate* the task to a modal expert
7. *Hire* a modal expert

When you have a degree of competency in the required non-preferred task, such informal redesigning may be accomplished by Sandwiching the task which uses your non-preferred competency between two tasks each of which draw on your true preference.

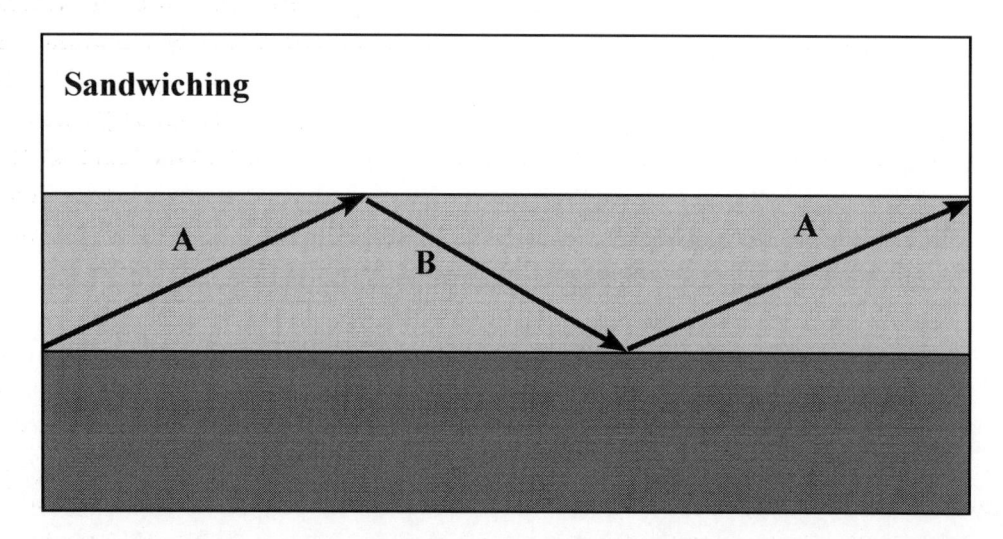

Sandwiching

The power of this simple yet highly effective approach is based on energy management. As such, Sandwiching is an important tool for managing your energy throughout the day. By using Sandwiching you can see that your energy is increased and uplifted. In this three hour example, the person again does the same three tasks – two A tasks which use his preference and energize him and one B task which uses a type of thinking other than his preference and drains him. By raising his energy with an A task prior to doing a B task which he knows will drain him, the person provides himself with a cushion of good feelings and additional energy first so that when he does do a B task, which brings him down, it only brings him back from feeling really good to a more neutral feeling. Moreover, by following the B task with a second A task he ends up feeling happy and comfortable.

Remember, engaging in non-preferred tasks Randomly, without self-charging the system before and after, often results in much of the day being spent between a down or negatively charged position and neutral. So, you might say this conscious ordering of tasks allows you to conserve a valuable resource – you. (Look back a few pages to see the Random graph.)

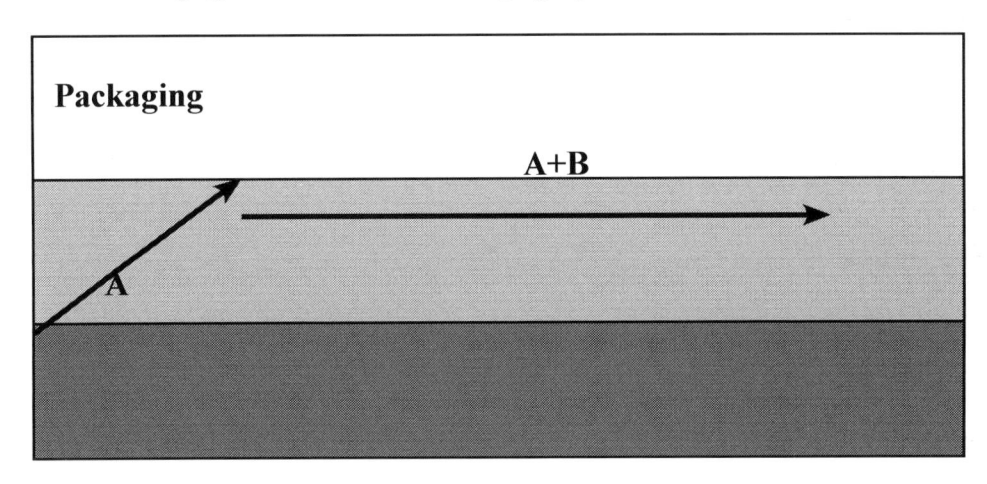

Packaging

A+B

A

A second informal strategy is called Packaging. Rather than doing tasks that use your preference before and after those which do not, Packaging invites you to use your preference to do something else, at the same time you are doing a job which requires you to use a non-preferred type of thinking. Packaging also helps you manage your energy. By using Packaging you ensure that your energy remains steady or stable. It is sustained. It doesn't rise much but it doesn't diminish either. In the three hour example illustrated, the person again does three tasks – two A tasks which use his preference and energize him and one B task, which uses a type of thinking other than his preference and drains him. He does the first A task to raise his energy. Then, he does the B task, which would otherwise drain him, packaged with another A task. This sustains his energy.

Two real-life examples of Packaging may help you understand how to use this technique. The first situation, in which Packaging can be used effectively, is when you are extraverted or balanced and have a task to do that uses your preference, but which is normally done in an introverted setting – in an isolated, out of the way or very quiet place. In many small businesses, for example, a Left Posterior Convexity is hired to do stocking inventory and order filling in a back room, alone. If the person happens to be an introverted Left Posterior Convexity that's fine and dandy. But if he's not, he's likely to become bored and lonely back there with the result that he finds himself wandering around the rest of the offices to find people to talk to and to find more activity and stimulation. In this kind of situation, providing the lone worker with a radio to listen to while he's working will make the job work for him.

Another example of Packaging was presented earlier in the book. Remember the Right Posterior Convexity librarians who did all their Left Posterior Convexity inventory work sitting around a table chatting? Here the face-to-face interaction and conversation with others, while these Right Posterior Convexities did a non-preferred task, kept their preference active and functioning efficiently while their auxiliary functioned inefficiently. Packaging helps us do a better job without the fatigue.

A third informal strategy involves conscious Scheduling. Two effective Scheduling techniques are:

- Schedule the non-preferred tasks at times of the day when you are generally, naturally up.
- Never schedule important non-preferred tasks at times of the day when you are generally low.

Other informal techniques that you can implement by yourself just before performing a non-preferred task are to:

- Remind yourself just before starting that it's something you don't prefer, but are *choosing* to do as part of a total job or position you want or for which you have accepted responsibility.
- Do a deep breathing exercise immediately prior to doing the non-preferred task in order to energize your brain.

When the above techniques are inappropriate or insufficient, your best step is to request help.

Requesting Help

Requesting help is generally the best solution when the task or person requires you to:

- use your greatest weakness (i.e. your Achilles heel located diagonally from your preference) or
- perform in a context that doesn't suit your stimulation needs.

Moreover, requesting and using help is not something to be ashamed of. Most jobs, whether in production, sales, problem-solving or management, are whole-brained. Breakthroughs like those presented in this book have shown that to do these jobs well you need to use every type of thinking. Today highly successful companies formally sanction or encourage executives and employees to help each other through team leadership, self-managing teams and whole-brain team building workshops or retreats.

Generally speaking, there are four ways to enlist the help you need:

- you can *Find and Use a Mentor* whose preference and introversion/extraversion match the task you have to do;
- you can *Trade* the task to a co-worker whose preference and introversion/extraversion match the job you have to do;

or, if you are a manager or supervisor:
- you can *Delegate* the task to someone who works for you and whose preference and stimulation needs match those required; or
- you can *Hire* a new employee (full time, temporary or contract) whose preference and stimulation needs match those in which you need help.

Finding and using a mentor was discussed in detail in Chapter 9 - Developing Competencies. One advantage of using a mentor is that, with his/her help and a bit of time and practice, you can develop a reasonable degree of competency in their area of giftedness and thereby become more self-sufficient. The disadvantage of using a mentor is that for a time you will need to devote more, rather than less, time to your non-preferred type of thinking, listening to and observing your mentor in action as well as practicing your new non-preferred language and skills.

By contrast, trading, delegating, and hiring an expert to do your non-preferred tasks, frees your time and energy to do what you do best. Although, of course, you don't increase your own requisite variety as you aren't developing any additional skills yourself. When deciding which strategy to use, consider both the immediate and long-term implications of each option. Generally speaking, if the task required is generic, one which you will need and can use to your advantage almost anywhere, i.e. selling or negotiating, you may want to use a mentor so that you learn to do it yourself and will have it in your personal tool kit in the future. Whereas, if the task is less generic it may be wiser to trade or delegate it to an existing staff person with the appropriate preference and introversion/extraversion or hire someone who can do it well.

Bringing it all together, you can manage your preferences by using this simple **3-Step Strategy for Managing Your Preferences.**

- Design your job so that at least 50 percent of what you do uses your preference and satisfies your introverted /extraverted need for high, moderate or low stimulation.
- Leverage your lead daily by using self-charging.
- Manage tasks that don't use your preference or satisfy your stimulation needs by redesigning how and when you do them: using sandwiching, packaging or scheduling; or by requesting help from someone with the necessary preference or introversion/extraversion.

All three steps are critical. They make it possible for you to be true to yourself and do your job well. They help you honor yourself and your preference while protecting your mental Achilles heel. Used in combination with the guidelines for communicating clearly detailed in the last chapter they can help you to transform uncomfortable or stressful situations into rewarding, energizing ones. They empower you to choreograph or orchestrate your life so you can thrive.

Helping Another Individual Structure High Performance At Work

When you've used these techniques for a few weeks, you'll appreciate their value. You'll know they increase your energy and effectiveness. You'll know that some are better suited to your present situation. And, if you are like most people, you will want to share them with others – simply because all of us like to share things that work. Encouraging others to manage their own mental preferences can be achieved with a proven four-step process that will be covered here.

Introduce them to this Whole-brain Model: It would be difficult or impossible for anyone to manage his own preference until he understands the model simply because most of us have been raised and educated to believe truly capable people can do everything. So, be sure you introduce them to: the principle of dominance, the four specialized types of thinking, extraversion and introversion, along with the underlying premise that each type of thinking and arousal level has a unique and valuable contribution to make to life. Be sure to clarify and emphasize how each type of thinking and arousal level contributes to the organization. Then, bring up the idea of whole-brained teams as an exciting and necessary part of the successful organization in the 21st century. And finally, always use illustrative examples people will recognize and appreciate from your own life and the company.

Teaching others the Three-Step Strategy is best done by introducing them to the strategy and subsequently providing them with examples of how you and others have accomplished each step.

Modeling evaluating, redesigning and requesting help openly will go far to encourage others that work done this way can be both satisfying and successful. Moreover, if you are the boss, demonstrating your commitment to this approach will ensure its safety for those who believe they must be able to do everything themselves.

Encouraging your staff to seek and use quadrant or modal mentors will be easiest if you can demonstrate to them that needing such help is okay. This is accomplished most easily by telling them about your own Achilles heel, how you sought and found someone with that preference to coach you and how that coaching has helped you be more effective. Similarly, **encouraging staff to seek and use translators** is best done by example. The more often you select and use a translator, the more doing so will feel okay to others. Additionally, if you can find ways to tell stories about your successful use of a translator that, too, will help.

Telling stories about yourself and others whose actions embody the new behaviors you want others to adopt is a powerful tool. If you are extraverted and have a lead in the Frontal or Right Posterior Convexity telling stories may come easily – after all it is a skill that uses your preference. If you don't feel comfortable telling stories, try reading these books. They will convince you that story telling is a valuable leadership skill. They may also inspire you to try it.

- Terry Deal's Corporate Cultures: *The Rites & Rituals of Corporate Life,* Addison-Wesley Publishing, 1982.
- Peg Neuhauser's *Corporate Legends & Lore: The Power of Story Telling as a Management Tool*, McGraw Hill, New York 1993.

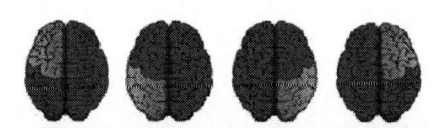

In summary, getting others to manage their own preferences is like parenting. It works best if you yourself are doing what you're asking others to do. If you try to be the exception to the rule, the person who is so gifted and intelligent that he doesn't need help, you aren't encouraging others to manage their preferences. If you focus on doing what you do best and regularly request help from others when doing things that don't use your preference, you are modeling what it means to be a high-functioning member of a whole brained team or family, a specialized, gifted participant in a complex and diversified human system.

Structuring High Performance as a Team

High performance teams comprised of peers each contributing a different strength were studied initially by NASA in the 60's. Getting a man on the moon and later manning the space shuttle were not tasks that could be successfully accomplished by the old top-down system. At that time American business was still functioning with the old hierarchical system of bosses, managers, supervisors and entry-level workers, all of whom were encouraged to believe the same myth, that really able or truly bright people can do everything. By the 1980's several natural resource and high-tech companies with a significant percentage of highly educated professional employees had learned that a highly educated work force did not follow dictates from on high in lemming proportions. These people experienced themselves more as adults than children and sought to be treated respectfully as peers to management with important contributions to make to decisions, policies, production, marketing, distribution and/or new product development. As employees they wanted and asked for a different type of organizational structure – one that would empower them as individuals and groups to take responsibility, solve problems and make decisions.

In the 1990's such requests were granted because almost overwhelming economic problems made layers of management a financial liability few companies can afford. American and global businesses sought to transform themselves so that high performance teams comprised of self-managing individuals could form and thrive. Today such teams are becoming the standard work unit. Unlike the semi-permanent team of the past that often took one to two years to get up to speed with the help of external consultants, today's project-focused teams often work together for only a few months or days. Consequently, there is an urgent need for the individual to know how to manage his own participation as a team member so that teams can function smoothly and effectively. Most especially, individual workers and managers need to know:
- how to belong,
- how and when to contribute,
- how to see and value others' contributions, and
- how and when to let others lead.

A key to success in this new approach to business is successfully identifying each person's specialized contributions in such a manner that everyone accepts the value of everyone else's contribution. In the past, a person's technical training and job experience helped others identify their value and contribution.

These are no longer adequate. We are now in an era of rapid and constant technological change. The cycle-time available for inventing, implementing, stabilizing and re-inventing is becoming shorter and shorter driven by an increased sensitivity to the market. Today, each person's role or contribution with respect to the overall process of change has become as important as his formal training and job experience. For this reason, people working with self-managed teams have become very excited about Brain Dominance because it helps everyone rapidly see where and how they and others contribute, as well as where and when they need to sit back and follow the leadership of others whose dominance fits other parts of the change cycle.

Linking Giftedness to the Rapid Change Cycle of the 21st Century	
Invent, Start, Begin, Birth	Frontal Right
Innovate, Push Into the Market, Compete	Extraverted Double Frontal
Stabilize, Implement, Maintain	Double Left
Market Liaison (feedback and/or feed forward person)	Right Posterior Convexity, Double Right
Process and Information Facilitator	Double Posterior Convexity

Because the members of successful high performance teams in business today need to recognize and value each other's individual contributions within this cycle of change, the model presented in this book can do a great deal to help self-managed teams function well. It offers easily understood and powerful organizing principles that everyone can relate to. By making it clear that each person has dependable strengths which link to the change cycle, the information makes it possible for any group or project team to identify their inventor, innovator, stabilizer and market liaison. One retired CEO, Dr. Robert Henry, who used the model in his organization during his final five years
even said *"Dr. Benziger's book is the best textbook available for the group that wants or needs to transform itself into an effective, self-managing, high performance team."*

If you are responsible for a team, or are a member of a team, keep in mind that structuring high performance for a team involves building on the self-managed strategies for improved individual effectiveness and performance. Given this information, employees become naturally more self-directed. Their ability to collaborate improves, along with their productivity, loyalty and enthusiasm. And, quite naturally, they improve the performance of the team to which they currently belong as well as assist future teams to transform themselves from a mere group of individuals who happen to work together into a highly effective high-performance team. To facilitate this happening more rapidly, you can choose to serve as a coach to transform and energize your team by adopting the same process presented earlier for helping individuals.

> **A Strategy for Helping Others Achieve High Performance**
>
> - Introduce them to this Whole-brain Model
> - Teach them the 3-Step Strategy for Managing Your Preferences
> - Model evaluating, redesigning and requesting help
> - Encourage them to seek and use Mentors and/or Translators

How you implement this process is important. Most especially, it's important you share and model your own efforts to manage your preference by understanding how your strengths and weaknesses have helped you. During the vast majority of the 20th century, global and American businesses were dominated by the belief that to succeed an individual must know, be and do everything well. Admitting and accepting weaknesses in a critical area was unacceptable. Now, today, in the 21st century, for a company or organization to transform, re-invent or re-engineer itself successfully, it is critical the people at the top demonstrate their commitment to a new, better and more useful guidepost.

> **Managing the Balance Between Creativity and Operations**
> **From a successful CEO – Advice for CEOs**
>
> - Have a Benziger Profile (i.e. the BTSA) done for every executive.
> - Introduce them to Dr. Benziger's model and ideas.
> - Make yourself an example.
> - Clarify your expectations.
> - Clarify your managers' role, i.e. as administrative-operations persons.
> - Clarify your creative persons' role.
> - Spend one-on-one time with key employees, developing their understanding and buy-in to the advantages of each person contributing from their preference.
>
> From a talk given by Charlie Leighton, Chairman, The CML Group
> at the Annual National Conference of Retailers, May 1990

At The CML Group, Charlie Leighton, CML's Founder and Chairman, maximized these strategies by inventing a process to manage the balance between creativity and operations. The 7-step process Leighton invented and used with tremendous success is an expanded version of the above 4-Step Strategy. The differences are revealing and show how successful business leaders respond to the need of the time. For Leighton, creativity was essential, but it had to be balanced with dependable operations. Here's what he did that worked.

> **New Guidepost for Corporate Cultures and Leadership**
>
> Dominance is normal and natural. No one truly knows and does everything equally well. We all do better in the long run when we each contribute from our strengths and look to others when our weaknesses are concerned.

For Leighton, corporate success in the 1990's was tied to the ability to establish and manage a balance of right and left-brained personnel. Establishing a balance can be done through hiring and slotting. Hire diverse thinkers. Then, make the differences work for you by placing people in jobs that use their preference. Slot people in a positive, empowering manner. Use and reward Left Posterior Convexity procedural thinkers for attending to operational and administrative details such as doing things by the book and doing things on schedule. Give your Frontal Lefts responsibility for making difficult operational and financial decisions. Ask and reward Right Posterior Convexities for attending to and developing strong employee morale and positive public, customer and community relations. Ask your Frontal Rights to take responsibility for shaping an energizing vision that will fuel your company and generate creative solutions to non-logical business problems, i.e. strategic planning, new product development, advertising, marketing, display, merchandising and packaging. Managing the balance effectively is still important whenever an increase in creativity is desired. Because introducing creativity into a company is usually a major shift in the company's culture, Leighton believed team-ship and collaboration between left and right-brainers must be openly modeled and repeatedly endorsed at the top. Listen again as Leighton tells us what he did that made a difference. And as you listen imagine doing each step yourself with your people:

- Invite an expert in to do BTSA profile for all your executives with the BTSA.
- Introduce all of your executives to the model and ideas presented in this book. This can be done by asking a KBA trained consultant to give an introductory workshop as Charles Leighton did, and or by giving each a copy of this book.
- Make your own profile and that of your partner or chief assistant public information for all your employees. Use your relationship with your partner as an example or model of how people with complementary preferences can work together effectively.
- Clarify your own expectations: that you don't expect your management personnel to be creative resources; that you don't expect your creative personnel to be financial or operational giants.
- Clarify repeatedly and openly your perception of your managers' role as supporters for your creative people, because their administrative and logical capabilities make it possible for them to handle problems that overwhelm creative types.

Leighton noticed and accepted that "Tom Wrubel, the founder of Nature Company, for all his genius, was simply overwhelmed when it came to managing lots of people and discussing the budget. And others of our founders and creative types have been frightened by legal negotiations and language." Leighton's solution was: don't make creative types attend budget meetings; seek ways to minimize the amount of negotiation they had to do; and as much as possible have legal language rewritten to use normal English.

- Clarify repeatedly and openly your perception of the role your creative people fill.
- Spend one-on-one time with all key employees, both left-brained and right-brained, to support them personally in developing an understanding and appreciation for the advantages of doing work that matches your preference and relying on others to assist you with tasks that depend on modes which you find difficult.

In summary, Leighton's actions as Chairman of The CML Group, intentional or intuitive, sought to maximize both individual and team performance at the top and within each of his companies by using the model presented in this book as a tool for clarifying roles and improving communications. Not surprisingly, The CML Group was as successful in the 1990's in retailing as GE has been in its field.

Creating New Teams

Consciously putting together two or more people who together have what it takes to get the job done is called *Pattern Blending*. Very often, when you need to put a group together to solve a problem, *Pattern Blending* can help. First identify the task your new team will be doing, and from that identify the skills the team will need to have. Compare the set of skills needed to what you know about each of the four specialized types of thinking and about introversion and extraversion, to identify which of the brain dominance patterns you need to put together to get the job done well. Then, select the appropriate people and bring them together using the approach Charlie Leighton developed and used so successfully, or the shorter strategy given below.

A Strategy for Helping Others Achieve High Performance

- Introduce them to this Whole-brain Model
- Teach them the 3-Step Strategy for Managing Your Preferences
- Model evaluating, redesigning and requesting help
- Encourage them to seek and use Mentors and/or Translators

Additionally, when assembling a team it is useful to know each person's feeling about being a team player. Generally, from a dominance perspective, Posterior Convexities are more team players than Frontals. But the way in which someone relates to teams and the sharing of power is not cut and dried. Extraversion, introversion and birth order strongly affect how comfortable a person is on a team as well as the structure of their participation. So, take time to review and consider the two charts below that summarize that information. And, particularly if you yourself are either highly extraverted or introverted, re-read Chapter 4 to remind yourself how others experience the world.

Extraversion, Introversion and Teams	
Extreme Extraverts	Independent star performers Deal makers, closers Not generally, team players
Moderate Extraverts	Like to be the boss
Balanced	Like to be on teams
Moderate Introverts	Function best as expert resources
Extreme Introverts	Independent workers Researchers Not generally team players

Birth order seems to be a powerful determinant of how people function on teams. Eldest and only children generally assume the role of the team leader or boss. Youngest children, in contrast, rarely want to be the boss. Combining birth order with the rest of the information in this book works well. It is not a primary part of this book and model as it is purely psychological and doesn't have a physiological foundation as preference and introversion/extraversion do. Those wishing to learn more on this topic, might read: *The Birth Order Book*, Kevin Leman, Dell Publishing, New York, 1985. Or, *Born to Rebel: Birth Order, Family Dynamics & Creative Lives*, Frank J. Sulloway, Pantheon Books, New York, 1996.

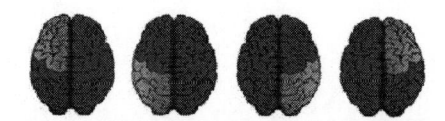

Birth Order and Team Participation	
Eldest	Wants to be the boss Wants to give orders rather than follow
Only	Wants to be the boss Wants to give orders rather than follow
Middle	Likes teams - Follows orders
Youngest	Rarely wants to be the boss

Summary

So now, you've not only learned a lot about your brain and how it works, you've also become familiar with a wide range of things you can do. In the first half of this final chapter, you learned how to leverage your preference through self-charging and to manage your weaknesses using seven different techniques so that you are happier and more energized as well as more effective. To truly benefit from this information and book you'll need to put what you've read into practice. Use the tools to improve your own life. When you've done that, and are feeling better, stronger, more powerful and effective, you will want to share what you have learned using the approaches presented in the second half of this final chapter.

Walk in Peace ~ Grow in Love

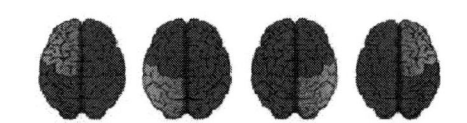

Appendices

Appendix A: The Tradition of Thinking About Thinking

Like most new ideas and inventions, the Benziger Model was not created in a vacuum. It is just one more evolutionary step in a long tradition of interlinked models, all of which seek to explain conscious human thinking and decision making. Two of the prin-cipal models in this historic tradition are the Native American Medicine Wheel, which is thousands of years old and held in high regard by native cultures, sociologists and anthropologists; and Carl Gustav Jung's 4-function model, developed by him in the 1920's and 30's to explain how people obtain, value and process information.

Interestingly enough, these two 4-modal models, developed centuries and continents apart, are very similar. The Indians' cold, unfeeling but wise "Buffalo" is much like Jung's cool analytic "Thinking" type. The introspection of their "Bear" is like the "Sensation" type's habit of looking within himself to see how he has done something before and/or "what worked" before. The innocent, trusting "Mouse" offers one perspective of the ever-hopeful, "Feeling" type. And, the far-sighted vision of the "Eagle" is an apt description of many "Intuitives". Moreover, both these models include information telling how each person is born with one natural preference, but will over his or her life-time grow in the ability to use his or her non-preferred or "shadow" functions.

Moreover, it is not surprising that both of these models have commanded reverence among those who

NORTH:	Buffalo, Wisdom, cold without feeling.
WEST:	Bear, Introspection and Looks-within Place.
SOUTH:	Mouse, Innocence and Trust, Touching.
EAST:	Eagle, Ilumination, clear farsighted vision, but close to nothing, always above & separated from life.
Carl Gustav Jung's Four Functions (1920's-30's) Jungian based models: Myers-Briggs (1962), Drake-Beam-Morin (1972), Keirsey-Bates (1978)	
THINKING:	objective, analytic, principles, criteria, critiques
SENSATION:	focus on past, realistic, down-to-earth, practical, sensible
FEELING:	subjective, personal, values intimacy, sympathetic & sensitive to harmony & to extenuating circumstances, humane
INTUITION:	hunches, futures, speculative, fantasy, imaginative

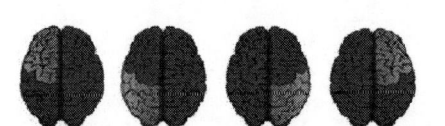

have lived and worked with them, for both have a timeless, universal quality. In fact, were it not for three considerations, each of which limits their utility, it would be easy to see these two models as the Alpha and Omega of this tradition. These limiting considerations are:

1. both models lack a diagnostic tool: diagnostic tools make it possible for individuals to identify their preferred style in a seemingly dependable manner;

2. both are generalized and "archetypal" in their nature: being achetypal they create in people a powerful feeling that they are true in a universal way. This positive attribute, makes them difficult for many people to apply them to specific life concerns such as: selecting or designing a job or career to insure personal satisfaction; selecting teams; selecting a partner; diagnosing and resolving marital problems; and

3. both lack scientific foundations: scientific foundations often convince "non-believers" to accept a model is real – that there are, in fact, real and innate differences in thinking styles, "which we cannot help," and that these differences play an important role in our lives.

Possibly for this reason, most of the models developed since Jung's time have attempted to address one or more of these limiting factors. For example, from the 1930's until well into the 1970's, many efforts were made to make Jung's model itself more available and useful to the average person by designing easy to use diagnostic tools to accompany it – along with easy to read books and training materials which clarify how the general model relates to life. Principle among these Jungian-based models are: the Myers Briggs Type Indicator (1962), Drake Beam Morin's I-SPEAK Survey (1972) and the Keirsey-Bates' Inventory in Please Understand Me (1978). Popular with many, these models are used by therapists, management consultants, trainers and church groups to help clients understand and accept the general differences between people in the hopes that it will improve their ability to accept these differences and to communicate effectively. These models have been very success-ful. They do not however offer any scientific basis for the four styles – nor do they address an important concept which Jung wrote about – Falsification of Type. As such, people are asked to accept that four specialized types exist and to appreciate all four without really understanding the value or contribution each makes.

Other models from this period were developed to explore, explain and predict specific social behavior. Within this group, there are three categories:

- those developed by educators to distinguish one "type" of student from another (often called "learning style inventories");
- those developed by organizational theorists to distinguish categories of employees (followers) and/or categories of leaders; and
- those developed by social scientists to explain specific problematic behaviors, such as criminality, conflict patterns, resistance to change and creativity.

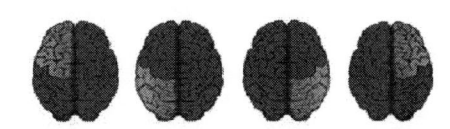

What is significant is that these behavioral models all reveal tremendous support for Jung's original four "functions." Nine of the ten models reviewed directly or indirectly identify logical analysis as a distinctive mode. Four of the ten pull out the ability to attend to details in a thorough manner (which is part and parcel of the sensation function). Eight of the ten directly or indirectly identify the personal feeling mode. And, four of the ten identify a future-oriented, speculative competency.

That this behavioral research identifies some categories which on the surface appear to be new, should not be surprising or confusing. Jung recognized that although each person had a lead function, each person also had predictable auxiliaries. The styles which appear to be new are in fact merely descriptions of someone who has developed an auxiliary along with his or her lead, or, occasionally, someone who is highly extraverted or introverted.

A more significant weakness of these behavioral models is that they often were developed by social scientists working with a highly particular sample of the population, such as: sales persons, criminals leaders in extant companies. Consider the following: suppose I asked you to identify the three "primary" colors on earth. If you sought to answer my question by going out into the world and observing the colors you found in the sky, the water, the grass, the leaves of trees, and the soil and sand of the earth itself, you would probably conclude that the three primary colors are blue, green and brown – because they are the three colors which are most frequently seen. If on the other hand, you were to structure your research such that you looked deeply into the true nature of color itself, you would discover that the true primary colors are: red, yellow and blue, and that although they do not all occur in their pure form with equal or great frequency, they are nonetheless the elements or units from which all colors are made. Just so, the Native Americans and Jung going deeply into human nature identified the true "primary" or universal units of human thinking, while the behavioral researchers, looking at external manifestations of our thinking, saw not the primary modes, but rather those patterns or combinations of modes which occur most frequently in the groups of human beings they were studying.

Thus, for a time it seemed that either one used a generalized model which described all the core modes but was not readily meaningful or useful to people in their day to day living; or one used a specific model which identified only the most frequent patterns as they related to a particular concern. Some breakthrough was needed which would provide those working with the model with the scientific foundations underlying what the tradition posited.

This came in the late 1950's and 1960's when the science and technology involved in brain research became sufficiently developed to make it possible for adherents of this long intellectual tradition to begin exploring its scientific roots. As might have been expected, the first attempts, which simply categorized people as either right- or left-brained, were sadly inadequate. And, although some people were excited by this bi-modal dichotomous choice, many rejected the model, knowing it was far too simplistic. Due to the limited capabilities of neurology's fledgling technology, it was not until the mid 1970's that the next link in the chain was added by Ned Herrmann. At that time Paul MacLean's Tri-Une or three-in-one Brain Model, identifying the brain as a unified system with three sub-systems:

the Cerebral Cortex, the Limbic System and the Reptilian Core, was en vogue. Herrmann's model identified four types of thinking and assigned each to one of four physical sites within the brain: the left cerebral cortex; the left limbic brain; the right limbic brain; the right cerebral cortex. Herrmann had developed his four modal model by sampling and analyzing the employees of General Electric where he worked at the time. He did not start out to validate Jung's model at all. For this reason, the similarity between Herrmann's four modes and Jung's functions is striking.

Jung	Herrmann
Analytical Thinking	Analytic Facts
Practical Sensation	Organized, sequential Form
Personal Feeling	Interpersonal Feeling
Intuitive Futures	intuitive Futures

In fact, it would be largely accurate to say that what Herrmann did in the 1970's in terms of describing the contents of the four modes was to ground Jung's theory in what was then known and hypothesized about the actual workings of the brain. As such, it was breakthrough. More importantly, because it claimed to be scientific, it was well received by American and European businesses which use it to identify innovative and "creative types," and to help employees understand their co-workers or identify the tasks they each do best.

By the mid-1980's, new and evolving technology enabled medical researchers to more accurately identify the actual specialized functions of much of the cerebral and limbic brain areas. It became clear that the Herrmann model was technically inaccurate, particularly with respect to the role it assigned the limbic brain. Today we know that the limbic brain does not actually think – not even in a sensitive, interpersonal way – nor does the limbic system manage our emotions. Emotions, according to Candace Pert, Ph.D. author of Molecules of Emotions Why You Feel the Way You Feel (1997), are managed by billions of molecules on every cell located throughout our body. While, the limbic system, according to Joseph LeDoux author of The Emotional Brain (1996)and The Synaptic Self (2002), makes a decision based on sensory input and when appropriate directs our autonomic system to switch on to respond to threats, with the result that sometimes our limbic system does not even send the information on to our cortex for us to think about so we do not create a memory of the situation. So, all actual thinking goes on in the cortex supported and enabled by the activity of both the limbic and reptilian brains. The limbic system, as it is presently understood supports our thinking in the following manner:

The LIMBIC SYSTEM enables or affects our THINKING by directing
our autonomic system to switch on to respond to threats by

- directing our autonimic system to switch on to respond to threats
- enabling us to form and store new memories in the cortex
- accessing existing memories from the cortex

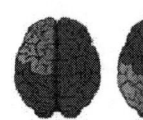

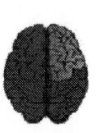

- focusing our attention
- energizing our thinking
- directing our thinking by engaging us emotionally
- fogging our thinking by engaging us emotionally
- signaling us to provide maternal care for our young
- shifting our cerebral activity under stress to the posterior convexity portion of the cerebral cortex.

And, the reptilian brain supports our thinking by bringing in new information from our environment, providing us with energy and drive, helping focus and direct our attention and sensing and asserting territotiality as follows:

The REPTILIAN CORE enables and affects our THINKING by

- bringing in new information from the environment
- providing us with energy and "drive"
- helping focus and direct our attention
- instinctively sensing and asserting territoriality

The above scientific findings on the role of our Limbic and Reptilian 'brains', in conjunction with the more in-depth research which has been carried on the cortex itself since the mid-1970's offer important insights into the structure of thinking.

As a next step in the tradition of thinking about thinking, the Benziger Model seeks to draw on and integrate current neurological information with the best historical information on how we think. Significantly, Benziger opted to not use Jung's labels for the four functions in an effort to help people value all of four equally – as a specialized type of thinking. She apologizes if this offends anyone, but hopes her choice empowers those whose natural lead function is not Jung's Thinking Function. In particular, Dr. Benziger acknow-ledges her debt to the work of:

- Carl Jung, whose insights on Falsification of Type supported her own observations and encouraged her to focus on the topic;
- Bernard Haldane whose observations of people in diverse social strata showed that each person was gifted in a generic, macro skill area which he referred to as their dependable strength which was flexible in that it could be applied to a variety of more specific, more specialized skills.
- Karl Pribram whose comprehensive and innovative under-standing of the human brain gave my thinking direction particularly with respect to sites for our functionally specialized types of thinking and for his insight that neuronal bridges explain why auxiliaries are auxiliaries and why a weakness can never be an auxiliary;
- Dr. Hans Eysenck whose ground-breaking work on our reticular activation system established the foundations for a deeper understanding of introversion and extraversion;

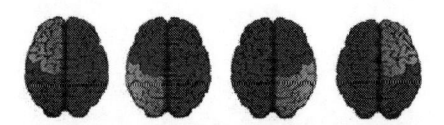

- Dr. Richard Haier whose work on the electrical efficiency of a person's natural lead function validated the existence of such a function and pointed to the tremendous costs which Falsification of Type was demanding on all who Falsified Type;
- Dr. Arlene Taylor whose work on Falsification of Type and its costs lead to the identification of the Prolonged Adaption Stress Syndrome (PASS).

The Benziger Model offers an understanding of and appreciation for the following:

- That we each have only one lead function or type;
- That the basis for this preference is grounded in an innate efficiency in the area of preference which is 100 times more efficient than other modes of thinking;
- That the costs of Falsifying Type are real and huge – not imagin-ary and minimal;
- The distinction between feeling (a cortex ability) and emotion (a limbic activity);
- That analytic and imaginative thinkers are more self-motivated and energetic because of the energy from focussing waves

Several of the popular models in this tradition are identified below. Where a mode described is similar to one of the four specialized types of thinking in the Benziger model the mode or combination of modes is noted using a two-letter abbreviation:

BL   Left Posterior Convexity   DR   Double Right = Right Posterior Convexity + Frontal Right
BR   Right Posterior Convexity DL   Double Left = Left Posterior Convexity + Frontal Left
FR   Frontal Right   DF   Double Frontal = Frontal Left + Frontal Right
FL   Frontal Left   DB   Double Posterior Convexity = Left Posterior Convexity + Right Posterior Convexity

HIGHLIGHTS IN THE TRADITION		
I. Generic Models		
Galen: The Four Humours 200 A.D. Used to understand human differences, and diagnose and treat illness		
MELANCHOLIC	sad, moody, anxious, reserved, rigid, quiet, sober, pessimistic, unsociable –descriptive of some introverts who have had difficult lives or been invalidated for being introverted, but can be true of anyone who has been heavily invalidated and has little hope that things will get better.	
PHLEGMATIC:	cool & self-possessed, passive, carefree, thoughtful, peaceful, controlled, reliable, even-tempered, calm.	BL

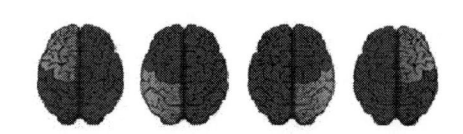

SANGUINE:	cheerful, sociable, out-going, talkative, responsive, easy-going, lively, carefree, willing and eager to lead – generally descriptive of extraverted persons.	E
CHOLERIC:	hot-tempered, aggressive, angry, touchy, restless, excitable, changeable, impul-sive, optimistic, active – descriptive of many extraverted frontals who regularly trigger Fight or Flight because they are meeting resistance	FR

Native American Medicine Wheel: "As old as the Native American"
Used to convey a symbolic, metaphoric understanding of lfe.

NORTH:	Buffalo, Wisdom, cold without feeling.	FL
WEST:	Bear, Introspection and Looks-within Place.(Also true of introverted persons)	BL
SOUTH:	Mouse, Innocence and Trust, Touching.	BR
EAST:	Eagle, Illumination, clear far-sighted vision, but close to nothing, always above and separated from life.	FR

II. Psychological Models

Carl Gustav Jung: Four Functions: 1930's

Jung's model was designed to assist an individual identify and understand his or her conscious and unconscious motivations and needs. (Many models have been developed from Jung's original work. These include: Myers-Briggs (1962), Drake-Beam-Morin (1972), Keirsey-Bates (1978).)

THINKING:	analytic, objective, principles, standards, criteria, critiques.	FL
SENSING:	past, realistic, down-to-earth, practical, sensible.	BL
FEELING:	subjective, personal, valuing intimacy, extenuating circumstances, humane, harmony.	BR
INTUITION:	hunches, futures, speculative, fantasy, imaginative.	FR
EXTRAVERSION:	an outwardly directed life-orientation which seeks to influence or control its environment.	E
INTROVERSION:	an inwardly directly life-orientation which seeks to inner understanding or experience.	I

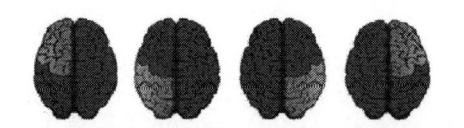

NATURAL LEAD	Each person has one lead function. It is innate and set It is their Preference.
NATURAL AUXILIARY	The two functions which are dependably available to assist the person's natural lead
NATURAL WEAKNESS	The function opposing the natural lead most difficult for a person to access
FALSIFICATION OF TYPE	When a person uses and regularly leads with a function other than his natural lead

Jean Shinoda Bolen   GODDESSES IN EVERY WOMAN: 1984
Identities dominant archetypes guiding female growth and development

ARTEMIS:	independent huntress, prefers wilderness, competitive	FR, E
ATHENA:	wise, decisive, warrior, tool maker	FL, E
DEMETER:	nurturer and spiritual guide	BR, E
HESTIA:	spiritual, centered, meditative	BR, I
HERA:	traditional, status & role conscious	BL, E
PERSEPHONE:	compliant, passive, chameleon-like	BL, I

Robert Moore & Douglas Gillette MASCULINE TYPES: 1990
Identifies four dominant archetypes guiding male growth & development

KING:	stability, order, fecundity	BL
WARRIOR:	goal-focussed, aggressive, alert, flexible, strategic, acts decisively, skilled with weapons	FL
LOVER:	feeling, connected, spiritual, nature lover	BR
MAGICIAN:	mystical, pattern-sensitive, insightful	FR

III. Educational Learning Style Models

David A. Kolb   LEARNING STYLES: circa 1974
Useful in assisting teachers to understand and communicate with students

ABSTRACT CONCEPTUALIZATION	analytical, evaluative, logical, rational.	FL
REFLECTIVE OBSERVATION:	tentative, watching, reserved, reflecting, observing, conservation	BL

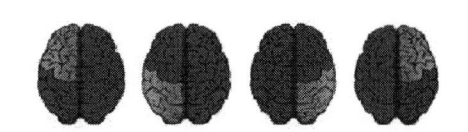

CONCRETE EXPERIENCE:	receptive, feeling, accepting, intuitive, present-oriented, experientialBR	BR
ACTIVE EXPERIMENTATION:	practical, doing, active, pragmatic, experimentation, responsible	FR
Anthony F. Gregorc LEARNING STYLES: circa 1977 Useful in assisting teachers to understand and communicate with students			
ABSTRACT SEQUENTIAL:	analytical and auditory, reads and thinks.	FL
CONCRETE SEQUENTIAL:	programmed by step-by-step demonstration needs well-organized, hands-on learning.	BL
CONCRETE RANDOM:	needs games, simultaneous, interpersonal and experiential learning opportunities.	BR
ABSTRACT RANDOM:	visual and questioning, discusses.	FR

IV. Organizational Employee and Leadership Models		
Irwin Thompson: ARCHETYPES IN HISTORY: circa 1970 Focus on theoretical insights			
HUNTER:	military general.	FL
LEADER:	administrative leader	BL
SHAMAN:	spiritual leader	BR
FOOL:	leader in impossible situations.	FR
Wilson Learning System SOCIAL STYLES circa 1975 Focus on increasing selling and influencing skills with bias towards perceived extraversion			
Analytic:	technical doer, provides detail, accuracy, needs to be told how	BL, I
Driver:	efficient, results-oriented, builds structure, wants to know goal	FL, E
Amiable:	feeling, agreeable, supportive, interpersonal	BR, I
Expressive:	intuitive, stimulating, dreams.	FR, E
Irv Rubin INFLUENCE STYLES: circa 1980 Focus on helping leaders be more effective by expanding options			
Reason	with logic.	FL
Assert	established goals.	BL

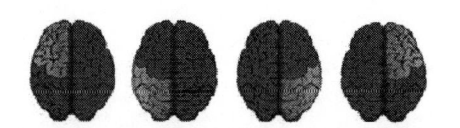

Bridge	with other people.	BR
Attract	with visions.	FR
Performax	DISC: circa 1985	
DOMINANCE:	authoritative decision-making, gets results in difficult circumstances	DF, E
COMPLIANCE:	critical thinking, attention to standards & key details.	DL, I
STEADINESS:	patient, calming, follows accepted work pattern, good listener.	DB, I
INFLUENCING OTHERS:	motivating, enthusing, expressive, group-oriented.	DR, E
Brian H. Kleiner:	TUNING INTO TEMPERAMENTS: circa 1986	
Science Oriented Thinking	logical & visionary combined.	DF
Responsible Judging	loyal, thorough, industrious, stabilizer	BL
Self-Actualizing, Intuition, Feeling	personal, sensitive to others	BR
Artistic-Sensation-Perceiving	creative, loner, risk-taker	FR
Harold Leavitt	EXECUTIVE STYLES In Praise of Pathfinders 1986	
	Focus on identifying excellent leaders	
IMPLEMENTER:	commanding and persuasive action.	DL
PROBLEM SOLVER:	logical and analytical.	FL
PATHFINDER:	impulsive and impractical visionary.	FR
V. Social Science Models		
Thomas-Kilman CONFLICT STYLES INVENTORY: circa 1965 Focus on enabling people to collaborate effectively to resolve conflict		
COMPETITION:	Manipulates and negotiates to win, not lose. (This could also describe any extreme extravert)	FL, E
COMPROMISE:	Adjusts goals according to a "fair" formula.	BL
COLLABORATION:	explores to find a win-win.	BR or DR
AVOIDANCE:	goes within, leaves, turns away from conflict. (This could also describe any extreme introvert.)	FR, I
ACCOMMODATION:	gives over to the other party gracefully.	BR

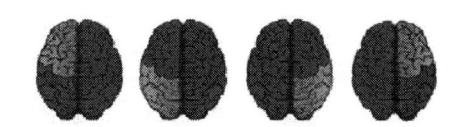

Frank Farley THRILL-SEEKING MODEL: circa 1970 Explores connection between creativity and criminality and risk taking		
BIG "T":	thrill-seeking, high stimulation needs, novelty, risk.	FR, E
LITTLE "T":	(This pattern is most true for extraverted FRs.) thrill avoiding, predictable, clarity, rigidity. (This pattern is most true for introverted BLs.)	BL, I

VI. Physiologically Based Models

Ned Herrmann WHOLE BRAIN MODEL © 1976

Focus on understanding and enabling creative thinking

CEREBRAL LEFT:	FACTS, analytical, mathematical, logical, technical, problem-solver.	FL
LIMBIC LEFT:	FORM, sequential, controlled, conservative, planner, organizer, administrative.	BL
LIMBIC RIGHT:	FEELING, interpersonal, emotional, musical, spiritual, talker.	BR
CEREBRAL RIGHT:	FUTURES, creative, imaginative, synthesizer, artistic, holistic, conceptualizer.	FR

Katherine Benziger Benziger's Whole Brain Model © 1987

Focus on validating each type of thinking as making a contribution to life and society; identifying and understanding Falsification of Type and its costs; and assisting individuals to live fuller and healthier lives by helping them to identify and let go of their habits of Falsifying Type, as well as leveraging their true preference.

FRONTAL LEFT	Direction; decision-making, analytical, logical
Left Posterior Convexity	Stable foundations and routine, sequential, orderly, procedural.
Right Posterior Convexity	Peaceful harmonious foundations, feeling, rhythmic, sensitive to nonverbals.
FRONTAL RIGHT	Creative adapting and internal imaging, abstract, imaginative, sensitive to patterns.
EXTRAVERSION:	natural life-orientation shared by 15% of humans in which the person seeks a heightened level of stimulation
INTROVERSION:	natural life-orientation shared by 15% of humans in which the person lives at such a heightened level of arousal that high levels of stimulation cause the individual to "back off" & "go within".
BALANCED	natural life-orientation shared by 70% of humans in which a person seeks a balanced environment The model posits a continuum of internal arousal managed by the reticular activating system

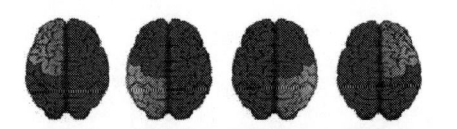

NATURAL LEAD	Each person has one lead function. It is innate and set. It is based on the cortical area responsible for the function or type of thinking being innately efficient – consuming one one-hundredth the energy of the other types
NATURAL AUXILIARY	The two functions which are dependably available to the assist the person's Natural Lead because they are hard-wired to their Lead by a neuronal bridge.
NATURAL WEAKNESS	The function diagonally opposite from the natural lead which is most difficult for a person to access because it's not connected to the lead by a neuronal bridge.
FALSIFICATION OF TYPE	When a person uses and regularly leads with any function other than his natural lead
COSTS OF FALSIFICATION	Prolonged Adaption Stress Syndrome (PASS): fatigue, hyper-vigilance, immune system alteration, memory impairment, altered brain chemistry, diminished frontal lobe function, dis-couragement or depression, self esteem problems

1. The lists of words used to describe many of these models in this essay are awkward combinations of nouns and adjectives. They are, however, the actual words used by the credited authors.

2. Information about the Medicine Wheel is from conversations with Shirley Barclay, a Native American who is also a practicing therapist, and the book Seven Arrows by Hyemeyohsts Storm, 1972.

3. Information about Jung's model comes from Benziger's mother, a practicing therapist who was reared by a student of Jung's, and from several books by and about Jung, including:
   - Contributions to Analytical Psychology, C.G. Jung. Harcourt, Brace & Company, 1928.
   - Psychic Energy: Its Source & Its Transformation with foreword by C.G. Jung, by M. Esther Harding. Random House, 1963.
   - Psychological Types, C.G. Jung. Princeton University Press 1971.
   - The Psychology of the Unconscious: A Study in Transformation & Symbolism of the Psyche: A Contribution to the History of the Evolution of Thought, C.G. Jung. Dodd Mead & Company, 1931.

4. For a partial listing of the models we have examined see the chart, Highlights in the Tradition, following this discussion.

5. Categories and adjectives listed to describe the Herrmann Model are taken from 'The Creative Brain' – an interview with Ned Herrmann, in ASTD's Training & Development Journal, 'Oct 1981 published by The American Society for Training and Development

6. Note: This is not an exhaustive listing of the tradition, which contains literally hundreds of models, including other traditional models, not unlike the Medicine Wheel.

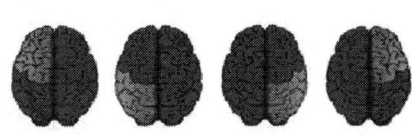

Appendix B: Physiological Bases for the Model

The model presented in this book has four key theoretical components: functional specialization, dominance and Falsification of Type and introversion : extraversion. The first of these, functional specialization, states that the brain is subdivided into discrete areas each of which has things it does best and is generally responsible for doing. The second, dominance, states that given our brain's functional specialization, all people are born with a physiological preference for only one specialized type of thinking. The third, Falsification of Type, states that when a person uses any type of thinking other than their natural preference most of the time, over time they suffer predictable, undesirable results. And finally, the fourth introversion : extraversion results from people being born with radically differing stable internal waking levels, which result in their needing very differing amounts of additional stimulation from their environment. In order to fully appreciate the neuro-scientific bases for the model, let's look at each of these components:

Part I: Functional Specialization

We have come to understand and appreciate our's brain's functional specialization over the past 150 years, beginning in the 1860's when a French surgeon named Broca noticed damage to a particular region of the left frontal lobe predictably resulted in a kind of speech difficulty known as aphasia. The area, now long accepted as the region of our brain naturally "encoded with the structure of language," is known today as Broca's area in honor of its discoverer. Following Broca, Werneke identified a second related area which he called "the language lump" in the left temporal lobe. Most of the research and discoveries were limited and disjointed, connected to one of two medical situations: a person came to a physician subsequent to an injury or stroke and the physician attempted to identify the damage done and map it based on the nature of the injury or stroke; or, a surgeon in the process of operating on some portion of the brain, would poke or probe a particular section to see how it reacted and what it did. As health care became more closely supervised the second kind of 'research' was stopped. It was not until the 1970's when EEGs became available that we began to be able to build a more comprehensive understanding of cortical functional specialization.

Nonetheless, by the late 1960's and early 1970's, people generally believed that the right and left cerebral hemishperes processed very different information in very different ways – that is, that they were functionally specialized.

In the mid to late 1970's, Ned Herrmann, working at General Electric, combined what was then state of the art EEG data on the functioning of the cortex with Paul MacLean's Tri-une Model and his own data on thinking styles. The result was a right-left brain model which had four modes – two right and two left: the left cerebral, left limbic, right cerebral, right limbic.

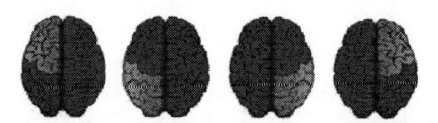

In 1981, Benziger contacted Herrmann and began to explore the connections between his model and her own observations working with clients in change management and conflict resolution. She became

the work of Jung and Thomas - Kilman. The implication of Herrmann's model was that two of Jung's functions, Thinking and Intuition, were actual thinking, while the remaining two of his functions, Sensing and Feeling, were actually limbic, or emotional.

In 1984, while teaching several workshops for the American Academy of Medical Directors, Benziger became convinced that there was no functional basis for believing the two "lower" modes were limbic in nature. Basically, several of the physicians had simply come to her and told her in no uncertain terms that the specialized capabilities which Herrmann attributed to the Limbic areas were simply inaccurate. As physicians, their combined expertise and certainty was irrefutable. The four functions which Jung had posited may indeed exist, but if they did they were not in the areas Herrmann had assigned to them.

Looking for answers, in 1985, Benziger sought advice and guidance from one of the world's foremost experts on the human brain, Dr. Karl Pribram. She presented him with her own anecdotal observations as well as Herrmann's model, adding that she believed Herrmann's model, developed independently from a statistical analysis of actual samples of people's thinking, had validity and as well corroborated Jung's model. Pribram, who had been a practicing neuorsurgeon prior to obtaining a PhD in Psychology and heading up Stanford's Behavioral Research Labs, is one of those rare individuals whose areas of expertise bridges across generally segmented specialities. An expert in brain structure and the known neurochemical bases of mental activity, as well as the various psychological models used to predict behavior, including Jung's, Pribram was able to make sense of the data in a way no one else had.

His observation was quite simply, that the four modes identified by Herrmann's model most probably reflected functionally specialized types of thinking, and that each was probably managed by one of the four equally sized areas in the cerebral cortex: the right and left frontal lobes, and the right and left posterior convexities (in older literature, these areas were identified as the sensory cortices) containing the occipital, parietal and temporal lobes. In establishing these locations, Pribram re-assigned Herrmann's four modes as follows:

Hermann Mode	Brain Site	Jungian Function
Left Cerebral	Left Frontal Lobe	Thinking
Left Limbic	Left Posterior Convexity	Sensing
Right Limbic	Right Posterior Convexity	Feeling
Right Cerebral	Right Frontal Lobe	Intuition

Pribram went on to add that the central or rondalic fissure which separates the frontal lobe of each hemisphere from that hemisphere's posterior convexity was already known to be one of the most significant divisions in our brain and that many scientists thought it was actually more significant than the hemispheric separation, the longitudinal fissure.

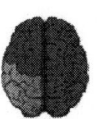

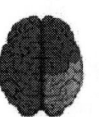

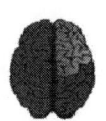

Almost as verification, Pribram added that Herrmann's description of Herrmann's left limbic mode did indeed fit some of what he was discovering about the structure of stored memories in the left posterior convexity. Namely that quite amazingly it seemed to have an internal specialized ability to sequence things.

Pribram went on to discuss with Benziger what he knew about the cortex which would support these locations as well as offer insights which might help substantiate more of Jung's model. Key was his obseration that access and communication between the four specialized areas was facilitated by neural bridges. He explained that the corpus collosum served as a very effective bridge between the Left Frontal and Right Frontal Lobes as well as between the Posterior Left and Right Posterior Convexities. Then, he added, an important point: a large bundle of nerves on the left connected the Broca and Werencke areas, facilitating speech, and a similar bundle connected mirror areas in the Right Hemisphere such that the Left Frontal Lobe and Left Posterior Convexity were able to communicate easily; as well as the Right Frontal Lobe and the Right Posterior Convexity. In essence, in theory, you could move circularly around the cortex in either direction, and come back to where you started – as in a Medicine Wheel.

What was not possible, Pribram added was to move diagonally in the cortex. One could not begin in the Left Frontal Lobe and move directly to the Right Posterior Convexity, or in the Left Posterior Convexity and move directly to the Right Frontal Lobe. Significantly, Pribram had substantiated the primary rule which Jung used when he explained for any single function, which functions were available as auxiliaries, and which single function was the weakest or inferior function and always most difficult for a person to access.

An intriguing point that Pribram made was that there are strong connections between the limbic brain (which among other things is the energetic brain) and each frontal lobe. His point was that some people are very energetic or active, while others appear to be more tranquil – along the lines of the Type A and Type B personalities – and that it would appear that those people who are naturally more frontal are also naturally more active.

Finally, Pribram commented on the EEG data which Herrmann and his team had gathered to support his model. The reason for the errors was, Pribram said, a technical one: EEG measurements done during late 70's years (15 years earlier), when the technology was new and unrefined, did not always manage to pick up or measure the functioning of the posterior convexity, particularly its deeper regions.

Since 1985, Benziger has continued to read widely and meet with active neuroscientists, to discover physiological data to corroborate or contradict Pribram's hypothesis and build a "neurologically sound" model of thinking to ground Jung's model. Fascinatingly, the data appears to corroborate his hypothesis – over and over again.

Functional Specialization in the Posterior Convexities

The temporal lobes, which run along the sides of the head, contain the auditory cortex (whose primary job is the analysis of sound) and some parts of the visual cortex. Also contained within these lobes (in the transverse convolutions of Heschl) are the musical centers. Although both right and left temporal lobes process sound, they do not attend to the same things. Research has shown that the left temporal lobe is most sensitive to words and verbal communication, while the right temporal lobe is more aware of non-verbal sounds (rain falling, a car honking its horn, fingernails scraping a chalkboard) and emotional utterances (crying, screaming, laughing). In the same vein, Damasio and Wyke's studies on music (referenced in The Mind) suggest that we naturally sing, play, and listen to music with the right hemisphere but that the left hemisphere takes over this function in those who are formally trained or who make it their profession.

The temporal lobes are also deeply involved with memory storage. And, memories aren't distributed randomly between right and left. In a recent study, experimental subjects were asked two different kinds of questions and monitored to see which hemisphere they accessed to come up with the answer. The subjects uniformly accessed the right hemisphere to answer "emotionally charged" questions ("Is your mother-in-law an interfering person?) and the left hemisphere to answer general information ones ("How many s's are there in Mississippi?"). Additional studies have substantiated these findings and strongly suggest that emotionally charged memories are stored on the right, whereas formal information is stored on the left. Also known as the "interpretive cortex", the temporal lobes are closely connected to the limbic system and, when stimulated, they produce the same kind of "cosmic/spiritual experiences" associated with the hippocampus. According to Karl Pribram, "A lesion in the temporal lobe near the amygdala can produce something akin to mysticism. There is a disruption in self awareness, a kind of consciousness without content, like the oceanic consciousness of the mystic state. The distinction between self and other disappears." (quoted from The 3-Pound Universe. p. 330) Unfortunately, the temporal lobes can be involved in negative experiences, too. For example, "panic attacks" are the result of a temporal-hippocampal malfunction (incoming sensory information is misinterpreted and this generates an intense fear response).

The parietal lobes, which are located on the top of the head, contain the somatic sensory cortexes which collect "feeling" (not emotional) information from receptors in the skin, joints, muscles, and tendons. They also deal with "body awareness" and damage to these lobes can literally cause us to lose awareness of our own bodies, in part or whole. The occipital lobes contain the visual cortex and damage to the back of the head, where these lobes are located, can result in blindness (even if your eyes themselves are undamaged).

In trying to understand the specialized thinking managed by our posterior convexities, it is important to remember that the Posterior Left is the site of the Wernicke's area, one of the two speech centers. If this area is damaged, we lose the ability to understand word meanings and to manage spoken and written grammar or syntax. We do not, however, lose our ability to articulate or to speak easily and fluently (which is governed by the Broca's area in the Frontal Left lobe). In other words, if we damage this area we can still talk well enough but nothing we say will make any sense. This condition, which is called aphasia, can have the interesting side effect of expanding our skill at reading non-verbals (a posterior right ability) to the point where we may be able to "understand" what someone "means" even if we cannot comprehend a single word they say. (For more information on this phenomenum, read "The President's Speech" chapter in Oliver Sack's book, The Man Who Mistook His Wife For A Hat).

In a study by Kimura (referenced in Two Sides of the Brain), it was found that damage to the Left Posterior Convexity produces apraxia, which is the inability to coordinate movement into a sequence (e.e. setting a table or performing any other routine incorporating multiple discrete acts.) and it is also known that lesions on the left parietal and temporal lobes disturb planning and sequencing skills. Again, the research matches Pribram's findings in his lab, which he shared with Benziger in 1985, that the left posterior convexity actively sequences information.

In the mid 1990's Dr. Susan Andrews, working with brain damaged patients in New Orleans, shared her own findings with Benziger that the ability to dress ourselves is managed in the Right Posterior Convexity. This was an intriguing and new piece of information – relating a penchant for dressing and changing clothes to the Right Posterior Convexity's Feeling Function. Benziger began to track it and found tremendous evidence that it was indeed an important if unnoticed part of the Feeling Function. Indeed, it was particularly useful when tracing the effects of Falsifying Type. Benziger found that Feelers who were Falsifying Type, often as Sensors using the Left Posterior Convexity more than their Right, seemed to suffer from shopping problems when immediately after a getting their pay checks they would go try on clothes for hours. For those with credit cards, the problem was complicated by the month round indirect availability of cash. These people often would follow a particularly exhausting and long day of Falsifying by an evening spent in clothing stores trying on clothes (and buying them).

During the 1990's a variety of highly specific findings further supported Pribram's hypothesis. Research done in Japan showed that incoming auditory information that matched words was sent to the left posterior convexity for processing, while information which did not, which appeared to be largely tonal or rhythmic, was sent to the right posterior. So it was appearing that it was not that all information went to all specialized types of thinking, but rather that at least in some cases, only the appropriate information was sent. This point was important. Pribram had told her that two rules applied to the physiology: (1) things were next to each other or very close because they needed to be; and (2) excluding things (saying no or stop) was as important if not more important as including (saying yes or go). Our brain excludes superfluous data from each specialized type of thinking to make the overall system most efficient.

Functional Specialization in the Frontal Lobes

If the cerebral cortex is the "new brain", then the frontal lobes are the "newest of the new" and, as such, they represent the most evolutionarily advanced part of us. Yet well into this century many neurologists believed they served no function whatsoever beyond being the site of the motor cortex. As it turns out, the frontal lobes are the part of the brain that generates goal-directed behavior and individuals who have damaged frontal lobes cannot create plans or choose actions to carry them out.

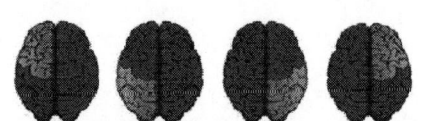

Furthermore, such individuals are easily distracted by irrelevant stimuli and inclined to randomly change actions for no reason.

The rash of pre-frontal lobotomies performed during the 1940's and 50's has given us ample opportunity to see what the loss of the frontal lobes costs the system. After this surgery, the lobotomized individual tends to be:

- Limited in his thoughts and actions to sequences he has already learned
- Unable to grasp the "key points" of a situation
- Prone to tantrums and fits of childish behavior
- Unable to focus his attention
- Lacking in verbal expressiveness and trivial and uninspired in his verbal contributions
- Easily distracted by irrelevant external stimuli
- Slow and deliberate in his movements
- Lacking in initiative and purpose
- Unable to consider and plan for the future
- Lacking in judgment
- Unable to defer immediate gratification
- Disturbed by changes in the environment and desirous of keeping everything "the same"

All of which reinforce the idea that the frontal lobes function as the seat of will, intention, and future-oriented behavior.

The Left Frontal lobe, as we have already mentioned, is the site of the other speech center (Broca's area) and is responsible for articulation. Damage to this area results in "telegraphic" speech (where the words come out one by one in a labored fashion). Studies have also shown this is the part of the brain that excels at math-ematics, at analysis, and at processing information in a logical way.

Conversely, the Right Frontal lobe has been shown to process information in a visual-spatial way (there is a visual-spatial complex on the right corresponding to the Broca's area on the left). Individuals who have damaged this area misjudge the size, direction, and distance of objects, they cannot copy simple shapes or arrange blocks or sticks to form a pattern, and they lose their ability to describe even well known routes. The frontal right is also the "expressive" part of the brain and a stroke or lesion in this part of the brain can cause a loss of all emotional inflection in the voice and an inability to laugh, cry, or express any other emotion. It is significant to note, however, that the ability to experience emotion is not impaired, only its outward expression. Additionally, there is no impairment in perceiving other people's emotions (the right posterior convexity's skills remain intact).

Anecdotal Support for Functional Specialization

Additional corroborating evidence can be found everywhere. Two recent examples are in Oliver Sacks book, The Man Who Mistook His Wife for a Hat. and in the forthcoming book by Michael Persinger, The Neuropsychological Bases of God Experiences.

In his lead story about Dr. P, Sacks observes that Dr. P was able to recognize some kinds of visual input but not others. Among those things which weren't recognizable to Dr. P were the faces of his wife and friends, his shoe, and much of his environment. Among the things which he could recognize were: abstract forms and shapes, stylized designs and caricatures, and on occasion a single human face or photograph with such strong lines so as to appear almost a caricature of itself. Although this seems confusing, the mystery dissolves as soon as the data is viewed through the lens of the Benziger model. Those things which are not recognizable to Dr. P are things processed by the right and left occipital lobes, located within the posterior convexity modes. We know specifically, for example, that faces in all their uniqueness are processed in the right occipital. Those things which are see-able, however, are distinctly part of the pattern sensitive Frontal Right. What is most interesting is that it is quite possible for another person suffering from the exact same condition not to see the things Dr. P could, simply because that other person might not have Dr. P's strong preference for the frontal right mode (an access strongly suggested by Dr. Sack's references to Dr. P's quirky and bizarre sense of humor.

In a pre-publication article on Michael Persinger's book, at least four different research projects are referred to, all of which suggest that spiritual experiences can be correlated with a heightened amount of electrical firing in the right temporal and parietal lobes. The suggested causes are stress, such as oxygen deprivation or a near-death experience, and meditation practices, such as Transcendental Meditation, both of which can affect the serotonin level in the brain. According to Persinger, increased nerve firing in the temporal regions produce feelings of intense "meaningfulness." It would be interesting to know whether those who have a distinct preference for the Right Posterior Convexity region also have a rate of nerve firing in this region which exceeds that of other people. If so, it would explain their generally heightened sensitivity to "spiritual values" and "meaning".

Another interesting point Persinger's work raises is that under stress, particularly life-threatening stress, the neural firing increases in both posterior convexities. We do not know why this happens, it may well be part of an evolutionary survival mechanism since, when we are subjected to severe stress, we need two things to survive: hope (which is perhaps what the spiritual experience offered by right temporal and parietal lobes is really all about) and the ability (as Churchill said) to "carry on." This latter ability is apparently encour-aged by the increased firing of the left posterior convexity and is consistent with the fact that, under stress, people tend to revert to old, routine ways of doing things.

Part II: Dominance

Benziger first became aware of Dr. Richard's Haier in 1987 and 1988, when he announced his findings on glucose uptake. Using PET Scanners, Haier discovered that what we have been referring to as brain dominance has its physiological roots in the chemistry of the brain and impacts 1) the speed at which neurons fire; as well as 2) how much energy they consume. Preeminent among the researchers in this area, Haier was invited to present his breakthrough findings on the glucose metabolic rate in the brain under differing circumstances at several medical and scientific conferences. Because his findings were so unexpected, they were not immediately accepted by the research community at large. By 1996, when Benziger met again with Pribram, Haier's findings had been replicated and proved to be correct. Pribram and his colleagues believed that he was an bright and capable researcher whose work was very credible. The Haier findings are this: the specialized type of thinking which we call a preference, enjoys a brain chemistry which causes the neurons in that area to fire more rapidly and at the same time to consume less energy resulting in a total energy consumption rate only 1/100 that of the other specialized areas. In other words, Preference is based on an almost unbelieveably high rate of innate efficiency. In a time when energy efficiency seems to be critical to the survival of mankind, it very interesting that a key to self-management is rooted in our internal energy management. It points to our need to learn to respect our brain's requirement that we sustain an energy efficient life.

Earlier work done in the 1990's and reported in an unpublished paper, "Cognitive Styles, EEG Waves and Brain Levels," by Drs. Lawrence L Schkade and Alfred R Potvin chairpersons respectively of Systems Analysis and Biomedical Engineering, a study was done at the University of Texas, in which EEG evidence was gathered correlating Herrmann's Cerebral Right (Pribram's Frontal Right) and Cerebral Left (Pribram's Frontal Left) modes (i.e. they did not seek to establish or measure what Herrmann was calling "limbic" activity) with actual brain activity. Only persons whose brain dominance pattern showed a clear preference for the left (selected not surprisingly from the accounting department) or the right (selected from the art department) were used. What happened was this. A list of activities were compiled which would use analytic and visual thinking in an alternating pattern. Although it is generally accepted that the left frontal lobe does math, analysis and logical processing and that the right frontal lobe does spatial thinking including geometry and artistic activities such as sketching, when these select subjects were asked to perform the selected list of activities an intriguing thing happened. When those who had an been identified by Herrmann's testing as strong analytic thinkers performed the list of "to do's" they tended to use a significant amount of frontal left thinking, even when the task could not benefit from it. And, when those who had tested out as strong internal image-oriented thinkers performed the list of "to do's" they tended to use a significant amount of frontal right thinking, even when the task could not benefit from it. In other words, they were trying to use their natural preference even if it couldn't do the task easily or well.

According to a story told to one of the authors by Herrmann, a double frontal, equally strong in both analytic thinking and internal imaging, additional illuminating data was discovered when he performed a similar list of to-do's while being monitored with EEG equipment. While performing an analytical or mathematical task his frontal lobes showed prominent activity in the frontal left and a quieting in the Frontal Right. Then, when he would shift to an activity best handled by spatial, pattern and image skills, his frontal left would show a marked decrease in the quantity of beta waves, sometimes shutting off almost entirely, while his frontal right was registering 100% beta. Thus, the study not only served to demonstrate the existence of dominance, but also spot-lighted another of Herrmann's theoretical contributions: the principle of situationalness. Otherwise stated: if a person has access to two modes, he or she will naturally use the mode best suited to the task.

Part III: Falsification of Type

Dr. Benziger, using her Benziger Thinking Styles Assessment (BTSA) to gather and study data on individuals who had been or were Falsifying Type, connected Falsification of Type to a condition of "prolonged or excessive adaption." In her summary report on the topic, Falsification of Type: It's Jungian and Physiological Foundations and Mental, Emotional and Physiological Costs, published in 1995, she stated that:
- the short term results of falsification tend to be increased irritability, headaches, and difficulty in mastering new tasks.
- the long term results of falsification include exhaustion, depression, lack of joy, of the brain, a vulnerability to illness

Subsequently, Dr. Benziger wrote an article on Rethinking Midlife Crisis and Depression in which she shared her findings on the connection between Falsification of Type and depression.

Working with Benziger for more than a decade Dr. Arlene Taylor worked in a hospital setting to identify and measure the full range of symptoms produced by Falsifying Type. In 1999 she announced that her work showed a collection of 8 symptoms, whose collective impact, could be seen as a distinct syndrome, Prolonged Adaption Stress Syndrome or PASS.

1. Fatigue. Prolonged Falsification of Type can require the brain to work up to 100 times harder, which can result in up to 100 times greater energy expenditure.
2. Hyper-vigilance. Prolonged Falsification of Type can create a state of hyper-vigilance as the brain goes on protective alertness.
3. Immune system alteration. Falsifying Type can be thought of as the individual living a lie at some level.
4. Memory impairment. Cortisol, released under stress, can interfere with memory functions.
5. Altered brain chemistry. The prolonged Falsification of Type can interfere with hypothalamus and pituitary function which, in turn, can interfere with hormonal balance.
6. Diminished Frontal Lobe Functions. Prolonged Falsification of Type can interfere with functions typically associated with the frontal lobes.
7. Discouragement or Depression. Prolonged Falsification can lead to the repeated triggering of the conserve/withdraw reaction form to stress. This can be especially true for high introverts although it can be observed in extroverts.
8. Self-Esteem Problems. Any or all of the other symptoms can be contributed to a perceived diminished overall success in life.

Dr. Taylor's findings corroborated Benziger's and reinforced their joint conclusion that some depression in the United States has been misdiagnosed, and should be more appropriately diagnosed as PASS.

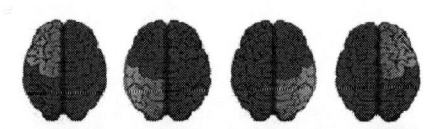

Part IV: Introversion : Extraversion

In this book Benziger embraces and applies the breakthrough findings of Dr. Hans Eysenck from the 1990's. Her own contribu-tion to this portion of the model is minimal, with the exception of one enlightening point: in working with people who've been either heavily invalidated or Falsifying Type for years, Benziger dis-covered that all people under chronic anxiety shift their normal towards introversion. This discovery differentiates those who are innately introverted from those who are introverted because they are chronically anxious from one of the above sources, or the presence of some other chronic anxiety-producing stressor in their lives.

Summary of the Physiological Bases for the Model

There is ample evidence to assert that all four key theoretical elements of the Benziger Model presented in the body of this book (functional specialization, dominance, Falsification of Type, intro-version : extraversion) are neurologically valid. 13 years ago, when Benziger's first book was written, the physiology underlying dominance, Falsification of Type and PASS, and introversion : extraversion were unknown. This book includes additional empower-ing information on the nature and structure of: dominance, Falsifying Type, PASS and introversion : extraversion. If this brief physio-logical overview has whetted your appetite for more "hardcore" information about the brain, look at Benziger's Physiological and Psychophysiological Bases for Jungian Concepts: An Annotated Bibliography, ©1996 or visit www.benziger.org.

Appendix C: Limbic & Reptilian Activation Indicators

I- Limbic/Reptilian states experienced as positive and "good":			
Happy	Passionate	Enthusiastic	Proud
Seductive	Ecstatic	Adoring	Certain
Loving/Loved	Eager	Safe/Secure	Reverent
Loyal	Nostalgic	Peaceful	Sentimental
Nurturing	Delighted	Playful	Playful
Joyous	Cheerful	Patriotic	Trusting
Content	Impressed	Excited	Calm
Pleased	Sleepy	Amused	Satisfied

II- Limbic / Reptilian states experienced as negative and "bad":			
Angry	Resentful	Irritated	Ambivalent
Furious	Smug	Hostile	Uncomfortable
Belligerent	Grief-stricken	Annoyed	Embarrassed
Controlling	Insecure	Arrogant	Fearful
Dominating	Judgmental	Cirtical	Invalidating
Dogmatic	Absolute	Antagonistic	Domineering
Contemptuous	Argumentative	Hateful	Willfull
Defensive	Jealous	Possessive	Guilty
Bored	Apathetic	"Shutdown"	Frightened
Envious	Hurt	Worried	Anxious
Emotional	Needy	Timid	Intimidated
Subservient	Sad	Invalidated	Desperate
Suspicious	Nervous		

III- Intense Reptilian / Limbic states, usually seen as "Very Bad":			
Paranoid	Obsessive	Delusional	Addicted
Hallucinating	Ritualistic	Territorial	Aggressive
Punitive	Submissive	Masochistic	Sadistic
Violent	Superior	Inferior	Repulsed
Disgusted	Glutonous	Reactive	Degraded
Humiliated	Horrified		

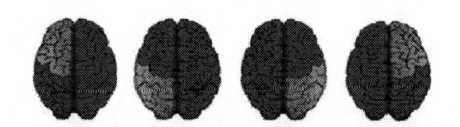

The two key points here are that (1) the more consistent positive activation a person experiences the greater the likelihood they are using their preference in a context which suits their natural level or introversion or extraversion; and (2) while chronic Negative Activation may be an indicator that a person is

- being heaviliy and chronically invalidated for their preference,
- being heaviliy and chronically invalidated for their natural introversion or extraversion, or
- is Falsifying Type.

Obviously there are a lot more words that could have been added (just as there are hundreds of shades, nuances, and variations on emotional states). If you think of additional words, please feel free to add them to this appendix.

Appendix D: A Glossary for the Jargon Lover

Additive Adaption
An adaptive pattern of behavior in which the person selectively increases the range of his or her access to include another mode or function such that the person uses the additional mode, but still leads his preference or natural lead function. See Type and Falsification of Type.

Atrophy
The inability to use an area or mode which develops as a result of avoidance, neglect or abstinence. This most often happens to a person's non-preferred mode when they marry someone whose strength in the mode enables them to "take care of those things" for their spouse. Since their non-preferred mode gets used less and less, what little strength the person originally had tends to "wither" away.

Auxiliaries
A term created by Jung to indicate the two functions which are available to an individual naturally to support his or her natural lead function or preference. When a person develops and uses these in support of the Natural Lead Function, or Preference, the effect is healthy and energizing.

Avoidance Pattern
A behavioral pattern in which someone avoids all activities which would engage a particular specialized type of thinking or mode – consciously or unconsciously.

Basal
Posterior Convexity of human cortex, what used to be called the sensory lobes.

Basal Lobes
The three lobes which make up the right and left posterior convexities of each cerebral hemisphere. The occipital, parietal, and temporal lobes. See Left Posterior Convexity and Right Posterior Convexity.

Benziger Breakthrough
A term invented by KBA Licensee to refer to a collection of ideas and tools created by Dr. Benziger during her thirty-three years of study.

Cerebral Cortex
The newest part of the tri-une brain. The seat of conscious thinking.

Competency
The ability to perform a skill in any of the four specialized types of thinking which generally exists as the result of usage and practice. We may develop Competencies in our non-preferred modes as well as in our Preference. Key life issues such as finding satisfaction and meaning often arise when an individual identifies strongly with a competency which is not also a preference.

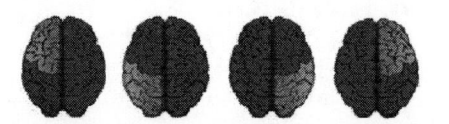

Creeping Dominance
The tendency to slip into or revert to your own thinking style or preference when communicating in a non-preferred mode. Creeping dominance may occur in your word choice, your speed of speech, your grammar, your perception of humor or your choice of examples.

Dominance
Dominance refers to a situation in which one or more of the four specialized cortical areas or functions dominates or controls the way in which a person thinks. Natural dominance occurs when the specialized type of thinking a person is his Preference – the mode in which his brain is naturally and significantly most efficient. Practical or Effective Dominance may involve either an expansion of the person's natural pattern in which the person continues to lead with his true Preference. If it involves the person abandoning his natural Preference or using it only in support of another function the individual is said to be Falsifying Type. See Falsification of Type.

Extraverted
Having a naturally low level of cortical arousal or inner wakefulness, which causes the individual to seek higher than normal levels of stimulation in order to "feel alive". Typical ways in which the extravert seeks stimulation include: trying to influence or control his or her environment, confronting others, engaging in competition, attending crowded parties or events "where the action is."

Falsification of Type
Jung's term for any situation in which a person has frequently and consistently ignored or denied his natural type or preference, in favor of a mode or function that is more generally modeled, accepted, rewarded by those around him. The cost of falsification identified by Jung was neurosis and exhaustion. Benziger's work on the psychological and physiological foundations for Falsification of Type scientifically substantiates and expands Jung's observations and beliefs. Indeed Dr. Benziger and Dr. Arlene Taylor have identified a lengthy set of symptoms, including depression, which they have found to be caused directly or indirectly by Falsification of Type.

First Law of Cybernetics
"The unit within the system with the most behavioral responses controls the system," is the first law of the science of cybernetics, otherwise known as the science of systems. It is used in brain dominance to explain why the multidominant individual tends to control and lead his environment as well as to rise to the top of many organizations. It is also used as an argument for developing whole brain access.

Frontal
Frontal and Prefrontal lobes on both sides.

Frontal Lobes
Prefrontal lobes are the furthest forward; and the Frontal are further back and continue until they reach the Posterior Convexity.

Frontal Left
The foremost lobe of the left cerebral hemisphere, adept at logical and analytical thinking, as well as the seat of grammar and the laws governing the structure of language. Generally identical to Jung's Thinking Function.

Frontal Right
The foremost lobe of the right cerebral hemisphere, adept at imaginative, adaptive and metaphoric thinking. This lobe generally processes internally generated images. Generally identical to Jung's Intuitive Function.

Function
Jung's umbrella term for the four different ways in which people tended to respond to their world: thinking, sensing, feeling, intuiting. Each of the four was identified by him as a function. His choice of the term has proven to be most apt, as each function appears to be physiologically based in a functionally specialized area of the human cortex, designed to take in highly specific types of information in order to perform the specific tasks.

Functional Specialization
A scientific term used to describe the manner in which the cerebral cortex is broken down into discrete areas each responsible for a different function. Brain dominance is an example of functional specialization – each area of the cortex has one type of thinking it does well, one type of job it does well and one type of data it perceives in order to do that job.

Half-Brained
Someone with a developed or effective dominance in any two of the four modes.

Homeostatic Balance
The concept that the body has ideal levels of oxygen, degree of acidity, temperature etc. which it needs to stay well. Stress can threaten the body by throwing it out of homenostatic balance

Introverted
Having a naturally high level of cortical arousal or inner wakefulness which causes the individual to seek lower than normal levels of stimulation in order to not feel overwhelmed. Over a period of years this need to not be overhelmed by external stimulation develops into an internally focussed thinking style which may seem withdrawn, meditative, quiet or even reclusive to more extraverted persons. Typical ways in which the introvert seeks to control the level of stimulation include spending time reading, reflecting or otherwise alone, avoiding or accommodating to others, competing mostly with oneself or a self image, going to small parties or out of the way places.

Left Posterior Convexity
The part of the human brain that used to be identified as the sensory lobes of the left cortex. This area occurs immediately behind the left frontal lobe of the human brain.

Likes Attract
The rule for friendships, also known as the "mirror rule", which says that people are most likely to choose friends who think the way they do and who have the same mental preference.

Limbic Brain
The middle brain as identified in Paul McLean's tri-une brain model. It is generally believed to be involved with emotions, body temperature and sex as well as with the memory storage and retrieval.. (For a detailed description of this portion of the brain and its function, see Appendix B.)

Mid-Life Crisis
A personal, internal emotional disturbance most frequently experienced in mid-life by those persons who abandoned their birth dominance in order to "fit in" and were most probably motivated by the need to find one's true "self."

Mid-Life Spread
A tendency to explore activities outside of one's dominance in midlife. It is motivated primarily by curiosity.

Misfit
Any person who lives or works in a situation in which they are different from everyone else. Often used to identify a child whose lead area is one in which neither of his parents has a strength.

Occipital Lobes
The most posterior lobe of each hemisphere responsible for processing the visual input from the eyes. Included in this model as a portion of the Right Posterior Convexity and left.

Opposites Attract
The rule for marriage which suggests that most people, particularly in an early or first marriage will marry a person whose strongest area is the same as their weakest.

Natural Lead Function
Jung's term for the one functionally specialized type of thinking or mode in which each of us enjoys relatively speaking tremendous natural efficiency. See: Preference.

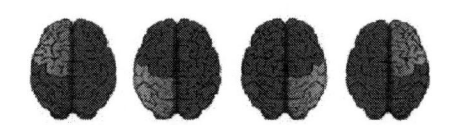

Parietal Lobes
Otherwise called the sensory lobes. Found behind the frontal lobes and separated from them by the central or rondalic fissure. Included in this model as a portion of the Right Posterior Convexity and left. Recent research substantiates that the right parietal lobes is the seat of what people call the "spiritual experience," which may be another reason why Right Posterior Convexities are so very interested in love and caring.

PASS
Prolonged Adaption Stress Syndrome. This is a collection of symptoms a person experiences when falsifying type for a significant length of time.

Posterior Convexity
Of the human brain refers to the parts of the human brain used to be called the sensory lobes. They occupy the back part of the human brain and are located immediately behind both frontal lobes.

Preference
The type of thinking in which someone is naturally highly efficient, their natural lead or natural dominance.

Replacement Adaption
The adaptive behavior in which a person abandons their preferred mode of thinking, usually because it's rejected by their environment, while adding another which they believe to be more acceptable. See: Falsification of Type..

Reptilian Brain
The inner or core area of the human brain. Popularized by Paul MacLean in his tri-une model and described by people working with stress reactions as the seat of the fight or flight response, which when out of control can harm a person's biochemistry. This area of the brain oversees and monitors the autonomic nervous system including the regulation of the heart rate and the pumping of the lungs. (See Appendix B for more detailed information)

Requisite Variety
Same as the First Law of Cybernetics. Strictly translated, the variety needed in order to gain control.

Right Posterior Convexity
The part of the human brain that used to be identified as the sensory lobes of the right cortex. This area occurs immediately behind the right frontal lobe of the human brain.

Quarter-Brained
Someone with a preference for only one of the four modes.

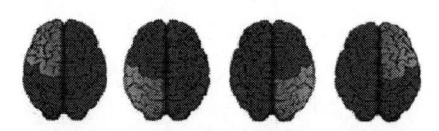

Secondary Access
Access which is neither strong enough to be rated as a part of the person's dominance nor weak enough to be called an area of avoidance. Typically, one can use a secondary area through consciously focusing one's will.

Temporal Lobes
Located within the Posterior Convexities. These lobes are lower down than the parietal lobes and nestled under the sylvian fissure on each side. A specialty of the left temporal appears to be the acquisition of words or a vocabulary. Both right and left temporal lobes process sound input.

The Smart-Dumb Rule
A rule which governs most people's choice of career as well as their procrastination. It states that we tend to choose to do what comes most naturally and to select tasks and careers which can be done by our most preferred mode in order to feel "smart" instead of "dumb."

The Mirror Rule
Same as "Likes attract." Points to who is our best friend and mirror, who naturally and effortlessly validates us.

Thriving
Successful, flourishing, prospering, according to Wiktionary.

Translators
People who have a practical or effective dominance in three or four specialized types of thinking. Typically, their developed access is strong in each of their developed modes such that they easily 'translate' between speakers using these different modes and thereby facilitate communication. See Dominance.

Triple-Brained
Having access to three of the four modes. See Translators.

Type
In Psychological Types Jung specifically links Type to Function saying there are 4 Types (4 predictable categories of people/personalities) 1 for each Function. As such Jung's 4 Types would be the same as Benziger's 4 specialized types of thinking or modes. See: Preference; Functional Specialization.

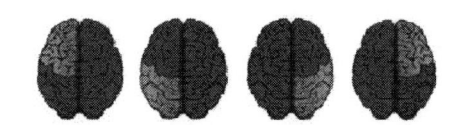

Jung's Types	Benziger's
Thinking	Frontal Left
Sensing	Left Posterior Convexity
Feeling	Right Posterior Convexity
Intuiting	Frontal Right

John Beebe, a contemporary Jungian writing on Integrity in Depth suggests it is more useful to use Type to identify both a person's natural lead function and their arousal level. Thus instead of merely saying Thinking, he suggests we say Extraverted or Introverted Thinking. Beebe thus identifies 8 Types: Extraverted Thinking; Introverted Thinking; Extraverted Sensation; Introverted Sensation; Extraverted Feeling; Introverted Feeling; Extraverted Intuition; Introverted IntuitionBy comparison, Myers-Briggs generates 16 types. They allow for both function and extraversion / introversion. And, as well they identify the auxiliary the person is using. Instead of simply Feeling as a Type as Jung and Benziger do, or extraverted Feeling and introverted Feeling as Types as Beebe does, Myers-Briggs identifies extraverted Feeling-Sensation; extraverted Feeling-Intuitive; introverted Feeling-Sensation; and introverted Feeling-Intuitive all as types.

Whole Brained
The practical developed ability to access all four modes, having sufficient competency to access and use each of the four modes situationally, as required by an environment or event.

Appendix E: Bibliography

Part I   Books and tapes by Katherine Benziger about the model.

Benziger, Katherine. Thriving in Mind.

Presents guidelines for communicating effectively. Exercises which allow you to apply the model to your work life while gaining insights into:
- which jobs are best for you and why;
- which jobs are a problem for you and why;
- why you have difficulty communicating or working with certain colleagues.

Stories and exercises relating the model to your home life:
- shedding light on problems between family members;
- offering ideas for improving the quality of your home life; and
- ideas for living with and helping your children.

Benziger, Katherine. The BTSA User Manual.

Presents a comprehensive discussion covering:
- the construction and properties of the BTSA
- the theory behind the BTSA
- details for administering the BTSA
- applications for the BTSA
- technical and statistical information on the BTSA's reliability and validity.

Benziger, Katherine. Falsification of Type.

Groundbreaking. Presents an in-depth analysis of this problem from both a psychological and physiological perspective, especially its role in weakening the immune system and self-esteem of the individual.

Benziger, Katherine. Increasing Your Own and Others High Performance - a set of 4 audio tapes.

Presents strategies for improving performance and effectiveness. Includes strategies for managing individual and group weaknesses.

Benziger, Katherine. Developing Positive Self-Esteem.

Introduces an empowering approach to helping yourself, for those wanting positive self-esteem.

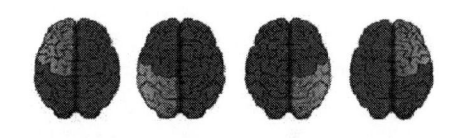

Benziger, Katherine. Maximizing Individual and Team Effectiveness.

Presents specific guidelines for applying the model to your own and other's lives. Additionally, this handbook functions as a useful concordance, assisting its reader-user to find pertinent material in other KBA publications and tapes.

Benziger, Katherine. Overcoming Depression.

Provides powerful and healing insights into the physiological basis of depression. A set of life skills which have been shown to be successful in overcoming depression.

Part II   Books by Carl Gustav Jung.

Jung, Carl Gustav. Psychological Types. New York: Harcourt, Brace & Company, Inc., 1926. (current versions always in print).

Presents an in-depth discussion by Jung of Extraversion, Introversion and the four modes or functions: Thinking (Frontal Left); Sensing (Left Posterior Convexity); Feeling (Right Posterior Convexity); and Intuiting (Frontal Right).

Part III   Books linking behavior and life situations to wellness referenced in Benziger's, Falsification of Type.

Chopra, Deepak. Ageless Body, Timeless Mind. New York: Harmony Books, 1993.

Discusses the critical link between sustaining homeostatic balance in our bodies and wellness; the role stress plays in throwing a person out of balance neuro-chemically; and the primary, natural way to sustain balance and thereby wellness, through responsive attention to the body's feedback about any situation, and thereby consciously navigating a path of increasing joy and wellness through homeostatic balance.

Csikszentmihalyi, Mihaly. Flow: the Psychology of Optimal Experience. Harper Collins Publishers, New York, 1991.

In KBA's efforts to teach people to thrive, being able to use developed competencies which we biochemically prefer sets us up for the experience Csikszentmihalyi describes as "flow." What is interesting is that Csikszentmihalyi himself, seems sufficiently unaware of the natural biochemical existence of a "preference", let alone the physiological basis of extraversion/introversion, that he is at a loss to explain why people experience flow doing such a variety of activities. His work is delightful and fun   as with The Man Who Mistook His Wife for A Hat, the reader already adept in the KBA model, the four modes, preference versus competency, introversion/extraversion and adaption or

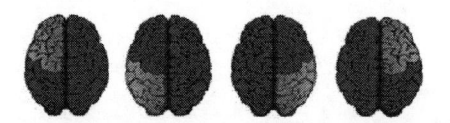

Justice, Blair, Ph.D. Who Gets Sick: How Beliefs, Moods and Thoughts Affect Your Health. Published by Jeremy P Tarcher, Inc., Los Angeles 1987.

Excellent book synthesizing the work of numerous researchers around the world. Goes far to explain how on a chemical level, using the automatic preservation systems of the sympathetic and parasympathetic components of the autonomic nervous system, a person's emotional tone is set chronically at anger, fear or grief. The overlap between this work and the KBA thinking styles model is presented on another KBA publication: Overcoming Depression. In general the triggers and learned behaviors detailed in Justice's book, tend in our society to be most frequently aimed at Right brained and introverted persons.

Sapolsky, Robert M. Why Zebra's Don't Get Ulcers. New York: W.H. Freeman & Co., 1994.

Similar to Chopra but much more technical - focusing on the neurochemistry of stress, especially glucocorticoid connection to neuron death.

Part IV   Other related reading for users of the Benziger model.

Cooper, Lynn A. and Shepherd, Roger N. "Turning Something Over in the Mind"., Scientific American, Dec. 1984, vol. 251, no. 6, pp. 106 115.

A discussion of the process of internal imaging and image rotation in time and space. A distinct study for indicating that some people are more adept at such imaging and image rotation than others.

Deal, Terrence E. and Kennedy, Allen A. Corporate Cultures: The Rites and Rituals of Corporate Life. Addison Wesley Publishing Company 1982.

A wonderful book filled with stories about the work place in which the specialized roles played by people with differing dominances is detailed by an excellent story teller. Again, the author wrote the book without the benefit of a model which would tell him what kind of person did each job but in studying his full spectrum of necessary contributors, you will find all aspects of the brain represented.

Edelman, Gerald M. Bright Air, Brilliant Fire: On the matter of Mind. Harper Collins Publishers, 1992.

Recent think piece on the relationship between mind and brain development.

Farley, Frank. "The 'Big T' in Personality". Psychology Today, May 1986.

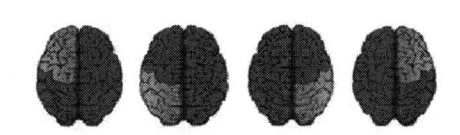

Identifies two types of persons identified physiologically by their levels of arousal: those with little need for stimulation who tend to be conservative and low risk takers; and those with a high need for stimulation who tend to be high risk takers as well as highly creative thinkers. Additionally, the author suggests that those with a high need for stimulation if stimulated sufficiently when young tend to develop into great creative contributors in society while those with such a need who are insufficiently stimulated as youngsters tend to become the "great criminals" of society.

Farley, Frank. "Psychobiology & Cognition: An Individual Differences Model". The Biological Bases of Personality & Behavior, vol. 1, Hemisphere Publishing Corp. and McGraw Hill Int'l, NY, 1985.

Describes two "extreme" behavior types: one characterized by a distinctly low level of arousability (and conversely a high need for stimulation) and the other by distinctly high level of arousability (and conversely a low need for stimulation). As identified by the activation level of their arousal systems, the first group is characterized by a "greater interrelatedness of cognitive processes, a greater transferability of ... representation" and ... a greater transmutative capability. Conversely, the second group is distinguished by a tendency towards sequential or serial thinking and less efficient transmutative capabilities.

Hooper, Judith and Teresi, Dick. The 3 Pound Universe. Laurel Press.

Studies God experiences as a result of repression of the Serotonin, and about judgment and initiative coming from the frontal lobes.

Konner, Melvin. The Tangled Wing: Biological Constraints on the Human Spirit. Holt, Rinehart & Winston, NY, 1982.

Is an encyclopedic description of the emotional system in humans, detailing the involvement of various portions of the limbic brain in emotions such as rage and lust, that is the pleasure/pain complex. Also discusses the involvement of the reptilian brain's elements as they are involved in our arousal system and in making energy available to us.

Loye, David. The Sphinx and the Rainbow. The New Science Library, Shambala Press, Boulder, 1983.

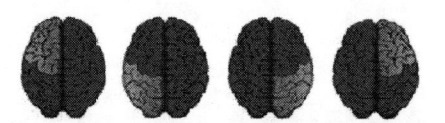

Discusses the involvement of the frontal lobes in analytical and spatial thinking. Identifies the frontal lobes as housing the two capabilities which he sees as necessary for evolution: to inhibit or anticipate our judgment and initiative, as well as for any future sensing or act of will, which he suggests takes the goal setting capability of the frontal right and left lobes. Additionally, he notes that the ability to problem solve to the extent of coming up with new answers is the territory of the frontal lobes. As such, Loye emphasizes again and again the importance of the differentiation between the frontal and posterior convexity lobes of each cerebral hemisphere.

Suggests that the spatial and artistic thinking occur on the right; that the expressive, non verbal gesturing including intonation and inflection, are managed by an area in the right frontal in a mirror image position to the Broca area on the Left (managing speech). Suggests that metaphor is a characteristic mode of the Right. And suggests that the "dynamic hasty" type (described as frontal) is involved with intuitive success in business.

As per the Posterior Convexity regions of the cerebral cortex, Loye suggests that they are non conceptual, more immediate and sensory based. Additionally, Loyc notes that emotional and non verbal memories are stored in the Right Posterior Convexity area.

As per the right left dichotomy, Loye comments that the Right devours information as a whole in contrast to the bit by bit processing of the Left.

Finally, in regard to the reticular formation which is involved in the arousal process (per Farley), Loye discusses the manner in which this creates, in the Frontal lobes, an excitation wave when new information is coming, in which both energizes and focuses the attention.

Minshull, Ruth. How to Choose Your People. Scientology Ann Arbor 1972.

An excellent book describing the full range of affected behaviors and implications of the tone scale. The author is particularly common sensible and gives practical examples from the work place.

Persinger, Michael. Neuropsychological Bases of God Beliefs. Praeger, NY, 1987.

Identifies a physiological experience known as the TLT (temporal lobe transient), during which a particularly rapid firing of neurons is measurable, which can be directly associated with "god experiences: and experiences of meaningfulness". He comments that such experiences can be found in temporal lobe epileptics frequently, but in all of us about every two years. He further suggests from his compilation of four major research projects in the area, that such experiences occur naturally immediately prior to death, during a near death experience, and during the first few days of mourning for a loved one who has died, as well as during particular types of meditation.

Restak, Richard. The Brain. Bantam Books, NY, 1984.

Identifies the conceptual, initiating and judging capabilities of the frontal lobes. Notes that natural musical abilities are managed by the right brain. Comments of the temporal lobe's involvement in hearing and the parietal lobe's involvement in feeling. Allocates memory accessing, memory storage enabling, emotional reactions and some nurturing and play instincts to the limbic brain.

Restak, Richard. The Brain has a Mind of Its Own. Harmony Books, NY, 1991.

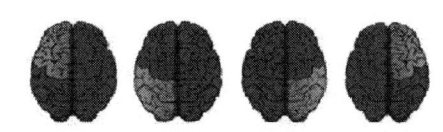

Restak, Richard. The Brain, The Last Frontier. Warner Books.

Discusses the arousal system as it involves the reptilian region and the frontal lobes; notes that emotionally charged memories such as those of a family experience are stored on the right.

Sacks, Oliver. The Man Who Mistook His Wife for a Hat. Summit Books, NY, 1970, 1985.

In a series of anecdotes about people with either diminutions of ability due to illness or injury or excess ability from birth to particular areas can point to the functional specialization of the brain. In particular he suggests how a person whose language area on the left has been damaged can learn to speak again using the right brain's musical ability. Also suggests that the ability to recall a particular face and the ability to recognize an abstraction (caricature) of that face are located in different areas, such that damage to the first does not imply damage to the second.

Schrade, Lawrence and Potvin, Alfred. Cognitive Style, EEG Wave Forms and Brain Levels (Report on Right Left Cerebral Specialization). Univ. of Texas, Human Management System 2, North Holland Publishing, 1981.

Suggests that the (frontal) left manages analytical, logical processing such as speech and that the (frontal) right manages spatial and artistic thinking. Also suggests that persons with differential preferences will attempt to process tasks in their area of preference regardless of the nature of that task, e.g. the degree of appropriateness whereby the task matches the mode, whereas a person with a broader range of dominance may indicate a differential selection of operation whereby they select and use the mode/region most appropriate to the task.

Scientific American, Special Issue: Mind and Brain. September 1992. A 140+ page update on the breakthroughs and insights of the early 1990's. This includes discussions on the brain's role in sex, vision, memory, learning, language, disorders, development and consciousness. Many key points are compatible with the KBA model.

Segalowitz, Sid J. Two Sides of the Brain. Prentice Hall, Englewood Cliffs.

Identifies articulation of language (speech) as a function managed by the frontal left lobe per Kimura's research. Notes that precision in psychomotor skills is attributable to the left frontal area. Locates expressiveness in the frontal right. Locates memory of non verbal sounds such as with wind or breeze, water flowing or the sound of a baby crying in the Right Posterior Convexity. Notes that the Left Posterior Convexity is largely involved in sequential thinking or the sequencing of information.

Smith, Anthony. The Mind. Viking Press, NY.

Notes that rhythmical information as music is processed by the temporal/Right Posterior Convexity, although as a person is instructed (formally) in music the management of this function is taken over by the frontal left.

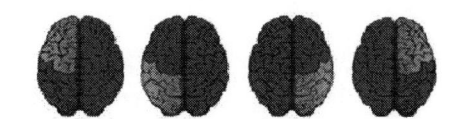

Index

Anger : 58, 64-65, 111, 156, 162, 165, 228 - 229, 251, 305

Anxiety: 5-6, 11, 17-18, 21, 37, 39, 86, 91-92, 94, 123, 186, 190, 199, 215, 293

Arousal Level: 90-91, 145, 264, 302

Augmenters: 90-91

Auxiliaries: 36, 40, 42-43, 46, 48, 95-98, 100-103, 106, 111, 113, 116, 118-120, 122, 124-125, 131-133, 139-140, 145-146, 150-156, 159, 161, 163-164, 171-173, 179-181, 188, 196, 199, 204-205, 208-212, 222, 229, 231, 237, 249, 258-260, 262, 274, 276, 279, 283, 286, 296, 302

Basal Left: see Left Posterior Convexity

Basal Right: see Right Posterior Convexity

Birth Order: 140, 172-173, 237-238, 269-271

Children: 26, 50, 58, 89, 97, 103, 109, 114, 143, 152, 154-155, 159, 162-166, 169-173, 176, 178-182, 184-186, 189, 194-198, 205, 213, 221, 225, 248-249, 251, 257, 265, 270, 303

Communicating: 57, 214, 222, 231, 245-246, 258, 263, 297, 303

Competencies: 8, 31, 36-37, 45-47, 49, 80, 93, 95-96, 111, 132, 145-146, 150-152, 162, 188, 190, 199, 205-207, 210, 216-217, 220-222, 227, 229-231, 258, 263, 296, 304

- Non-Preferred Competencies: 36, 46, 190, 199, 215, 229-231, 258
- Preferred Competencies: 36, 45, 230

Counseling: 112-113, 155, 164, 179, 182-183, 233

- Co-Counseling: 182
- Peer Counseling: 179, 182-183
- Re-Evaluation Counseling: 182

Counseling: 112-113, 155, 164, 179, 182-183, 233

Creativity: 22, 52, 68, 87, 99, 178, 195, 221, 228, 267-268, 273, 282

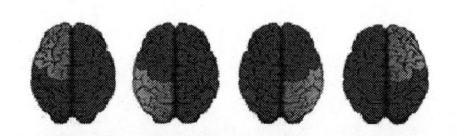

Csikszentmihaly, Mihaly: 94, 188, 214, 254, 304

Delegate: 260, 263

Depression: 5-6, 18-21, 94, 124, 162, 171, 173, 190-192, 199, 202, 204, 215, 283, 292, 297, 304-305

Diminishers: 90-91

Drop Out: 181

Effectiveness: 30, 35, 72, 95, 131, 143, 148, 230, 237, 244, 253-254, 264, 266, 303-304

Efficiency: 8, 29, 45, 48, 51-52, 54, 64, 96, 181, 198, 220, 277, 291, 299

Englander-Golden, Paula: 181, 183

Extraversion: 11, 17, 29, 31, 86-91, 124-125, 128-129, 133, 143, 146-147, 167, 170, 173, 187-188, 194, 200, 215, 254, 262-264, 269-270, 276, 280, 284, 293, 295, 302, 304

Eysenck, Hans: 17, 29, 90-92, 276, 293

Falsification of Type: 5, 18-21, 40, 45-46, 94, 123, 162, 190-192, 194, 199-204, 214, 273, 276-277, 282, 284, 292-293, 296-297, 230, 303-304

Feeling : 7, 10, 15, 22, 25-27, 33, 35, 39, 41-42, 55, 58-61, 79-81, 90, 98, 110-112, 117, 123, 125-126, 130, 132, 134, 136, 139-140, 156-157, 165, 169, 177, 182, 187, 203, 205, 207-208, 210-211, 218, 221, 228, 234, 250-251, 256-258, 261, 269, 271-275, 277-282, 285, 287-288, 298, 302, 304, 307

Feynman, Richard: 64-65, 69

Flow: 77, 94, 188-189, 214-215, 254, 304

Friends: 6, 14-15, 49, 53, 60, 66, 82, 103, 109, 124, 132, 143-147, 150-153, 155-156, 162, 164, 165, 168, 171, 173, 181, 187, 192-193, 198, 202, 207, 209-212, 221, 231-232, 245-246, 248-250, 258, 290, 299, 301

Function: 8-9, 11, 19-20, 25, 27-28, 40, 43-44, 52-53, 59-60, 63, 67-68, 70-71, 73, 74, 86, 95, 106, 113, 119, 123, 131-132, 134, 141, 143, 145, 156, 198, 200-202, 205, 210-215, 220, 237, 239, 254-255, 265-266, 270, 272, 274, 276-277, 279, 283, 285-289, 292, 296-299, 301-302, 308-309

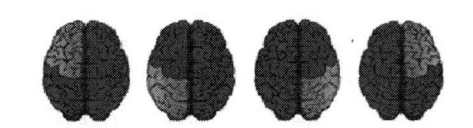

Frontal Left: 8, 10-11, 14, 16, 22, 25, 27, 36, 40, 42-43, 46, 48, 56, 70-85, 89, 95, 97-98, 100-101, 103, 105-108, 115-116, 119-121, 123, 128-129, 131-133, 135, 137-139, 141, 144, 147, 149-151, 153, 155, 157, 160, 163-164, 172-173, 175, 177, 179, 181, 185, 189, 193, 196-197, 199, 203, 205, 207-213, 222, 224, 226, 228-229, 231, 236, 239, 243-245, 249, 251-252, 255, 259, 277, 282, 287, 291, 298, 302, 304, 308-309

Frontal Right: 6, 8, 10, 12, 15-16, 22, 25, 27, 36, 40-43, 46, 48, 56, 62-69, 76-80, 82, 85-86, 89, 98, 100-103, 106-109, 111-113, 116, 118-121, 123-124, 126-128, 130-133, 135, 137-139, 141, 147, 149, 151, 153, 155, 159-161, 163, 166-167, 171-172, 174, 177-178, 180-181, 184-185, 189, 193, 195-198, 203-205, 207-210, 212, 221-222, 226-229, 232, 234-236, 238, 242-243, 249-250, 255, 259, 266, 277, 282, 290-291, 298, 302, 304, 306, 308

Gallagher, Kathleen: 184, 186

Haier, Richard: 8, 29, 277, 290-291

Hire 51, 86, 120, 128, 163, 260, 263, 268

Hiring: 68, 140, 263, 268

Introversion: 11, 17, 29, 31, 86, 88-92, 124-125, 128-129, 133, 143, 146-147, 167, 170, 173, 187-188, 190, 192-194, 196, 200, 215, 254, 262-264, 269-270, 276, 278, 282, 284, 293, 295, 302, 304

Invalidation: 6, 156, 168, 181, 195, 202, 229

Jackins, Harvey: 182-183

Joy: 22, 38, 42, 94, 124, 177, 188, 190, 198, 214-215, 230, 253, 292, 304

Jung, Carl: 5, 9-11, 17, 22, 26, 29, 40, 43, 81, 91-92, 94, 149, 193-194, 198-199, 203, 211, 215-217, 272-276, 278, 283, 285-286, 296-299, 301-302, 304

Justice, Blair: 190, 305

King, Jr., Dr. Martin Luther: 69, 75, 12, 279

Left Posterior Convexity: 7, 11, 14, 16, 22, 25-26, 40, 42-43, 46, 48-54, 62, 70, 76-81, 95-98, 100-101, 103, 105-106, 108-109, 111-113, 115, 119, 121, 123-125, 128-129, 131-132, 134-138, 149, 151, 153-155, 159-164, 168, 170-172, 174, 176, 178-181, 184-186, 195, 197, 199, 205-209, 211-213, 220-221, 224, 228, 231-232, 240, 246-247, 250, 254, 259, 261-262, 268, 277, 282, 285-286, 288, 290, 296, 299, 302, 304, 308

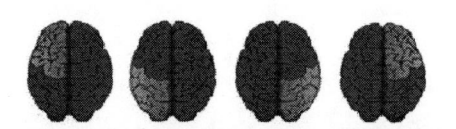

Leveraging: 5-6, 35, 254, 282

Management: 5, 17-19, 74, 87, 97-98, 114, 119, 128, 130, 135-137, 139, 141, 191, 210, 236, 243, 257, 259-260, 262, 265, 268, 273, 284, 291, 308-309

Managing: 35, 50, 73, 82, 134, 142, 150, 153, 160, 233-234, 236, 251-252, 254, 256, 258-260, 262-263, 265--269, 303, 307

Managing Teams: 262

Marriage: 143, 147-149, 151-152, 154, 157-164, 166, 194, 213, 299

Maslow, Abraham: 11-12, 22, 30, 68, 149, 194

Mediation: 172, 179, 182

Mentor: 173, 198, 216-217, 220, 228, 260, 262-264, 267, 269

Mid-life Crisis: 128, 160, 299

Mirror Rule: 143-147, 173, 286, 299, 301, 307

Nardi, Dario: 9, 22-23

Natural Lead: 11-12, 29-30, 36-37, 40, 46, 48, 52, 56, 80, 98, 100-102, 106-107, 109-112, 116, 119-120, 122, 124-125, 131-132, 135, 139, 145, 157, 159, 163, 205, 212, 214-217, 231, 276-277, 279, 283, 296, 299-300, 302

Natural Weakness: 36, 42, 46, 48, 109, 122, 150, 211, 258, 260, 279

Neuro-science: 9, 14-15, 17, 22-23, 25-26, 94, 215

Package: 57, 134, 260

PASS (Prolongued Adaption Stress Syndrome): 19, 21, 123, 125, 191-192, 194, 199, 201, 203, 215, 277, 283, 292-293, 300

Petrie, Zenith: 90-91

Pilon, Grace: 184-186

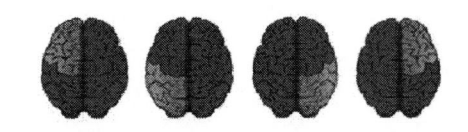

Preference: 5, 7-8, 10-11, 13-14, 18, 29-31, 36-37, 39-40, 42-46, 48, 52, 55-57, 62, 64, 82, 86, 89-90, 94-95, 97-98, 100-104, 106, 108-114, 116-136, 139-143, 145-148, 151-155, 159-167, 170-176, 178-181, 187-188, 192, 194-199, 203-217, 220, 222-223, 229-234, 236-237, 239, 245, 252-265, 267-272, 277, 279, 282, 284, 290-291, 295-297, 299-301, 304, 308

Pribram, Karl: 8-10, 26, 67, 228, 276, 285-288, 291

Right Posterior Convexity: 6-8, 10, 12, 15-16, 22, 25-26, 40, 42-43, 48, 55-60, 62, 66, 76-81, 96-98, 102-103, 109, 111-113, 116-119, 121, 124-125, 132-139, 141, 144, 147, 149-151, 153, 155-157, 159, 161, 163-164, 166-168, 171-172, 174, 176-177, 179-182, 184-186, 189, 194-199, 205-214, 221, 224-225, 227-229, 231, 233-235, 238-239, 241, 245, 248-249, 252, 255, 257-259, 262, 264, 266, 277, 285-286, 288-290, 296, 299-300, 302, 304, 307-309

Sandwich: 130-131, 260, 263

Satir, Virginia: 181, 183

Say It Straight: 181, 183

School: 49, 89, 93, 107, 113-117, 123, 125-127, 137, 141, 153-154, 168, 174, 178-187, 193, 195, 197-198, 203-204, 207, 209, 212-213, 225, 254, 257

Self-charging: 254-258, 261, 263, 271

Self-esteem: 19-20, 30, 80, 95, 140-141, 143-144, 165, 167-168, 181, 187-189, 192, 195, 198-199, 202, 205, 215, 229-230, 237-238, 253, 292, 303

Sensing: 10, 22, 26, 30, 80, 203, 276, 278, 285, 302, 304, 306

Supervising: 97

Taylor, PhD, Arlene: 7-8, 12, 19, 94, 123, 191-192, 199, 201, 277, 292, 297

Teams: 216, 265, 271, 304

Thinking: 7-10, 12, 15, 17, 22-27, 29-35, 42, 44-45, 49-52, 55-60, 62, 64-68, 70, 72-73, 75-76, 80-86, 88, 90, 101-103, 106-107, 118-119, 128-129, 131-132, 135, 139, 141-143, 145, 147, 151, 158-162, 165, 167, 173, 175, 178, 181, 187-188, 192, 195, 197-198, 202-203, 206-208, 210, 213, 215-218, 220-224, 227-229, 236-237, 239, 249, 251, 254-259, 261-264, 269, 272-278, 281-288, 291-292, 296-302, 304-308

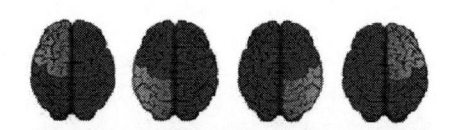

Trade: 259, 261-262

Transcendental Meditation: 181, 298

Turkel, Studs: 93

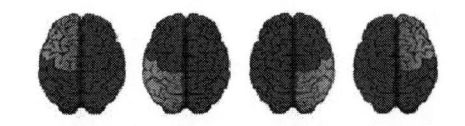

KBA's Life-Building Tools

KBA's life building tools, developed by Dr. Beniziger to help people apply her work, are all based on the synthesis of state of the art knowledge from neurochemistry, neurophysiology and psychology. The most significant and central tool is the Benziger thinking Styles Assessment or BTSA. All other tools have been designed to facilitate the effective application of this tool to a wide range of life situiatuations. The BTSA is explained in detail below. Following that description is a comprehensive list of available products, along with ordering instructions.

The Benziger Thinking Styles Assessment

People are more productive, as well as happier and healthier, when the use, and are rewarded for using, their natural mental preferences. This is even truer when their natural extraverted or introverted needs are simultaneously understood, valued and rewarded.

Although these statements seem self-evident, they are not as easy to apply as you might think. Many people adapt early in life, developing and using one or more non-preferred types of thinking more than their natural preference, as a result of environmental pressure and/or opportunities. Such early Falsification of Type may even result in an individual identifying so strongly with such skills and competencies that they forget their natural or true identity. When this occurs a person is apt to suffer from chronic self-esteem problems, low-grade depression and/or burnout.

For this reason, we recommend the BTSA be used in conjunction with Thriving in Mind by anyone seriously interested in using the model to help themselves and others. The assessment, which is lengthier and more complex than the self-assessment at the beginning of this book, is designed to help you sort out your true natural preferences from any developed but non-preferred competencies. Upon completing the assessment you will receive a 24-28 page Personal Feedback Document including a personal analysis of your thinking style, your strongest and weakest modes, your extraverted and/or introverted needs and your life patterns of adaption.

Everyone can benefit from knowing more about themselves. The insights and self-knowledge provided by the BTSA can help us select more appropriate jobs, set more appropriate personal and professional goals or expectations as well as understand, accept and work more effectively with others whose preferences differ from our own.

KBA's Life-Building Tools	
Item	**Contribution**
• BTSA Assessment and eBTSA (the electronic version) available at www.benziger.org	Gathers data about you or another person. The BTSA Feedback explains the data in a manner that allows you to learn about yourself or another person in a positive affirming way.
• Thriving in Mind: The Natural Key to Sustainable Neurofitness	Presents guidelines for communicating effectively. Exercises which allow you to apply the model to your work life while gaining insights into: • which jobs are best for you and why; • which jobs are a problem for you and why; • why you have difficulty communicating or working with certain colleagues. Stories relating the model to your home life: • shed light on problems between family members; • offer ideas for improving the quality of your home life; and • offer ideas for living with and helping your children.
• Thriving in Mind: the Workbook	A companion workbook for Thriving in Mind. Provides exercises that help the reader apply the content of Thriving in Mind to their everyday life, at home and on the job.
• The BTSA User Manual	Presents a comprehensive discussion covering: • the construction and properties of the BTSA; • the theory behind the BTSA; • details for administering the BTSA; • applications for the BTSA; • technical and statistical information on the BTSA's reliability and validity.
• Falsification of Type	Groundbreaking. Presents an in-depth analysis of this problem from both a psychological and physiological perspective, especially its role in weakening the immune system and self-esteem of the individual.
• Increasing Your Own and Others high Performance (a set of 2 double-sided audiotapes)	Presents strategies for improving performance and effectiveness. Includes strategies for managing individual and group weaknesses.

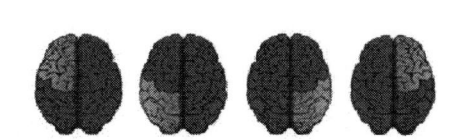

• Developing Positive Self-Esteem	Introduces an empowering approach to helping yourself to increase self-esteem.
• Overcoming Depression	Provides powerful, healing insights into the physiological basis of depression. Provides a set of life skills that have been shown to be successful in overcoming depression.
• Physiological and Phychophysiological Bases for Jungian Concepts – An annotated Bibliography	Provides the reader a more in-depth understanding of the physiological bases of the KBA/Benziger Model.

All books in KBA's Core Library available in Color and Black & White now, can be ordered from CreateSpace and from Amazon (US, Canadian dollars), Amazon Great Britain (GBP pounds), Amazon for Continental Europe (Euro).

KBA, LLC • The Human Resources Technology Company
"Helping people thrive around the world."
www.benziger.org

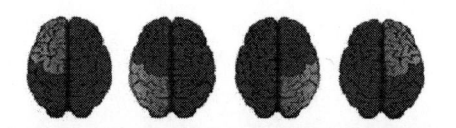

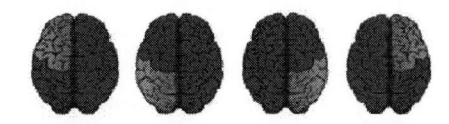

Living true to Type, keeps your brain operating in cool blue!

Living true to type
Keeps your brain Operating in cool blue.
It is healthy and promotes wellness! It is sustainable!

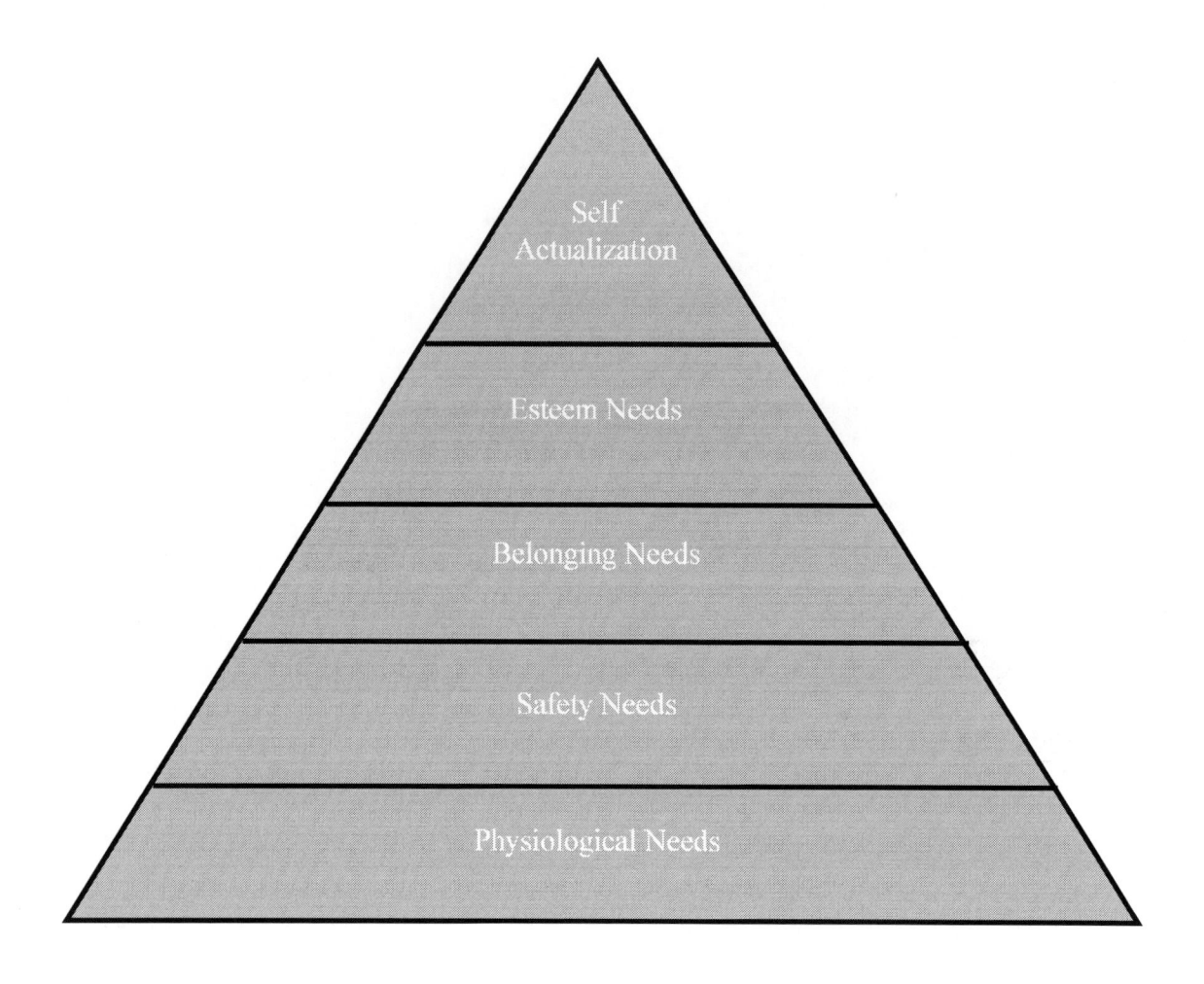

- Self Actualization
- Esteem Needs
- Belonging Needs
- Safety Needs
- Physiological Needs

Falsifying Type, makes your brain red hot – fries your brain!

Falsifying type
Forces Your brain to Overheat & Fries your brain.
It is not healthy! It is not sustainable!

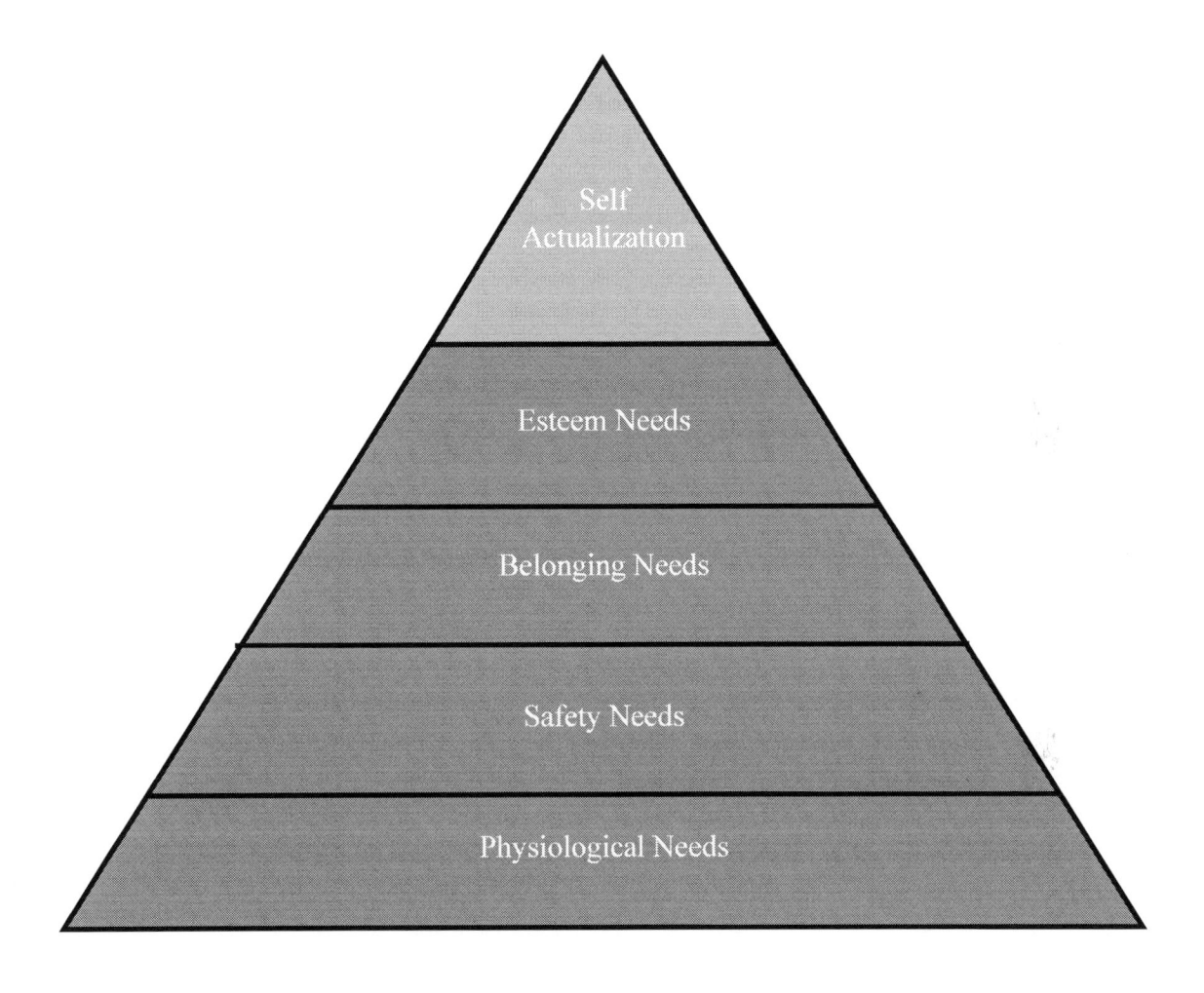

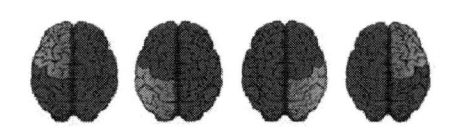

- Self Actualization
- Esteem Needs
- Belonging Needs
- Safety Needs
- Physiological Needs

Printed in Great Britain
by Amazon.co.uk, Ltd.,
Marston Gate.